I0010121

Automotive Cybersecurity Engineering Handbook

The automotive engineer's roadmap to cyber-resilient vehicles

Dr. Ahmad MK Nasser

BIRMINGHAM—MUMBAI

Automotive Cybersecurity Engineering Handbook

Copyright © 2023 Packt Publishing

All rights reserved. No part of this book may be reproduced, stored in a retrieval system, or transmitted in any form or by any means, without the prior written permission of the publisher, except in the case of brief quotations embedded in critical articles or reviews.

Every effort has been made in the preparation of this book to ensure the accuracy of the information presented. However, the information contained in this book is sold without warranty, either express or implied. Neither the author, nor Packt Publishing or its dealers and distributors, will be held liable for any damages caused or alleged to have been caused directly or indirectly by this book.

Packt Publishing has endeavored to provide trademark information about all of the companies and products mentioned in this book by the appropriate use of capitals. However, Packt Publishing cannot guarantee the accuracy of this information.

Group Product Manager: Pavan Ramchandani

Publishing Product Manager: Prachi Sawant

Senior Content Development Editor: Adrija Mitra

Technical Editor: Irfa Ansari

Copy Editor: Safis Editing

Project Coordinator: Neil D'mello

Proofreader: Safis Editing

Indexer: Subalakshmi Govindhan

Production Designer: Shankar Kalbhor

Marketing Coordinator: Marylou De Mello

First published: October 2023

Production reference: 2031023

Published by Packt Publishing Ltd.

Grosvenor House

11 St. Paul's Square

Birmingham

B3 1RB, UK.

ISBN 978-1-80107-653-1

www.packtpub.com

To my extraordinary mother, Amal Awada, whose influence ignited within me, from a young age, a profound inquiry into the limits of my abilities.

To my father, Mohamad Kheir, whose serene demeanor under intense pressure instills in me the belief that within oneself lies the strength to face the impossible.

To my wife, Dr. Batoul Abdallah, who set the academic bar high, motivating me to always strive for more both academically and professionally.

And finally, to my beloved son, Yahya, and daughter, Dalia, who displayed remarkable patience while I dedicated my nights and weekends to completing this book.

– Dr. Ahmad MK Nasser

Contributors

About the author

Dr. Ahmad MK Nasser is an automotive cybersecurity architect with a long experience in securing safety-critical systems. He started his career as a software engineer, building automotive network drivers, diagnostics protocols, and flash programming solutions. This naturally led him into the field of automotive cybersecurity, where he designed secure firmware solutions for various microcontrollers and SoCs, defined secure hardware and software architectures of embedded systems, and performed threat analysis of numerous vehicle architectures, ECUs, and smart sensors. Ahmad holds a B.S. and an M.S. in electrical and computer engineering from Wayne State University, as well as a Ph.D. in computer science from the University of Michigan in Dearborn. He is currently a principal security architect for NVIDIA's autonomous driving software platform.

About the reviewers

Heinz Bodo Seifert received his master of science in electrical engineering from the University of Siegen in 1994. He has worked in the automotive industry since 1997 for companies such as GM, Audi, and Stellantis, as well as tier-one companies such as Magna Electronics, developing automotive systems. At Audi, he was responsible for running global test fleets to collect vehicle performance data. At Magna Electronics in Auburn Hills, Michigan, he led the advanced engineering department and was responsible for developing functions and technologies that are due to emerge in the automotive field in the coming years. At Torc Robotics, he leads the safety and cybersecurity efforts for the Torc self-driving truck.

Robert Kaster is a chief technical expert at Bosch, leading the Americas' regional cross-divisional automotive product security team. In his 27 years at Bosch, he submitted more than 100 invention records, was awarded 18 patents in automotive safety and security, and was recognized as CC-NA's inventor of the year three times.

He designed more than 40 million braking controllers and implemented more than $70 million dollars in first-year cost savings. He worked at Chrysler for five years in the pre-prototype electronic controller design team. Robert serves on the Auto-ISAC board of directors and led the effort to set up the Auto-ISAC in Europe.

He has bachelor's ('89) and master's ('95) degrees from the University of Michigan in electrical engineering and computer science and is working to complete a PhD in automotive cybersecurity in January 2024.

Table of Contents

2

Cybersecurity Basics for Automotive Use Cases ⠀⠀⠀⠀⠀⠀⠀⠀43

3

Threat Landscape against Vehicle Components ⠀⠀⠀⠀⠀⠀⠀⠀87

Part 2: Understanding the Secure Engineering Development Process

4

Exploring the Landscape of Automotive Cybersecurity Standards   125

5

Taking a Deep Dive into ISO/SAE21434   161

6

Interactions Between Functional Safety and Cybersecurity   197

Part 3: Executing the Process to Engineer a Secure Automotive Product

7

9

ECU-Level Security Controls   311

Index   349

Other Books You May Enjoy   368

Preface

The subject of automotive cybersecurity involves many concepts, engineering methods, and technologies, some of which are unique to the automotive domain while others are shared with adjacent fields. The unique aspects are derived from the fact that the vehicle belongs to the family of cyber-physical systems. In such systems, embedded computers integrate with sensors and networking components to control physical processes, which then provide feedback to the computing environment. While sharing concepts with the domain of information security, breaches of cyber-physical systems result in physical impacts that can cause the unsafe operation of the system with the potential for injury and loss of life. When you choose to work in the field of automotive cybersecurity, you are not only responsible for protecting the security of the driver's data, and the intellectual property and reputation of members in the supply chain, but more importantly, you are responsible for protecting the lives of those driving the vehicle or coming within its vicinity.

The complexity of producing vehicles that are secure by design goes beyond the technology challenges and spans several factors that are unique to the automotive industry. These include the complexity of the automotive supply chain, the legacy systems and practices that are hard to change, the limited allocated budgets for deploying security controls, the ever-shrinking program schedules, the limited computing resources, and the stringent power consumption requirements. All of these factors must be considered while meeting strict regulatory requirements and standards, which makes the job of automotive cybersecurity engineers both exciting and exhausting at the same time. To make matters worse, there is a severe shortage of automotive cybersecurity professionals, and all these while vehicles are becoming more connected, putting them at increased risk of cyber attacks. While software-defined vehicle transformation is underway, the trend of increased autonomy and connectivity will not be successful if vehicles are not developed on a secure foundation. Just like in adjacent domains, such as banking, cloud computing, and enterprise systems, when an opportunity for financial gain exists, hackers will find a way to penetrate even the most sophisticated defenses.

To ensure that the automotive industry does not go down the path of other industries in which the rate of fixing vulnerabilities is outpaced by the rate of creating them, there is a need for a systematic approach to cybersecurity engineering that is on par with the quality management and functional safety approaches that have an established record within this industry. You may have heard the phrases "secure by design" and "built-in security" versus "bolt-on security." These are good mottos that we aim to put into practice throughout this book. Adopting cybersecurity within the engineering life cycle presents many challenges, which this book tries to tackle. The worst-case adoption scenario involves identifying threats but failing to act on risk reduction due to concerns about schedule and cost. Organizations that take this approach usually create a false sense of security by relying on a heavy-handed process that produces reams of paperwork to document risks and risk treatment decisions without investing in the technology needed to mitigate critical risks. Consequently, relying on processes that prioritize paper evidence over technical analysis and thorough argumentation of security risks creates a belief by engineering teams that the cybersecurity process is merely a checkbox exercise that adds no value. It is also possible to create an over-zealous security culture that produces security solutions that are too complicated to achieve in practice. In fact, security experts can lose credibility when they offer too many esoteric solutions that are impractical to implement or that cannot be defended when scrutinized for fulfilling an actual need. It is thus the job of the cybersecurity professionals to strike the right balance between security, technical feasibility, cost, effort, and overall impact on schedule. That is why one of the goals of this book is to define a practical approach for building secure systems that integrate seamlessly with existing engineering processes and tools while producing effective results.

There is no doubt that today, there exists a sizeable knowledge gap. To close this gap, the automotive industry either recruits security professionals with limited automotive knowledge or trains automotive engineers with limited security knowledge. This book aims to bridge the gap between the two groups of professionals by providing a balanced approach that reduces security risks to reasonable levels while working within the acceptable parameters of producing sellable automotive systems.

Throughout this book, you will notice that we do not dwell heavily on theory, and sometimes concepts may intentionally be over-simplified in favor of highlighting their practical aspects. It is the intent of this book to expose you to the widest set of cybersecurity topics that are relevant to this domain so you may later choose the level of depth you want to pursue in areas of interest. You might already be a practicing professional or someone who is just getting into the field. Either way, sooner or later, you will discover that what may be more challenging than producing technical security solutions is convincing people of the risks that need mitigation and why the pain they must endure now is justified in the long run. Having a formalized security engineering approach can help reduce the amount of subjectivity during these difficult conversations to avoid endless debates about what is considered a reasonable risk. That is why this book aims to reframe the security conversation through a common language that stresses objectivity while focusing on cybersecurity risk reduction.

> **Note**
> The views and opinions expressed in this book are solely those of the author and do not necessarily represent or reflect the views of current or past employers.

Who this book is for

This book is for automotive engineers and security professionals who are expected to make their systems cyber-resilient through compliance with industry standards (specifically ISO21434 and UNECE REG 155-156). You may have a background in functional safety and are wondering what it means to develop a system that is both safe and secure. You may have a background in developing non-safety-relevant production software and are wondering how to add security-related features. You may also be a person who has a security background and is trying to transition into the automotive domain. Regardless of your background, this book is intended to provide you with a practical approach to automotive cybersecurity engineering that can be applied within a reasonable time frame and effort in a way that leverages your organization's existing processes.

To ease the understanding of the concepts in this book, you will need to be familiar with basic automotive development processes that are applied through the V-model and basic principles of computer security. By the end of this book, it should be apparent to you why cybersecurity matters for automotive systems, how to integrate cybersecurity engineering with your development process, how to perform cybersecurity engineering activities efficiently within the time and engineering constraints of your system, and how to deploy cybersecurity controls at various layers of the vehicle and the ECU architecture. It is therefore the strategy of this book to demystify cybersecurity for automotive engineering teams and help them find ways to make cybersecurity an integrated property of their systems rather than a burden that must be de-prioritized to push products out of the door.

What this book covers

Chapter 1, Introducing the Vehicle Electrical/Electronic Architecture, covers the vehicle E/E architecture, which comprises the computing nodes, communication channels, sensors, and actuators distributed over several functional domains. Understanding the various E/E architectures of vehicles is essential to gain a perspective on how the vehicle can be attacked. This section examines the E/E architecture of several vehicle types and introduces the reader to different types of computing nodes, networking protocols, sensors, actuators, and security-relevant interfaces.

Chapter 2, Cybersecurity Basics for Automotive Use Cases, covers the basic principles of cybersecurity and cryptography, which are important to understand before tackling the problem of securing automotive systems. For people skilled in the art of cybersecurity, this chapter can be skipped; but for others, it is a prerequisite to help set the stage for other chapters. The reader is introduced to cryptographic methods with a general explanation of how each one can be applied to an automotive use case. The chapter then switches to common security principles that should guide the design of any secure system.

Chapter 3, Threat Landscape against Vehicle Components, follows on from *Chapter 1*, where the reader gained insights into the vehicle E/E architecture and the various components it supports. In this chapter, the reader walks through the various threats that exist for each component and vehicle subsystem. Understanding the threat landscape helps us understand why automotive cybersecurity is critical and establishes the groundwork for later chapters that aim to address those threats. The chapter walks the reader through each category of threats and then explores the common security weaknesses that make those threats viable. We take a top-down approach, starting with cybersecurity weaknesses at the vehicle level and then zooming in to various components and subcomponents at the ECU level.

Chapter 4, Exploring the Landscape of Automotive Cybersecurity Standards, covers engineering automotive systems, which require compliance with a myriad of quality and safety standards. With the introduction of cybersecurity to automotive systems, the automotive engineer is expected to be well versed in the various automotive cybersecurity standards. This section introduces standards such as ISO21434, REG155, REG156, TISAX, and SAE J3101. The reader is given a breakdown of each standard along with the rationale for why compliance is necessary.

Chapter 5, Taking a Deep Dive into ISO/SAE21434, covers ISO/SAE21434, which is the de facto standard for automotive cybersecurity engineering. It guides the reader through the complete secure development life cycle as well as cybersecurity management and risk governance. This chapter will walk through all the sections of the standard and explain why each one is important and how it shapes the product engineering life cycle.

Chapter 6, Interactions Between Functional Safety and Cybersecurity, covers functional safety, which is a differentiating aspect of automotive systems when compared to IT systems. The vast majority of automotive ECUs have a certain degree of safety relevance, which pulls into the picture various standards, such as ISO26262 and SOTIF. Building secure systems that are safety relevant requires close cooperation between the two engineering approaches. A disjointed approach is guaranteed to result in high costs, and inconsistencies that can lead to a project's failure. This chapter describes the various areas where safety and security engineering approaches overlap and where they need to be reconciled. A basic understanding of functional safety is a prerequisite to reading this chapter.

Chapter 7, A Practical Threat Modeling Approach for Automotive Systems, covers threat modeling, which is at the core of any secure engineering process. It is the driver for understanding threats against the system and deriving cybersecurity goals, controls, and requirements necessary to treat those threats. Due to the safety aspect of automotive systems, general threat modeling approaches from IT systems are not suitable for automotive security analysis. To bridge that gap, several automotive-centric threat modeling methods have been proposed. In this chapter, we explore the different threat modeling methods available and how they integrate the safety aspects. We show common challenges in applying a TARA to a complex system. Then, we present an optimized approach that accounts for various types of automotive systems and components to produce a comprehensive set of security requirements that ensure system security.

Chapter 8, Vehicle-Level Security Controls, explores the various security controls and techniques available to build cyber-resilient automotive systems. The book started with exploring threats and weaknesses and then detoured into applying a systematic cybersecurity engineering process to identify risks that require treatment. This chapter delves into each technology area and presents the most common methods used to create mitigations at the vehicle level considering the complete vehicle life cycle. It also presents common pitfalls to avoid when implementing those controls.

Chapter 9, ECU-Level Security Controls, applies a similar approach to *Chapter 8*, which focused on security controls applied at the vehicle level, but this time at the ECU level. Keeping up with the principle of defense-in-depth requires us to build resilient vehicle components at the ECU and sub-ECU levels. This chapter takes a layered approach to securing the ECU and its sub-components. We will examine the various technologies available, understand their challenges and pitfalls, and then discuss how to use them securely.

To get the most out of this book

This book is most effective when read while working on a real automotive project that has cybersecurity relevance. Doing so will help you connect with the many challenges mentioned in this book from the various perspectives presented. While we tried our best to provide the background on as many concepts presented in this book, if you find yourself unfamiliar with a specific topic, then we advise you to spend time researching it before moving on to other chapters in the book as the concepts are built up one chapter at a time. In fact, it helps to create your own library of references so you may come back to it in the future when you find yourself working on a certain topic. And remember, cybersecurity is a field of life-long learning.

Midway through writing this book, we discovered the wonder of **Large Language Models** (**LLMs**) and their extraordinary ability to process and generate text. The topic of generative AI for accelerating cybersecurity work deserves a book of its own, but for now, let us share some firsthand lessons that should be considered to optimize and streamline your automotive cybersecurity work.

If we pause to briefly ask, "What is knowledge-based work?" then the answer can be explained through three main activities: searching for information, comprehending the information, and producing new information. It turns out LLMs can be a perfect assistant in all three categories of knowledge-based work. Given how knowledge intensive the field of cybersecurity is, the integration of LLMs offers a transformative approach to streamlining cybersecurity efforts, particularly in the automotive industry. At the crux, LLMs excel in indexing and making text-based data—such as security requirements, architecture descriptions, and code—semantically searchable. Moreover, these AI models can synthesize, evaluate, and summarize critical information, offering an invaluable toolset for cybersecurity analysis.

As a cybersecurity professional, you might be overwhelmed with the volume of workload that you have to manage, such as security requirements, threat models, and risk analysis. AI promises to improve the workforce imbalance by providing with models that can improve the efficiency of security analysis and work product generation to demonstrate the achieved level of cybersecurity assurance. As you build your threat models, threat catalogs, and weaknesses databases, you will generate a wealth of text that is perfect for an LLM to index, compare, and even flag duplication. For example, threats can be transformed into embedding vectors, enabling similarity searches based on text descriptions of other threats. This effectively can serve as a recommendation system that proposes threats that you should consider based on how you described your feature, architecture, or attack surface.

When it comes to producing the ISO 21434 work products, it is possible to rely on the few-shot learning capability of LLM models to transform text describing a security objective, a transferred risk, or even a desired security outcome into a formal work product such as a cybersecurity goal, a claim, or a security requirement. All it takes is a few well-vetted examples of each of these work products and the LLM can transform the input text into well-written, close-to-compliant output. When performing threat analysis and risk assessment, you will find in many cases that you are constantly searching for existing cybersecurity controls or prior weaknesses and threats that should be considered. Integrating the ability to search for these work products within your TARA tool significantly reduces the time it takes to research whether a security control already exists or an assumed risk has already been captured for a given attack path. Even coding weaknesses can be found with the help of an LLM by presenting the code and asking the model to identify vulnerabilities and argue about why the code is free from vulnerabilities. Finally, generating test cases from requirements emerges as a potent use case, deployable after supplying example pairs showing test cases along with their parent security requirements. As you read this book, you are encouraged to think of these and other use cases that can be streamlined with the help of LLMs.

Download the example code files

You can download the example code files for this book from GitHub at `https://github.com/PacktPublishing/Automotive-Cybersecurity-Engineering-Handbook`. If there's an update to the code, it will be updated in the GitHub repository.

We also have other code bundles from our rich catalog of books and videos available at `https://github.com/PacktPublishing/`. Check them out!

Conventions used

There are a number of text conventions used throughout this book.

`Code in text`: Indicates code words in text, database table names, folder names, filenames, file extensions, pathnames, dummy URLs, user input, and Twitter handles. Here is an example: "The first check (`signatureVerificationResult == 0x3CA5965A`) determines whether `signatureVerificationResult` has the correct and expected value."

A block of code is set as follows:

```
if (signatureVerificationResult == 0x3CA5965A)
{
    // Hamming distance check passed, now perform a second check using
    // the inverse of the variable
    if (~signatureVerificationResult != 0xC35A69A5)
    {
        Log_fault(error_type);
    }
    else
    {
        Allow_application_to_run(); // Attacker wants to get here
                                    // through glitching
    }
}
```

Bold: Indicates a new term, an important word, or words that you see onscreen. For instance, words in menus or dialog boxes appear in **bold**. Here is an example: "**SAE J2497** is a communication protocol used in commercial trucks to allow the exchange of data between the tractor and the trailer, such as the ABS trailer status lamp."

> **Tips or important notes**
> Appear like this.

Get in touch

Feedback from our readers is always welcome.

General feedback: If you have questions about any aspect of this book, email us at customercare@packtpub.com and mention the book title in the subject of your message.

Errata: Although we have taken every care to ensure the accuracy of our content, mistakes do happen. If you have found a mistake in this book, we would be grateful if you would report this to us. Please visit www.packtpub.com/support/errata and fill in the form.

Piracy: If you come across any illegal copies of our works in any form on the internet, we would be grateful if you would provide us with the location address or website name. Please contact us at copyright@packt.com with a link to the material.

If you are interested in becoming an author: If there is a topic that you have expertise in and you are interested in either writing or contributing to a book, please visit authors.packtpub.com.

Share Your Thoughts

Once you've read *Automotive Cybersecurity Engineering Handbook*, we'd love to hear your thoughts! Please click here to go straight to the Amazon review page for this book and share your feedback.

Your review is important to us and the tech community and will help us make sure we're delivering excellent quality content.

Download a free PDF copy of this book

Thanks for purchasing this book!

Do you like to read on the go but are unable to carry your print books everywhere?

Is your eBook purchase not compatible with the device of your choice?

Don't worry, now with every Packt book you get a DRM-free PDF version of that book at no cost.

Read anywhere, any place, on any device. Search, copy, and paste code from your favorite technical books directly into your application.

The perks don't stop there, you can get exclusive access to discounts, newsletters, and great free content in your inbox daily

Follow these simple steps to get the benefits:

1. Scan the QR code or visit the link below

https://packt.link/free-ebook/9781801076531

2. Submit your proof of purchase
3. That's it! We'll send your free PDF and other benefits to your email directly

Part 1:
Understanding the
Cybersecurity Relevance of the
Vehicle Electrical Architecture

In the first part of the book, we aim to understand the cybersecurity relevance of vehicle **electrical/electronic** (E/E) architectures to gain perspective on how such systems can become vulnerable to attacks and the relevant threats that apply. After walking through the evolution of vehicle E/E architecture, we introduce basic cybersecurity concepts that will aid us in later chapters when we perform security analysis and derive security controls. We end the first part of the book by surveying the threat landscape to give us a clear idea of the security problem that lies ahead.

This part has the following chapters:

- *Chapter 1, Introducing the Vehicle Electrical/Electronic Architecture*
- *Chapter 2, Cybersecurity Basics for Automotive Use Cases*
- *Chapter 3, Threat Landscape against Vehicle Components*

1
Introducing the Vehicle Electrical/Electronic Architecture

The vehicle **Electrical/Electronic (E/E)** architecture refers to the set of electronic components, electrical wire harnesses, networking technologies, and software applications that coalesce to manage a diverse suite of vehicle functions tasked with controlling the vehicle and user experience.

While the combination of software and electronics has revolutionized how vehicle features are designed and deployed, it gradually produced a rich attack surface that made vehicles vulnerable to cyber threats. Therefore, understanding the fundamental concepts of the E/E architecture is a prerequisite to analyzing vehicle security. To help provide the necessary background, first, we will explore the various hardware platforms supported in the **electronic control unit** (ECU) and the corresponding reference software architectures. Next, we will examine how ECUs can be grouped into domains (which are distinct functional subsystems that have specific responsibilities) along with the networking technologies needed for their communication. With the ECUs and network layers defined, we will turn our attention to the sensors and actuators that enable the vehicle to sense the environment and react to it. Finally, we will put all these components together in the different vehicle architecture topologies while showing current and future trends in this area. Following this hierarchical approach should help us gain perspective on how the vehicle can be attacked.

As we dive through the E/E architecture layers, we will pose a series of questions in the form of discussion points to help you explore threats against your vehicle components. A brief answer list will be provided at the end of this chapter. The next few chapters will offer deeper insights into these discussion points as we navigate the cybersecurity threat landscape.

Note that this chapter does not attempt to offer a comprehensive list of every possible E/E architecture and component, but rather focuses on the aspects that are most relevant to vehicle cybersecurity. If you are well acquainted with vehicle E/E architecture concepts, this chapter can be considered a review to set the stage for cybersecurity analysis.

In this chapter, we will cover the following main topics:

- Overview of the basic building blocks of the E/E architecture
- Electronic control units
- ECU domains
- Exploring the in-vehicle network
- Sensors and actuators
- Exploring the vehicle architecture types

Overview of the basic building blocks of the E/E architecture

Before we explore the multiple layers of the E/E architecture, we must start with **ECUs**. These ECUs are grouped into ECU domains, which are interconnected by a suite of in-vehicle network communication channels. The ECUs are further connected to sensors and actuators through a mixture of hardwired and network-based connections. The combination of ECUs, sensors, actuators, and network channels can be arranged in different configurations, giving rise to several variants of the vehicle E/E architecture. *Figure 1.1* shows a simplified example of an E/E architecture:

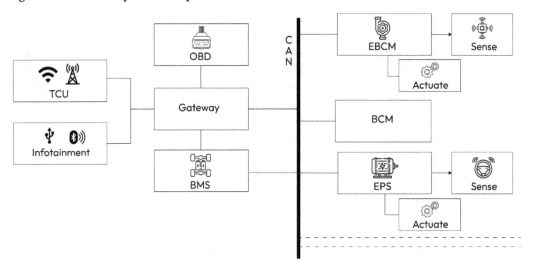

Figure 1.1 – Simplified vehicle architecture view

Our first stop will be ECUs.

Electronic control units

ECUs are at the heart of the E/E architecture and consist primarily of the processing elements and electronic components necessary to perform one or more vehicle functions, such as steering, information display, seat control, and more. In the simplified view of *Figure 1.1*, we can see seven ECUs interconnected through the vehicle network (for demonstration purposes only). One such ECU is the **electronic braking control module (EBCM)**, which is responsible for active safety functions such as **anti-lock braking systems (ABSs)** and **electronic stability control (ESC)**. Another ECU is the **battery management system (BMS)**, which is commonly found in electric vehicles.

Figure 1.2 – Closed box view of an ECU

The electronic components of the ECU are housed in a sealed enclosure that is designed to withstand harsh environmental conditions such as heat, vibration, and electromagnetic interference. The black connector shown in *Figure 1.2* enables the ECU to interface with the rest of the vehicle E/E architecture through a set of cables known as the **wire harness**. Mapping the pin out of the connector is the first step to determine which signals are relevant for cybersecurity. The power inputs, physical network bus lines, hard-wired sensor inputs, and actuation outputs are among the typical assets that are considered for protection against security threats.

If you were to crack open the ECU enclosure, as shown in *Figure 1.3*, you would find a PCB populated with various passive and active electronic components, such as relays, solenoids, resistors, capacitors, diodes, the **power management integrated circuit (PMIC)**, network transceiver memory chips, and, most importantly, a **microcontroller (MCU)** or **system on chip (SoC)**.

Figure 1.3 – Open box view of an ECU

Due to their power, cost, and timing performance constraints, most ECU types are driven by an MCU that realizes the vehicle functions through software running on one or more CPU cores embedded within the MCU.

SoCs, on the other hand, integrate several components into one chip to offer higher computation resources with larger memory and networking capabilities, making them well suited for applications such as infotainment and autonomous driving systems.

> **Discussion point 1**
>
> Can you think of any assets that are worth protecting once the PCB layout is exposed?
>
> *Answers to all discussion points are provided at the end of this chapter.*

To answer the preceding question, let's first dive a bit deeper into the hardware architecture of MCU-based ECUs before moving on to SoCs.

Looking at MCU-based ECUs

An MCU-based ECU executes software through one or more symmetric CPU cores that fetch code and data from the MCU's internal flash memory. Code execution from the internal flash is a key requirement to meet the hard real-time constraints of these ECUs. Even when external flash memory is used, it is normally restricted to storing data such as images or audio files, as is the case with an instrument cluster ECU.

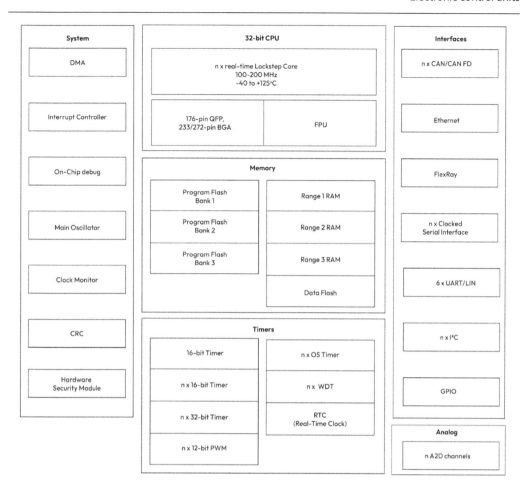

Figure 1.4 – A typical MCU block diagram

MCUs come in many variants, each tailored for a specific vehicle ECU application type. For example, an MCU for engine control will have many high-precision timer units, while an MCU for body control will have a large number of general-purpose **input/output (I/O)** pins. When analyzing the cybersecurity threats of a specific ECU, it is important to understand the different peripherals that are available as they may introduce a unique set of assets and attack surfaces. *Figure 1.4* shows a block diagram for a typical 32 bit microcontroller with multiple peripherals and networking interfaces.

Looking back at *Figure 1.3*, we can start to explore the assets that can be probed for by an attacker who has possession of the ECU. For one, the MCU's memory contents are an interesting target for exposure. This is where the ECU control software and calibration data are stored and therefore are of value at least to the ECU supplier, who may wish to protect their intellectual property against illegal access. Together with the vehicle's **original equipment manufacturer (OEM)**, they both want to prevent probers from discovering exploits that can be leveraged in more sophisticated attacks. However, since the memory is embedded inside the MCU, by having possession of the open ECU, an attacker cannot directly probe the memory contents. Instead, they will have to explore ways to leverage the **on-chip debug** features or serial flash programming interfaces to gain access to the memory's contents.

> **Discussion point 2**
>
> Looking at the block diagram in *Figure 1.4*, can you guess what might be another asset that is of interest to an attacker who has possession of our ECU?

Looking at SoC-based ECUs

At first glance, the main difference between the SoC and MCU is the increased level of complexity and the diverse set of peripherals offered. For one, the SoC has a combination of CPU clusters that serve different use cases. The application CPUs feature multiple symmetric cores that target computationally intensive functions such as perception, path planning, and sensor fusion. On the other hand, the real-time CPUs feature multiple symmetric cores that target safety-critical functions such as fault monitoring and error reporting. In addition to the common network peripheral types of an MCU, we expect to see a higher number of network interfaces with higher bandwidth (for example, Ethernet 1 GB/10 GB links and PCIE). One significant difference with the MCU-based architecture is that code execution is out of DRAM as opposed to the embedded flash. Additionally, eMMC and QSPI flash interfaces are commonly used to support loading code and data from external storage devices. As is the case with the MCUs, SoCs come in different variants as they aim to serve specific vehicle use cases. For example, you will find that SoCs for ADAS applications are equipped with computer vision and deep learning accelerators, while SoCs for infotainment are equipped with video encoders/decoders for media streaming:

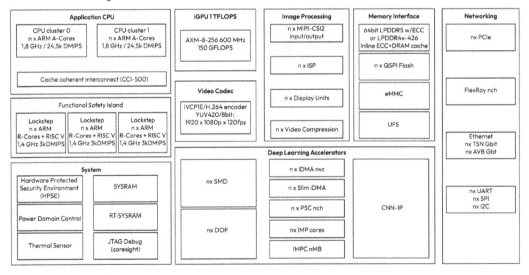

Figure 1.5 – Typical block diagram of an automotive SoC

In addition to storing typical software and calibration data, an SoC has additional unique objects of value, such as machine learning models that are programmed in storage, as well as stored camera images, videos, and vehicle logs that may contain users' private data. Machine learning models are valuable intellectual property to the ECU supplier and the OEM that helped create them. On the other hand, camera images and video data are important to vehicle owners who care about protecting their privacy. Vehicle logs serve many purposes and can be especially useful in accident investigations. Furthermore, since memory is exposed on the PCB, an attacker can attempt to directly dump the contents of the eMMC or probe the QSPI lines to extract memory contents.

> **Discussion point 3**
>
> Looking at the block diagram in *Figure 1.5*, can you spot other assets that are interesting to an attacker who has possession of an SoC-based ECU?

Continuing with our "peeling the onion" exercise, let's look at the MCU and SoC software layers.

Looking inside the MCU and SoC software layers

The most differentiating feature of MCU-based automotive ECUs is their hard real-time performance requirements and their high degree of determinism, both of which are critical to controlling time-sensitive operations such as **braking**, **deploying airbags**, **steering**, and **engine combustion**. As a result, an MCU periodic software task may only deviate within milliseconds, and sometimes even microseconds, from its nominal execution rate before the application starts violating its safety and reliability objectives.

Before **AUTomotive Open System ARchitecture** (**AUTOSAR**) was founded, if you wished to examine the software architecture of an ECU, you would have to work in a software team at the OEM or for an automotive supplier. But thanks to the AUTOSAR consortium's efforts of creating a standardized basic software architecture and standard application interface layer, security professionals can gain insights into a typical ECU software architecture simply by learning the basics of the AUTOSAR software architecture.

> **Note**
>
> AUTOSAR is a worldwide development partnership of vehicle manufacturers, suppliers, service providers, and companies from the automotive electronics, semiconductor, and software industries.

Let's start by looking at the MCU-based software architecture based on the AUTOSAR classic variant:

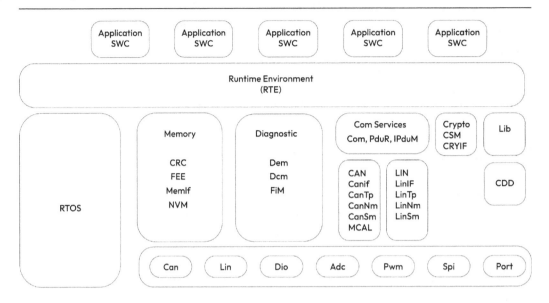

Figure 1.6 – Simplified AUTOSAR classic software block diagram

At the heart of the AUTOSAR classic software architecture is the AUTOSAR real-time operating system. The AUTOSAR operating system offers several memory, timing, and hardware resource isolation and protection guarantees to support safety-critical applications. As we will see in the following chapters, some of these safety features are also useful for hardening AUTOSAR-based applications against cyber threats.

Another signature feature of AUTOSAR classic is the hardware abstraction layer, which exposes the MCU features through well-defined interfaces to ensure software portability across different hardware platforms. Configuring the **microcontroller abstraction layer** (**MCAL**) correctly and with security in mind is a critical part of reducing the attack surface against the rest of the AUTOSAR layers.

Besides the MCAL, several AUTOSAR software layers are critical for security. For example, if the Com services layer is improperly configured, it can be abused by a software application to send spoofed messages to other ECUs on the shared CAN network. Similarly, the memory stack can be exploited to tamper with the non-volatile memory contents. The diagnostic layer can cause fake diagnostic data to be erased or inserted, or even worse, critical diagnostic services to be unlocked under unsafe conditions. Even without a deep knowledge of the AUTOSAR Crypto services layer, we can guess that cryptographic keys and critical security parameters could be exposed or at least be used illegally if this layer is not properly configured or implemented.

Discussion point 4

Can you spot additional AUTOSAR layers that may be critical for security? Hint: Think about the ECU mode management.

Before moving on, let's look briefly at the AUTOSAR **runtime environment (RTE)**, which separates the base software modules from the application software components. This standardized application interface layer makes it possible to interchange application software components between automotive suppliers if they abide by the RTE interface definitions. The RTE configuration dictates how application software components interact with each other, as well as with the basic software modules. Therefore, tampering with the RTE configuration has significant impacts on the ECU software security.

Note that an AUTOSAR classic-based ECU software is built as a single software executable image, along with one or more calibration images.

An important software subsystem for MCU-based ECUs that is not covered by AUTOSAR is the *flash bootloader*, which manages how the ECU software is started and updated, two areas that are critical for security:

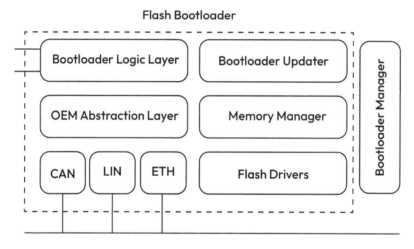

Figure 1.7 – Block diagram of a typical bootloader architecture

At startup, the flash bootloader performs basic hardware initialization and may control which software partition is executed based on the partition validation check results. Manipulating this stage can result in the startup of a tampered application or the improper safety and security initialization of the system. During runtime, the bootloader provides the functionality to reprogram the software and calibration images either through a diagnostic client or through an **over-the-air (OTA)** application. Illegal access to the flash bootloader update mechanisms can result in the ECU being programmed with unsafe or maliciously crafted software. Let's assume the bootloader manages two partitions – one that contains a backup image and one that contains a recently updated image that must be booted. The bootloader memory flags that determine which software partition to boot after reset are critical for security because if they're tampered with, this can result in the execution of an invalid or corrupt software image. Additionally, flash drivers containing the routines to erase and reprogram flash contents are important for security as they can be misused to reprogram or erase the ECU software or calibration data.

Discussion point 5

Investigate the software layers of the bootloader to see whether you can spot any services that can be abused by an attacker so that they can reprogram or erase the software.

Once again, let's turn our attention to our SoC-based ECUs and look inward at the software architecture. Luckily, AUTOSAR has also standardized a software architecture that targets such systems through the AUTOSAR adaptive variant. While AUTOSAR adaptive has not reached the level of market adoption as AUTOSAR classic, it still serves as a useful reference. A key feature of this software architecture is the transition from signal-based software design to a **service-oriented architecture (SOA)**. Rather than a monolithic software image built for a specific ECU with a pre-generated RTE, AUTOSAR adaptive offers a flexible architecture that allows for dynamically updated and deployed applications. Another key feature is its reliance on high-bandwidth networking technologies such as Ethernet:

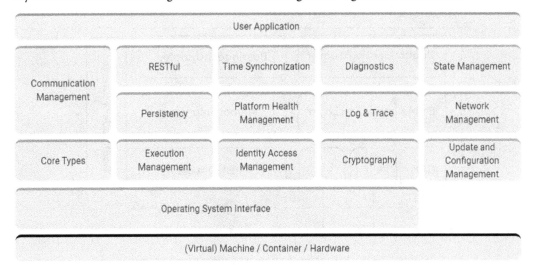

Figure 1.8 – AUTOSAR adaptive block diagram (credit: AUTOSAR)

The adaptive architecture offers the main set of basic services needed to enable computationally intensive user applications. Rather than defining its own operating system, AUTOSAR adaptive defines an operating system interface layer that is compatible with any POSIX PSE51-compliant operating system. This ensures the portability of the AUTOSAR adaptive implementation across various operating systems and hardware platforms. The POSIX PSE51 profile represents the core set of POSIX APIs, which include support for features such as thread priority scheduling, thread-safe functions, synchronized I/O, real-time signals, semaphores, shared memory, **inter-process communication (IPC)** message passing, as well as a few utilities. Moreover, AUTOSAR adaptive can be hosted directly on a single hardware platform or as a virtual machine, sharing the platform with other operating system instances. A brief look at the AUTOSAR adaptive software architecture shows several security-related concepts. For one, data read or written to the non-volatile storage through the persistency cluster can be considered security-relevant. Error information reported through the platform health management cluster to enable the user application to take safe action is also worthy of protection. Communication data handled through the communication management cluster is another interesting area to consider when you're analyzing the security of an adaptive-based system.

> **Discussion point 6**
>
> How about the logs captured by the Log and Trace cluster? What does the cryptography cluster manage, and could these assets be vulnerable? How about the Update and Configuration Management cluster?

Before we finish this section, we must look at how SoC-based ECUs are booted and updated:

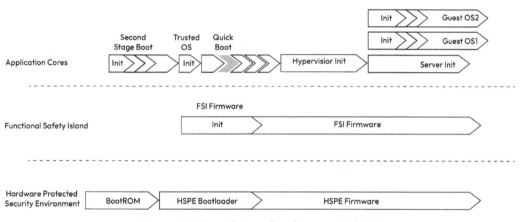

Figure 1.9 – Example boot flow from a typical SoC

Unlike the flash bootloader of the MCU-based ECU, SoC-based ECUs rely on a series of bootloaders that load software and calibration data from the external non-volatile memory into DRAM and other internal volatile memory types before handing control over to the respective cores that run the loaded firmware and software. The boot process typically starts with a MaskROM boot partition, which performs the initial hardware configuration, loads the next boot stage, and then jumps to the next boot partition after verifying its integrity and authenticity (assuming secure boot is enabled). This process continues until all firmware is booted in a staged fashion up to the point where the hypervisor kernel is started (if multiple virtual machines are supported). The hypervisor, using a loader utility, then loads one or more guest operating systems in memory and allocates the necessary CPU, memory, and hardware resources to allow the guest operating system to function as an isolated virtual machine. The latter is then responsible for launching its applications and managing its resources. Alternatively, if the operating system is running directly on the hardware (also known as a host OS), then a hypervisor is not needed. The boot sequence is one of the most security-critical execution paths of the ECU because any exploitable weakness in the boot chain can result in the execution of malicious software, which can spell disaster for a safety-critical ECU.

When it comes to reprogramming the firmware and software binaries, different types of update solutions exist, including OTA. AUTOSAR adaptive provides one reference architecture through its update and configuration management cluster. This enables updates through a diagnostic client in addition to an OTA application. As you might have guessed, this functionality is also security-critical as it exposes the software platform to the possibility of malicious software updates and the execution of potentially dangerous code.

Now that we have been introduced to the general hardware and software architecture of ECUs, let's explore the various ECUs and the domains in which they are grouped based on their related functionality. This will prove useful in later chapters as we analyze the threats that impact such ECUs.

ECU domains

An ECU domain is a grouping of ECUs that collaborate to achieve a common vehicle-level function, such as propulsion control or active braking. Such a grouping improves the efficiency of communication by limiting communication messages to the ECUs that are most co-dependent, thus reducing network congestion caused by non-domain-related messages. As the vehicle architecture evolves, ECU domains may be arranged in different configurations (as we will see in the last section of this chapter). For now, our focus is on understanding the various ECUs that are typically found in a standard vehicle architecture.

> **Note**
>
> The following list of ECUs is meant to be representative of ECUs found in vehicles rather than a comprehensive one with the aim of highlighting the security relevance of each.. Some ECU names can change as OEMs differ in the way they partition vehicle functions across different control units.

Fuel-based powertrain domain

The fuel-based powertrain domain is responsible for producing power in an **internal combustion engine** (ICE) and transmitting it to the wheels. An attacker who can gain access to any ECU in the powertrain domain may be able to affect the vehicle's longitudinal motion, which has an obvious safety impact. However, the more common attack target of this domain is engine tuning to illegally increase performance, which has the side effect of increasing vehicle emissions.

Engine control module (ECM)

A vehicle engine's performance is precisely regulated by the ECM, which pulls data from sensors layered throughout the engine. Among the control functions of the ECM are the engine starting procedure, spark plug ignition, fuel injection, and the cooling process.

Transmission control module (TCM)

The TCM uses different gear ratios to convert a fixed engine speed and torque into a variable driving speed and torque in automatic transmission vehicles. The TCM determines when to shift gears to optimize the vehicle's performance, balancing factors such as fuel efficiency, power, and engine protection. This is based on a variety of input data, such as engine speed (RPM), vehicle speed, throttle position, and load on the vehicle.

Electric drive powertrain domain

This domain is responsible for battery charging and managing and distributing electric power to the motors, as well as the other electronics that require varying power levels. Like the fuel-based powertrain domain, protecting this domain against security breaches is essential to prevent several hazards, such as erratic vehicle motion control and unsafe battery management. The latter is a unique problem for electric vehicles with the potential to cause catastrophic thermal events if the batteries are not operated safely.

Battery management system (BMS)

The BMS's primary function is to manage the **state of charge** (**SoC**) and **state of health** (**SoH**) of the battery pack by controlling the charging and discharging of the battery cells. It also monitors the battery pack's status for hazardous conditions such as overheating or high current events to ensure fail-safe action is taken before it leads to a catastrophic failure.

Onboard charger

The onboard charger's primary role is to convert the AC power provided by the **electric vehicle supply equipment** (**EVSE**) into DC power, which can then be used to charge the vehicle's battery pack. This involves controlling the rate of charging to ensure the battery is charged safely and efficiently.

Additionally, it provides communication between the EVSE and the vehicle's charging system. This is done using a power-line communication protocol, which allows data to be sent over the electrical power lines. This can be used to negotiate the charging rate based on factors such as the vehicle's current state of charge, the capacity of the EVSE, and the temperature of the battery [8].

DC-AC converter

In electric vehicles, the high-voltage DC-AC converter, also known as the inverter, converts DC output from the battery pack to AC power for the electric motor(s).

Powertrain electronic control unit (PECU)

This ECU manages the speed and acceleration of the electric motors by controlling the supplied voltage frequency and magnitude.

Chassis safety control domain

The chassis safety control domain encompasses a variety of ECUs and in-vehicle sensors with a clear focus on active and passive safety management. Since the ECUs in this domain are responsible for vehicle safety, it can be argued that this domain is at the top of the list for security professionals regarding what needs to be protected against cyberattacks.

Electronic braking control module (EBCM)

The EBCM is a specialized module that supplies brake pressure to the wheels to achieve several active safety functions, such as ABS, ESC, and automatic emergency braking.

Airbag control module

As a passive safety system, airbags protect occupants from bodily harm in the case of a collision by inflating the airbags through controlled explosions of the squibs embedded in the airbag.

Electronic power steering (EPS)

The EPS is responsible for providing electronic steering assistance to the driver through the actuation of steering motors. The EPS can provide several enhanced driver assistance features, such as lane departure warnings and lane correction.

Advanced driver assistance (ADAS) control module

While several ADAS functions can be integrated within the EBCM and EPS, a dedicated ECU is common in more modern vehicles to achieve higher levels of autonomy.

This module can command the ECM, EBCM, and EPS to control engine torque and apply braking and steering based on the situation at hand. It integrates inputs from multiple sensors, which makes it possible for the ADAS ECU to perform autonomy functions such as automated parking and autonomous highway driving, to name a few.

Interior cabin domain

The interior cabin domain encompasses the comfort features expected from a modern vehicle. At first glance, this domain may seem less critical for security. On the contrary, due to its ability to control physical security, this domain is among the most targeted by attackers today as a breach of this domain translates to vehicle break-in and theft.

Body control module (BCM)

The BCM manages the remote keyless entry and access to the vehicle's interior. Additionally, it can control seat positions and power windows, light controls, and windshield wipers.

Climate control module (CCM)

The primary function of the CCM is to provide heating and cooling of the cabin. It typically heats the air with a heater core and cools the air with an evaporator and a refrigerant that absorbs heat from the cabin's air.

Infotainment and connectivity domain

The vehicle functions that engage the driver through the **human-machine interface** (**HMI**) are usually grouped in the infotainment domain. ECUs in this domain include the vehicle's head unit, the central console, as well as the driver-facing instrument cluster. You have probably guessed by now that this domain is also security-critical due to the rich user interfaces it offers.

In-vehicle infotainment (IVI)

The IVI offers entertainment and information delivery to drivers and passengers. The IVI system accepts user input through touchscreens and physical controls and serves the occupants with audio, video, and navigation data. In some cases, the instrument cluster can be integrated with the IVI to provide the driver with a digital display of vehicle information such as speed, fuel level, and more. IVI systems enable vehicle occupants to connect their phones through Bluetooth and USB, making them an attractive target for attackers.

Telematics control unit (TCU)

The TCU is the primary remote access point to the vehicle and therefore is considered high on the list of security-critical ECUs. Among its features are the reception of GPS signals and providing connectivity through cellular and Wi-Fi communication to facilitate OTA updates, as well as the transmission of remote messages such as telemetry data and emergency assistance requests.

Cross-domain

The interconnection of all domains can be viewed as its own domain whose primary objective is providing reliable communication across the previously mentioned domains when message exchange is needed.

Central gateway (CGW)

While some vehicles may rely on individual ECUs to act as gateways between two or more vehicle subsystems, a more common trend is to dedicate a single gateway ECU to perform this function. When a CGW is used, it behaves as an in-vehicle router by allowing ECUs from different network segments to communicate with one another. The CGW translates data across different network systems, such as **CAN to CAN**, **CAN to Ethernet**, and **CAN to LIN**. Due to its access to all vehicle domains, the CGW can play an important role in security by segmenting the network architecture and dropping unwanted traffic.

> **Discussion point 7**
>
> Can you think of some unique assets of the CGW? Hint: Network filter rules are one such asset.

Now that we have explored the different ECUs and ECU domains, it's time to dive into the networking technologies that enable them to exchange information.

Exploring the in-vehicle network

The plethora of ECUs, sensors, and actuators gave rise to a diverse set of in-vehicle networking technologies. A common goal of these technologies is the need for reliable communication with deterministic behavior under harsh environmental conditions within low-cost constraints. The bulk of the ECUs rely on signal-based communication through automotive bus systems such as **Controller Area Network** (**CAN/CAN-FD**), FlexRay, Ethernet, and **Local Interconnect Network** (**LIN**). The increased demand for network bandwidth is constantly driving the in-vehicle networks to transition to higher bandwidth solutions such as Ethernet and GMSL.

While securing in-vehicle networks shares common challenges with general network security, the real-time performance constraints and limited payload sizes present unique challenges for many of the automotive networking protocols. In the following section, we will survey the most common automotive networking technologies and touch upon their unique security challenges. Understanding the primary features and common use cases of these protocols will serve as a basis for analyzing the security of the in-vehicle networking protocols in the following chapters.

CAN

It is hard to work on vehicle security without learning about how CAN works and the various security problems it suffers from. CAN is a serial communications protocol that is perfect for real-time applications that require dependable communication under harsh environmental conditions. It has been and remains a popular communication protocol due to its low cost and excellent reliability. CAN is used in a variety of vehicles, including commercial trucks, cars, agricultural vehicles, boats, and even aircraft:

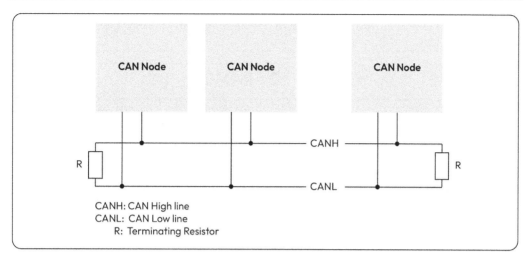

Figure 1.10 – Typical bus layout with multiple CAN nodes sharing a single CAN channel

The CAN physical layer supports bitwise bus arbitration, which ensures that the CAN node transmitting with the lowest CAN ID wins the arbitration, causing the other nodes to wait until the bus is idle before re-attempting transmission. This arbitration scheme can be potentially harmful if CAN nodes misbehave by attempting to acquire bus access greedily.

Another important feature of CAN is its built-in error handling strategy, which ensures that nodes experiencing transmit errors enter a bus-off state to stop disturbing other nodes. This minimizes bus disturbance and allows for application layer strategies to retry transmission after a back-off period. These rules are upheld if the CAN controller is conforming, as is the case with standard CAN-based devices. Note that in later chapters, we will examine the threat of non-conforming CAN controllers, which are intentionally designed to violate the physical and data link layer protocols. In those cases, the malicious CAN node can inject bit flips, creating continuous availability issues with the physical CAN channel.

When it comes to the flavors of CAN, there are three versions: CAN 2.0, CAN-FD, and the latest, CAN XL. CAN 2.0 is the most used since it's the legacy protocol but its maximum payload size of eight bytes and a typical baud rate of 500 kbps makes it unsuitable for more bandwidth-hungry applications. As a result, CAN-FD was added, offering a larger payload of up to 64 bytes and a faster payload data rate, which is typically 2 Mbps. The final variant of CAN is CAN XL, which offers a maximum payload size of 2,048 bytes and up to 20 Mbps. Note that while each CAN protocol advertises a higher theoretical baud rate limit, factors such as bus length, bus load, signal quality, and EM interference force a lower typical baud rate to ensure the reliability of communication.

The CAN FD message's frame format is shown in the following figure to help you visualize what a CAN frame looks like:

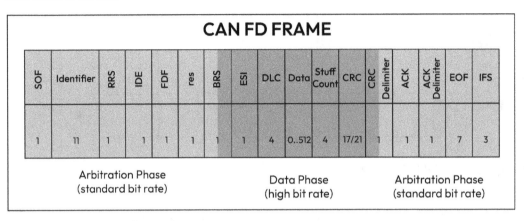

Figure 1.11 – CAN FD bit frame layout

CAN node receivers use the CAN identifier to determine how to interpret the **payload content**, also known as the **PDU**. The CAN ID is important for setting up acceptance filters so that a receiver can determine which messages it wants to receive or ignore. In addition to the CAN ID, the transmitter specifies the DLC field, which indicates the payload size, and the data field, which contains the actual payload. Note that the CRC field is automatically calculated by the CAN controller to ensure the receiver detects flips in the CAN frame occurring at the physical layer. Above the CAN data link layer, several CAN-based protocols exist, such as the *transport protocol*, *diagnostic protocol*, *network management*, and *OEM-defined PDU Com layers*. Diagnostics are particularly interesting for security as they allow an external entity with access to the **onboard diagnostics (OBD)** interface to send potentially harmful diagnostic commands. In later chapters, we will take an in-depth look at how the OBD protocol can be abused to tamper with emissions-related diagnostic tests, as well as OEM-specific diagnostic services. Another important use case of CAN is the transmission and reception of safety-critical PDUs that include sensor data, vehicle status messages, and actuation commands.

> **Discussion point 8**
>
> Given the small payload size of CAN 2.0 messages, and the low tolerance for message latency, can you think of a suitable way to protect the message integrity from malicious tampering?

FlexRay

A big driver for the automotive industry to transition to FlexRay was the desire for a more deterministic communication protocol that could offer guaranteed bandwidth to safety-critical messages. Unlike CAN, which allows the transmitter with the lowest CAN ID to always win the arbitration, FlexRay allocates time slots based on a **Time Division Multiple Access (TDMA)** structure:

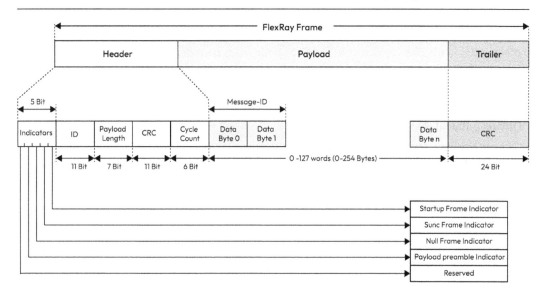

Figure 1.12 – FlexRay frame layout

Another benefit of FlexRay over CAN and CAN FD is the maximum payload of 254 bytes. Moreover, FlexRay offers a redundant configuration for the communication channel to reduce the possibility of failure with a data rate of up to 10 Mbps per communication channel. Where redundant communication is not critical, the redundant channel can be leveraged to boost the data rate to 20 Mbps. FlexRay features a static slot and a dynamic slot to allow fixed messages in reserved time slots to be transmitted, as well as dynamic messages that can be transmitted non-cyclically. The payload length has the same value for all messages transmitted in the static slot. On the other hand, the dynamic slot can have payload lengths of varying sizes.

> **Discussion point 9**
>
> Could the dynamic slot be abused by a malicious FlexRay node?

The payload preamble indicator field indicates whether a frame is a dynamic or static FlexRay message. In a dynamic message, the first two bytes of the payload are the message identifier, which allows for precise identification of the payload and finer control of acceptance filtering. The NULL frame indicator is used to send a message with a payload of zeroes to indicate that the transmitter was not ready to provide data within its allocated time slot. The CRC field is automatically calculated by the FlexRay controller to ensure channel errors are detected by the receiver. Critical to the correct operation of the FlexRay protocol is the use of time synchronization. Without this, senders will start transmission in the wrong time slots and the protocol will lose its reliability. In a FlexRay cluster, at least two FlexRay nodes must act as the synchronization nodes by transmitting a synchronization message in a defined static slot of each cycle. All FlexRay nodes can then compute their offset correction values using the **fault-tolerant midpoint** (**FTM**) algorithm. The FTM algorithm is used to ensure that the nodes in the FlexRay network are synchronized to exchange data in a coordinated and reliable manner. The

FTM algorithm works by using a central node, known as the FTM, which acts as a reference point for the other nodes in the FlexRay network. The FTM node sends periodic synchronization messages to the other nodes in the network, which, in turn, use these messages to adjust their internal clocks to match the clock of the FTM node.

> **Discuss point 10**
>
> Can you think of a unique attack method that the FlexRay cluster is exposed to? Could the FTM algorithm be abused by a malicious node to cause a loss of network synchronization?

LIN

A LIN bus is a single-master, multiple-satellite networking architecture based on the **universal asynchronous receiver-transmitter** (**UART**) protocol and is typically used for applications where low cost is more critical than data transmission rates. In a LIN network, the master sends a command containing a synchronization field and an ID, while the satellite responds with a message payload and checksum. Like CAN 2.0, the payload size is up to 8 bytes but at a much lower bit rate, typically 19.2 kbps:

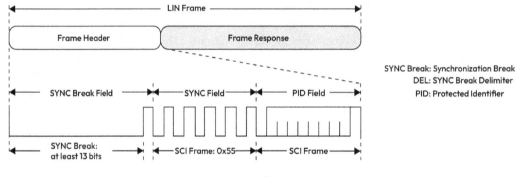

Figure 1.13 – LIN frame structure

LIN communication is based on a schedule table maintained by the LIN master, who uses it to issue LIN header commands directed at specific LIN satellites. LIN is perfect for sensor and actuator networking applications such as seat control, window lifters, side-view mirror heating, and more. A typical vehicle network will contain a CAN node that is also a LIN master acting as a gateway between the CAN network and the LIN sub-network. This enables such a master to control the LIN satellites by sending them actuation commands and diagnostic requests. Therefore, the LIN master node is a critical link in exposing deeply embedded sensors and actuators in the rest of the vehicle through a CAN-LIN gateway node.

> **Discussion point 11**
>
> Can you think of a way the LIN bus can become exposed to security threats?

UART

The UART communication protocol supports the asynchronous transmission of bits and relies on the receiver to perform bit sampling without the use of a synchronized clock signal. The transmitting UART node augments the data packet being sent with a start and stop bit in place of a clock signal. The standard baud rate, which can go up to 115,200 bps, is 9,600 bps, which is adequate for low-speed communication tasks:

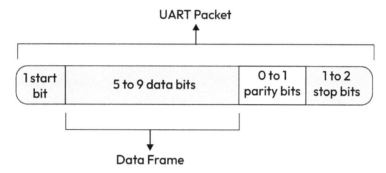

Figure 1.14 – A UART packet showing start, stop, data, and parity bits

UART is typically used in automotive applications to open debug shells with an MCU or SoC, which naturally makes it an interesting protocol for attackers to abuse.

SENT

The **Single Edge Nibble Transmission (SENT)** bus, known as SAE J2716, provides an accurate and economical means of transmitting data from sensors that measure temperature, flow, pressure, and position to ECUs. The SENT bus is unique in that it can simultaneously transfer data at two different data rates of up to 30 kbps, outperforming the LIN bus. The primary data is normally transmitted in the *fast channel*, with the option to simultaneously send secondary data in the *slow channel*.

A typical SENT frame consists of 32 bits, as shown in *Figure 1.15*, and breaks up the data into 4-bit nibbles that are terminated by a CRC to ensure frame integrity against corruption errors:

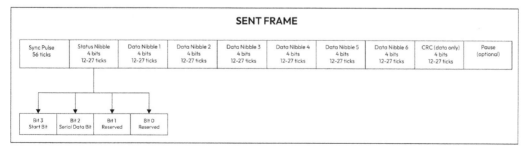

Figure 1.15 – SENT frame format

Although SENT is robust, easy to integrate, and has high accuracy, the SENT messages can still be affected by noise, timing problems, and subtle differences in implementations, which limits its use to specific sensor types.

GMSL

Gigabit Multimedia Serial Link (GMSL) is a high-speed multigigabit serial interface used originally in automotive video applications such as infotainment and **advanced driver assistance systems (ADASs)**. It allows for the transmission of high-definition video and audio signals between components within the vehicle, such as cameras, displays, and audio processors. It uses a serializer on the transmitter side to convert data into a serial stream, and a deserializer on the receiving side to convert the serial data back into parallel words for processing. GMSL can transfer video at a speed of up to 6 Gbps:

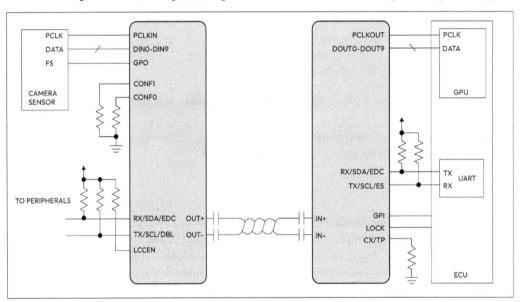

Figure 1.16 – GMSL use case diagram based on analog devices (ADI) GMSL deserializer

Figure 1.16 shows a typical configuration of a camera application where a serializer chip (shown on the left) is connected to a camera sensor, while a deserializer chip (shown on the right) is connected to the ECU. In addition to its use in audio and video transmission, GMSL technology is used in automotive applications to transmit other types of data, such as high speed sensor data and control signals.

I2C

Inter-Integrated Circuit (**I2C**) is a two-wire serial communication protocol mainly used for communication between an MCU or SoC and a peripheral such as a camera sensor or a memory chip (EEPROM) that is positioned near the controlling unit. I2C supports data rates of up to 5 Mbps in ultra-fast mode and as low as 100 kbps in standard mode. I2C comes with an address frame that contains the binary address of the satellite device, one or more data frames of 1 byte in size that contain the data being transmitted, start and stop conditions, read/write bits, and ACK/NACK bits between each data frame:

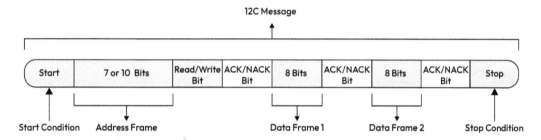

Figure 1.17 – I2C message layout

Ethernet

The constant growth of bandwidth demands due to content-rich use cases has led the automotive industry to gradually adopt Ethernet through a set of IEEE standards known as Automotive Ethernet [9]:

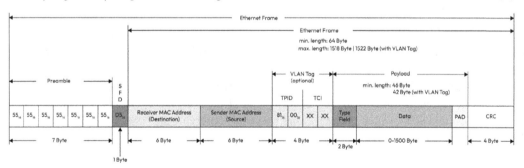

Figure 1.18 – Ethernet frame layout

Ethernet-based communication offers high bandwidth with great flexibility for integration with standard products outside the automotive domain. Automotive Ethernet covers a data rate range starting from 10 Mbit/sec standardized through 10Base-T1S up to 10 Gb/sec standardized through 10Gbase-T1. This makes it suitable for a range of automotive use cases, from time-sensitive communication to high-throughput video applications.

One of the primary differences between Ethernet and automotive Ethernet is the physical layer, which is designed to handle stringent automotive EMC requirements. Another difference is the introduction of the IEEE **time-sensitive networking** (**TSN**) standard, which offers preemption to allow critical data to preempt non-critical data, time-aware shaping to ensure a deterministic latency in receiving critical data, **precise timing** (**PTP**) to synchronize clocks within the network, per-stream filtering to eliminate unexpected frames, frame replication, and elimination, as well as an audio-video transport protocol for infotainment-related use cases.

J1939

SAE J1939, defined by the **Society of Automotive Engineers** (**SAE**), is a set of standards that defines how ECUs communicate via the CAN bus in heavy-duty vehicles:

Layer	Name	Standard
7	Application	SAE J1939-71 (applications)
		SAE J1939-73 (diagnostics)
6-4	Presentation, Session, and Transport	Not used but included in the Data Link layer
3	Network	J1939-31
2	Data Link	J1939-21
1	Physical	J1939-11

For communication among ECUs within the truck network, the standard ISO 11898 CAN physical layer is used. However, for communication between the truck and the trailer, a different physical and data link layer based on ISO11992-1 is used.

At the data link layer, J1939 supports peer-to-peer messages in which the source and the destination address are provided in the 29-bit CAN ID. It also supports broadcast messages, which contain only the source address. This allows multiple nodes to receive the message. A unique feature of J1939 over traditional CAN is the **Parameter Group Number** (**PGN**) and **Suspect Parameter Number** (**SPN**). Unlike passenger vehicles that rely heavily on OEM-defined PDUs, J1939 comes with a set of standard PGNs and SPNs, which makes it easier for people observing the J1939 CAN bus to decode the meaning of the messages.

Let's look at an example PGN and its corresponding SPNs, as defined in the *SAE J1939 standard*.

The PGN 65262 is reserved for engine temperature and given a fixed transmission rate of 1s, a PDU length of 8 bytes, and a default priority of 6. The 8 bytes are distributed as follows:

Start Position	Length	Parameter Name	SPN
1	1 byte	Engine Coolant Temperature	110
2	1 byte	Engine Fuel Temperature 1	174
3-4	2 bytes	Engine Oil Temperature 1	175
5-6	2 bytes	Engine Turbocharger Oil Temperature	176
7	1 byte	Engine Intercooler Temperature	52
8	1 byte	Engine Intercooler Thermostat Opening	1134

The SPN is the equivalent of a signal ID that's commonly used in signal-based communication for passenger vehicles. J1939 standardizes the SPN name, description, data length, and even the resolution to ensure the raw-to-physical interpretation is performed correctly.

When transferring data that is larger than 8 bytes, you will need to use the transport protocol, which in J1939 supports message transfers of up to 1,785 data bytes. This is done through two modes: connection mode data transfer, in which **ready-to-send** (**RTS**) and **clear-to-send** (**CTS**) frames are used to allow the receiver to control the data flow, and a **broadcast announce message** (**BAM**), which allows the sender to transmit messages without the data flow control handshake.

Discussion point 12

Can you think of ways the handshake messages can be abused by a malicious network participant?

The transport protocol supports diagnostic applications, which rely on a set of **parameter groups** (**PGs**) reserved for handling different diagnostic services. PGs designated as **diagnostic message** (**DM**) types fulfill the UDS protocol, which is commonly used for passenger vehicle diagnostics. When observing a diagnostic frame over J1939, you can easily look up the diagnostic trouble code by observing the SPN field (which contains the unique identifier of a fault parameter) and the FMI field (which contains the type of failure detected).

Finally, source address management and mapping to an actual function are handled by the network management layer. Unlike passenger vehicle network management protocols, which are designed to support ECU sleep and wakeup, J1939 uses network management to define how ECUs get admitted to the network and how device addresses are administered in dynamic networks. A simple form of J1939 network management is the transmission of the `Address Claimed` parameter group (PGN 0x00EE00) of every ECU after booting and before the start of communication. With `Address Claim`, the device name and a predefined device address are exchanged to describe the network topology. For a detailed understanding of the address claiming protocol, we encourage you to read *J1939-31* (see *[1]* in the *Further reading* section). For now, let's be aware that this ability to claim certain addresses can present security challenges if a network participant is not behaving honestly.

So far in this chapter, we've surveyed the most common in-vehicle networks. We intentionally left out external network types such as Wi-Fi, Bluetooth, 5G cellular, GNSS, and RF communication. We will explore threats that emanate from these communication domains in the following chapters. Now that we have learned how to interconnect components through the vehicle network, let's explore some special vehicle components that allow an ECU to sense and react to changes in the vehicle's environment.

Sensors and actuators

The MCU and SoC-based ECUs discussed in the previous sections would be of very little use if it were not for the sensors that feed into their control algorithms and the actuators that are driven by the output of those algorithms. Sensors and actuators enable numerous vehicle functions that enhance both the driver experience and safety aspects, such as adaptive cruise control, automatic emergency braking, and more. When it comes to sensing, modern vehicles may contain upward of 100 sensors both embedded within the ECUs as well as within the vehicle's body. Sensors transform a variety of physical conditions, including temperature, pressure, speed, and location, into analog or digital data output.

Understanding the physical properties of the sensor and its vehicle interfaces allows us to determine how it can be affected by a cyberattack. In the following subsection, we will sample a variety of sensors to gain a perspective on how they sense inputs and the interfaces by which they transmit and receive data:

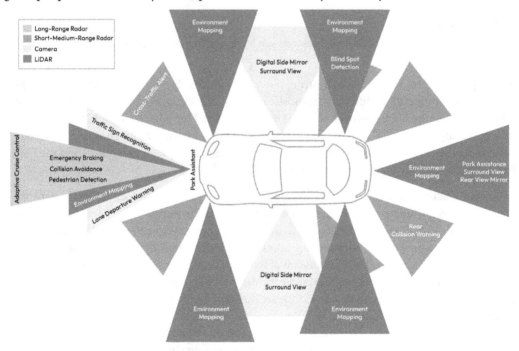

Figure 1.19 – Sensors mapped to ADAS functions providing 360-degree sensing capability

Sensor types

The sensors shown in *Figure 1.19*, in addition to a sample of internal sensors, are described here:

- **Cameras**: These enable a range of vehicle functions, such as digital rear-view mirrors, traffic sign recognition, and a surrounding view on the center display. A camera sensor produces raw image data of the surroundings by detecting light on a photosensitive surface (image plane) using a lens placed in front of the sensor. Camera data is then processed by the receiving ECU to produce the image data formatted for the camera applications. Typically, an image resolution of 8 megapixels is supported with a frame rate of up to 60 FPS. In most cases, the raw image data is serialized from the sensor over the GMSL link and deserialized by the host ECU with data transfers of up to 6 GB per second. A separate control channel is typically supported to configure and manage the sensor using a low-speed communication link such as I2C. Certain specialized cameras produce classified object information such as lane, car, and pedestrian. In all cases, attacks against cameras can impact the vehicle's ability to correctly identify objects, which can have a serious safety impact. Additionally, user privacy can be violated if the camera data is illegally accessed.

- **Light Detection and Ranging (LiDAR)**: This is a remote sensing technology based on the principle of emitting pulses of laser light and measuring the reflection of target objects. The interval taken between the emission and reception of the light pulse enables the estimation of the object's distance. As the LiDAR scans its surroundings, it generates a 3D representation of the scene, also known as a point cloud. LiDAR sensors are used in object detection algorithms and can support the transmission of either raw or pre-processed point cloud data. Such sensors typically interface to the host ECU through a 1000Base-T1 Ethernet link. Attacks against LiDAR can impact the vehicle's ability to detect objects, which can have a safety impact.

- **Ultrasonic sensors**: These are electronic devices that measure the distance of a target object by emitting ultrasonic sound waves and converting the reflected sound into an electrical signal. Ultrasonic waves are sound waves transmitted at frequencies higher than those audible to humans and have two main components: the transmitter (which emits the sound using piezoelectric crystals) and the receiver (which transforms the acoustic signal into an electrical one). Ultrasonic sensors typically interface with the host ECU via CAN. Attacks against the ultrasonic sensors can impact the vehicle's ability to detect objects during events such as parking, which can have a safety impact.

- **Radio Detection and Ranging (Radar)**: This is based on the idea of emitting EM waves within the region of interest and receiving dispersed waves (or reflections) from targets, which are then processed to determine the object range information. This allows the sensor to determine the relative speed and position of identified obstacles using the Doppler property of EM waves. A radar sensor's resolution is much more coarse than a camera's and typically interfaces to the host ECU via CAN or Ethernet. Like LiDAR, Radar is used in autonomous driving applications, so attacks impacting its data have implications for vehicle safety.

- **GNSS sensors**: These use their antennas to receive satellite-based navigation signals from a network of satellites that orbit the Earth to provide position, velocity, and timing information. These sensors typically interface with the host ECU via CAN or UART. Attacks on GNSS sensors can impact the vehicle's localization ability, which is critical for determining the vehicle's location within a map to establish a sense of the road and buildings. Also, GNSS input is necessary for receiving global time, which, if compromised, can interfere with the vehicle's ability to get a reliable time source.

- **Temperature sensors**: These are used for sensing temperature, typically using a thermistor, which utilizes the concept of negative temperature coefficient. A thermistor with a negative temperature coefficient experiences lower resistance as its temperature increases, which allows you to correlate a change in temperature to a change in the electric signal flowing through the thermistor. Other techniques besides a thermistor exist, such as **infrared (IR)** sensors, which detect the IR energy emitted by an object and transmit a signal to the MCU for processing. Temperature sensors are used in many automotive applications both inside the MCUs and SoCs as well as on the PCB board itself. They are essential for temperature monitoring to satisfy safety requirements. Temperature sensors embedded within the MCU typically provide temperature readings through a simple register read operation, while external temperature sensors can be interfaced to the MCU via **general-purpose input/output (GPIO)** pins, **analog-to-digital converters (ADCs)**, or I2C. Attacks on temperature sensors can impact the ECU's ability to monitor its temperature, potentially leading to undetected overheating situations, which can be hazardous.

- **Vehicle dynamics sensors**: These enable active and passive safety ECUs to determine the vehicle's motion state, which factors into the algorithms for controlling steering, braking, and airbag deployment. Attacks on any one of these sensors will have a direct safety impact as the control algorithms consuming their data would be making erroneous calculations that would likely result in an unsafe control action. Here is a sample of the most common sensors that are used within this domain:

  - **Inertial measurement units (IMUs)** sense the physical effects of motion along six dimensions: yaw, roll, and pitch rate as well as lateral, longitudinal, and vertical accelerations. This helps the vehicle determine when it is experiencing hazardous events, such as slipping on ice or roll-over. IMUs leverage MEMS technology to sense acceleration through the capacitive change in the micromechanical structures of the sensor. They are typically interfaced with the host ECU via CAN.

  - The steering angle sensor design is typically based on **Giant Magnetoresistance (GMR)** technology. It is positioned onto the steering shaft to measure the steering angle value. The sensor outputs both the steering angle value and steering angle velocity over CAN. Wheel speed sensors use a Hall-sensing element in a changing magnetic field to produce an alternating digital output signal whose frequency is correlated to the wheel speed. The wheel speed sensor is typically hardwired to the host ECU, normally the EBCM.

- The brake pedal sensor, also known as the angular position sensor, is normally based on a magnetic field sensor, which enables contactless pedal angle measurement. This is typically used in the regenerative braking of hybrid and electric vehicles. This sensor is hardwired to the host ECU, normally the EBCM.

The accelerator pedal sensor, also known as the rotary position sensor, uses a magnetic rotary sensor with a Hall element to measure the angular position. The sensor is hardwired to the host ECU, normally the ECM. In addition to sensors mounted inside the vehicle, a wide range of sensors exist that are integrated directly within vehicle electromechanical components such as the **engine's mass air flow rate sensor**, which is used for electronic fuel injection. Another important engine sensor is the **exhaust gas oxygen sensor**, which enables the exhaust emissions catalyst to operate correctly. Attacks against these types of sensors can have environmental impacts due to their role in emissions control.

Understanding the sensors that are used within your vehicle, their physical characteristics, and the method by which they are interfaced with ECUs is important for understanding the threats that may apply to those sensors. Therefore, you are encouraged to make an inventory of all the sensors related to your ECU as preparation for the next chapters when we study threats impacting sensors.

The sensor inputs to the control algorithms of an ECU would be of very little value if not for the components that convert the ECU output into physical action. In the next subsection, we will focus on these types of components and learn how they can be controlled by the ECU.

Actuators

An actuator is a component that can be electronically controlled to move a mechanism or a system. It is operated by a source of energy, such as an electric current, hydraulic fluid pressure, or pneumatic pressure, which is then converted into motion. The ECU contains the electronic components necessary to interface with the actuators and apply the software-driven control algorithms. Understanding how actuators are controlled and the effect they can have if misused is important for vehicle cybersecurity. Here's a sample of some of the common actuators that we expect to find in a vehicle:

- **AC servo motors**: These are electrical devices that are driven by an ECU to accurately rotate mechanisms within the vehicle. These motors are used in many use cases within the vehicle, such as assisting steering by controlling the motion of the steering column, as demanded by the EPS.

- **Brushless DC motors**: In powertrain applications, brushless DC motors can be found in the shifting function of the transmission, as well as the torque distribution controller in transfer cases and differentials. Several possible interfaces exist to control these motors, such as **Pulse Width Modulation (PWM)** and CAN.

- **Electric window lift drives**: These enable the opening and safe closing of windows. They typically offer self-locking gear units to prevent windows from being forced open from the outside. These drives are normally interfaced with the BCM through LIN.

- **Seat drives**: These use one - or two-stage gear motors to control seat adjustment. It is normally controlled by the BCM through LIN.

- **Sunroof drive**: It produces high torque to control the sunroof's position through a motor and gear system that is controlled by the BCM.

- **Fuel pump**: This is electrically controlled by the ECM to provide the engine with fuel at the required pressure.

- **Injectors**: These are solenoid-equipped injection nozzles that the ECM manages. The ECM determines the basic fuel injection time based on intake air volume and engine RMP, as well as the corrective fuel injection time based on engine coolant temperature and the feedback signal from the oxygen sensor during closed-loop control.

While actuators are normally not directly accessible by an attacker, it is important to understand the impacts of attacks targeting them and whether feasible attack paths exist to reach them.

Now that we have explored the various ECUs, sensors/actuators, and networking technologies that enable their communication, we will consider the different topologies that shape how these components are interconnected and used.

Exploring the vehicle architecture types

The different ways an E/E architecture can be built impact the vehicle attack surface, as well as the attack feasibility associated with certain attack paths. As we will see in *Chapter 3*, some E/E architectures are more vulnerable to cyberattacks than others.

Throughout the years, the E/E architecture has evolved from a highly distributed one with direct mapping between vehicle functions and ECUs to a more centralized architecture where vehicle functions are consolidated into a few yet computationally powerful domain controllers. *Figure 1.20* shows the expected progress of E/E vehicle architectures. It starts with the highly distributed architecture, which consists of highly interconnected function-specific ECUs. The second evolution represents the domain-centralized architecture, which utilizes domain-specific ECUs that consolidate the features of multiple ECUs into fewer ones. The next generation is the zone architecture, which consists of vehicle computers or zone ECUs connected to the rest of the control units, sensors, and actuators:

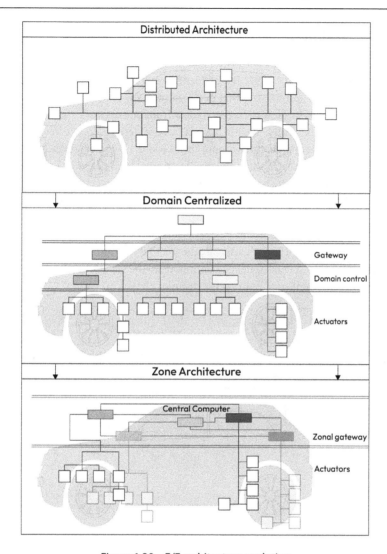

Figure 1.20 – E/E architecture evolution

Let's zoom in on the three main types of E/E vehicle architectures to better understand their differences and gain insights into some of their security weaknesses.

> **Note**
>
> OEMs take different approaches to how they advance their vehicle architectures, so it is possible to find vehicle architectures that are in a transitional stage between architecture classes presented here. At the time of writing this book, the story of the vehicle architecture evolution has not been finished yet, so a different architecture class may still emerge.

Highly distributed E/E architecture

This type of architecture clusters ECUs with similar functionality or inter-dependent functionalities in shared network segments using CAN, LIN, or FlexRay so that messages can be exchanged. You may find several ECUs in this architecture that perform message relay functionality in addition to their primary vehicle functions to allow messages to flow from one network segment to another – for example, CAN to CAN or CAN to LIN. Such ECUs can be considered as local gateways that allow you to add new ECUs to the vehicle architecture without the need for a complete redesign of the in-vehicle network. A side effect of this approach is that the proliferation of local gateways creates weaknesses in network isolation as these gateways are not designed to limit unwanted access to the newly added ECUs. To reduce the addition of dedicated network channels, the designers of this architecture may allow ECUs with a high degree of difference in security exposure to be grouped in the same sub-network. For example, you may find the infotainment ECU adjacent to the braking ECU, which should make you uneasy. Another common aspect of this architecture is that the OBD connector, which enables a diagnostic client to send and receive diagnostic commands to the vehicle, is directly connected to an internal vehicle network segment such as the powertrain or chassis domain:

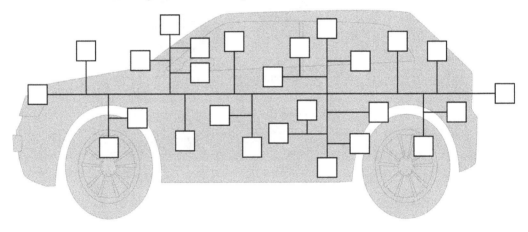

Figure 1.21 – Highly distributed architecture

> **Discussion point 13**
>
> What could go wrong if infotainment ECUs are adjacent to safety-critical ECUs in a network segment? Why is the OBD connector a source of concern?

Domain-centralized E/E architecture

Challenges in terms of the cost and maintenance of highly distributed E/E architectures gave rise to the domain-centralized E/E architecture when security was not even a concern yet. The primary feature of this architectural variant is that you can group ECUs in well-defined vehicle domains and separate communication between the domains through dedicated gateways. The domains we introduced in the previous sections can be seen in *Figure 1.22* connected through an Ethernet backbone to support high-bandwidth message transfer across the different domains:

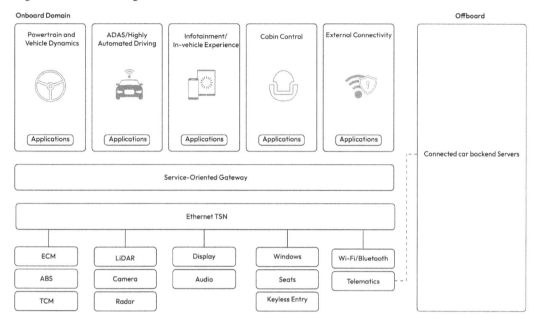

Figure 1.22 – Domain partitioning in a centralized architecture

One of the main features of the centralized architecture is the availability of a central multi-network gateway with a high-speed networking backbone such as Ethernet, which is preferred due to the high volume of data transferred between domains as well as off-board systems. This gateway, which can serve as a vehicle's central networking hub, is capable of enforcing network filtering rules that prevent one domain from interfering with others. A typical CGW contains multiple CAN/CAN-FD interfaces, along with multiple Ethernet interfaces with support for time-sensitive communication. The backbone enables features such as **Diagnostics over IP** (**DoIP**) to support high-bandwidth use cases such as parallel flashing and diagnostics of multiple ECUs.

> **Discussion point 14**
> What role does the CGW play in improving the E/E architecture's security?

Domain control unit

A **domain control unit** (**DCU**) combines multiple small ECUs into a single ECU with a more powerful processor, larger memory, and more hardware peripherals and network interfaces. DCUs are a key enabling feature of software-defined vehicles, where vehicle features can be enabled or disabled through software updates without the need for a hardware upgrade. DCUs typically rely on high-performance MCUs and SoCs.

Due to a common computational platform being shared among different applications, these systems need to consider a larger threat space, which gives rise to concerns regarding spatial and temporal isolation:

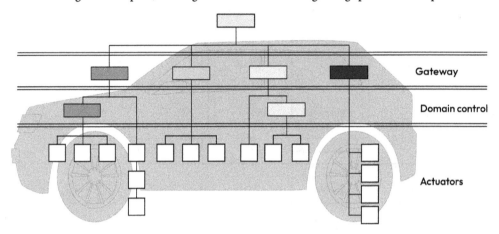

Figure 1.23 – DCU architectural view

From a software perspective, a domain controller is expected to execute an application subsystem that runs within a POSIX-based operating system alongside a high safety integrity-compliant MCU within a real-time operating system. One common implementation of this architecture uses an AUTOSAR adaptive instance, alongside one or more AUTOSAR classic instances, as shown in *Figure 1.24*. Assumptions about the security of real-time instances must be reconsidered in this type of architecture because of a common hardware platform being shared:

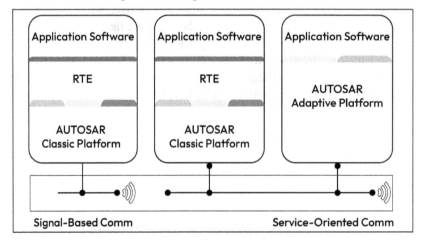

Figure 1.24 – Multiple software platforms in a single DCU

Discussion point 15

Do you think that a DCU is more vulnerable to attacks compared to the ECUs that run AUTOSAR classic only?

Central compute cluster

This high-performance vehicle computer is built upon heterogeneous execution domains, integrating CPUs, GPUs, and real-time cores to support computationally intensive applications, such as autonomous driving, infotainment, and the cockpit, all within a common hardware platform. An example of a central compute cluster is NVIDIA's autonomous driving platform, as shown here:

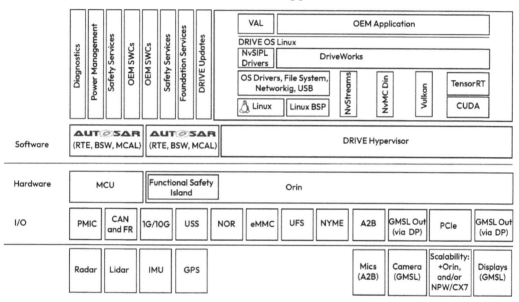

Figure 1.25 – Software partitioning of the NVIDIA vehicle computer (credit Nvidia)

This type of architecture supports multiple instances of AUTOSAR classic for the real-time safety applications that are executed on the real-time cores. A separate CPU cluster is hosted through a hypervisor that supports one or more POSIX-compliant operating systems. Typically, a safety-certified operating system such as BlackBerry's QNX manages autonomous driving applications, while Linux and Android operating systems are used to offer cockpit and infotainment services. These systems offer a rich set of peripherals and network interfaces to enable applications for computer vision, object detection, sensor fusion, and many cloud-supported services, such as mapping and software updates.

Discussion point 16

Can you think of the security weaknesses of this type of architecture? What happens when applications of varying security levels are hosted within a single computer?

Zone architecture

The zone controller is an essential element of this design as it connects a large number of actuators and sensors to a CGW and vehicle computer. Zones are distributed based on the location in the vehicle (for example, the front driver location can be a zone and the rear right passenger location can be another zone). A zone supports various functions, and local computing handles each of these functions to the best extent possible. Typically, a central computing cluster (introduced in the previous subsection) is linked to the sensors and devices through networked zone gateways. A backbone network connects the zones to the central computing cluster:

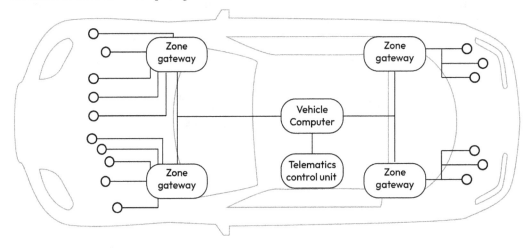

Figure 1.26 – Top-level view of the zone architecture

The domain-centralized E/E vehicle architecture can scale well if the sensors and actuator placement remain very close to the ECUs. However, as new vehicle functions are added, vehicle architects must duplicate sensors and add more cabling and interfaces, which becomes very costly.

This resulted in the advent of the zone architecture, which aims to distribute power and data effectively across the vehicle while reducing the wiring cost, vehicle weight, and manufacturing complexity. This approach classifies ECUs by their physical location inside the vehicle, leveraging a CGW to manage communication. Rather than duplicating sensors, the CGW can transport sensor data across zones, reducing overall costs. Furthermore, the physical proximity of sensors to the zone controllers reduces cabling, which saves space and reduces vehicle weight, while also improving data processing speeds and power distribution around the vehicle. This makes the networked-zone approach desirable as it provides better scalability and flexibility, as well as improved reliability and functionality.

> **Discussion point 17**
>
> Are there downsides from a security standpoint of having so much data processed by the CGW? How about the single central vehicle computer – could it present security risks?

Commercial truck architecture types

Before concluding our discussion on E/E architectures, we need to touch upon a special vehicle category that is quite important for security. Commercial trucks may not get the glamour that passenger vehicles get, but when security is considered, the consequence of a breach in a commercial truck weighing up to 40 tons can have far more catastrophic effects than a passenger vehicle. The E/E architecture of commercial trucks trends in a similar fashion to passenger vehicles, with the main difference being the existence of one or more trailers that have electromechanical systems, such as trailer braking and trailer lamps. Due to the longer development cycles for commercial trucks, their architectures typically include more legacy components, making it harder to adopt security features. Another differentiating aspect of commercial trucks is the reliance on the J1939 protocol for in-vehicle communication. Moreover, the usage of SAE J2497 is common for communicating with the trailers through **power-line communications** (**PLC**), creating a unique attack surface. When it comes to ECU types, while the domains are largely the same, the types of actuators differ due to the larger vehicle size. For example, the braking system relies on pneumatic pressure rather than brake fluid pressure. Throughout the remaining chapters of this book, we will point out special threats and considerations that apply to commercial trucks when appropriate.

Summary

In this chapter, we surveyed the various types of E/E architectures, their respective networking technologies, and the various sensors, actuators, and control units that make it possible for the vehicle to perform its functions. This deep dive gave us a solid base for understanding how automotive electronic systems are built, which is essential when exploring how they can be forced to fail through malicious attacks. In discussing each layer of the architecture, we shed some light on the assets that are worthy of protection and the consequences of a successful attack. While this chapter has given us a good basis for what needs to be protected, we should be aware that E/E architectures are constantly evolving, which makes the attack surface a constant variable. Nevertheless, the fundamentals we learned here should enable us to adapt to those changes as we encounter new attack surfaces and threats.

In the next chapter, we will review the fundamental security concepts, methods, and techniques necessary for analyzing and securing our automotive systems.

Answers to discussion points

Here are the answers to this chapter's discussion points:

1. Typical components on the PCB that require protection are memory chips, MCUs, SoCs, networking integrated circuits, and general-purpose I/Os that control the sensors and actuators.

2. An attacker with physical possession of an MCU-based ECU will be interested in compromising networking interfaces such as CAN and Ethernet.

3. An attacker with physical possession of an SoC-based ECU will be interested in compromising the PCIe link, the eMMC chip, and the QSPI flash memory.

4. Mode management software is highly security-relevant. An attacker who can influence the ECU mode can cause serious damage. For example, transitioning the ECU into a shutdown state while the vehicle is in motion will have safety impacts. Similarly, interfering with the ECU's ability to stay in sleep mode can impact the battery life and cause operational damage.

5. Certain bootloaders offer support for reprogramming the flash bootloader itself. While this capability is convenient for patching bootloader software after production, it creates an opportunity for attackers to replace the bootloader with a malicious version that bypasses signature verification checks during a normal download session – not to mention the possibility of leaving the ECU in an unprogrammable state if the flash bootloader is erased without a backup copy.

6. Logs and program traces are favorite targets for attackers as they can contain valuable information that can be leveraged during a reconnaissance phase to discover secrets and reverse engineer how a system works. Similarly, software that handles cryptographic services is a good target for abuse to exfiltrate or misuse cryptographic secrets. The software cluster handling update management is certainly a target of interest due to it serving as an attack surface for tampering with the ECU software.

7. Routing tables, CAN filter rules, and Ethernet switch configurations (if supported within the CGW or managed by the CGW) are all valuable targets for attack.

8. Absent support for cryptographic integrity methods and the usage of network intrusion detection and prevention systems can be quite effective in blocking unwanted traffic from reaching the deeper network layers of the vehicle. We will learn more about this in the following chapters.

9. A malicious FlexRay node can abuse the dynamic slot to send a large number of messages to monopolize the allotted bandwidth. It can also repeatedly request the dynamic slot, even if it does not need it to prevent other nodes from using the dynamic slot.

10. A malicious FlexRay node can introduce disruptions with the FTM process, leading to synchronization issues through incorrect time reporting and transmission delays or collisions.

11. LIN interfaces can be relatively easy to access through the vehicle cabin, such as seat controllers. Additionally, the CAN-LIN gateway is a primary access point to reach the LIN bus.

12. A malicious network participant can inject spoofed RTS and CTS frames to disrupt the communication protocol.

13. Given the rich feature set of the infotainment ECU and its connectivity capabilities, it is a more likely target for attack. If the infotainment ECU is on the same network segment as a safety-critical ECU, then an attacker only needs to compromise the infotainment ECU to be in direct contact with the safety-critical ECU. It is generally a good practice to create layers of security defense to reduce the likelihood that a single security breach can impact vehicle safety. On the other hand, the OBD connector provides direct access to the vehicle's internal network. It is common for vehicle owners to plug in OBD dongles to allow them to gain insights into their vehicle driving patterns, as well as receive fault code notifications. These dongles act as attack vectors against the internal vehicle network due to their Bluetooth or Wi-Fi connectivity.

14. The CGW plays the role of network isolation and filtering. It is also an ideal candidate for implementing intrusion detection and prevention systems for the internal vehicle network.

15. A DCU that is running AUTOSAR adaptive alongside AUTOSAR classic is likely to be exposed to more attacks than a typical ECU that is running AUTOSAR classic alone due to its feature-rich nature and its support for dynamic application launching. This does not mean that it has to be less secure if it is designed properly to account for all the threats in a systematic fashion.

16. Having a heterogeneous set of operating systems that offer a high degree of configurability and advanced features certainly increases the likelihood of security weaknesses becoming exploitable. Additionally, each execution environment is known to run applications with varying degrees of security levels, from Android apps to time-sensitive applications running within a real-time operating system environment. This requires careful consideration to ensure that the system provides adequate spatial and temporal isolation capabilities to limit unwanted interference.

17. In the case of the CGW handling high-throughput data, it can become susceptible to denial of service attacks that aim to exhaust its networking resources. Having a single central vehicle computer may function as a single point of failure. Therefore, it is important for such systems to internally support several redundant compute and networking layers.

Further reading

To learn more about the topics that were covered in this chapter, take a look at the following resources:

- [1] SAE J1939 Network Layer: `https://www.sae.org/standards/content/j1939/31_202306/`.

- [2] Learning Module J1939: `https://elearning.vector.com/mod/page/view.php?id=406`.

- [3] M. Integrated, 28-bit gmsl deserializer for coax or stp cable. `https://www.analog.com/en/products/max9272a.html` [Online, Accessed 23-December-2022].

- [4] J. Deichmann, G. Doll, and C. Knochenhaue, Rethinking car software and electronics architecture. [Online]. Available: `https://www.mckinsey.com/industries/automotive-and-assembly/our-insights/rethinking-car-software-and-electronics-architecture`.

- [5] M. Tischer, The computing center in the vehicle: Autosar adaptive, Translation of a German publication in Elektronik automotive, special issue "Bordnetz", September 2018 [Online]. [Online]. Available: `https://assets.vector.com/cms/content/know-how/technical-articles/ AUTOSAR/AUTOSAR Adaptive ElektronikAutomotive 201809 PressArticle EN.pdf`.

- [6] M. Rumez, D. Grimm, R. Kriesten, and E. Sax, An overview of automotive service-oriented architectures and implications for security countermeasures, IEEE Access, vol. 8, 12 2020.

- [7] M. Iorio, M. Reineri, F. Risso, R. Sisto, and F. Valenza, "Securing some/ip for in-vehicle service protection," IEEE Transactions on Vehicular Technology, vol. 69, pp. 13 450–13 466, 11 2020.

- [8] ISO 15118-1:2019 Road vehicles – Vehicle to grid communication interface – Part 1: General information and use case definition.

- [9] ISO 15031-3:2016 Road vehicles – Communication between vehicle and external equipment for emissions-related diagnostics – Part 3: Diagnostic connector and related electrical circuits: Specification and use.

- [10] OPEN Alliance Automotive Ethernet Specifications: `https://www.opensig.org/about/specifications/`.

2
Cybersecurity Basics for Automotive Use Cases

In *Chapter 1*, we peered into the vehicle E/E architecture layer by layer to understand its layout, interfaces, networks, and various electronic components. While doing so, we got a glimpse of the objects of value that needed protection and some of the adverse consequences of successful attacks. In this chapter, we will review some fundamental security concepts, methods, and principles that are especially applicable to automotive use cases. Building this foundation is a prerequisite for the later chapters, where we will explore vehicle threats, the methodology for treating them, and the technical cybersecurity controls to mitigate them.

If you are skilled in the art of general cybersecurity, this chapter will give you an automotive perspective on how to apply the security fundamentals to automotive use cases. If you're not, this chapter should be treated as a crash course in cybersecurity to enable future learning. Rather than presenting you with an academic view of cybersecurity, we will use practical examples to tie the concepts of this chapter to real-world scenarios that you are likely to encounter when securing an automotive system. We will start by defining the various attack classes that a vehicle must defend against. Then, we will introduce the high-level security objectives and cover confidentiality, integrity, authenticity, accountability, and availability of vehicle assets while at rest, in motion, and in use.

Next, we will survey cryptographic mechanisms and concepts to show how they can be applied to automotive use cases. In some cases, we will refer to some mathematical concepts underlying certain cryptographic algorithms to help you gain perspective on what prerequisites will be needed if you choose to pursue a more in-depth study of the field of cryptography. Finally, we will present the set of security principles that must be considered when designing cyber-resilient automotive systems. By the end of this chapter, you should have a good grasp of the security fundamentals that are needed when studying the security of an automotive system.

In this chapter, we will cover the following main topics:

- Exploring the attack classes
- Identifying security objectives
- Cryptography applied to automotive use cases
- Security principles

Exploring the attack classes

In the context of automotive systems, an attack is an action that's performed by an adversary that aims to either compromise the vehicle information or the vehicle's ability to carry out its operational, security, or safety objectives. Perhaps you are wondering why someone would want to attack a vehicle in the first place. As we have seen from famous hacks of enterprise and IT systems, one main motivation for attackers is financial gain. A classic attack example is to roll back the vehicle odometer to cheat the leasing company from mileage overage charges. A more recent type of attack on vehicles is bypassing electronic security systems to facilitate vehicle theft. Another financially motivated attack is modifying vehicle features to gain better performance or unlock features that the **original equipment manufacturer (OEM)** hides behind a paywall. But not all attackers are financially motivated as some organized crime or even nation states may be interested in mounting attacks that cause targeted crashes and mass casualties. Throw in the prospect of autonomous driving and heavy-duty trucks, and you can start seeing a bigger attack space in which attackers are motivated to cause mass chaos against people and infrastructure. But before we get carried away with imagining nefarious attack objectives, let's understand how to classify attacks. From a computer security perspective, attacks can be classified as either passive or active. Let's dive into the various categories under each of these attack types.

> Tip
> Attack types should not be confused here with attack techniques. To learn about attack techniques, you are encouraged to check out the MITRE corporation's **Industrial Control Systems (ICS)** Attack Matrix (see *[22]* in the *Further reading* section at the end of this chapter) due to its relative similarity to the automotive control systems.

Passive attacks

When performing passive attacks, the attackers' primary objective is to gather information about the target without being discovered. Whether it is an IT network or a vehicle network, a passive attack will involve some form of eavesdropping or reconnaissance activity. Taking the example of the in-vehicle networks that we explored in *Chapter 1*, a passive attack against such networks involves a malicious network participant who is listening on the communication channel and recording **Controller Area Network (CAN)**, FlexRay, or Ethernet frames. *Figure 2.1* shows a sample CAN network trace in which an attacker managed to record messages from the engine and braking **electronic control units (ECUs)**.

Once the network traffic has been recorded, the attacker can later replay those frames to manipulate vehicle functionalities – for example, they can cause an unsafe change regarding the engine or ABS functions. The other nodes on the vehicle network are unable to detect this type of attack because listening to the network traffic is considered normal behavior:

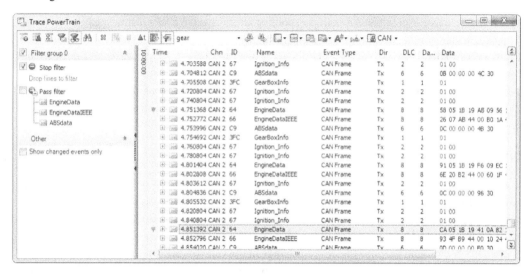

Figure 2.1 – CAN message traffic captured using Vector CANalyzer

Another common type of passive attack is intercepting software updates that are intended to modify the vehicle software. An attacker who positions themselves between two parties without their knowledge is commonly referred to as a **man-in-the-middle** (**MITM**). In the software update scenario, an MITM can capture a software binary package with the intent of analyzing its contents. If the attacker can disassemble the binaries, they may discover a vulnerability that can be exploited through a different attack path. In the next few sections, we will learn how to limit the impact of passive attacks through cryptographic methods that can conceal data and reduce the likelihood of undetected message replay.

Note

MITM attacks are also used in active attacks, where the MITM aims to modify the data that they are intercepting, as we will see next.

Active attacks

Active attacks require interference with the target through modification, deletion, insertion, or blocking of data or system functions. While attackers interfering with a target ECU or vehicle network are normally not worried about being detected, in cases of nation state or sophisticated threat agents, they may be interested in hiding their traces to prolong the exploit as long as possible. Let's explore the various types of active attacks.

Spoofing

With spoofing, the attacker's objective is to masquerade as another party when communicating with the target, making the target believe that the communication is coming from a trusted source. When the target does not properly verify the identity of its peers or the source of the data that its consuming, spoofing attacks become possible. An example spoofing attack is when a fake diagnostic tester initiates a diagnostic session and requests a restricted diagnostic service. If the ECU does not verify the identity of the diagnostic client, the fake client can masquerade as a legitimate diagnostic tester, resulting in the execution of privileged services such as rolling back the odometer to a lower mileage value. Another popular spoofing attack is constructing messages with CAN identifiers that belong to other ECUs on the CAN network. The receiving ECU is unable to determine if the message truly originated from the source ECU or has been constructed by another entity masquerading as the source.

Replay

The attacker's objective is to cause the target to react to old data. If the target ECU does not check for data freshness, then replay attacks become possible. As we saw with passive attacks, a successful eavesdropping attack results in the attacker possessing communication messages that can be replayed at the time of the attacker's choosing. One of the easiest ways to influence a vehicle network is to replay old CAN messages to cause the desired change in the vehicle's behavior, such as increasing the engine's torque. Another example is replaying diagnostic commands that have been captured from a diagnostic client to access privileged services.

Tamper

The attacker's objective is to interfere with the target by inserting, deleting, or modifying its data or system functions. Tampering attacks in automotive systems can affect the ECU configuration settings, the ECU firmware or calibration data, sensor input data, vehicle network inputs, and more. To tamper with the ECU firmware, the attacker may launch a passive attack to capture the unmodified ECU firmware. Then, through careful analysis, the attacker can determine the parts of the firmware that need modification to produce the desired adverse effect. Finally, the attacker needs a way to program the tampered ECU firmware into the target, such as through a replay of the flash programming sequence (through the flash bootloader), but this time using the tampered ECU firmware. The attacker may also be an MITM who can intercept the data, modify it, and retransmit it without the knowledge of the original sender and target receiver. For vehicle network messages, tampering attacks can target the physical layer to manipulate individual message frame bits.

Denial of Service

The attacker's objective is to reduce or completely disable the functions of the target. **Denial of Service (DoS)** attacks have a wide scope in automotive systems. An example of a powerful DoS attack is erasing the ECU firmware, resulting in a bricked ECU. With network data, a common DoS attack is transmitting back-to-back CAN messages with the highest priority CAN identifier to deny other ECUs access to the shared CAN bus. In other scenarios, the attacker may terminate a programming session by injecting invalid diagnostic frames that violate the programming sequence and trigger the ECU to terminate the diagnostic session. If done repeatedly, this type of attack would deny an ECU the ability to update its software. Resource exhaustion attacks are a branch of DoS attacks that aim to reduce the target's ability to perform its normal functions by exhausting its computational resources. For example, a target ECU that gives high priority to externally initiated requests to store data in persistent storage can easily deplete its CPU runtime bandwidth and non-volatile memory capacity as it is overwhelmed by requests for storing data in persistent storage. It is also noteworthy that frequent erasing and programming requests to non-volatile memory can be a powerful attack method to wear out the memory, causing it to eventually fail.

Side channel attacks

A special type of attack is one that aims to exfiltrate sensitive data through covert channels, also known as side channels. Like any computer system, automotive systems leak information through various side channels, such as timing, temperature, power, and shared cache memory. Although we have not discussed the topic of cryptographic material yet, one of the primary objectives of side-channel attacks is to discover the contents of cryptographic keys inside an ECU or a smart sensor by observing variations in the side channel. These attacks can be launched from outside the target (if the attacker has physical possession of the device) or from within the target, such as in the case of a multi-tenant domain controller or vehicle computer.

The topic of side-channel attacks is quite rich and therefore we will only present a brief overview focusing on the main areas that impact automotive systems. Typically, the attacker modifies the target hardware so that power or electromagnetic traces can be captured that can be correlated to the key material. Based on the knowledge of the crypto algorithm in use, the attacker can exfiltrate the full key material if enough power traces are captured. *Figure 2.2* shows an example trace of the power variations of an ECU while a key is in use with the **Rivest-Shamir-Adleman (RSA)** algorithm. This type of analysis exposes the plaintext secret bits of the key while the key is in use by the target hardware:

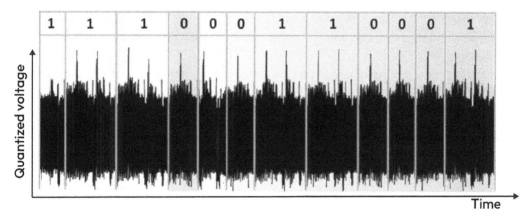

Figure 2.2 – A trace based on simple power analysis (SPA) to extract
the private key used with an RSA implementation

Side-channel attacks are normally grouped with fault injection attacks. A special category of fault injection attacks, called *glitch attacks*, can alter the hardware state, causing changes in the software control flow to bypass critical code sections. As a result, we may observe that the CPU skips a specific instruction, leading to certain security critical features being bypassed. One such example is bypassing the boot authentication checks, enabling an attacker to execute non-genuine software on the ECU.

Figure 2.3 shows a typical setup where the **device under test** (**DUT**) is subjected to electromagnetic wave pulses through a glitch controller:

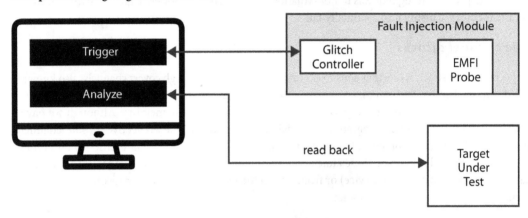

Figure 2.3 – A typical setup for fault injection attacks (credit: Riscure)

The probe is positioned at the proper location to yield the desired perturbation in the silicon. This type of fault injection causes a cryptographic function to produce observable changes in the output of the ECU, causing the eventual leakage of secret keys if the ECU is susceptible to these types of attacks. Due to the relative ease and declining cost of acquiring fault injection and side-channel analysis equipment, automotive designers must consider these types of attacks as viable and plan the proper countermeasures.

> **Dig deeper**
>
> To gain a better perspective of side-channel attacks mounted from within a single compute environment, look up **Spectre** and **Meltdown** vulnerabilities *[24]* to see how attackers can abuse the hardware behavior to infer information about tenants sharing the same computing platform. For externally mounted side-channel attacks, you are advised to look up **simple power analysis** (**SPA**), **differential power analysis** (**DPA**), and **electromagnetic fault injection** (**EMFI**) attacks, which leverage the power and electromagnetic fault injection-based analysis to discover cryptographic key material.

Having explored the main attack types, we will now turn our attention to the high-level security objectives that an ECU must consider throughout the vehicle's life cycle.

Identifying security objectives

A common way to analyze the security of a system is to evaluate if it has achieved its security objectives. These objectives can be grouped into five classes: **integrity**, **authenticity**, **confidentiality**, **accountability**, and **availability**. A typical automotive system will aim to achieve a subset of these objective classes. In the following subsections, we will explore each class of security objectives and give examples of how they apply to automotive systems.

Integrity

If you have worked in functional safety, then integrity is a familiar concept that ensures data is protected from corruption due to random or systematic faults in a system. In the context of cybersecurity, integrity has a more general meaning as it is concerned with protecting data not only from accidental corruption but also from malicious tampering. At a high level, a vehicle aims to protect the integrity of its data and safeguard its ability to correctly control its functions within the desired safety and performance constraints.

Recall that when we explored the architecture of the ECU, we mentioned that the validity of the software and firmware binaries stored in non-volatile memory had significant importance for the secure operation of the vehicle. If someone can replace or modify such binaries, then the behavior of the vehicle will change, with serious consequences to overall vehicle safety. Therefore, one of the primary vehicle security objectives is to protect the integrity of the software binaries that are programmed in ECUs. Another use case is protecting the data integrity of in-vehicle network communication between ECUs, sensors, and actuators. The malicious tampering of any safety-critical message can result in the ECU consuming incorrect data or applying incorrect actuation commands, which can have catastrophic impacts on road user safety.

For an automotive system to perform its control functions correctly, it must consume uncorrupted data and maintain the integrity of its software execution environment, which includes task schedules, system variables, CPU state, and other parameters that contribute to the correctness of its runtime execution environment.

Authenticity

Authenticity protection aims to verify the origin of data as well as the identity of a peer or a client. Authenticating the origin of data and the identity of peers ensures that a vehicle system will neither consume data from an untrusted source nor will it grant illegal access to untrusted peers. In practice, several automotive use cases exist in which authenticity is violated. One such use case is when a CAN message is received – the data origin is inferred automatically by examining the CAN identifier. Without a means to verify the true origin of a CAN message, a malicious node can masquerade as another network node. In the next section, we will see how message authentication codes help in protecting the authenticity of data.

Another use case that involves missing or inadequate client authentication involves the diagnostic protocol. Recall in the *Exploring the in-vehicle network* section of *Chapter 1*, we discussed the **Unified Diagnostic Services (UDS)** protocol, which enables a diagnostic tool (the client) to access diagnostic services from an ECU. If the ECU accepts any diagnostic service request without verifying the identity of the requester, this will result in the extraction of security-sensitive data such as firmware image contents or performing unsafe diagnostic routines while the vehicle is in motion. To enable client authentication, the UDS protocol supports two diagnostic services for access control protection through access-level or user-level authentication (*service 0x27* and *0x29*, respectively). A rule of thumb is that whenever a privileged service is being offered, client authentication must be considered a security objective.

> **Note**
> Legacy implementations of the UDS protocol relied on rudimentary seed and key access control mechanisms that utilized short-length seed values and simple key calculation methods that are easy to circumvent.

Confidentiality

This objective is concerned with concealing the content of data to prevent its exposure to unauthorized parties. A modern vehicle has many data objects that should remain confidential. An obvious one is the user's private data that is stored within an ECU – for example, phone contacts synchronized over Bluetooth with the infotainment ECU. Another is the intellectual property in the form of software algorithms, or machine learning models typically found in autonomous driving systems. When cryptography is used within a vehicle application, protecting the confidentiality of cryptographic key material becomes a must.

Accountability

This objective is concerned with tracing an action to a unique entity without the possibility of repudiation of the action. In automotive systems, the most common case for the accountability objective is protecting the crash records that are logged during an accident by an **electronic data recorder (EDR)**. If the crash records can be easily replaced, modified, or deleted, then the accountability objective cannot be achieved. You might think that the data authenticity objective should be sufficient to assure accountability. However, accountability requires stronger guarantees on the data origin that go beyond the authenticity objective by ensuring repudiation of origin is not possible. In the next section, we will explore some cryptographic methods that help us achieve this objective.

Availability

This security objective aims to ensure the system functionalities are available even when the system is under attack. When an attacker downgrades or causes a system to go completely offline, they have succeeded in compromising the availability objective. An example attack method that violates the availability objective of an ECU is the full or partial erasure of software binaries in an ECU. Depending on the functions of the target ECU, this could leave the entire vehicle in an inoperative state.

In the next section, we will explore how cryptographic methods can help us satisfy the aforementioned objectives when applied to automotive use cases.

Cryptography applied to automotive use cases

The study of mathematical procedures that process or alter data to conceal and authenticate information and its sources is known as **cryptography**. The field has had a fascinating past with a decisive influence in protecting national secrets during critical periods of world history. The great advances in **Information Technology** (**IT**) called for stronger cryptographic methods as an enabling technology for greater connectivity and information sharing. More recently, cryptography has gained an added sense of allure due to the rise of cryptocurrency, which has garnered the attention of millions of people from all walks of life. In this section, we will try to demystify some of the basic concepts of cryptography and show how to apply them to common automotive use cases to achieve some of the security objectives presented earlier in this chapter. This section is meant to give you an introduction to important concepts that should make it easier for you to pursue more advanced studies in this area. Whenever possible, we will refer you to the *Further reading* section so that you can explore certain algorithms and concepts in more detail.

Building blocks

A **cipher** is a function that reads in information (plaintext) together with a secret value (key) and produces an unintelligible piece of data (ciphertext) of the same length as the plaintext input. If the same ciphertext is presented to the cipher algorithm along with the same key, then the original plaintext is reproduced. The process of producing the ciphertext is called **encryption**, while that of recovering the plaintext from the ciphertext is called **decryption**. When the same key is used for both encryption and decryption, the cipher algorithm is referred to as symmetric cryptography while the key used in the operation is called a symmetric key. There are two types of symmetric key-based ciphers: **block** and **stream** ciphers.

Block cipher

In a block cipher, a fixed-size block of data is used by the cipher algorithm. If the block size is 16 bytes, for instance, then 16 bytes of plaintext will be encrypted each time the block cipher is called. A message larger than a single block size is segmented into multiple blocks before being processed by the block cipher during an encryption or decryption operation. *Figure 2.4* shows a block cipher in which a block of b bits of a plaintext message is fed in with a secret, (K), to produce a block of the equivalent size of ciphertext. The decryption step utilizes the same block cipher but this time, the input is the ciphertext along with the same key, (K), while the output is the original plaintext message:

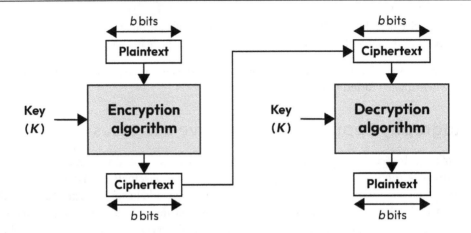

Figure 2.4 – Encryption and decryption steps performed by a block cipher

One block cipher that is widely used in automotive applications is the **Advanced Encryption Standard** (**AES FIPS 197**). It uses a block size of 16 bytes and supports keys of 128, 192, and 256-bit length. The number of rounds in AES depends on the key size – for example, AES-128 consists of 10 rounds. Each round of AES consists of several processing steps, including substituting, permutating, mixing the input plaintext, and transforming the key. As such, each round involves different transformations, providing confusion and diffusion in the cipher.

> **Experiment online**
>
> To see the values of AES rounds for a given plaintext input message and test key, visit https://www.cryptool.org/en/cto/aes-step-by-step. Notice how selecting different key sizes produces different numbers of rounds and how the encryption rounds are mirrored by the decryption rounds.

Due to its established security properties, AES is supported in most modern ECUs through cryptographic hardware accelerators. Automotive applications commonly use AES with either a key length of 128 or 256-bit keys, depending on the desired security strength. Although AES is quite robust, one downside for automotive systems is the added latency for encryption and decryption, which can be undesirable in real-time applications. Another downside is the susceptibility of the AES implementation to side-channel attacks.

For more details on the AES implementation and its internal structure, you can refer to *[4]*.

Stream cipher

Unlike block ciphers, a stream cipher encrypts data one bit (or one byte) at a time. In essence, a stream cipher creates a keystream using the supplied key. The plaintext data and the resulting keystream are then XORed to produce the ciphertext, as seen in *Figure 2.5*. Since the bitstream inherits its secrecy from the key input, when XORed with the plaintext, the output is the unintelligible ciphertext. As shown in *Figure 2.5*, the decryption path requires the usage of the same key to produce the same bitstream (k_i). XOR has two nice properties that make it useful for retrieving the plaintext back from the ciphertext. XORing a value with itself produces zero while XORing a value with zero leaves the value unchanged. Therefore, when the ciphertext is XORed again with the bitstream (k_i), the bitstream component of the ciphertext ($p_i \oplus k_i$) is XORed with the same bitstream (k_i), leaving us with ($p_i \oplus 0$), which is Pi:

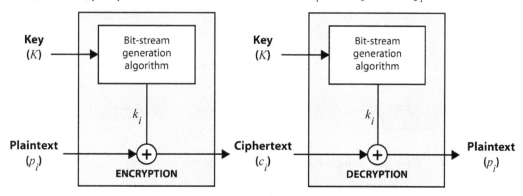

Figure 2.5 – Stream cipher encryption and decryption steps

An example stream cipher that is gaining popularity in automotive applications is **Chacha**, commonly used as part of the **ChaCha20-Poly1305** algorithm, which provides both encryption and authentication. Its main benefit over AES is the lower processing time needed, which makes it suitable for resource-constrained devices with low tolerance regarding communication latency.

Cipher modes

A mode of operation is essentially a method for customizing the cipher algorithm for a particular application while meeting specific security objectives. Rather than explain each cipher mode, we will focus on the four modes that are most commonly used in automotive use cases. These modes are typically used with symmetric block ciphers such as AES FIPS 197.

Electronic codebook (ECB)

The **electronic codebook** (ECB) mode is the simplest one, handling plaintext one block at a time and encrypting each block with the same key. The encryption operation produces a *codebook* where, for a given key, every b-bit block of plaintext maps to a specific ciphertext. In *Figure 2.6*, C_1 is always produced from P_1 for a given key, K:

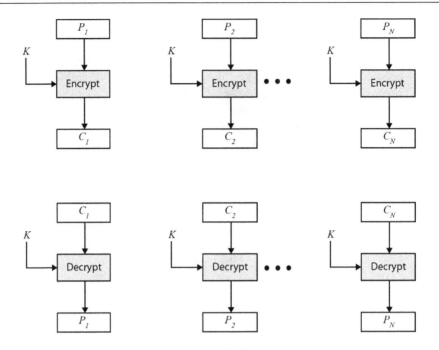

Figure 2.6 – ECB mode encryption and decryption operations

If the message is longer than the block size, we simply divide the message into b-bit blocks (P_1, P_2, ..., P_N) and pad the final block where necessary. Similarly, decryption is carried out by feeding the ciphertext blocks (C_1, C_2, ..., C_N) one block at a time into the block cipher using the same encryption key.

One downside of ECB is that a multi-block plaintext message consisting of a repeating pattern will produce a ciphertext with a repeating pattern of code words. If the attacker already possesses a few plaintext-ciphertext pairs, they can recognize repeating ciphertexts and substitute them with the plaintext values they already possess. With highly structured input messages, the ciphertext will leak information about the original message, as is elegantly demonstrated in the ECB Penguin project *[5]*. Therefore, we do not recommend using ECB mode in automotive use case.

Cipher block chaining (CBC)

Given the weakness of ECB mode, we need a method where a repeating plaintext block produces distinct ciphertext blocks. The **cipher block chaining** (**CBC**) mode is one method that meets this criterion by XORing the previous ciphertext block with the current plaintext block being encrypted, as shown in *Figure 2.7*. An **initialization vector** (**IV**) is XORed with the first block of plaintext to create the first unique ciphertext block. This scheme ensures that each subsequent XOR operation produces unique ciphertexts, even if the same plaintext message is encrypted again with the same key. The last block in CBC mode must be padded to a full b-bit length if it is a partial block, just like in ECB mode:

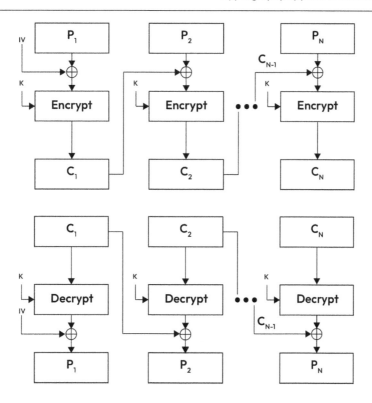

Figure 2.7 – Cipher block chaining steps during encryption and decryption

To recover the first block of plaintext after decryption, the IV is XORed with the results of the decryption method. While the IV does not have to be kept secret, it must be unique for each message encryption under the same key. A common way to generate a unique IV is to use a timestamp or a monotonic counter that does not roll over. For automotive applications, monotonic counters are are usually concatenated with a cryptographically secure random number (salt) to produce an unpredictable and non-repeating IV.

CBC mode is commonly used for encrypting files, software binaries, and the cryptographic key material of an ECU.

Counter (CTR)

When parallelism of the encryption process is desirable, **counter mode** (CTR) is the preferred choice over CBC mode. In this mode, a nonce (a number that's used once) is first created by concatenating a random number with a monotonic counter. The resulting nonce is encrypted using the key (K), and the output is XORed with a block from the plaintext message, as shown in *Figure 2.8*. For each subsequent encryption operation, the nonce is incremented and the process is repeated to produce the next block of ciphertext. Since no chaining between the encryption steps is needed, a large message can be encrypted or decrypted in parallel steps. Decryption follows a similar procedure but this time, the output of the nonce encryption is XORed with the ciphertext block to retrieve the corresponding plaintext block. Once again, having a unique nonce for a given key is essential to maintaining the security of the encrypted message:

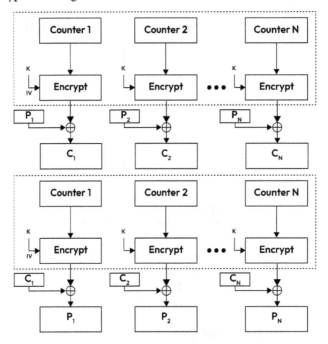

Figure 2.8 – Counter mode encryption and decryption steps

The automotive use cases of CTR mode are like those of CBC mode.

So far, these cipher modes helped us achieve the security objective of data confidentiality. Later, we will look at a special cipher mode that in addition to confidentiality provides data integrity and authenticity. But before that, we need to gain some perspective on cryptographic functions that help us achieve the data integrity objective.

One-way hash functions

With any computer system, including an ECU, there is a need to detect when the contents of a data object have changed from their original unaltered state. Having a fingerprint that uniquely identifies the contents of the data object is a useful scheme to determine when unwanted alteration has occurred.

A hash function, H, provides such fingerprinting capabilities by mapping an input message, M, of a finite length, L, to a fixed length digest, also called a hash value, h, as shown in *Figure 2.9*. In the context of automotive applications, M can be any piece of data, from a binary file containing the ECU firmware, a filesystem, video data, or even a camera frame:

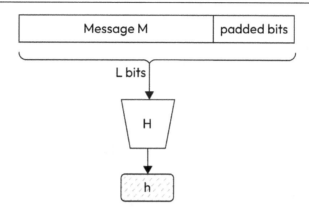

Figure 2.9 – Converting a message, M, of arbitrary length, L, to a fixed message digest, h, where (h = H(M))

To qualify as a strong cryptographic hash function, H must satisfy the following properties:

- A slight modification to the message should result in a significant change in the hash value so that the new hash value appears unrelated to the hash value of the original message (this is referred to as the avalanche effect).

- Given a hash value, h, it should be computationally infeasible to guess the original message, M, only from the knowledge of M's hash value, h. This property is called pre-image resistance and can be useful when you're concealing the contents of the original message, such as when you're storing hashes of passwords rather than the passwords themselves.

- Given a hash value, h, of a message, $M1$, it should be computationally infeasible to find a second message, $M2$, that produces the same hash value, h. This property is called the second pre-image resistance and it is necessary to prevent someone from creating a tampered message whose hash matches the original message hash value.

- It must be computationally infeasible to find a pair of messages that produce the same hash value. This property is referred to as collision resistance and helps prevent the forgery of messages by finding matching hashes.

- The output of the hash function should pass tests for pseudorandomness, making the hash value appear as a random bit stream. This property is necessary because in many cases, hash functions are used as **pseudorandom functions** (**PRFs**) for key derivation and random number generation.

The most used hash functions in automotive applications that satisfy these properties belong to the SHA-2 and SHA-3 families, both of which were standardized through FIPS 180-4 and FIPS 202, respectively. Conversely, SHA-1 has been deprecated by NIST for being shown to be insecure and therefore must not be used for any future automotive applications.

Experiment online

To see a step-by-step demonstration of how the SHA256 algorithm generates hash values from plaintext input messages, visit `https://www.cryptool.org/en/cto/sha2`. Make sure you go through all the steps to get the final hash digest.

Integrity through cryptographic hash functions

Hash functions form the basic building blocks of numerous security applications that aim to protect data integrity:

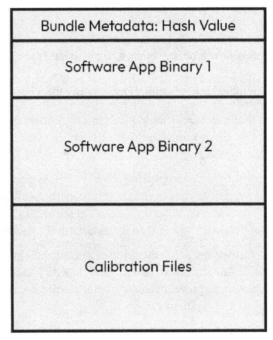

Figure 2.10 – Hash value appended to a software update bundle

In *Figure 2.10*, we can see a sample bundle of ECU software binaries and calibration files that are grouped together. The bundle metadata typically contains length and address information about each data block. A hash value corresponding to the grouped binaries and metadata uniquely identifies all the data within the bundle. To verify that none of the contents of the bundle have been corrupted, the entity consuming the data must calculate the hash value and compare it to the one supplied in the bundle. A mismatch indicates that the contents have been changed. However, in this use case, if an attacker can modify any data block within the bundle, they may also recalculate the matching hash value and replace it with the new valid value. To allow us to trust the hash value, we need to incorporate a secret that makes the hash value impossible to forge without knowledge of the secret. In the next section, we will see how this can be achieved using message authentication codes.

Message authentication code algorithms

As we saw earlier, generating a hash value does not depend on any secret input (for example, a key) and as such, a hash value is necessary but not sufficient to detect tampering with a message. To prevent the hash value from being forged, we need a method that introduces a secret into the process of generating the unique code that identifies the message. This code is referred to as the **message authentication code** (**MAC**) and can only be produced with knowledge of a shared symmetric key. Similar to hashing, the party generating the MAC provides the code alongside the message, while the party verifying the MAC computes the code and compares it to the one supplied with the message. If the two parties possess the same symmetric key, then the supplied and calculated MAC must match. The secrecy of the shared symmetric key ensures the message integrity is protected from the point of generating the MAC to the point of verifying the MAC.

Message authentication codes support two of our security objectives: integrity and authenticity. Integrity is protected because a change in the original message would cause the calculated MAC value to differ from the original MAC. On the other hand, authenticity is protected because only the parties that are sharing the symmetric key can generate a valid MAC, thereby protecting the message's origin.

Let's examine two of the most commonly used MAC algorithms in automotive applications.

Hash-based message authentication code (HMAC)

The keyed-hash message authentication code is standardized in FIPS 198-1 *[8]* and defines how to generate unique message authentication codes using a hash function and a secret key:

```
HMAC(K, M) = H[(K+ ⊕ opad) || H[(K+ ⊕ipad) || M]]
```

First, we choose a secure hash function such as SHA-256 to act as our function, H. Then, we pad the shared secret key, K, with zeroes to produce a value, K+, to align it with the block size of the hash function. Next, K+ is XORed with an input pad (`ipad`), which has a constant value of 00110110 (36 in hexadecimal). The result is concatenated with the message (M) and a hash value is calculated over the concatenated value. Next, the same padded key, K+, is XORed with the **output pad** (`opad`), which is another constant with the value of 01011100 (5C in hexadecimal). The result is concatenated with the hash value produced in the first step. The resulting value is then fed into the same hash function to produce the final HMAC.

Note that if we replace the hash value in *Figure 2.10* with the HMAC, then the party verifying the integrity of the software update bundle can determine that the contents have remained uncorrupted from the point of the HMAC creation to the point when the HMAC was verified.

Cipher-based message authentication code (CMAC)

Another commonly used MAC algorithm in automotive applications is CMAC mode, which is standardized in NIST SP 800-38B. CMAC is constructed using an approved block cipher such as AES.

To use CMAC, you simply provide an input message, the length of the input message, and the cryptographic key. The output is a message authentication code of width equal to the block cipher's size. Behind the scenes, the CMAC algorithm uses the provided key to generate two subkeys, *K1* and *K2*. *K1* is used when the input message is an integer multiple of the cipher block length and *K2* is used when it is not. Details on how the subkeys are generated can be found in the NIST standard *[9]*. For demonstration purposes, we will focus on how the CMAC gets generated while assuming the subkeys are already derived and the message length is a multiple of the block cipher length:

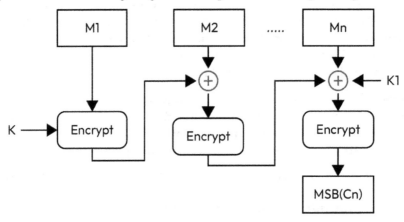

Figure 2.11 – CMAC generation when the message length is a multiple of the block cipher length

As shown in *Figure 2.11*, the output of each block cipher is XORed with the next input block until the final block is reached. There, *K1* is XORed with both the ciphertext input and the final block plaintext. The result is encrypted with the block cipher to produce the CMAC tag. Depending on the desired tag length, the most significant bits of the generated tag are extracted, and the rest can be discarded:

```
C1 = E(K, M1)
C2 = E(K, [M2 ⊕C1])
...
Cn = E(K, [Mn ⊕Cn-1 ⊕K1])
T = MSBTlen(Cn)
where
T = message authentication code
Tlen = bit length of T
```

When the input message is not an integer multiple of the cipher block length, a similar flow is applied, with the exception that the final block is padded with zeroes so that it aligns with the cipher block's length; here, *K2* is used instead of *K1*.

One of the common mistakes when implementing the CMAC algorithm is not providing the same level of protection for the subkeys (*K1* and *K2*) as the shared symmetric key, *K*.

> **Tip**
> To avoid the scenario that a receiving entity that shares a symmetric key is misused to generate valid MAC tags, a key usage policy must be enforced to restrict the usage of the MAC keys in the receiving party for verification only.

Authenticated encryption with GCM

The **Galois counter mode (GCM)** belongs to a family of authenticated encryption modes that offer both encryption and authentication in a single algorithm. Performed in a two-step process, GCM encrypts a plaintext message and then calculates an authentication tag of the ciphertext. This allows the receiver to verify that the ciphertext has not been tampered with before recovering the plaintext. It is also possible to skip the encryption step and only perform authentication, in which case the mode is called GMAC. GCM has several uses in automotive applications, such as protecting the confidentiality and authenticity of smart sensor data, such as camera frames. GCM is also commonly used for securing Ethernet communication using the MACsec protocol *[21]*. When confidentiality is not a concern, GMAC mode is preferable for performance reasons.

The GCM algorithm takes the following inputs: a secret key (K), a unique initialization vector (IV), the plaintext message (P), an optional additional authenticated data denoted as *Auth Data*, and the length information of both the plaintext message and the Auth Data. Auth Data is useful in communication protocols where part of the message needs authentication protection but must be transmitted in plaintext (such as the IP address of a packet). The output of GCM is the ciphertext and the corresponding authentication tag:

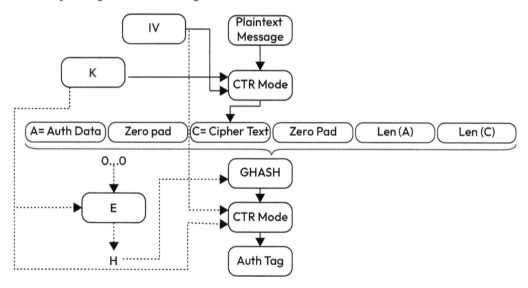

Figure 2.12 – Steps for performing GCM-based authenticated encryption

As shown in *Figure 2.12*, the plaintext message is converted into ciphertext using CTR mode, also referred to as GCTR, using the input, *IV*, and key, *K*. Note that, for simplicity, we have not shown the encoding of *IV* based on whether a 96 or a 128-bit initialization vector is used.

Following the encryption step, the Auth Data, ciphertext, and length information, along with zero-padded bits (if needed), are all fed into the GHASH function. Zero padding is used to ensure the resulting string is a multiple of the block size. Details on how to perform the GHASH function are outside the scope of this book but can be found in *[3]*. A 128-bit zero block is encrypted using the same key, *K*, to generate *H*, which is then fed into the GHASH function. The output of the GHASH function is encrypted once more using CTR mode to produce the authentication tag.

For the decryption step, the authentication tag is an input parameter. The tag is calculated first using the same process as the encryption operation and is then compared to the tag passed by the caller. If they match, the decryption will proceed similarly to CTR mode-based decryption.

As in the case of CBC and CTR mode, the uniqueness of *IV* must be ensured to maintain the security of the cipher mode.

Typical use cases of message authentication codes

In automotive use cases, a MAC is commonly used to protect the integrity of in-vehicle messages, vehicle log data, as well as security-sensitive user-generated data that is persisted in storage. *Figure 2.13* shows how the secure onboard communication protocol leverages a MAC to protect the authenticity and freshness of **protocol data units** (**PDUs**) transferred over the in-vehicle network. Before message transmission, the PDU is concatenated with a freshness value and processed into a MAC generation algorithm (for example, AES CMAC). The output tag is truncated to fit within the message length and appended to the PDU data, along with the used freshness value. The receiving node first verifies that the received freshness value is equal to the expected value, and then verifies the MAC tag by comparing the supplied MAC with the one they computed using the shared symmetric key. If the truncated MAC tags match, the message is accepted as authentic and fresh; otherwise, it is rejected. Recall that message replay attacks are only possible if the MAC is covering the PDU data alone (excluding the freshness value).

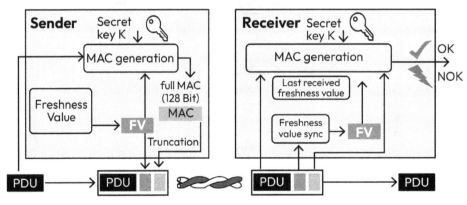

Figure 2.13 – Secure OnBoard Communication Protocol defined by AUTOSAR (credit AUTOSAR)

Note that with CAN messages, MAC generation must also cover the CAN ID, CAN **data length code** (**DLC**), and PDU contents. This prevents an attacker from being able to manipulate any part of the message without detection by the receiving party. Since the CAN ID is the value that identifies the source of the message, verifying the MAC of the entire message would also verify that it has been generated by the correct source.

There are two challenges with using MACs in automotive systems. For one, the time taken to generate and verify the MAC adds latency that may be too large to tolerate for real-time embedded systems. Furthermore, at high data rates, the computational burden to generate and verify MACs becomes significant, such as the case of authenticating camera sensor frames transmitted at multiple gigabits per second. One way to address these challenges is by relying on inline cryptographic accelerators that process the MAC in hardware on the fly during message transmission and reception.

> **Note**
> Classic CAN PDUs can only fit eight bytes, making this method impractical. Therefore, MAC-based authentication is more commonly used with CAN FD and CAN XL, which offer much larger payloads.

Random number generators

Random numbers are an enabling mechanism for several cryptographic functions and security protocols. They are often used to generate cryptographic keys, nonce values, or random challenge values to be used in a challenge-response protocol. Random numbers can be produced through two main methods: true random number generators standardized through NIST SP800-90B and deterministic **random number generators** (**DRBG**) standardized through NIST SP800-90A. The former utilizes a hardware mechanism that harvests randomness from a physical process such as the variations in a clock oscillator. The latter relies on pseudorandom functions that are initialized with a true random seed to produce a random bit stream that is ideally indistinguishable from a true random bit stream. DRBGs are favored due to their high performance compared to hardware-based random number generators. Therefore, the latter is typically used to generate a random seed that serves as an input for the DRBG, as shown in the next section.

One unique property of DRBGs is that given the same seed, they produce the same bitstream sequence. Therefore, it is essential to keep the seed secret and update it frequently.

> **Need for high entropy**
> When choosing a microcontroller or an SoC, pay attention to the hardware capabilities for generating randomness specified through the entropy level. The higher the entropy, the more uniformly distributed the bits in the hardware-generated bit stream, which is an important property.

NIST SP800-90A *[6]* standardizes three types of DRBGs: Hash, HMAC, and CTR-based. In the next section, we will explore the CTR-based DRBG.

CTR-DRBG

Recall that one of the properties of a secure block cipher is that the generated ciphertext appears to be random, displaying no correlation with the source plaintext message. This property is leveraged to construct a DRBG using the block cipher at its core, as shown in *Figure 2.14*:

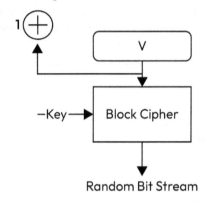

Figure 2.14 – Generating a random bit stream using counter mode

Typically, the user requests several random bits to be generated by the DRBG and supplies a random seed that is decomposed of two values: *Key* and *V*. Assuming that AES is the block cipher, a random seed generated from a hardware random generator [SP800-90B] is divided into a 128-bit key and a 128-bit *V*. The output bit stream can be simply constructed like so:

```
While (len(Temp) < total_requested_bits >
Temp = E(Key,V)
Random_Bit_Stream = Random_Bit_Stream || Temp

V =  V + 1
```

After each block of bits is generated, *V* is incremented and fed back to generate the next random block, which, in turn, is appended to the bit stream until all the requested bits have been generated.

It is important to abide by the maximum number of generation requests specified in the NIST standard to maintain the security strength of the DRBG.

Public key cryptography

Earlier, we examined symmetric key cryptography, which relies on the same secret key for encryption and decryption, thus requiring that the key be kept secret and shared only with the intended parties. Managing such secret keys can be challenging, especially for automotive systems, where ECUs in millions of vehicles need to receive the right key set to securely exchange data with the other ECUs or clients they depend on. In contrast, public key cryptography, also known as asymmetric key cryptography, uses a pair of keys: a public key and a private key. The public key can be freely shared with anyone, while the private key must be kept secret. Using public key cryptography, we can achieve the following security objectives: confidentiality, integrity, authenticity, and accountability. The latter is a unique advantage over symmetric key cryptography because the party that uses the private key to perform a cryptographic operation cannot later deny doing so since it is the only party that should possess the private key.

A public key cryptosystem leverages a hard mathematical problem that makes it computationally infeasible to determine the private key from the public key. Among the most popular classic public key cryptosystems are **elliptic curve cryptography** (**ECC**) and RSA. ECC is based on the algebraic structure of elliptic curves over finite fields *[25]*. The security of this type of cryptosystem relies on the fact that it is computationally infeasible to find the discrete logarithm of a randomly chosen element in a large cyclic group. The problem of finding the discrete logarithm is known as the **discrete logarithm problem** (**DLP**). On the other hand, the security of the RSA cryptosystem hinges on the difficulty of factoring a large composite number into its prime factors. To break RSA, an attacker would need to find a way to factorize the composite number used in the public key into its two prime factors, which is a hard problem for classical computers. The primary advantage of ECC over RSA is the smaller key size, which produces an equivalent level of security. Note that a sufficiently powerful quantum computer can perform the factorization problem efficiently, making RSA insecure in a post-quantum world. ECC is also not considered quantum safe. We will discuss post-quantum cryptosystems in more depth later.

For the sake of brevity, we will only focus on the RSA algorithm to get a closer look at how a public key cryptosystem works.

The RSA algorithm

To understand the RSA algorithm, we must start with the fundamentals of how the encryption and decryption operations are performed:

```
Given a plaintext message M < n
To generate the ciphertext:
C = Me mod n
To recover the plaintext message:
M = Cd mod n
```

The process of encryption requires the exponentiation of the plaintext message, M, using the public key exponent (e) modulo (n).

Exponentiating the ciphertext using the private exponent (d) modulo (n) produces the original message, M, which constitutes the decryption process. To see why this is true, first, expand C in the following equation:

```
M = Cd mod n = (Me)d mod n = Med mod n
```

This equation holds if e and d are multiplicative inverses of the modulo, $\phi(n)$, where $\phi(n)$ is the Euler totient function. This can be represented as follows:

```
φ(n) = φ(n)= (p-1)(q-1) where p and q are prime numbers
ed mod φ(n)= 1 which is equivalent to:
ed ≡ 1 mod φ(n)
with gcd(φ(n),e) = 1 and 1< e < φ(n)
```

The resulting private key is {d,n}, while the public key is {e,n}.

Rather than diving deeper into the mathematics behind these equations, let's walk through a commonly used practical example for RSA encryption and decryption using two small prime numbers:

1. First, we pick two prime numbers, p = 17 and q = 11.

2. Next, we calculate n as the product of the two prime numbers: n = p*q = 17 * 11 = 187.

3. Then, we need to calculate $\phi(n)$= (p - 1)*(q - 1) = 16 * 10 = 160.

4. To select e so that it is less than $\phi(n)$ = 160 and relatively prime to $\phi(n)$, we must choose e = 7.

5. Finally, we choose d so that d * e ≡ 1 (mod 160) and d < 160. This results in d = 23 because 23 * 7 = 161 = (1 * 160) + 1, which satisfies the aforementioned equation.

The resulting keys are public key Pub = {7, 187} and private key Priv = {23, 187}.

Now, let's pick the plaintext value to encrypt to be M=101. The resulting ciphertext is 84.

If we repeat the same operation but this time using the ciphertext as the input and private key exponent as the key, we will recover the original plaintext message – that is, 101.

In this simple example, we used a private key and public key pair that can be expressed using 8 bits; however, in a real-world application, an RSA key must be at least 2,048 bits long. The minimum RSA key size must be selected based on the required security strength up to the point when the ECU is nearing its end of life. We'll cover crypto periods later, but for now, keep in mind that choosing key lengths must be done as per the expected lifetime of the vehicle.

Experiment more online

To try out generating your own public and private key pair, as well as performing step-by-step RSA-based encryption, visit https://www.cryptool.org/en/cto/rsa-step-by-step.

Public key cryptography use cases

Now that we understand the general principles behind public key cryptography, we will explore three of their primary applications.

Encryption/decryption

Using the recipient's public key, a message can be encrypted by the sender and transferred to the recipient who, in turn, decrypts it with their private key. Public key cryptography for encrypting and decrypting large data is not widely used in automotive systems due to the lack of efficiency of this operation compared to symmetric key-based counterparts.

Digital signature

Recall the usage of hash functions to protect message integrity. Rather than producing an HMAC with a symmetric key, we can encrypt the hash value using the private key, as shown in *Figure 2.15*. The resulting value is concatenated with the message and transmitted to the receiver. Since only the signer owns the private key, the encrypted hash behaves as a digital signature:

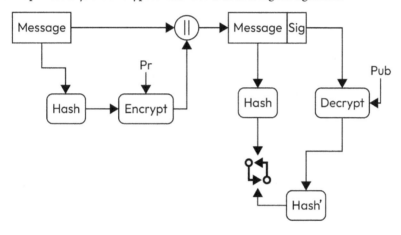

Figure 2.15 – Digital signature generation and verification sequence

On the other end, the receiver calculates the hash value of the received message normally. Then, using the transmitter's public key, they decrypt the signature to recover the expected hash value (*Hash'*). The two hash values are compared, and if they match, then the receiver confirms that the message contents have not been tampered with and that the message originated from the owner of the private key.

Digital signatures are widely used in automotive applications, for example, to verify the integrity of binaries that were downloaded during a flash programming or OTA session. Similarly, a digital signature can be used to verify that the software binaries have not been tampered with before booting the system. Digital signatures have an advantage over MAC for protecting firmware integrity. In the case of MAC, attackers are motivated to recover the shared symmetric key used in the MAC generation of the binaries. Since the key must be stored on the device itself to perform the MAC verification, the attacker can invest significant time in recovering the key, especially if that key is globally used to authenticate firmware for all ECUs of a certain class. In contrast, digital signatures only require the public key to be stored in the ECU. The private key can remain securely stored in the backend, such as in a **hardware security module** (**HSM**). Exposure of the public key does not reduce the security of the private key, making digital signatures a more secure choice for protecting the firmware's integrity.

> **Note**
>
> In embedded systems the term HSM is used to refer to a hardware-protected security environment that is embedded within an MCU or an SoC. However, in the context of the backend or the factory environment, the HSM is a standalone appliance that provides hardware-protected secure storage of cryptographic keys. These are used to sign software images and generate keys that are provisioned in the ECU during vehicle production and software deployment over the air.

Another emerging use case for digital signatures where MAC alone is inadequate is the storage of crash records logged in a vehicle **electronic data recorder** (**EDR**). An investigator of a serious crash expects to access the driving logs to determine if the vehicle or the driver should bear any responsibility for the event. Without a way to verify the source of the data, the driver can claim that anyone could have replaced the crash records in the EDR using, for example, a reprogramming tool. While a MAC would detect tampering with the data, since the symmetric key used to generate the MAC is shared with other parties, it is not enough to prove that the data was strictly produced by a specific party. Unlike the symmetric key, only the signing party possesses the asymmetric private key and therefore, signed logs may be used as evidence of accountability.

Key exchange

Another use of public key cryptography is for exchanging key material to produce a shared symmetric key. The exchanged key is strictly used for a specific session and is valid for a brief window of time, earning it the name **ephemeral key**. Once the session is terminated, the ephemeral key is destroyed. Ephemeral keys are preferred over long-term shared secret keys because they are not exposed to the same risk of side-channel leakage. Recall from our attack types that side-channel analysis can reconstitute the key material by correlating data from side channels such as power, **electromagnetic fault injection** (**EMFI**), or time-based analysis. By frequently exchanging new ephemeral keys, the attacker's ability to discover the key's contents is severely hampered since they have fewer data to analyze. The **Diffie-Hellman** (**DH**) key exchange algorithm is a popular method for securely establishing a shared secret between two parties. The party initiating the key exchange generates a public and private key pair and then sends the public key to the other party. The recipient also generates a public and private key pair and sends back its public key to the first party. Each party then proceeds to compute the shared secret key using the private key and the public key of the other party. Thanks to the mathematical properties of the DH algorithm, each party computes the same key without the need to exchange any secret key material in advance, as shown in *Figure 2.16*:

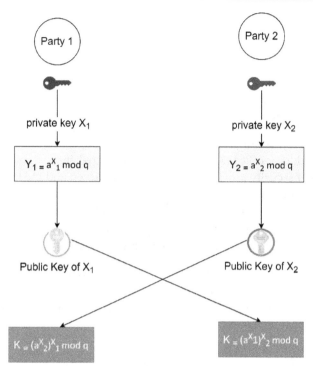

Figure 2.16 – Diffie-Hellman key exchange protocol between parties X1 and X2

DH leverages the difficulty of the discrete logarithm problem, which makes it infeasible to discover k given only a and a^k, as shown here:

```
Y = a^k mod q
```

Follow these steps to establish a shared secret key:

Start by choosing a large prime number, q:

```
Select a < q where a is a primitive root of q
```

Party 1 generates a private, public key pair:

```
Private key: X₁ < q
Public key: Y₁ = a^X₁ mod q
```

Party 2 generates its own private, public key pair:

```
Private key: X₂ < q
Public key: Y₂ = a^X₂ mod q
```

Party 1 and 2 exchange the public key portion: Y1 is sent to party 2 and Y2 is sent to party 1.

Then, to generate the shared secret key, each party performs exponentiation of the public key of the second party using their private keys:

$$K = (Y_2)^x{}_1 \bmod q = (Y_1)^x{}_2 \bmod q$$

If you are not sure why these two equations are equivalent, then expand Y_1 and Y_2 – you will see that multiplying the exponents produces the same result.

In automotive systems, it is common to see the DH key exchange combined with **elliptic curve cryptography (ECC)**, which is called ECDH. The latter is preferred due to the smaller size of ECDH keys, the higher level of security provided through elliptic curves, and the higher flexibility. An example use case for the use of ECDH is in establishing a shared secret between an ECU and a smart sensor (such as a camera) that needs to exchange encrypted and authenticated messages. Due to the latency of establishing the shared secret, DH-based algorithms are limited to automotive applications in which the latency of establishing the session is not a critical factor.

You might think that a vehicle could exchange keys among all ECUs during startup to mitigate the risks of key disclosure. However, as we mentioned in *Chapter 1*, automotive systems have real-time constraints, and waiting until all the keys have been exchanged to initiate communication would extend the vehicle startup time significantly.

Key management

As the cryptographic mechanisms increased in security, the attackers turned their attention to compromising the security of the cryptographic keys. Instead of attempting to brute-force attack a cryptographic algorithm, an attacker will look for ways to recover the keys while the key is either at rest or in use. Therefore, apart from picking the right security algorithm, it's important to know how the keys are managed throughout the life cycle of the product.

The problem of key management can be split into the following areas:

- Managing long-term symmetric keys
- Managing ephemeral symmetric keys
- Managing asymmetric keys

Long-term symmetric keys are generated offline through a secure mechanism with the help of a **hardware security module (HSM)** and are provisioned in a secure environment into the target device. Long-term symmetric keys suffer from a few problems. For one, they are intended to be used for a very long time, and therefore they are especially at risk of disclosure through covert channels such as timing, electromagnetic, or power side-channel analysis. In many cases, it is impractical to revoke and update those keys due to how they are programmed, such as when they're stored in **one-time programmable memory (OTP)**. The primary way to reduce the risk of long-term secret key loss is to limit how they are used in the system. One such practice is limiting the keys for use only to derive other keys (using key derivation functions). Another common practice is to make such keys device-specific to ensure that even if the key is extracted, it cannot be used globally on other devices.

When dealing with ephemeral keys, the expectation is that the device will generate such keys using a mechanism such as the key exchange algorithms presented earlier. While ephemeral keys are preferred over long-term secret keys, they do present unique challenges, such as improperly configured session length and previously used ephemeral keys being discarded improperly. Therefore, it is recommended to discard such keys after a session is terminated and prevent the reuse of old keys from previous sessions. Also, carefully choosing the session's duration is mandatory to avoid the case that an ephemeral key is used beyond a safe crypto period, after which key leakage through side channels is possible.

Finally, managing public keys in automotive use cases faces two main challenges: how to trust the authenticity of the public key and how to prevent it from being replaced. To solve these challenges, we will take a deeper look at how certificates can be used to help with managing and distributing public keys.

X.509 certificates

The security of public key cryptography hinges on the trust we place in the authenticity of the public key:

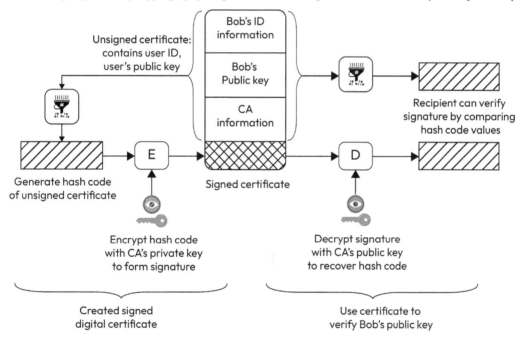

Figure 2.17 – Creation and usage of an X.509 certificate

In *Figure 2.17*, if Bob signs a message using his private key and shares the public key with Alice, who wants to use it to verify a digital signature, Alice can only trust the validity of the signature if she is certain that the public key truly originates from Bob. To establish trust in the origin of the public key, a certificate-based scheme is defined through the X.509 standard, which requires the use of a trusted **certificate authority** (**CA**). In our example, to generate an X.509 certificate that attests to Bob's identity, Bob must use a CA that can establish a chain of trust for him. If Bob can prove his identity to the

CA, then the CA can generate a certificate containing Bob's public key, along with a digital signature generated using the CA's private key. The X.509 certificate's contents are simply hashed and encrypted to produce the certificate signature. Before using Bob's public key, Alice must verify the certificate's validity by verifying the certificate signature using the CA public key, which Alice already trusts.

> **Question**
> How does Alice trust the CA public key in the first place?

In automotive use cases, a so-called root public key is provisioned in the ECU in a secure environment, such as the chip vendor's factory or the vehicle assembly line. This root public key functions as the CA public key because after it has been provisioned, a public key certificate presented to the ECU must contain a signature that was signed with the matching root private key. A typical ECU may contain more than one root public key to allow different stakeholders to establish trust with the ECU. For example, the chip vendor may inject their root public key to verify certificates submitted by someone attempting to perform failure analysis. An OEM may also inject a root public key that can be used to validate the certificates of service shops. Since root public keys require hardware storage capabilities, it is recommended to always reserve multiple slots for such keys in case of a future need for revocation. There are multiple uses of an X.509 certificate in automotive applications, such as authenticating a smart sensor, an OTA backend, or an electric vehicle charging station.

The following diagram shows the fields you will normally find in an X.509 certificate:

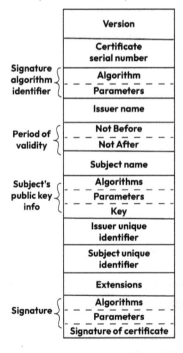

Figure 2.18 – X.509 certificate fields, as defined by the ITU standard

Let's take a look at them in more detail:

- **Serial number**: A discrete integer value that, in combination with the issuer name, uniquely identifies the certificate.

- **Signature algorithm identifier**: The algorithm and any associated parameters that were used to sign the certificate.

- **Issuer name**: The name of the CA that issued and signed this certificate.

- **Period of validity**: This contains the time window during which the certificate is valid. The receiver must always check if the certificate is within the validity period before use.

- **Subject name**: This is the name of the entity that has the matching private key.

- **Subject's public key information**: This includes the subject's public key, as well as the name of the algorithm this key should be used with, and any associated parameters.

- **Issuer unique identifier**: This uniquely identifies the issuing CA.

- **Subject unique identifier**: This uniquely identifies the subject.

- **Extensions**: These were added in version 3 of the standard and allow extra fields to be defined within the certificate.

- **Signature**: This covers all the fields of the certificate. The name of the signature algorithm is contained in this field as well.

> Tip
> Before using the public key of an X.509 certificate, verify the certificate's signature, along with all the fields that ensure you are using an unexpired certificate from a genuine source.

Before we wrap up the topic of key management, let's consider one more area related to how symmetric cryptographic keys can be created.

Key derivation functions (KDFs)

A KDF is a function that generates (that is, derives) keying material using an input consisting of a (secret) key and additional data to ensure the generated keys are different, even though the same secret input is used. A KDF typically relies on a **pseudorandom function** (**PRF**) that is called multiple times to produce the desired number of cryptographic keys. A **key derivation key** (**KDK**) is the cryptographic key that is used as an input to a key derivation function. The KDK that's used as input to one of the key-derivation functions may be produced by a DRBG or may be obtained from the output of an authorized automated key-establishment scheme. The keying material for the KDK may also come in part from another KDK. NIST recommends several key derivation schemes, including the counter mode KDF presented next.

KDF in counter mode

In this mode, a counter is used as input to the PRF as the function iterates over the input parameters. For this illustration, we chose the HMAC as the PRF. Let's look at the steps of deriving the key material from an input key (K_{in}):

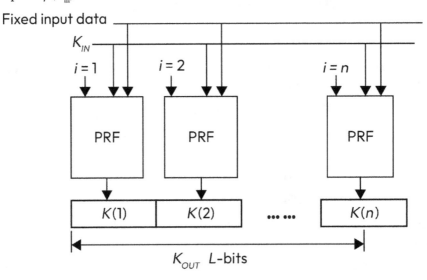

Figure 2.19 – KDF structure in counter mode

At the core of each iteration, the PRF takes the following parameters as input:

- KIN: The key derivation key
- i: Counter value
- Label: A string identifying the purpose of the derived keying material
- Context: A bit string that uniquely identifies the derived key material, such as the identities of parties who are deriving the key
- L: The requested bit length of the output key, which is represented as a bit string

In each iteration, a block of the key material is produced using the key derivation key (KIN), the counter value (i), and the fixed input data, as shown in *Figure 2.19*:

```
K(i) := PRF (KIN, [i] || Fixed input data)
```

Here, Fixed input data is the concatenation of the label, a separation indicator, 0x00, the context, and [L] (Label || 0x00 || Context || [L]).

After each iteration, the output is concatenated with the previous result, as follows:

```
result := result || K(i)
```

At the end of all the iterations, the **output key** (K_{out}) is constructed by keeping the leftmost L bits of the derived key material and discarding the rest.

KDFs are commonly used by chip vendors who need to generate unique device keys using a common secret, and a device-specific constant. If an OEM chooses to treat the KDK as a master key from which ECU keys are derived, then the fixed data is chosen to uniquely identify the target ECU. This allows the OEM to quickly derive the keys of any ECU by looking up the fixed data and the knowledge of KDK. When used as a master key, protecting the KDK becomes even more critical than protecting the derived keys as the disclosure of such a key would result in total loss of security for all ECUs that depend on that master key. A more secure way to use key derivation functions is to make the KDK unique per device by leveraging a hardware-defined unique key.

> Tip
> KDKs must be used only for key derivation purposes, never for multiple purposes such as data encryption or authentication.

NIST defined security strength

NIST maintains a list of cryptographic mechanisms that are secure for usage, along with the minimum key length required for a specific crypto period [17]. This factors in the increased computational power of adversaries and their abilities to recover key material over time. When developing automotive systems, we must always assume the maximum vehicle lifetime when choosing crypto algorithms and key lengths to avoid finding ourselves with a broken security system that is hard or impossible to upgrade when the vehicle is already on the road. An important implication of crypto period awareness is that automotive systems must be built with the ability to update keys in the field when a key is nearing the end of its allowed crypto period. Moreover, when choosing cryptographic algorithms that support multiple key lengths, we must ensure that the higher security strength is supported at the time of design, even if that strength is not immediately needed. For example, an automotive ECU should offer AES 128- and 256-bit key support to future-proof the vehicle against advances in cryptanalysis.

Note that while security through cryptography does increase the overall security of our systems, it is how we implement such mechanisms that determines whether our systems are truly secure or not. In most cases, you will find that a security mechanism did not fail because it was inherently insecure, but rather because it was either misused or implemented incorrectly.

Chinese cryptography

So far, the cryptographic algorithms we have presented are ones approved by NIST. When selling vehicles in the Chinese market, we must be aware of Chinese cryptographic standards that are mandated by the Chinese State Cryptographic Authority. These mechanisms mirror the NIST-approved algorithms but require additional support in terms of software and hardware:

Chinese Cryptography Function	Supported Functions
SM2	Elliptic Curve Diffie-Hellman key agreement and signature using a specified 256-bit elliptic curve
SM3	A 256-bit cryptographic hash function
SM4	A 128-bit block cipher with a 128-bit key
SM9	Digital signature, key exchange, and identity-based encryption

Table 2.1 – Mapping Chinese cryptography functions to their use cases

Therefore, when designing ECUs that must operate in Chinese vehicles, support for Chinese cryptography standards must be considered.

Before we conclude the topic of cryptography, we will touch on post-quantum cryptography to ensure that our vehicles are adapting to advances in quantum computing.

PQC algorithms

A report released in April 2016 by the **National Institute of Standards and Technology (NIST)** highlighted the need for new standards to replace cryptosystems based on discrete logarithm problems and integer factorization that are weak against Shor's quantum algorithm regarding prime factorization. The security of public key cryptosystems, which are widely used in communication protocols, digital signing processes, authentication frameworks, and more, will be compromised if the shift is not made before sufficiently powerful quantum computers are implemented. As a result, **post-quantum cryptography (PQC)** alternatives emerged as the quantum-resistant replacement for cryptosystems such as RSA, ECC, ECDSA, ECDH, and DSA cryptosystems.

After several rounds of evaluating candidate PQC algorithms, NIST has standardized two post-quantum stateful hash-based signature schemes known as LMS and XMSS. NIST has also settled on the four algorithms shown in the following table to be standardized while additional algorithms continue to be evaluated:

Function/Use	Algorithm
Digital signatures	CRYSTALS-Dilithium
	FALCON
	SPHINCS+
Public key encryption	CRYSTALS-KYBER
Key encapsulation mechanism	CRYSTALS-KYBER

Table 2.2 – PQC algorithms slated for NIST standardization

Given the long lifetime of a vehicle (more than 15 years), there is an urgency in the automotive industry to equip the ECUs being designed today with the support of PQC algorithms to ensure their crypto agility in response to advances in quantum computing. If you are designing your ECU today and deciding on which cryptographic algorithms to support, you are advised to watch the NIST standardization efforts for PQC algorithms closely to ensure that your design can adapt when needed. The transition to PQC algorithms is expected to be costly and will require careful planning. Many factors contribute to this, such as the expected increase in memory, computing resources, and key sizes for the new algorithms. Replacing proven security algorithms with ones that are still being evaluated also presents a risk that should not be ignored.

> **Note**
>
> Symmetric key-based ciphers are not included in this list because quantum computers do not present an immediate advantage over classical computers in weakening their security. Therefore, AES is still considered secure. If you'd like to read how AES will be impacted in the distant future, please read Lov Grover's paper [27] on the quantum search algorithm.

A deep dive into LMS and XMSS is outside the scope of this book, but you are encouraged to read the NIST recommendation for stateful hash-based signature schemes [18] to understand how these algorithms differ from classical digital signature schemes.

Before we wrap up this section, we would like to suggest that you experiment with the OpenSSL library to see the algorithms you learned about here in action. A great resource for quickly getting set up with OpenSSL is `https://www.cryptool.org/en/cto/openssl`.

Security principles

As we saw in the previous section, cryptography provides a foundation for achieving our security objectives. But besides security through cryptography, several equally important security principles ensure that the established trust provided through cryptography is sustained throughout the life of the product. In this section, we'll explore a subset of NIST-recommended security principles that we deem most relevant to automotive systems. You are encouraged to read the full list [23] and find additional principles that may apply to your system.

Defense in depth

Building automotive systems that are resilient to cyberattacks requires a multi-layered approach to security that holistically secures the vehicle, starting with external supporting systems such as the cloud and backend infrastructure, down to securing the smallest hardware and software components that are relevant to cybersecurity within the vehicle. Relying on a single security protocol or control can create a single point of failure. In contrast, by using a diverse set of defenses and employing them around every critical component, the system can prevent, detect, and respond to various attack vectors.

At the vehicle level, this means securing the backend, supporting tools (for example, diagnostic clients), off-vehicle communication, vehicle interfaces (such as OBD-II ports), and in-vehicle networks. At the ECU level, this means building security mechanisms throughout the hardware and software architecture layers. By creating barriers at different levels of the vehicle and ECU architecture, an attacker is required to defeat multiple, diverse security controls to achieve their objective, with each layer designed to stop intrusions or detect anomalies, increasing the robustness of the overall security posture. As we will see in *Chapters 8* and *9*, building effective cybersecurity controls requires a repetitive systematic process in which residual risks are identified after each added measure, and additional controls are applied until the overall risk has reached an acceptable level.

Domain separation

Domain separation is a fundamental security principle that dictates the need for different levels or domains of security for different types of data or operations. By keeping different parts of a system separated, we limit the impact of a security breach to just one part of the system and prevent it from spreading to other, potentially more safety and security-critical areas. At the ECU level, domain separation is achieved by having a separation between a trusted execution environment and a normal execution environment. Even if the normal execution environment is compromised, the trusted execution environment should remain capable of protecting the cryptographic secrets as well as critical operations that prevent a total compromise of the system assets. At the vehicle level, ECUs are grouped by their type of functionality, as we saw in the domain-separated E/E architecture. This separation is done physically through different in-vehicle networks, such as CAN or LIN. This provides an inherent degree of isolation as compromising one ECU doesn't immediately give an attacker access to all other ECUs in the vehicle. However, with the advent of more sophisticated, connected, and centralized vehicle computer systems, physically separating domains is not always possible or desirable due to factors such as cost, space, or efficiency. In such cases, logically separating domains becomes extremely important. This often involves using virtualization technologies, which allow multiple **virtual machines** (**VMs**) and virtualized resources to be created on a single physical machine. Each VM operates as a separate virtual ECU with its own operating system and software, creating a strong logical barrier. So, even if one VM is compromised, the breach remains contained within that virtual machine and doesn't affect the underlying physical machine or other VMs running on it. In this model, you could have one VM running the infotainment system, another handling communication with external networks, and yet another controlling the safety-critical functions, such as braking and steering. Even if the infotainment system is compromised, the attacker would not be able to directly affect the other VMs thanks to the logical separation provided by virtualization. In all cases, domain separation must be coupled with a reduction in the number of interactions between the domains to further reduce the likelihood of unwanted interference.

Least privilege

It is desirable to assign privileges and abilities to each software or hardware component based on the minimum set needed to perform their intended function. By carefully segmenting and controlling access rights, a compromise in one area does not necessarily grant an attacker access to other parts of the system. This localized containment means that breaches can be more easily detected, managed, and remedied without impacting the whole system. For example, in an SoC running multiple applications in the host operating system, if two applications need to write logs to persistent storage, then only these two applications must be given the ability to do so. If other applications are given the same ability, then a compromise of one of those applications would give the attacker the ability to tamper with persistent storage, which could have been prevented if the principle of least privilege had been practiced. Similarly, limiting network access to the applications in the guest operating system that require it would mean that a compromised VM cannot be used to attack other parts of the network. This is especially important as more ECU functions get centralized within larger domain control units and vehicle computers. In those scenarios, if any application can send any CAN message or Ethernet frame, then it is very difficult for the receiver to detect that the message did not originate from the legitimate communication partner. With MCU-based ECUs, least privilege can be implemented by reserving higher CPU privilege levels to the real-time operating system and trusted elements while executing all other user applications in the lowest privilege mode. Similarly, segmenting the application so that network and hardware resources are allocated to applications that need them eliminates opportunities for abuse and unwanted interference.

Least sharing

This principle is related to the least privilege principle but focuses on limiting how system resources are shared to the minimum set of users that need it. Enforcing this principle minimizes the risk that a resource can be abused by an entity that becomes malicious due to having unnecessary access privileges to the shared resource. On the other hand, unrestricted access to shared resources creates weak points that are hard to manage. Even a trusted entity can become a risk if compromised; therefore, by only allowing necessary access, this principle limits the damage that can be done if an entity becomes malicious. For example, if only two applications need access to specific sensors (for example, a camera image sensor), restricting access to those applications will prevent the sensors from being tampered with by other applications within the system. Similarly, if two communication endpoints need to exchange messages, then creating a virtual network between these endpoints prevents interference from other network endpoints that may try to eavesdrop or spoof the communication.

It is important to note that the setup phase of the ECU is critical for configuring access rights and assigning shared resources to their respective entities to reduce the likelihood of unwanted interference during the runtime phase. Wherever possible, keeping such configuration immutable during runtime is highly desirable to maintain the security benefits of the least sharing principle.

Mediated access

A typical automotive system will contain several resources that must be shared – for example, network interfaces, image processing engines, general-purpose **input/output** (**I/O**), and other peripherals that need to be accessed by mutually distrustful applications. Enforcing access mediation ensures that critical resources can't be easily tampered with by a single process or application that becomes malicious. One example approach for mediated access is the use of a client-server architecture in which the resource is managed by a server that exposes a limited set of services for interacting with the resource. This architecture allows the server to perform plausibility checks and verify access before accepting the request from a given client.

Protective defaults

The automotive supply chain consists of many layers that require close collaboration between suppliers and integrators. At each step of the supply chain, there is an opportunity for a component to be misconfigured in a way that reduces the overall security of the system. Therefore, it is imperative to deliver components with the maximum protection enabled by default, and with clear documentation on the risks of modifying the default configuration. For example, flash bootloader software should be delivered with the default security settings, which enforce digital signature verification of downloaded software images. There are cases where the protective default cannot be enabled, such as if a chip vendor must deliver the MCU or SoC in an unlocked state to allow key provisioning. In such a case, it is expected that the chip supplier will provide documentation that describes how to enable the security mode and the recommended practices on how to inject the key material with minimal risk of key tampering.

Anomaly detection

This principle requires that any anomaly in the ECU or the vehicle environment that meets a certain level of criticality is promptly detected to allow for an anomaly handling policy to be applied. A typical automotive product will experience a set of anomalies throughout its lifetime. These anomalies are frequently due to accidental faults such as random or systematic failures, which are thoroughly studied in functional safety. However, certain anomalies originate from malicious causes, such as the MAC verification failure of a secure message, or a failed authentication attempt of a diagnostic client. Having the ability to detect such anomalies and logging them for future inspection is a useful practice for analyzing attack patterns across a vehicle or even an entire vehicle fleet. Anomaly detection is not limited to the overall vehicle level but can be implemented at each layer of the architecture to permit the execution of local security policies. An example security policy is to disable access to communication keys if the boot authentication check fails during startup. This prevents an attacker who tampers with the ECU software from being able to communicate with other ECUs.

Distributed privilege

Certain critical operations should require multiple authorized entities to act in a coordinated manner before the operation is allowed to occur. One example of applying distributed privilege is separating **Over-the-Air** (**OTA**) functions into multiple roles. Rather than having a single backend server manage the entire OTA operation, separating the functions into a signing server, a time server, and a deployment server ensures that multiple security breaches are needed to successfully deploy software updates to a vehicle. Another example is the use of multiple signing authorities over software images that are checked during secure boot. An ECU supplier may choose to sign the images with their own key, even though the OEM also plans on signing the same images with their own key as well. This ensures that the OEM can't modify software that the supplier intends to remain unchanged.

Hierarchical protection and zero trust

When choosing which parts of an automotive system to protect, it is imperative to decide which entities of the system are assumed to be trusted. While practicing zero trust is a desirable approach, for systems with limited capabilities, doing so is not always possible. Therefore, we should aim for a minimal set of trusted parties. For example, in a multi-VM vehicle computer, the hypervisor must be considered trusted to set up the VMs and enforce spatial and temporal isolation. In a single operating system instance that is running mutually distrustful applications, the operating system itself can be considered the trusted party. When the hardware supports even stronger isolation, such as in the case of confidential computing, we can reduce our assumptions of trust. To read more about confidential computing, please refer to [19].

Minimal trusted elements

Along the lines of zero trust is the principle of minimal trusted elements, which aims to reduce the number of trusted elements that must remain secure for the overall system to be considered secure. The more elements that the system must trust to maintain its security, the more ways there are to breach the overall system security. Since trusted elements must be developed with a high level of security rigor, it is desirable to focus our resources on building as few trusted elements as possible. In an automotive ECU, at a minimum, the root of trust (namely the hardware-protected security environment defined in [20]) must be treated as the trusted element.

Least persistence

An automotive system leverages many resources that may only be needed for a brief window of time. The principle of least persistence requires that resources are disabled whenever they are not in use to further shrink the attack surface and eliminate opportunities for misuse. One way to apply this principle is to disable resources by default and only enable them once they are needed. For example, a system that must provide Wi-Fi and Bluetooth connectivity while also performing autonomous driving operations should consider shutting down the Wi-Fi and Bluetooth ASIC as soon as it is no longer needed. This reduces the window of opportunity for an attacker to abuse such interfaces to impact the safety-critical components of the system. However, practicing this principle in real-time systems is challenging because re-enabling resources after they have been disabled incurs a timing penalty, which in many cases cannot be tolerated. Therefore, we must practice this principle selectively by weighing the risks against the benefits.

Protective failure

Any automotive system is expected to fail at some point in time. However, a failure must never result in a complete loss of security. If designed with the protective failure principle, a component that fails is ensured to protect its assets during and after the failure occurs. For example, a cryptographic key that is stored in a secure hardware engine should not be exposed because of a hardware failure in the secure engine. Another example of this is when a self-test of a cryptographic function fails – further attempts to use the cryptographic functions should be rejected to prevent misuse of a malfunctioning cryptographic function. Enforcing this principle requires that systems are designed with the ability to detect failures promptly to allow protective measures to be executed promptly.

Continuous protection

When designing a system, a common pitfall is considering security during runtime mode and ignoring other states in which the vehicle can be exposed to threats. The continuous protection principle requires that protection mechanisms are active and uninterrupted across all system states and modes where protection is needed. For example, if an ECU is transitioned to a decommissioned state, any secrets that were provisioned in the ECU must be wiped clean to prevent their eventual leakage to someone who has physical possession of the ECU. This principle, however, allows certain protections to be intentionally overridden where such an override is justified, such as during the debug state, where control flow manipulation is desired to troubleshoot a problem. Note that even in the debug state, certain protections are still applicable, such as preventing access to cryptographic keys or erasing such keys to prevent their misuse.

Redundancy

Redundancy is a principle that applies to both safety and security to ensure system reliability and availability by replicating certain critical functions. The obvious downside of redundancy is the added cost, which limits how widely it can be used. An important aspect of redundancy is the diversity of the redundant elements to prevent common cause failures resulting from a single event from producing the same failure in the redundant elements. In the context of vehicle cybersecurity, redundancy can be achieved by replicating cryptographic keys in secure storage. This ensures that if a cryptographic key is corrupted or maliciously erased, the ECU is still able to access a copy of the key to perform the related cryptographic functions. Another example is using redundant fuse arrays to ensure that a device's life cycle state is not permanently corrupted, preventing the system from being able to boot. Similarly, using multiple redundant storage partitions for software ensures that a successful attempt to erase software does not leave the system in a bricked state.

Use of standardized cryptography

A common mistake in using cryptography is relying on proprietary algorithms or the misuse of standard cryptographic algorithms. Security through obscurity has been shown time and again to be a failed strategy. Attackers have many tools at their disposal to discover weaknesses in cryptosystems and deciding to rely on unproven secret cryptosystems will most likely result in an unhappy ending. Similarly, when cryptographic functions are used without paying attention to the constraints required by the standards, the security of such functions is severely reduced. Therefore, you must invest time in not only implementing cryptographic functions correctly but also in following the standard recommendations and avoiding common pitfalls.

In general, security principles are a powerful way to avoid common design mistakes and to ensure we are following security best practices. Having a good grasp of such principles enables us to build a strong foundation for building automotive systems that are resilient to cyberattacks. It is recommended that a tailored set of security principles is created for a given program to guide engineers during the design process and to establish a common baseline of secure design. Throughout this book, we will be referring back to these security principles when addressing a security threat or applying cybersecurity control.

Summary

In this chapter, we started by defining the different attack types that must be considered when building secure automotive systems. These attack types form a reference for future attacks that we will explore during the threat analysis phase. We then introduced the five main security objectives that any automotive system aims to achieve. These objectives will serve as parent objectives for our vehicle-level security goals. Next, we provided a crash course on cryptography and showed how to use its mechanisms to satisfy several of our security objectives. To complement these cryptographic mechanisms, we sampled the most common security principles that should influence the design of automotive systems. By covering these topics, we have established a good base for understanding security fundamentals and how they relate to automotive use cases.

While this chapter is by no means a comprehensive resource on all these topics, it should serve as an enabler to help you explore each topic more deeply on your own. Nevertheless, having covered the basics, we will now turn our attention to analyzing the various threats and attack surfaces that our vehicle is exposed to, which will conclude *Part 1* of this book.

Further reading

To learn more about the topics that were covered in this chapter, take a look at the following:

- *[1]* https://csrc.nist.gov/Projects/cryptographic-standards-and-guidelines.

- *[2] The Codebreakers*, by *Kahn*.

- *[3] Handbook of Applied Cryptography*, Discrete Mathematics and Its Applications, by Alfred J. Menezes (Author).

- *[4] Cryptography and Network Security, Principles and Practice*, by William Stallings.

- *[5]* https://github.com/robertdavidgraham/ecb-penguin.

- *[6] NIST SP800-90A: Recommendation for Random Number Generation Using Deterministic Random Bit Generators*: https://csrc.nist.gov/publications/detail/sp/800-90a/rev-1/final.

- *[7] NIST SP800-90B: Recommendation for the Entropy Sources Used for Random Bit Generation*: https://csrc.nist.gov/pubs/sp/800/90/b/final.

- *[8]* National Institute of Standards and Technology (2008) *The Keyed-Hash Message Authentication Code (HMAC).* US Department of Commerce, Washington, DC, Federal Information Processing Standards Publication (FIPS) 198-1: https://doi.org/10.6028/NIST.FIPS.198-1.

- *[9]* Dworkin MJ (2005) *Recommendation for Block Cipher Modes of Operation: the CMAC Mode for Authentication.* National Institute of Standards and Technology, Gaithersburg, MD, NIST Special Publication (SP) 800-38B, Includes updates as of October 6, 2016. https://doi.org/10.6028/NIST.SP.800-38B.

- *[10]* Kelsey JM, Chang S-jH, Perlner RA (2016) *SHA-3 Derived Functions: cSHAKE, KMAC, TupleHash, and ParallelHash.* National Institute of Standards and Technology, Gaithersburg, MD, NIST Special Publication (SP) 800-185. https://doi.org/10.6028/NIST.SP.800-185.

- *[11]* Singh, S. *The Code Book: The Science of Secrecy from Ancient Egypt to Quantum Cryptography.* New York: Anchor Books, 1999.

- *[12]* NIST SP800-38D: https://doi.org/10.6028/NIST.SP.800-38D.

- *[13]* Erik Dahmen, Katsuyuki Okeya, Tsuyoshi Takagi, and Camille Vuillaume. *Digital signatures out of second-preimage resistant hash functions.* In Johannes Buchmann and Jintai Ding, editors, Post-Quantum Cryptography, volume 5299 of Lecture Notes in Computer Science, pages 109-123. Springer Berlin/Heidelberg, 2008.

- *[14]* Mihir Bellare and Phillip Rogaway. *Collision-resistant hashing: Towards making UOWHFs practical.* In Burton Kaliski, editor, Advances in Cryptology – CRYPTO '97, volume 1294 of Lecture Notes in Computer Science, pages 470–484. Springer Berlin/Heidelberg, 1997. 10.1007/BFb0052256.

- *[15]* https://csrc.nist.gov/Projects/Random-Bit-Generation.

- *[16]* Ralph Merkle. *A certified digital signature.* In Gilles Brassard, editor, Advances in Cryptology-CRYPTO' 89 Proceedings, volume 435 of Lecture Notes in Computer Science, pages 218–238. Springer Berlin/Heidelberg, 1990.

- *[17]* https://nvlpubs.nist.gov/nistpubs/SpecialPublications/NIST.SP.800-57pt1r5.pdf.

- *[18] NIST SP800-208*: `https://doi.org/10.6028/NIST.SP.800-208`.

- *[19]* `https://confidentialcomputing.io/`.

- *[20] Requirements for hardware-protected security for ground vehicle applications (work in progress)*. [Online]. Available at `http://standards.sae.org/wip/j3101/`.

- *[21] IEEE standard for local and metropolitan area networks-media access control (mac) security*, IEEE Std 802.1AE-2018.

- *[22]* `https://attack.mitre.org/techniques/ics/`.

- *[23]* `https://nvlpubs.nist.gov/nistpubs/SpecialPublications/NIST.SP.800-160v1r1.pdf`, *Appendix E*.

- *[24]* A. Johnson and R. Davies, *Speculative Execution Attack Methodologies (SEAM): An overview and component modelling of Spectre, Meltdown and Foreshadow attack methods*, 2019 7th International Symposium on Digital Forensics and Security (ISDFS), Barcelos, Portugal, 2019, pp. 1-6, doi: 10.1109/ISDFS.2019.8757547.

- *[25]* Hankerson, Darrel, Alfred J. Menezes, and Scott Vanstone. *Guide to elliptic curve cryptography*. Springer Science & Business Media, 2006.

- *[26] Cryptography lecture series*, by Professor Christof Paar: `https://www.youtube.com/playlist?list=PL2jrku-ebl3H50FiEPr4erSJiJHURM9BX`.

- *[27]* Grover, Lov K. *From Schrödinger's equation to the quantum search algorithm*. American Journal of Physics 69.7 (2001): 769-777.

3

Threat Landscape against Vehicle Components

The more connected features that modern vehicles offer, the richer the attack surface gets, and the more diverse the threat space becomes. Examining the threat landscape is an essential step in understanding the cyber risks that modern vehicles are exposed to and the required cybersecurity controls to reduce or eliminate that risk. The intent of this chapter is not to serve as an exhaustive reference on all possible cybersecurity threats and attacks that impact a modern vehicle, but rather to serve as a representative catalog of threats to be considered by practitioners in the field. Whether you are a vehicle manufacturer, an **electronic control unit** (ECU) supplier, or a component supplier, you are encouraged to build upon the threats presented here to create a tailored threat catalog that fits your vehicle systems and update it frequently to aid engineers who are performing security analysis. A secondary goal of this chapter is to establish the motivation for the secure engineering approach, which will be the topic of the next part of this book.

When classifying threats against vehicle interfaces and components, it's useful to view the vehicle as a multi-layered system. The top layer provides external connectivity to both the backend and supporting systems. This layer consists of the ECUs and sensors that are exposed to direct attacks by anyone who can interact with the exposed vehicle interfaces. The next layer is the network topology, which determines how easy or difficult it is for a top-layer threat to propagate to the deeper layers of the vehicle. Following that layer, we encounter the in-vehicle network and protocols, each of which comes with a set of known weaknesses that shape how a threat can traverse through different vehicle domains. In the final layer are our deeply embedded ECUs, internal sensors, and actuators, each of which is subject to a unique set of threats and weaknesses.

Note that while we may hint at some methods or practices to mitigate a threat, we will intentionally avoid an in-depth discussion on the applicable countermeasures. This will be discussed comprehensively in the last two chapters of the book as a culmination of the application of the secure engineering method.

In this chapter, we will cover the following main topics:

- Threats against external vehicle interfaces
- Threats against the E/E topology
- Threats against in-vehicle networks
- Threats against sensors
- Common ECU threats

Threats against external vehicle interfaces

Before diving into real-world threats, let's first define what a **threat** is and how it differs from an **attack**. Simply put, a threat represents the possibility of achieving an adverse effect on the vehicle stakeholders, through the exploitation of a security vulnerability or weakness. For example, an ECU that receives data over an insecure channel is exposed to the threat of data tampering by a threat agent with access to the vehicle network. On the other hand, an attack is the actual exploitation of a vulnerability or a weakness to realize the threat. For example, the threat of vehicle network data tampering can be realized by an attack in which network messages are intercepted, modified, and retransmitted to the target ECU. To derive attacks for a specific threat, it helps to identify the underlying vulnerability or weakness that makes the threat viable, turning the possibility of compromise (threat) into a realized action (attack). Now that we know the difference between threats and attacks, we first examine the threats against external-facing ECUs.

> **Note**
> Discovering new vulnerabilities and finding ways to exploit them requires a certain level of expertise, tooling, and knowledge in relation to the target. These aspects will be considered in depth in later chapters when we study methods to quantify the attack feasibility of a given threat.

The unique aspect of this type of ECU is that it is directly reachable through a wired or wireless vehicle interface, such as USB, Wi-Fi, or Bluetooth. A typical modern vehicle may contain several external-facing ECUs such as the telematics unit, **in-vehicle infotainment** (**IVI**), and the autonomous driving system. Having external connectivity exposes these ECUs to threats ranging from those that require direct physical access to those that can be carried out virtually from any point in the world. A primary source of remote-based threats is the backend, which we will examine next.

Backend-related threats

Backend servers play a myriad of roles in the support of connected vehicles such as administering over-the-air software and map updates, aggregating vehicle health reports across a vehicle fleet, and even performing real-time tracking of drivers for commercial fleet management. A consequence of having continuous connectivity to cloud services is that when a backend server is compromised, the vehicle and its occupants are exposed to the threat of malicious remote interference, which can result in loss of vehicle function or even a crash. Another possible threat is the extraction of sensitive vehicle data, which includes the exposure of driver location or the loss of intellectual property belonging to the vehicle manufacturer.

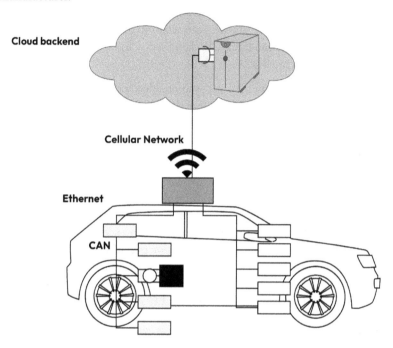

Figure 3.1– A simplified view of two-way communication between the vehicle and a cloud backend

To understand how such threats can materialize, we consider the following common attack methods that impact the backend environment:

- **Insider threat**: If an employee or a contractor with authorized access to the backend server uses their privileges for malicious purposes, they could potentially issue malicious vehicle software updates, send corrupted map data, and exfiltrate sensitive vehicle data. Insider threats can be particularly difficult to detect or prevent, as the perpetrator often has legitimate access to the system or network and may be able to bypass certain security controls.

- **Social engineering**: Server administrators can be manipulated through social engineering techniques to open malicious links in phishing emails, leading to the compromise of the backend server that is handling vehicle data and remote vehicle management.

- **Spoofed vehicle ID**: Backend servers are exposed to the threat of a masquerading vehicle in which an attacker assumes the identity of a real vehicle to trick a server into accepting communication requests. Depending on the services available to the vehicle, an attacker may be able to perform a successful remote code injection to launch further attacks against other vehicles or simply retrieve the data of the vehicle whose identity is being misused.

- **Service disruption**: When vehicle backend services are disrupted, the effects can be felt through the automotive supply chain such as dealerships, automotive suppliers, and even assembly plants. For vehicles that depend on connectivity to function, this can lead to drivers losing access to features they paid for, such as the ability to receive map updates and vehicle health reports. To disrupt those services, attackers can resort to distributed denial of service attacks in which a swarm of machines can target a backend server to exhaust its resources and prevent it from serving legitimate requests.

- **Vehicle data loss or exfiltration**: Like any web-enabled server, vehicle backend servers are vulnerable to attacks that leverage cross-site scripting, **Structured Query Language** (**SQL**) injection, server misconfiguration, and a slew of other vulnerabilities. When successful, breaches to vehicle backend servers may result in the loss of sensitive data, such as personal driver data, financial information, cryptographic secrets, and intellectual property, which can lead to financial losses and damage to the organization's reputation.

- **Malicious software updates**: The ability of the vehicle to update its software periodically is a strong security mechanism that ensures vehicle systems can be periodically patched to handle security breaches. However, this ability is also a powerful attack surface to maliciously modify the vehicle software. A primary source of threats using **over-the-air** (**OTA**) updates originates from a compromised backend server, which can issue malicious software updates. Besides the backend threats, attackers with remote vehicle access can potentially intercept and manipulate updates to introduce malicious code or to alter the ECU's behavior.

Let's take a closer look at the most common attack methods against the OTA process:

- **Eavesdropping attacks**: If the update package is not transferred securely from the backend to the target ECU, an attacker may intercept the update package and extract its contents.

- **Denial of software updates**: This can be achieved through a **man-in-the-middle** (**MitM**) attack that blocks network traffic traversing through one of the network segments connecting the backend and the final target ECU. Rather than blocking an update that would trigger a download retry, an MitM attacker can instead slow the transfer of data blocks in such a way that does not produce a timeout in the target ECU, causing the update to never finish. Here, the attacker can abuse the communication protocol, for example, by repeatedly requesting the retransmission of a specific data block to prolong the update process.

- **Rollback and freeze attacks**: Weak authentication with the legitimate backend can enable the attacker, who captures a valid software update to masquerade as the backend, triggering an update request to revert to an older version. If the vehicle does not enforce version checks, it can revert to an older, unpatched version, which re-enables certain vulnerabilities. Another way this can be abused is through the repeated issuance of the old update to keep the vehicle in a busy state, unable to receive the legitimate update, which effectively freezes the update process.

- **Resource exhaustion**: An attacker who gains access to the software update service can issue an update that is larger than the storage capacity of the vehicle. If the target ECU lacks the proper memory safety checks before committing the update to storage, the attacker can overwrite the backup software partition, or even cause the software update to crash.

- **Mix and match**: Even when digital signatures are enforced to prevent the installation of unauthentic software, an attacker can resort to grouping validly signed software images in a bundle that would be incompatible with a specific vehicle. If the vehicle does not enforce compatibility checks, this type of update can result in a malfunction once the software is booted and starts execution.

Protecting the vehicle backend environment entails standard security procedures that are applied to IT based systems such as strong role-based access controls, firewalls and intrusion detection systems, as well as frequent software updates to patch to vulnerable systems. Using secure communication channels that enforce strong end-to-end authentication and encryption is a must, especially when offering OTA services. Due to the highly distributed nature of the automotive supply chain, it is also crucial to regularly review and monitor data-sharing practices, to ensure that data is only shared with authorized parties in a secure manner. Finally, having procedures in place to quickly respond to and recover from attacks or other disruptions can minimize the impact of a successful breach on the backend.

Connectivity threats

Both wired vehicle interfaces, such as the USB ports of an infotainment system and **onboard diagnostics (OBD)** ports, as well as wireless interfaces such as cellular modems and Wi-Fi chipsets, are vulnerable to a wide range of security threats. In this section, we survey the most common attacks over these interfaces.

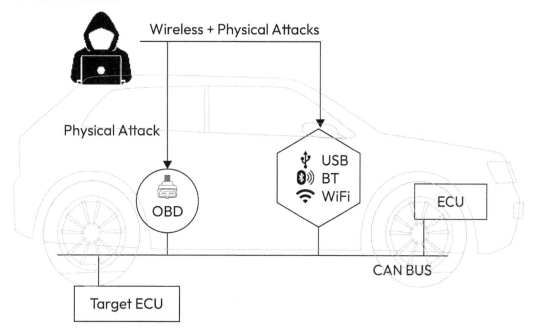

Figure 3.2 – Abuse of vehicle exposed interfaces to mount attacks against a target ECU

Cellular

Telematics ECUs serve as the vehicle's primary method of external connectivity through cellular modems. While cellular connectivity offers a convenient way to reach the vehicle anywhere that a cellular service is available, this also means that the window of opportunity to launch attacks over the cellular link is practically unlimited. This makes the telematics ECU a primary target for attack; therefore, investment in significant resources should be made, to ensure that the telematics ECU is as secure as possible.

Typical services offered through the telematics unit are OTA updates, vehicle health reporting, geofencing, fleet monitoring, and emergency calls. This means that the vehicle can be exposed to a range of threats from tampering with vehicle software, blocking vehicle health reports, disclosing vehicle driving patterns (including location) to denying the emergency call service. The latter has life-threatening consequences if the driver is unconscious and cannot receive medical help in time.

To realize these threats, attackers can target the cellular network connecting the vehicle using three main attack methods:

- **Location tracking**
- **Communication interception**
- **Service downgrade**

The tools used in carrying out the attacks fall under the umbrella of **cell-site simulators** (**CSSs**). These operate on different cell network generations, starting with 2G, which only supported calls and text, and 2.5G, which added data transmissions such as email and text. With 3G and LTE, faster data rates were possible, which made video transmission possible. 4G and 5G marked a significant jump in data rate and improved security.

Let's look at a basic type of communication interception attack in which a CSS will be used to track a vehicle's location. In this attack, the CSS boosts its signal strength to trick the vehicle's cellular modem into connecting to the CSS, rather than to a legitimate cellular tower. The CSS then proceeds to request the modem's identity and receives the **International Mobile Subscriber Identity** (**IMSI**) stored on the SIM card of the modem. Upon receiving the IMSI number, the CSS can terminate the connection to allow the cellular modem to connect to the real network.

Figure 3.3 – A CSS masquerading as a cell tower

> **Note**
>
> In 4G and later generations, a cellular modem will not connect with random base stations only due to the high signal strength, and therefore the attack requires more steps to establish a connection with a CSS. In addition, with 5G, the IMSI is not shared directly.

To carry out a more sophisticated attack for communication interception, which would allow tampering or eavesdropping on data being transmitted to and from the vehicle, the CSS needs to play the role of an **MitM**. In this attack, which is only illustrated using 2G networks, the CSS first transmits a **location update request** (**LAC**) to the cell tower, which in turn asks the CSS to identify itself. The CSS responds using the captured IMSI number from the previous attack. Next, the tower issues a cryptographic challenge that requires the CSS to know the secret key stored in the SIM card of the vehicle cell modem. The CSS will simply relay that request to the cell modem, which will prepare the correct response to be relayed this time by the CSS back to the network. Now, the CSS has successfully authenticated itself to the network as the vehicle modem. In the next step, when the network requests the usage of encryption to transmit the data, the CSS simply responds with the option to use no encryption, allowing it to now receive the data in plaintext.

While this attack is only possible with 2G networks, it is still important to consider, due to it being a service downgrade attack. Here, the attacker can jam the 3G or 4G bands, forcing the cell modem to downgrade to 2G in search of a reliable signal. This makes it possible to exploit the 2G authentication weakness.

In addition to attacks that target cell connectivity protocols, a vehicle is exposed to attacks over higher-layer protocols such as SMS, through spoofing, flooding, and malware injection. Consider a vehicle that uses the SMS protocol to wake up the telematics unit, which in turn can wake up other ECUs to perform a remotely triggered function such as reporting the vehicle location. By sending the cellular modem in the telematics unit, a carefully timed sequence of SMS messages, the vehicle battery can eventually be depleted.

With SMS flooding, an attacker sends a large number of SMS messages to a specific vehicle modem in an attempt to overwhelm it, thereby disabling external connectivity through the cellular network. Finally, if the SMS protocol implementation in the cellular modem contains security vulnerabilities, an attacker can abuse the protocol to perform remote code injection attacks, with the intent of compromising the telematics unit to construct a more advanced attack chain against the rest of the vehicle electronic systems.

Wi-Fi

Similar to cellular, Wi-Fi can be used as an alternative method to remotely access vehicle services, such as delivering OTA updates (as shown in *Figure 3.4*) through a home or commercial Wi-Fi link (for example, in a fleet service center). The OEM chooses which services to expose over Wi-Fi to reduce cellular data usage. Alternatively, Wi-Fi can be offered as a vehicle hotspot for the vehicle occupants. In-car Wi-Fi can be supported through the cellular network either through the telematics cell modem or through aftermarket devices such as the **Verizon Hum** (see *[21]* in the *Further reading* section at the end of the chapter). Controlling built-in Wi-Fi hotspots typically involves utilizing certain mobile applications or the multimedia touch screen in the vehicle. The latter creates an additional attack vector against the IVI system.

When Wi-Fi is used to establish connectivity to backend servers, the vehicle is exposed to the typical threats that impact Wi-Fi networks. For example, if the Wi-Fi network is not properly configured or secured (for example, due to weak passwords or outdated encryption schemes), an attacker may be able to gain access to the network and intercept or manipulate traffic between the vehicle and the backend.

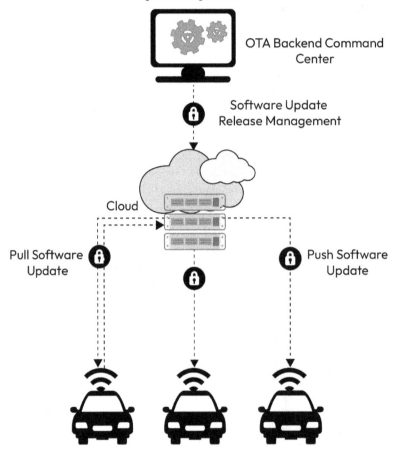

Figure 3.4 – Delivering OTA updates using the Wi-Fi link

When used as a hotspot for vehicle occupants, weak Wi-Fi network configuration, coupled with the lack of proper network segmentation can enable an attacker, who is in the vicinity of the vehicle, to gain access to other segments of the network connecting the vehicle to the backend.

A unique source of threats over vehicle Wi-Fi originates from aftermarket hotspots that can be plugged into the OBD port to provide the vehicle occupants with internet and remote vehicle access. By plugging into the OBD port, these aftermarket devices can send the driver vehicle diagnostic alerts when they detect a **diagnostic trouble code** (**DTC**) and can enable remote vehicle tracking to help the vehicle owner locate the car in case it is stolen. These features of convenience expose the vehicle to the threat of remote access to the vehicle **Controller Area Network** (**CAN**) bus and unwanted vehicle tracking. Unlike OEM telematics units, these devices are not validated for a specific vehicle type and may have been developed to a lower security standard than required; therefore, consumers must be wary of introducing them into their vehicles. Regarding older models that were never designed to be web-connected, this almost guarantees that a breach of the Wi-Fi hotspot will have serious consequences for the vehicle operation, due to the absence of network filtering at the **on-board diagnostics** (**OBD**) port.

Mobile-application-based attacks

It is common for vehicles to offer vehicle services access through mobile phones that allow a user to retrieve vehicle health information, check on the next service, enable remote start, unlock the doors, or even in some cases initiate low-speed driving, for example, to summon the vehicle in a parking lot. With each such service, there exists the threat of illegal access, private data extraction, and vehicle interference.

Weak authentication in APIs that offer vehicle services to mobile applications makes the vehicle vulnerable to attacks, which range from violation of driver privacy to unlocking the vehicle or even gaining control of the vehicle operation. One such incident occurred with the *Nissan Leaf*, which could be remotely compromised through the Nissan mobile application. The researchers discovered that the Leaf's **application interface** (**API**) only checks the **vehicle identification number** (**VIN**) to enable remote access to car features. An attacker who can retrieve the VIN could then control features such as climate settings, depleting the vehicle battery, or accessing driver information such as vehicle travel time.

Another type of mobile app attack exploits the lack of access termination after access is no longer needed, such as vehicle rental return. If the vehicle provides no option to terminate access once a phone is linked to the car, the renter can retain access indefinitely, allowing them to monitor the vehicle location and even start it remotely, which is guaranteed to spook the next driver that rents the vehicle.

Bluetooth

Several types of Bluetooth standards are commonly used in vehicles ranging from Bluetooth 2.0 to Bluetooth 5.1, as well as **Bluetooth Low Energy** (**BLE**). BLE, introduced as part of the Bluetooth 4.0 specification, was designed for power efficiency, making it suitable for use in devices that require long battery life. Bluetooth has been used for many years to connect the smartphone to the vehicle's hands-free function. It can also be used with telematics units for initial setup through a mobile phone. Unfortunately, Bluetooth vulnerabilities are still being discovered, making them a useful target when attacking vehicles.

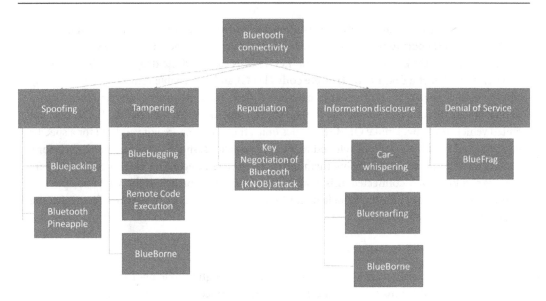

Figure 3.5 – Classification of Bluetooth attacks

Below we survey some of the common attack methods that may be used against Bluetooth in the vehicle:

- **Car Whisperer:** A tool that can be used to exploit vulnerabilities in a vehicle's Bluetooth implementation to eavesdrop on communication.

- **Bluesnarfing:** Exploits vulnerabilities in the **object exchange protocol (OBEX)** in a victim's device that is set to *discoverable to others* mode.

- **Bluebugging:** As you might guess from the name, this is similar to bugging a landline phone but through Bluetooth instead. It exploits vulnerabilities to gain unauthorized access to the victim's device's command interface, allowing the attacker to access data on the device.

- **Bluejacking:** A type of attack in which an unauthorized device attempts to send unsolicited messages (such as spam or malicious software) to Bluetooth-enabled devices (such as a smartphone within range).

- **BlueBorne:** Exploits vulnerabilities in the Bluetooth stack to inject code into the target device's operating system through a buffer overflow vulnerability, without the need for pairing, making it critical.

- **Key Negotiation of Bluetooth (KNOB) attack:** Exploits a weakness in the encryption key negotiation protocol of Bluetooth to downgrade the entropy of the encryption key of a target device, potentially to as low as 1 byte. The low-entropy keys are then subject to brute force attacks to discover the key content and enable the exposure and tampering of encrypted and authenticated data, respectively.

- **BlueFrag**: A set of attack scenarios that takes advantage of the Bluetooth fragmentation process, in which a device breaks up large data packets into smaller fragments to be transmitted over the Bluetooth connection. An attacker can exploit this process by sending large data packets that cause the targeted device to crash, or by injecting malicious code into the fragments to gain control of the device.

- **Bluetooth Pineapple**: An attack on the protocol's feature of inquiry and paging that tricks the target device into connecting to an attacker's device, rather than the intended device.

Note that Bluetooth-enabled diagnostic dongles are commonly used to allow the vehicle owner to scan for diagnostic faults through a mobile phone. If such dongles contain a Bluetooth vulnerability, the attacker who can successfully connect to the dongle will be able to inject messages directly into the CAN network through the OBD port. It's therefore best practice to remove such devices when the vehicle is in motion. Furthermore, to reduce the risk of Bluetooth-based attacks against IVI systems, it is recommended to continuously monitor for known vulnerabilities and patch systems frequently. Additionally, relying on high-assurance Bluetooth implementations can reduce the likelihood of high-severity bugs.

Universal Serial Bus (USB)

USB is typically offered in IVI systems to allow users to plug in their devices such as a mobile phone. It can also be found on ECUs that require extended storage such as autonomous driving systems or telematics units.

Figure 3.6 – Attack methods that can be carried out through the USB port

Updates through USB are a common backup method to software updates over the air. This creates an opportunity to install malicious software through a compromised USB storage device that can exploit authentication weaknesses in the software update protocol.

With the support of USB 3.x devices, faster data transfer speeds and larger data buffers are supported using **Direct Memory Access (DMA)** controllers. When copying data from a USB storage device into system memory using DMA, the attacker can exploit improperly configured or missing memory isolation through the **Input/Output Memory Management Unit (IOMMU)** to inject a malicious payload. Once the payload has been successfully copied by the DMA controller into the system memory, the attacker can gain root access to run commands with *escalated privileges* or add a backdoor for later exploit. An effective way to eliminate the risk of USB attacks is to disable the USB port after the ECU has transitioned into the production state.

OBD

The OBD port, introduced in *Chapter 1*, is a standard, mandated feature in vehicles that allows state and federal governments to assess the status of the emission control mechanisms, and also allows mechanics to access the vehicle's internal systems for troubleshooting and repair. However, the OBD port can also be used by attackers to gain unauthorized access to the vehicle's internal network, resulting in the manipulation or disruption of vehicle operations.

The OBD interface is designed to send diagnostic commands from an OBD client to an ECU. The OBD port is normally interfaced with a central gateway that intercepts both CAN and Ethernet-based diagnostic commands, before routing them to the target ECU. The gateway plays an important role in filtering unwanted traffic coming from the OBD port. Weak or missing filters in the gateway or even a lack of network segmentation can enable an attacker, who plugs in a CAN tool through the OBD port, to send unsafe messages to internal ECUs such as braking and steering commands. One way to carry out this attack is through OBD dongles, which are Bluetooth-enabled devices that allow a vehicle owner to diagnose their own vehicle. If left connected while driving, the dongle can collect information such as vehicle speed and ECU fault data. Unfortunately, this ability also creates an attack surface, allowing remote access to the vehicle's internal network. In the UDS protocol section, we will take a closer look at attacks that can abuse the diagnostic protocol, which can be carried out through the OBD port. This makes the securing of the OBD interface an important security objective.

Radio frequency

The **remote keyless entry** (RKE) system is an electronic lock that restricts access to vehicles using a wireless key fob carried by the user to remotely lock, unlock, and start your car's engine using **radio frequency** (RF) signals. This exposes the vehicle to the threat of unauthorized access to remotely unlock the vehicle over the RF channel with the intent to steal the vehicle or its contents.

RKE systems come in two variants: the **one-way RKE**, in which only the key fob can send commands while the vehicle is in receive mode, and the **two-way RKE**, where both the key fob and the vehicle can exchange messages. With two-way RKE, a vehicle may support either active or passive unlock. The passive unlock RKE systems automatically transmit signals, allowing a car door to be unlocked as the vehicle owner approaches the vehicle and/or touches the door handle without the need for any action on the part of the vehicle owner. On the other hand, active RKE systems require that the vehicle owner manually presses the fob to transmit the command signal. One-way RKE only supports active mode, as shown in *Figure 3.7*.

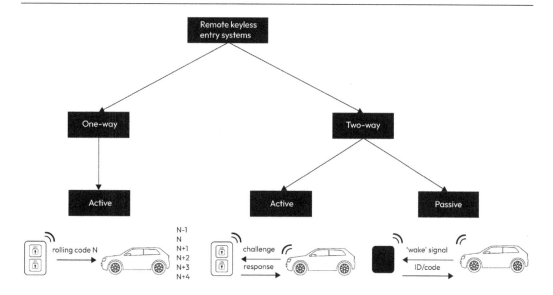

Figure 3.7 – One-way and two-way RKE systems

To understand how RKE systems can be attacked, we will examine the **RollJam and Replay** attack against the one-way RKE system.

In the normal scenario, a large incrementing counter is maintained by the vehicle side. The key fob generates a counter value and encrypts it along with some payload data that identifies the key fob and the requested action (unlock door, beep horn, etc.), and then transmits the signal to the vehicle side. The receiver on the vehicle side decrypts the signal and then compares the received counter to the validity window. A counter within the validity window causes the fob action to be performed, otherwise, the signal is rejected.

Several documented attacks can lead to the compromise of the RKE, based on the underlying protocol for performing the lock/unlock sequence.

This method is vulnerable to wireless jamming attacks, one of which is widely known as the Replay and RollJam attack, shown in *Figure 3.8*.

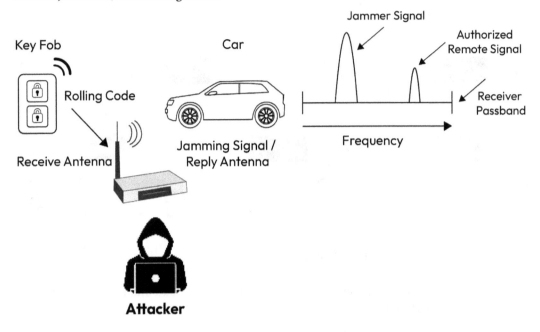

Figure 3.8 – Replay and RollJam attack

The Replay and RollJam attack is realized through the steps shown in *Figure 3.9*. First, the driver presses the key fob button to unlock the vehicle. During this time, the attacker records the signal while jamming the vehicle to prevent the RKE system from detecting the command. Expecting the vehicle to flash the brake lights or sound a chirp, the driver assumes that the signal was not received and presses the button once more. The attacker repeats the same jamming to record the second unlock command. With two unlock commands, the attacker now plays the first command to give the driver the illusion that they have successfully unlocked the vehicle. The driver continues to use and drive the vehicle, then steps out and locks it. With the driver out of the way, the attacker now plays the second unlock command to gain access to the vehicle and successfully steals it.

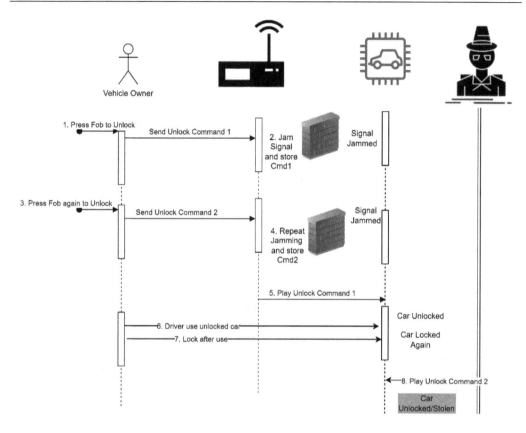

Figure 3.9 – Replay and RollJam attack flow diagram

Another possible attack against RKE systems is the **RollBack time-agnostic** attack, which enables the attacker to capture a signal once and replay it as often as needed in the future. You are encouraged to research this attack by referring to *[14]*. The final RKE attack we discuss is a simple relay attack against passive RKE systems. This attack involves sending signals from one place to another to give the impression that one entity is near the vehicle when it is not. The attack typically doesn't have to decode or alter the message signal. All that is needed is a simple delay, as we will see next.

This attack can be carried out in four steps, usually by two people working together, as shown in *Figure 3.10*. First, the thief stands within close proximity to the vehicle and uses specific devices to relay received signals to the second thief. The second thief stands as close as possible to the house, where the key fob is located, operating the second device. This second device transmits the relayed signal into the house to be received by the key fob stored in the house. The key fob replies in the normal manner, fooling the remote keyless system into thinking the owner is close and allowing the first thief entry into the vehicle.

Figure 3.10 – The four steps of implementing the relay attack against passive RKE

As demonstrated in this section, external vehicle interfaces make up a rich attack surface for malicious actors to establish a foothold within the vehicle E/E architecture. In some cases, breaching an external interface is sufficient to achieve the attack objective, as in the case of the RKE-based attacks. However, for other interfaces, a successful breach is just the first step in building the attack chain targeting the internal vehicle systems. In the next section, we proceed with the next layer of the E/E architecture to evaluate how the E/E topology plays a role in propagating threats to the rest of the vehicle domains.

Threats against the E/E topology

In *Chapter 1*, we explored the various E/E architecture types from the highly distributed, to the domain centralized, and finally, the zone architecture. In this section, we will highlight the threats against each type of architectural layout.

Highly distributed E/E architecture

A typical weakness of such architecture is that security-critical ECUs may be reached from multiple attack surfaces, without the possibility of cleanly separating the domains. One of our security principles in *Chapter 2* was **domain separation**, which required the physical and logical separation of the domains of various levels of security needs.

An example of a weak architecture is that of the famous Jeep hack in which the infotainment ECU was on the same network segment as the brake ECU *[28]*.

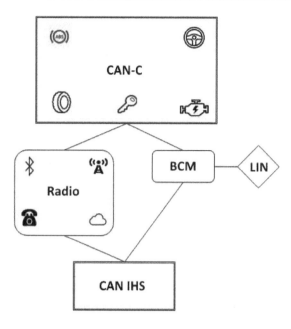

Figure 3.11 – 2014 Jeep Cherokee architecture (source is [28])

This enabled an attacker who managed to compromise the infotainment ECU to start directly interacting with the brake ECU over the insecure CAN network. The primary way of dealing with this weakness is to switch to a domain-controlled architecture. If that is not feasible, then serious security hardening is needed for all the primary attack surfaces, in the hope of shielding the rest of the vehicle ECUs from malicious interference.

Domain-centralized E/E architecture

With the vehicle domains being physically separated through different in-vehicle networks, we achieve a reasonable degree of isolation. An attacker who aims to reach a safety ECU in the chassis domain needs to breach an external vehicle interface such as the telematics unit, in addition to the central gateway, before being able to interfere with an ECU on the chassis domain.

However, poor implementations of this type of architecture can still cause serious security risks. One such weakness is in vehicle architectures where the OEM allows users to bring their own aftermarket devices to plug into one of the internal network segments. This type of solution can defeat the segmentation offered through the central gateway if the aftermarket device is directly interacting with internal vehicle systems. Another example is the weak or missing network filtering in the central gateway, giving an attacker with OBD access the ability to directly reach a chassis domain ECU by using the gateway as the relay.

While the centralized architecture provides better isolation across network segments, if not implemented correctly, it can lose the benefits of domain isolation. Furthermore, the central gateway behaves as a single point of failure. An attacker who can take over the central gateway is now free to interact with any ECU on any vehicle domain.

Central vehicle computer architecture

Consolidating multiple vehicle functions into a vehicle computer introduces its own set of challenges. It is not uncommon to find a vehical computer that integrates vehicle infotainment with ADAS functions. With such architecture, physical separation within the vehicle computer is no longer possible, so we must depend heavily on logical separation. This calls for a high degree of resource separation through mechanisms such as virtualization and confidential computing. A mistake in the configuration of the system can lead to direct interference between the rich execution environment, such as the Android OS, and the more safety-critical environment that is running on a safety-qualified operating system, such as Blackberry's QNX or PikeOS.

Having examined the role of the E/E topology in the level of threat exposure, we now take a closer look at the various in-vehicle networking technologies to highlight their weaknesses and how they can be leveraged by an attacker to interfere directly with target ECUs.

Threats against in-vehicle networks

In-vehicle networking protocols enable ECUs, sensors, and in some cases, actuators to communicate under strict real-time and low-cost constraints. However, since the primary design objective of these networking protocols is efficient and deterministic communication, it is not unusual for some of these protocols to exhibit serious security weaknesses. In this section, we examine the weaknesses and in-vehicle networking protocols and highlight the corresponding attacks that can exploit them.

CAN

A simple Google search on **CAN** security yields hundreds of papers and articles on how CAN is not secure. While earlier versions of CAN such as CAN 2.0 and CAN FD did not consider security while the protocol was being defined, a more recent variant called CAN XL [REF29] now offers a security extension that protects the data link layer. Nevertheless, CAN XL is in its infancy, so we have to judge the security of the CAN protocol based on the first two variants. To cover the CAN threats, we will explore both the physical and the data link layers.

CAN physical layer

Abusing the characteristics of the CAN physical layer is an easy way of creating a disturbance in the CAN network. One such method is to abuse the CAN bus-off mechanism by injecting an invalid bit pattern, targeting specific frames. First, let's see briefly how CAN bus-off works. Each CAN node keeps an error counter that is incremented when the transmitter observes an error on the bus. If the transmitters observe an error in their own frame, then they increment their error counter by 8; otherwise, they increment it by 1. The intent of this strategy is to cause a node that has a physical failure to reach the error count limit earlier than the other nodes and force it to enter bus-off mode. In this mode, the transmitter is expected to stop sending messages for a period of time to allow the fault to be resolved before attempting to join the network again. If the fault were transient, then the transmitting node would be able to resume transmission successfully; otherwise, it would again experience the same error behavior, forcing it to enter bus-off again. OEMs implement different fault-handling strategies, such as short periodic retries, followed by long periodic retries to avoid continuously disturbing the bus if the node has experienced a permanent failure. Now, an attacker who can manipulate the CAN physical layer can induce faults that mimic those causing a bus-off condition. This type of attack requires special abilities such as using a non-conforming CAN controller or reconfiguring the CAN pins as **general purpose I/O (GPIO)** to inject faults through software control. This is essentially a denial-of-service type of attack that causes an ECU to temporarily or permanently lose the ability to send and receive CAN messages. Another objective of this attack is to target specific messages to prevent an ECU from performing its function such as corrupting a brake command message during an emergency braking event. It should be clear that this type of attack requires a high degree of skill and specialized equipment, as well as physical access to the CAN bus.

CAN data link layer

Since the CAN protocol sends all messages in plaintext format, and since the CAN ID is used to identify the message source, the CAN data link layer several network layer threats. First, spoofing is possible because any network participant can construct a CAN message with the ID of any other node, which makes it possible to spoof other ECUs. Second, since all the data link layer fields such as the **data length code (DLC)** and the payload are sent as plaintext, an attacker can construct or replay a message with a payload of their choosing, causing the receiving node to react to a maliciously crafted message. Third, thanks to the arbitration mechanism that allows the ECU to send the frame with the lowest CAN ID to win the arbitration, a malicious network participant can flood the bus with zero ID messages to prevent other ECUs from gaining access to the bus and essentially all normal communication.

When secure communication is enabled by appending MAC values to the payload, an additional attack is possible through resource exhaustion by forcing an ECU to perform a high workload of MAC verification requests to deplete runtime resources. To launch any one of these attacks, an attacker needs to first establish a foothold within the in-vehicle network for example by compromising the telematics unit, OBD WiFi dongle or any other ECU with external connectivity. In Chapter 8, we will see how to apply vehicle level cybersecurity controls to address those risks.

FlexRay

In *Chapter 1*, **FlexRay** was described as a deterministic, time-triggered protocol that offers a bandwidth of up to 10 Mbps per channel in the redundant configuration. The data frames are sent and received within predefined time slots, and all the ECUs connected by this protocol are synchronized to the global time. The FlexRay frame consists of a payload, a header segment, and a trailer segment. The slot ID, payload length, cycle counter, and so on are all included in the header segment, while the frame data is encapsulated in the payload segment, followed by the frame **cyclic redundancy check (CRC)** in the trailer segment. Like CAN, FlexRay is subject to both physical and data link layer threats. At the physical layer, the attacker needs to manipulate the FlexRay transceiver transmit pin to corrupt frame bits. As a result, the receiving nodes will be unable to receive frames, which may trigger re-synchronization attempts. If the physical bus manipulation persists, the re-synchronization will fail, effectively making the link unavailable. Due to the deterministic nature of the FlexRay network, an attacker could target specific time slots to create this disturbance and prevent a certain node from sending its messages. On the other hand, the data link layer shares several threats with the CAN bus, such as frame ID spoofing, data tampering, frame replay, and denial of service.

These attacks are possible due to the lack of authentication and encryption of any of the frame segments. During the static slot transmission, a FlexRay node that has been compromised may masquerade as another FlexRay node by faking the header segment ID. Similarly, that node can construct a malicious payload, without the receiving node being able to detect that the frame is from an illegitimate source. To carry out such attacks, the malicious node has to define the target messages in its own communication schedule and choose transmission cycles that do not contain the legitimate message. Since the legitimate message will still come through, the attacker will need to create collisions with this message to completely trick the receiver into consuming the malicious message.

Due to the time slot allocation and synchronization features of FlexRay, a few attacks are unique to the FlexRay protocol. A denial-of-service attack can be carried out if the attacker creates collisions with synchronization frames. After a number of failed re-synchronization attempts, the affected nodes will lose synchronization, leading to their loss of the ability to communicate on the channel.

Similarly, an attacker can create bus collisions by modifying their transmission schedule to send messages during static slots belonging to other nodes. This produces a similar result to the previous attack. If the dynamic slot is enabled, the attacker can attempt to block other nodes from using that slot by continuously sending frames with high priority or by creating collisions.

Due to the redundant nature of the FlexRay network, if the management of the channels is properly isolated, then these types of attacks should be harder to carry out as the attacker would need to breach the separation of control of both channels.

Ethernet

As with IT networks, Automotive Ethernet is susceptible to MAC address spoofing, payload manipulation, and denial of service. When transmitting confidential information over the Ethernet, an additional threat of information disclosure is applicable.

Ethernet networks are also vulnerable to the **virtual local area network (VLAN)** attacks listed here, which can violate network isolation and potentially compromise the security of the vehicle:

- **VLAN hopping**: This type of attack involves an attacker sending packets with modified VLAN tags to bypass security restrictions and gain unauthorized access to sensitive network segments

- **VLAN tag injection**: This type of attack involves an attacker injecting their own VLAN tags into a packet to place it on a different VLAN from that which it should be on

- **VLAN double tagging attack**: This type of attack involves adding extra VLAN tags to a packet, making it traverse different VLANs to which it should not have access

To protect against these types of attacks, it is important to implement security measures such as VLAN **access control lists** (**ACLs**) and port security that limit the ability of unauthorized devices or users to access or modify VLAN tags.

Automotive Ethernet protocols offering **quality of service** (**QoS**) are susceptible to malicious nodes that can disrupt traffic shaping or priority handling by ignoring protocol rules.

> **Note**
>
> Automotive Ethernet QoS protocols allow for traffic prioritization, where vital communications, such as safety messages, take precedence over less important data, such as infotainment video streaming. Additionally, the protocols support bandwidth management and latency reduction and help in avoiding network congestion, which could lead to network data loss.

In the case of the **Precision Time Protocol** (**PTP**), an attacker can intentionally manipulate timestamps to interfere with time synchronization. When the Ethernet is used to transfer time-sensitive sensor data, such attacks can have a severe impact on the overall vehicle safety, as the sensor data may be fused from incorrect points of time that do not reflect the reality of the vehicle environment. Misuse of the PTP protocol can potentially lead to a violation of time synchronization, which can be achieved through one of the following attacks:

- **Time-skew attack**: This type of attack involves an attacker modifying the PTP messages to change the time displayed by the clock

- **MitM attack**: This type of attack involves an attacker intercepting PTP messages and modifying them in transit

- **Replay attack**: This type of attack involves an attacker intercepting PTP messages, recording them, and replaying them later

- **Master clock spoofing attack**: This type of attack involves an attacker spoofing the master clock, allowing them to control the time that all the devices on the network will synchronize to

To protect against these types of attacks, it is important to implement security measures such as PTP message authentication and cryptographic protection.

Ethernet **Time-Sensitive Networking** (**TSN**) is an extension of the traditional Ethernet that provides a set of features for enabling real-time communication and QoS in automotive and industrial control systems. Misuse of the Ethernet TSN protocol can potentially lead to a violation of QoS features, which can have safety implications for the vehicle:

- **Denial of service (DoS) attack**: This type of attack involves an attacker sending a large number of packets to a specific device or network in an attempt to overwhelm it and cause it to fail.

- **Priority inversion attack**: This type of attack involves an attacker manipulating the priority levels of packets to cause a lower-priority packet to prevent a higher-priority packet from being transmitted.

- **Traffic shaping attack**: This type of attack involves an attacker manipulating the traffic flow to cause certain packets to be delayed or dropped. This can disrupt the real-time communication and QoS features of the Ethernet TSN network.

To protect against these types of attacks, it is important to implement security measures such as network segmentation, ACLs, and packet filtering to limit access to the Ethernet TSN network to authorized devices only. A common security mechanism that is increasingly used in automotive applications is enabling MACsec, which offers frame authenticity, integrity, freshness, and confidentiality protection.

The Unified Diagnostic Services (UDS) protocol

The **UDS protocol** introduced in *Chapter 1* enables a diagnostic client to access a variety of vehicle services that impact vehicle data and operation. A diagnostic client can either be an external tool, such as in the service shop, or an internal ECU that behaves like an onboard diagnostic tester to perform tasks, such as aggregate fault data from various ECUs or initiate programming sessions. The UDS protocol relies on the transport protocol, which enables the transmission and reception of segmented messages over different communication protocols such as CAN.

To learn about the threats enabled through the UDS protocol, we need to analyze the services that UDS supports. The most relevant attacks that can be carried out through UDS are as follows:

- **Manipulation of vehicle code and data**: This can be achieved through the initiation of a flash programming session using the **requestDownload** and **TransferData** services, as well as memory erasure through the **RoutineControl** service.

- **Vehicle code and data extraction**: This can be achieved through the **requestUpload** service, which allows a client to read out code and firmware, by providing the address and length of the blocks to upload to the tool.

- **Vehicle mode manipulation**: This attack can be achieved by issuing a **resetECU** request to trigger a soft or hard reset, which can be dangerous if allowed while the vehicle is in motion.

- **Vehicle parameter tampering**: This attack can be achieved through the WriteDataByIdentifier request, which allows a client to change the stored values of select parameters. If such parameters contain sensitive data such as the odometer value, then this can have financial and legal implications.

- **Vehicle operation tampering**: This attack can be carried out if a diagnostic routine that is reserved for troubleshooting or testing an actuation capability is triggered, while the vehicle is in operational mode. This can be achieved through the call to the RoutineControl service, with the specific routine identifier that would trigger such a function.

- **Vehicle configuration tampering**: Many times, diagnostic routines are used in the factory to configure the vehicle in a specific way or to provision cryptographic secrets. Abuse of diagnostic routines during vehicle assembly or service at the shop can result in a potentially unsafe or insecure configuration.

Similar to the UDS protocol being a target for abuse, the transport protocol underneath it can also be attacked through carefully crafted messages that can violate the protocol requirements and result in terminated connections. You are encouraged to study the transport protocol and determine the ways in which it can be abused.

SAE J1939 protocols

In *Chapter 1*, SAE J1939 was described as being widely used in commercial vehicles such as trucks and buses. Built on top of CAN, the J1939 application layer inherits the weaknesses of CAN, making it vulnerable to message tampering, spoofing, DoS, and replay attacks. Similarly, the J1939 diagnostic layer inherits the authentication weaknesses of the UDS protocol.

Therefore, in this section, we will look at two unique attacks that are derived from the way in which the J1939 protocol is designed:

- **Address claim attack**: For vehicles that enable the network management protocol, this attack is possible due to the protocol's address claim procedure, which allows a dishonest network participant to claim that a requested source address is already assigned to it. The protocol uses the **NAME** field to determine the priority of the node claiming the address. Therefore, if a legitimate node is requesting source address X, an attacker can simply respond that it already owns address X and that its **NAME** field is a higher priority value. As a result, the legitimate node must again send a request for another source address, Y, hoping that is not already claimed. But the attacker will simply respond again that the address is claimed and will fake the **NAME** field using a higher priority value. Repeating this procedure effectively blocks the legitimate node from being able to claim any address and makes it unable to transmit frames.

- **Network congestion attack**: The protocol requires that all nodes respond to a global request for Address Claimed messages. A malicious node can frequently send such a request, with a high priority to trigger a broadcast storm of Address Claimed messages. Based on the number of nodes sharing the bus, the attacker can cause a 100% busload relatively quickly, which would significantly delay other safety-critical messages that must be received within a predetermined maximum time latency, before the vehicle starts shutting down functions that depend on those messages.

Given the preceding attacks, perhaps it is not surprising that several OEMs may choose to completely remove the support for the network management protocol or disable significant portions of it.

SAE J2497 (PLC4TRUCKS)

SAE J2497 is a communication protocol used in commercial trucks to allow the exchange of data between the tractor and the trailer such as the ABS trailer status lamp. The protocol leverages the **power line communication** (**PLC**), due to its relatively low cost and reliability over long distances. One popular use case is the transmission of the trailer's ABS status lamp to the tractor ABS control module, which is then displayed on the instrument panel for the driver to see. This allows the driver to know the status of the ABS system on the trailer, which is crucial when a failure has occurred with the trailer braking system.

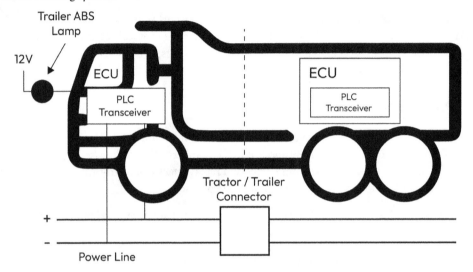

Figure 3.12 – PLC bus layout between a tractor and one trailer

Researchers have identified several attacks against this protocol:

- **RF interference**: Using devices that generate **RF** interference, an attacker can disrupt the communication between the tractor and the trailer. This can lead to the driver not receiving important information about the trailer's braking system or receiving incorrect information. When the attacker uses a device that sends RF signals on the same frequency band used by the PLC system, they could disrupt the communication between the tractor and trailer, or even inject false data into the communication stream. This type of interference can occur when radio waves from an external source, such as a nearby transmitter, are picked up by the PLC system's antenna and cause errors in the communication between the tractor and trailer.

- **Physical spoofing**: Using a device that mimics the signals of the tractor or trailer, the attacker can generate or replay messages to masquerade as a legitimate party. A replay attack in this context involves intercepting and recording a legitimate transmission between the tractor and trailer and then replaying that message to one or both parties at a later time.

- **Physical line manipulation**: This attack can be referred to as a bit-banging attack and requires the addition of hardware to manipulate the signal on the data lines of the communication link. Due to the severe impact of a successful attack against commercial vehicles, physical attacks must be taken seriously, especially when we consider the types of hazardous loads the trailer may carry.

Attacks on J2497 can be mitigated by a host of physical countermeasures that reduce the likelihood of RF interference, as well as physical security countermeasures, such as inspecting tractor and trailer cables periodically to ensure no nefarious devices have been inserted to cause bus manipulation.

Threats against sensors

As we saw in *Chapter 1*, sensors play a critical role in the ability of the vehicle to determine its current state and to apply the correct control, given a specific driving situation. Attackers who want to influence the vehicle's ability in performing its functions will find that sensors form a rich attack surface. Vehicle sensors are often connected to the vehicle's network, which can make them vulnerable to cyberattacks potentially leading to accidents or other safety issues. In addition, sensors in vehicles often collect and transmit data, which could be vulnerable to tampering or manipulation. Attackers could potentially alter sensor data to mislead the vehicle's control systems or gain access to sensitive information.

We differentiate between two types of sensors, based on the level of exposure to external attacks *[18]*:

- **Environment sensors**: For example, **Light Detection and Ranging** (**LiDAR**), ultrasonic, camera, **Radio Detection and Ranging** (**Radar**) systems, and **global positioning system** (**GPS/ GNSS**) units. These are typically located on the vehicle body and come into direct contact with the environment.

- **Vehicle dynamics sensors**: For example, **tire pressure monitoring systems** (**TPMSs**), magnetic encoders, and inertial sensors. These sensors can be embedded throughout the vehicle cabin, chassis, and various components.

Regardless of their location within the vehicle, sensors are exposed to a wide range of threats such as physical and network-based tampering, counterfeiting, DoS, and, in some cases, information disclosure, such as the case of camera sensors carrying users' private data. First, we look at each threat type and how it impacts the sensors, then, we will examine the specific threats among a sample of the most targeted sensors:

- **Counterfeiting**: Perhaps the most serious threat to sensors is the possibility that a genuine sensor could be replaced by an unapproved sensor. In the case of highly critical safety systems, if the sensor is not from a trusted source, the safety concept itself may be violated. In a worst-case scenario, the counterfeit component could be designed to behave maliciously under certain conditions to induce a safety-critical failure. Therefore, detecting counterfeit sensors is important, especially to vehicle manufacturers, who want to ensure that the vehicle operates as intended.

- **Sensor miscalibration or configuration**: For some sensors, calibration or configuration is needed at startup to ensure the sensor operates within the correct parameter boundaries. An attacker who can re-calibrate or re-configure sensors to an improper parameter range or configuration setting may affect the vehicle's ability to perform the correct control operations.

- **Physical attacks**: Sensors in vehicles are vulnerable to physical tampering or damage, which could compromise their accuracy or reliability. For example, attackers could potentially cover or remove sensors, or damage their wiring or connectors. Out-of-band attacks can cause a sensor to malfunction, such as aiming lasers at a LiDAR sensor which is also known as a **blinding attack**.

- **Network attacks**: Many sensors transmit their data over a shared network such as the Ethernet or CAN bus. This type of sensor data is exposed to the same threats as any network message such as spoofing, tampering, and DoS.

- **Replay attack**: In this type of attack, an attacker intercepts and records legitimate sensor data, and then replays it later to disrupt or mislead the control system.

- **MitM attack**: This type of attack involves an attacker relaying false sensor data to the control system through a malicious entity, positioned between the legitimate sensor and the target ECU, thus acting as an MitM. This typically occurs with local gateway ECUs that must relay vehicle sensor data from the main network to a private bus.

- **Spoofing attack**: This type of attack involves an attacker sending false sensor data to the control system, in an attempt to disrupt or mislead the control system. Spoofing GNSS signals, for example, has been shown to disrupt navigation systems in ships by replacing signals with fake locations. A similar scenario could exist on targeted vehicle systems to cause a failure in localization.

- **Jamming attack**: This type of attack involves an attacker transmitting a powerful signal to disrupt or interfere with the normal operation of a sensor. For example, the attacker may use a jamming device to transmit noise or interference at the same frequency as the radar or ultrasonic sensor, making it difficult for the sensor to accurately detect and interpret signals. GNSS jamming is another type of attack that can prevent the vehicle from relying on such signals to determine its current location.

- **Acoustic interference attack**: This type of attack involves using sound waves to cancel out the ultrasonic signals emitted by a sensor, making it difficult for the sensor to detect objects. Another possible acoustic-based attack targets the **inertial measurement unit** (**IMU**) sensor by injecting sound waves [19] that alter the digitized sensor signal, as shown in *Figure 3.13*.

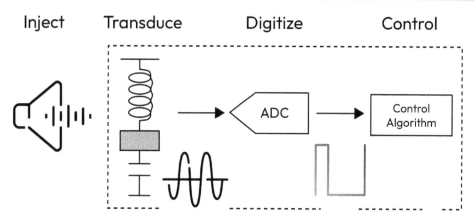

Figure 3.13 – Acoustic attacks against IMU sensors

Common ECU threats

When looking at threats against external vehicle interfaces, we indirectly analyzed threats that impact external facing ECUs, such as telematics, IVI, and autonomous driving systems. In this section, we will expand our focus on threats that apply to both internal and external facing ECUs, based on the most common weaknesses of these systems.

Debug ports

ECUs offer several methods to access debug capability during development and, in some cases, after the ECU has been installed on a production vehicle. The JTAG interface is commonly used to debug and test the internal operation of an ECU. Attackers who gain access to the JTAG interface can extract the ECU software for offline analysis to identify vulnerabilities that can be exploited in the field. Another popular attack is attempting to recover global secrets, such as long-term cryptographic keys that are accessible in a debug mode. In addition to these attacks, ECU suppliers may have proprietary test modes that are intended for use in the factory. These can have a higher degree of access to critical security functions and can be mistakenly assumed to be secure, due to their hidden nature. An attacker with access to such interfaces can replace keys in protected memory such as eFuse and OTP.

> Note
>
> **Electronic fuse (eFuse)** and **one-time programmable (OTP)** memory are used in embedded systems to safeguard critical information such as encryption keys and device identities. eFuses are programmable fuses that can be irreversibly blown to store binary data, while OTP memory allows data to be written only once, preventing subsequent alteration. Both mechanisms ensure that sensitive data is securely locked and resistant to tampering.

Another popular method for debug access is through UART-based debug shells that may be left behind from the development phase, which allows an attacker to open a terminal and run tests that execute privileged commands. These may expose many powerful features such as exercising the cryptographic interfaces for test purposes or the extraction of memory content, both RAM and flash-based.

In larger ECUs, it is not uncommon to discover power shells that are accessible through the Wi-Fi or Ethernet, for example, using **Secure Shell (SSH)**. The latter can be easily misconfigured, for example, through weak passwords, or enabling login as root. Typically, such shells are used to quickly update software or extract large files used for debugging and analysis. If left open after the system has been installed on a production intent vehicle, the attackers will have a suite of highly effective tools to tamper with the vehicle software and data. Therefore, it is generally best practice to disable or lock debug interfaces, as well as completely remove power shells, to prevent their malicious re-enablement once the ECU has been installed in a production vehicle.

Flash programming

Flash programming tools that allow the reprogramming of non-volatile memory over a serial flash programming interface can be used as an attack vector if the programming interface is not properly protected. Such an interface is typically used in the factory to install software and calibration data. It may also be misused postproduction to extract software and calibration data through the memory upload features.

As mentioned earlier in the UDS protocol section, flashing over the diagnostic protocol is commonly carried out to update the ECU software after it has been initially installed. The lack of proper access controls to enter the flash programming session is one way this attack method can be exploited. Additionally, leaving behind flash programming libraries opens the door to malicious applications that can conveniently call flash commands, to read, erase, or write the contents of the flash during runtime. The danger of such attacks is that they can introduce malicious code or alter the ECU's behavior, potentially compromising its functionality and leading to hazardous events. If for example, **flash erase** commands during runtime are accessible to a malicious application, an attacker can perform repeated erase function calls to wear out the flash, essentially leaving it in an unprogrammable state. This makes it crucial to remove flash libraries from the system once they are no longer needed and to lock erase functionality after flash programming access is terminated.

> **Note**
>
> The ability to install malicious software and calibration data is one of the most security-critical attacks that must be prevented. The malicious reprogramming of calibration data may be mistakenly viewed as a less serious problem. Besides the safety impact of tampering with the calibration data, such attacks can result in the violation of emissions standards, which can result in hefty fines.

Power and mode manipulation

Tampering or disabling the power input to an ECU is a serious threat that, at best, can result in the loss of convenient vehicle functions and at worst can result in the disruption of a safety critical operation such as steering or braking. This can happen when the power management ECU is compromised, allowing an attacker to selectively disable power to target ECUs. Similar to power source tampering, mode management tampering is another powerful method that can lead to loss of functionality or the extraction of secrets during the transition to an less secure state. One common method of attack is to abuse the network management protocol over CAN to frequently wake up ECUs, resulting in the draining of a vehicle's battery. Another attack method is to trick an ECU to switch to a special system state with reduced functionality, while the vehicle still needs that system to be fully operational. Carefully analyzing the ECU state transitions is an important method for enforcing controls on when a transition may occur.

Tampering with machine learning algorithms

Vehicle systems that rely on machine learning algorithms such as computer vision in autonomous driving applications are exposed to several threats that corrupt or confuse machine learning models. Adversarial machine learning attacks involve crafting specific inputs (in this case, images) that have been altered slightly to deceive a model into making an incorrect prediction or classification. For example, researchers have shown that by introducing noise to an image, such as placing stickers on a stop sign, it is possible to fool machine learning algorithms to misclassify that object, effectively leading to the vehicle crossing the road without stopping. In addition to attacks that aim to trick machine learning algorithms, the machine learning models themselves are subject to the threat of tampering and disclosure. Since they must be stored in non-volatile memory, they are at risk of physical and logical tampering. Similarly, if someone can gain access to the storage contents, they can extract machine learning models with the purpose of stealing valuable intellectual property.

Software attacks

Domain controllers and vehicle computers execute software with different degrees of safety and security criticality. This creates the risk that one flawed or corrupted process can interfere with another process. In a multi-virtual machine environment, the threat can emanate from a less secure virtual machine that aims to interfere with a safety-critical virtual machine. Attackers can attempt to abuse CPU cycles to prevent a safety VM from performing its functions. Similarly, they may attempt to access shared resources such as network interfaces, or hardware peripherals that control a safety and security-critical process. Attackers can also target the persistent storage to overwrite memory records or snoop on data that is meant for another application or VM.

We will survey the various software-based attack methods as follows:

- **Illegal access to restricted services**: Lack of enforcement of access controls within an operating system can expose an ECU to the threat of a malicious application, using privileged services that are not part of its intended function. Assume the ECU offers a service to reprogram keys in a keystore through a privileged service. If the service is accessible by any application within a given VM, then a single corrupted process can reprogram or delete keys.

- **Tampering and spoofing of Inter-Process Communication (IPC)**: Similar to network-based communication, internal messages exchanged across an OS process or virtual machine boundary are subject to the threats of spoofing, tampering, replay, and DoS. The difference, however, is the method by which these attacks are mounted. Assuming weak or missing authentication of IPC peers, a malicious process within a VM or from a compromised VM can attempt to initiate communication with another process, with the aim of sending fake data or tampering with an existing communication channel. The same threats apply to non-virtualized systems in which IPC messages are exchanged for example between tasks running on different CPU cores.

- **Shared cache attacks**: A shared cache memory attack is possible when multiple processes share a common cache memory, as is the case in domain controllers and vehicle computers. The shared cache creates an opportunity for a malicious process to illegally access sensitive data or disrupt the workload of another process. One such attack leverages the shared cache memory to infer information on the memory access patterns of other processes and extract sensitive data. For example, an attacker could use a cache side-channel attack to infer the encryption key used by another process, by observing the shared cache memory and measuring the time it takes for the cache to access certain memory addresses. Another type of shared cache attack is called the cache eviction attack. This type of attack leverages the shared cache memory to evict useful data from the cache to fill it with its own data, thereby causing a safety process to be slowed down and creating latencies. This can be serious for safety-critical systems that aim at producing deterministic behavior.

- **DMA attacks**: A **DMA** attack bypasses the system's memory protection mechanisms to directly access and manipulate the embedded system memory (DRAM or SRAM) as well as the hardware engine's internal memory, such as the cryptographic accelerator. This can be achieved by exploiting weak security isolation, which allows one DMA user to access memory that is not intended to be shared. Once the attacker has access to the memory area, they can exfiltrate or modify the data, which can result in serious consequences to safety.

- **DoS against shared resources**: With multi-core ECUs that segment their CPUs across multiple applications or virtual machines, the shared cores are exposed to malicious applications or VMs that can aim to consume more CPU runtime resources than originally intended. This can be made possible if the CPU cluster is not properly allocated across applications of varying degrees of security and safety or if the priorities are not set in such a way as to limit the effect of one process or VM behaving badly.

- **Persistent storage tampering**: ECUs normally use persistent storage to store logs, diagnostic data, or even images and videos. Such data is exposed to the risk of illegal access by an unauthorized application within the system, due to weak or missing access controls. This can result in the exposure of sensitive IP or the exposure of user confidential data. With illegal write access, an attacker can falsify crash or driving records, and manipulate the odometer mileage and other diagnostic data that may need to be preserved. In addition to illegal access, the write operation exposes the system to the threat of runtime resource exhaustion, by keeping the system busy performing endless write requests on slower memory peripherals such as eMMC. In flash-based embedded devices (such as MCUs), erase operations can be particularly harmful if an unauthorized software application manages to perform a complete erase command of flash contents or repeated write commands, with the intent of exceeding the maximum number of programming cycles, causing the flash to be permanently damaged.

Disclosure and tampering of cryptographic keys

In *Chapter 2*, we discussed several cryptographic functions that help us achieve our security objectives. The security of these functions hinges on the secrecy and integrity of the cryptographic keys. In this section, we will consider common threats against the confidentiality and integrity of cryptographic keys.

Supply chain

Provisioning ECUs with cryptographic keys in the manufacturing environment is subject to supply chain and insider threats. The **microcontroller unit** (**MCU**) or **system-on-chip** (**SoC**) is usually delivered in an insecure state, where no security controls are enforced to permit the manufacturing facility to inject the first set of keys. With the assumption of a secure provisioning environment comes the risk that the keys may have been injected with fake identities and key sets before the chip has been secured. If assumptions are made about the manufacturing environment being secure, a malicious insider may gain access to the provisioning services and install keys of their choosing, such as a fake root public key. This would allow an attacker to subsequently perform software updates, using forged signatures that will be validated by the fake root public key.

A common mistake in installing keys in production is mistakenly installing or leaving development keys in the ECU. Those keys, which were used to validate functionality during development, may be easily guessed, as they normally depend on commonly used known answer tests. If left in production, an attacker can leverage that knowledge to extract secrets encrypted in those keys or establish secure communication sessions using the development keys.

Side-channel and fault injection

Side-channel and fault injection attacks are methods used to compromise the security of cryptographic keys in an ECU, by exploiting information leaked from the system during its normal operation, such as power consumption and electromagnetic emissions. Side-channel attacks extract secret information by observing the physical characteristics of a system during encryption or decryption, such as power consumption, timing, or electromagnetic radiation. Fault injection attacks introduce errors into a system's operations by physically manipulating hardware, for example, through voltage or electromagnetic glitches to cause the target to leak cryptographic secrets or exhibit behavior that can help infer the cryptographic key material. Long-term cryptographic keys are especially at risk of such attacks because once exposed, they can be abused indefinitely unless the ECU provides a revocation method.

Software attacks against cryptographic keys

Software attacks in this context originate from a compromised or malicious program that is being executed within an ECU runtime execution environment. Here, we survey some attacks that can result from a compromised application that aims to expose or abuse a certain key.

When cryptography is implemented purely in software, the key handling is exposed to the threat of illegal access through missing or weak access separation. For example, if the key is buffered in the RAM, an application that has shared access to that memory can simply read out the key value. Additionally, direct handling of cryptographic keys in software creates opportunities for timing side-channel analysis in which one process can infer the key values through careful measurement of the time taken to use such keys.

Another software-based attack is the replacement of root public keys with those of an attacker's choosing. If the root public key is stored in normal storage such as flash memory, an attacker who has access to the flash programming libraries can issue an erase and programming command sequence to install a root public key of their choosing. Services that allow the erasure or invalidation of key material are vulnerable to illegal access by a malicious application that aims to render the system inoperative due to its inability to use the keys, for example, to decrypt content during boot or establish secure communication sessions with peers or clients during runtime.

Even when keys are not being handled directly in the software, the lack of key usage policies can allow any application running within the system to abuse the key. For example, a key may be intended to be used only to verify the MAC values of the CAN messages that the ECU is receiving. Without enforcing this policy, another application could request the key to be used for MAC generation. This subsequently allows it to construct a validly authenticated message that it could transmit to another ECU, which would have no way of knowing that the message came from a malicious source.

Summary

In this chapter, we investigated the threats that affect all the layers of the E/E architecture that were introduced in *Chapter 1*. Doing so has enabled us to understand the full spectrum of threats and attacks that automotive systems must consider. The obvious question that follows the threat and attack enumeration is *what security countermeasures are required to mitigate such threats*?

It would have been tempting to simply provide a catalog of threats and mitigations. However, in a real vehicle, new threats and attacks are continuously emerging. Addressing those threats requires a systematic engineering approach that provides us with assurances that we not only addressed those threats but we adequately uncovered all the applicable threats and followed a measurable approach to reducing risk to a tolerable level. This is the focus of *Part 2* of the book where we address security assurance through a process-driven approach. This is to stress that the problem of automotive cybersecurity must be addressed from both angles: process and technical measures.

In the next chapter, we will start with a survey of the automotive standards that guide us toward building resilient automotive systems to address known cybersecurity threats (presented here) and future unknown threats.

References

- [1] No, U.R. (2021). 155 [Uniform provisions concerning the approval of vehicles with regards to cyber security and cyber security management system].

- [2] Le, V.H., Hartog, J.D., Zannone, N. Security and privacy for innovative automotive applications: A survey. Comput. Commun. 2018, 132, 17–41.

- [3] Kim, S., Shrestha, R. In-Vehicle Communication and Cyber Security. In Automotive Cyber Security; J.B. Metzler: Stuttgart, Germany, 2020; pp. 67–96.

- [4] Nilsson, D.K., Larson, U.E., Picasso, F., Jonsson, E. A First Simulation of Attacks in the Automotive Network Communications Protocol FlexRay. In Proceedings of the Advances in Computer Science and Education; J.B. Metzler: Stuttgart, Germany, 2008; Volume 53, pp. 84–91.

- [5] Kishikawa, T., Hirano, R., Ujiie, Y., Haga, T., Matsushima, H., Fujimura, K., Anzai, J. Vulnerability of FlexRay and Countermeasures. SAE Int. J. Transp. Cybersecur. Priv. 2019, 2, 21–33.

- [6] Khatri, N., Shrestha, R., & Nam, S.Y. (2021). Security issues with in-vehicle networks, and enhanced countermeasures based on blockchain. Electronics, 10(8), 893.

- [7] Kishikawa, T., Hirano, R., Ujiie, Y., Haga, T., Matsushima, H., Fujimura, K., Anzai, J. Intrusion detection and prevention system for flexray against spoofed frame injection. In Proceedings of the 17th Escar Europe: Embedded Security in Cars Conference (Konferenzveröffentlichung), Detroit, MI, USA, 19–20 November 2019; pp. 59–73.

- [8] Mousa, A.R., Noureldeen, P., Azer, M., Allam, M. Lightweight Authentication Protocol Deployment over FlexRay. In Proceedings of the 10th International Conference on Predictive Models in Software Engineering, Turin, Italy, 17 September 2014; pp. 233–239.

- [9] van de Beek, G.S. (2016). Vulnerability analysis of the wireless infrastructure to intentional electromagnetic interference. University of Twente.

- [10] Parameswarath, R.P. & Sikdar, B. (2022, June). An Authentication Mechanism for Remote Keyless Entry Systems in Cars to Prevent Replay and RollJam Attacks. In 2022 IEEE Intelligent Vehicles Symposium (IV) (pp. 1725-1730). IEEE.

- [11] Van De Moosdijk, J. & Visser, D. (2009). Car security: remote keyless "entry and go".

- [12] Alrabady, A.I. & Mahmud, S.M. (2005). Analysis of attacks against the security of keyless-entry systems for vehicles and suggestions for improved designs. IEEE transactions on vehicular technology, 54(1), 41-50.

- [13] https://uptane.github.io/papers/uptane-standard.1.1.0.pdf

- [14] Kamkar, S. "Drive It Like You Hacked It: New Attacks and Tools to Wirelessly Steal Cars", Presentation at DEFCON 23, https://bit.ly/3j0NZKc, Aug 2015.

- [15] Murvay, P.S. & Groza, B. (2018). Security shortcomings and countermeasures for the SAE J1939 commercial vehicle bus protocol. IEEE Transactions on Vehicular Technology, 67(5), 4325-4339.

- [16] Ricciato, F., Coluccia, A. & D'Alconzo, A. (2010). A review of DoS attack models for 3G cellular networks from a system-design perspective. Computer Communications, 33(5), 551-558.

- [17] Traynor, P., Enck, W., McDaniel, P. & La Porta, T. (2006, September). Mitigating attacks on open functionality in SMS-capable cellular networks. In Proceedings of the 12th Annual International Conference on Mobile Computing and Networking (pp. 182-193).

- [18] El-Rewini, Z., Sadatsharan, K., Sugunaraj, N., Selvaraj, D.F., Plathottam, S.J. & Ranganathan, P. Cybersecurity Attacks in Vehicular Sensors. United States. https://doi.org/10.1109/jsen.2020.3004275

- [19] Tu, Y., Lin, Z., Lee, I. & Hei, X. (2018). Injected and delivered: Fabricating implicit control over actuation systems by spoofing inertial sensors. In *27th USENIX Security Symposium (USENIX Security 18)* (pp. 1545-1562).

- [20] https://research.nccgroup.com/2022/05/15/technical-advisory-tesla-ble-phone-as-a-key-passive-entry-vulnerable-to-relay-attacks/

- [21] https://www.verizon.com/solutions-and-services/hum/

- [22] https://cdn.vector.com/cms/content/know-how/_application-notes/AN-ION-1-3100_Introduction_to_J1939.pdf

- [23] https://www.sae.org/standards/content/j2497_201207/

- [24] Ivanov, I., Maple, C., Watson, T. & Lee, S. (2018). Cyber security standards and issues in V2X communications for Internet of Vehicles.

- [25] https://www.sciencedirect.com/science/article/pii/S221420961930261X

- [26] https://ieeexplore.ieee.org/document/6407456

- [27] https://medium.com/codex/rollback-a-new-time-agnostic-replay-attack-against-the-automotive-remote-keyless-entry-systems-df5f99ba9490

- [28] Miller, C. & Valasek, C. "Remote exploitation of an unaltered passenger vehicle". Black Hat USA 2015.S 91 (2015): 1-91.

- [29] https://www.can-cia.org/can-knowledge/can/can-xl/

Part 2: Understanding the Secure Engineering Development Process

In this part, you will learn about the importance of applying a systematic engineering approach to achieving cybersecurity resilience in automotive systems. We start by surveying the various cybersecurity-related standards that are relevant to the field of secure engineering. We then take a focused approach to the ISO/SAE 21434 cybersecurity standard, which serves as the primary standard for establishing and applying a cybersecurity management system. We then dive into the interactions between the functional safety and cybersecurity domains to identify synergies and conflicts between the two.

This part has the following chapters:

- *Chapter 4, Exploring the Landscape of Automotive Cybersecurity Standards*

- *Chapter 5, Taking a Deep Dive into ISO/SAE21434*

- *Chapter 6, Interactions between Functional Safety and Cybersecurity*

4

Exploring the Landscape of Automotive Cybersecurity Standards

Designing cyber-resilient automotive systems calls for more than a surface-level understanding of the automotive security threat environment. It necessitates an orderly, process-driven approach that guarantees every facet of vehicle development, production, and operation is guarded against cybersecurity threats. To that end, standardization bodies have published numerous standards on the process and technical measures for protecting vehicles and their supporting systems throughout the vehicle's life cycle. Such standards establish the state of the art to help organizations understand gaps in their engineering processes and technology offerings. They also provide a framework for maintaining a consistent level of security across the automotive supply chain by adhering to a common set of procedures and practices. Besides complying with the state of the art, abiding by standards helps reduce debate among practitioners through a common framework that uses a common language. The standard landscape is constantly evolving and for that reason, we are certain that by the time you read this book, there will be additional standards besides the ones that are described here that will deserve your attention. Generally, automotive security standards can be divided into three main categories according to the level of compliance needed: primary, secondary, and supporting standards. The first group defines general security frameworks for which compliance is mandatory due to regulations. The second group addresses specific areas of vehicle security for which compliance depends on the automotive manufacturer's needs. The third group consists of standards and resources that aid in complying with the first two types of standards.

In this chapter, we will provide a snapshot of the most relevant automotive cybersecurity standards and resources, as shown in *Figure 4.1*. For each standard, we will describe the standard's purpose, the intended audience, and the general scope. These standards should be viewed as keys to the world of cybersecurity standards and resources, therefore, this list shall not be considered conclusive by any measure:

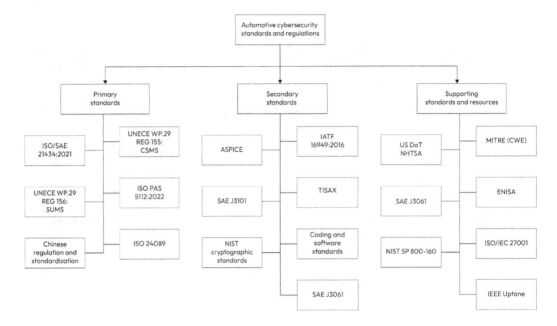

Figure 4.1 – Standards in the scope of this chapter

In this chapter, we will cover the following main topics:

- Primary standards
- Secondary standards
- Supporting standards and resources
- Useful resources and security best practices

Primary standards

Three binding standards govern the cybersecurity aspects of how vehicles and their supporting systems are developed, produced, and maintained. Non-compliance with those standards can lead to legal and financial implications for OEMs and suppliers, so let's take a deeper look.

UNECE WP.29

Different government and international bodies have mandated cybersecurity standards and regulations that govern OEMs within their geographic region. The **United Nations Economic Commission for Europe (UNECE) World Forum for Harmonization of Vehicle Regulations (WP.29)** has defined two such regulations that apply to members of the UNECE region *[17]*. The first regulation concerns the mandate for automotive manufacturers to implement a **Cybersecurity Management System (CSMS)** *[3]*, while the second concerns the regulation for establishing a **Software Update Management System (SUMS)** *[6]*. These regulations cover four distinctareas, which include managing the vehicle cybersecurity risk, securing vehicles by design to mitigate risks along the entire supply chain, detecting and responding to security incidents across the vehicle fleet, and providing safe and secure software updates while ensuring that vehicle safety is not compromised. Specifically, SUMS introduces a legal basis for regulating **Over-the-Air (OTA)** updates to onboard vehicle software due to its criticality both as an attack vector for tampering with vehicle software and as a security mechanism to apply security patches to vehicle systems.

REG 155: CSMS

In response to the emerging threats against connected vehicles, REG 155 mandates the establishment of a CSMS for both the automotive manufacturer and its supply chain concurrently. The UN regulation provides a comprehensive framework for the automotive sector to address the growing concern of cybersecurity risks in road vehicles. It aims to ensure that the necessary processes are put in place to identify and manage these risks during the full product life cycle *[3]*.

To sell vehicles in markets where UNECE WP.29 regulations apply, manufacturers must demonstrate to national technical services or homologation agencies that they have established a CSMS that meets the requirements of REG 155 and that they have adhered to the CSMS. A successful implementation of the CSMS must achieve the following objectives:

- Perform a risk assessment to identify critical vehicle components

- Implement mitigation measures to treat the identified risks

- Provide evidence of the effectiveness of these measures through testing

- Implement measures to detect and prevent cyberattacks through monitoring activities, and support for data forensics specific to the vehicle type

- Share reports of monitoring activities with the relevant homologation authority:

Figure 4.2 – Achieving type approval through a two-stage approach

When compliance comes up, the main concern of OEMs and suppliers is how to perform assessments of their products to fulfill the regulation's requirements. The cybersecurity assessment of automotive products requires a two-stage approach:

1. As shown in *Figure 4.2*, the first aspect of the assessment involves auditing and certifying the vehicle manufacturer's CSMS. This step evaluates the manufacturer's processes, procedures, and overall approach to managing cybersecurity risks in the development, production, and maintenance of road vehicles.

2. The second aspect of the assessment involves measuring the adherence of the automotive product to the CSMS by evaluating the effectiveness of the procedures at the product level in reducing cybersecurity risks to a reasonable level. This step evaluates the specific cybersecurity measures that are implemented in each vehicle and verifies that they are effective in protecting against potential cyber threats.

This two-stage approach ensures that both the manufacturer's overall approach to cybersecurity and the specific measures implemented in individual vehicles are thoroughly evaluated and certified *[5]*.

A successful audit and assessment earn the OEM the right to attain type approval for a vehicle as an indication that it is safe and secure for usage in UNECE WP.29 regions. Additionally, this regulation impacts suppliers of cybersecurity-relevant components who need to aid the OEM in proving compliance with the CSMS by adhering to it themselves, thereby showing evidence that cybersecurity risk is managed adequately across the entire supply chain. Passenger cars, vans, trucks, buses, and light four-wheelers that have autonomous driving capabilities starting from SAE Level 3 onwards are included in the vehicle categories that must attain type approval. To aid OEMs in ensuring cybersecurity risk is adequately considered, the regulation includes guidance regarding a baseline of threats and vulnerabilities that should be considered and defended against. This is captured in Annex 5, which provides the minimum set of cybersecurity threats that a vehicle manufacturer or component supplier must consider when developing their systems. *Figure 4.3* provides a snapshot of the threats and vulnerabilities that should be in scope for the security analysis:

> Tip
> When performing a threat analysis and risk assessment, consult the threat types in *REG 155* to ensure that at least all the applicable threats have been accounted for by your product.

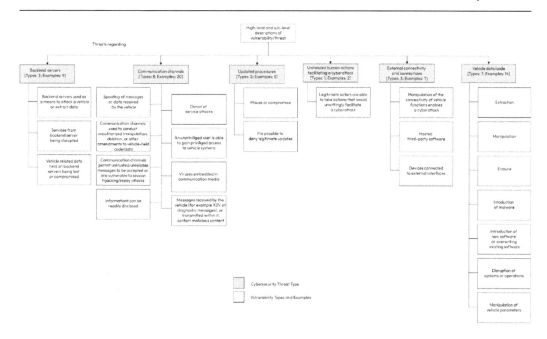

Figure 4.3 – REG 155 Annex 5 cybersecurity threats and vulnerability types

In addition to the threats and vulnerabilities to be considered, REG 155 provides a list of common mitigations to aid OEMs and suppliers in choosing the right technical countermeasures. Examples of these mitigations are the usage of secure communication channels, the removal of debug capabilities, and reliance on cryptographic functions.

> **Tip**
>
> Start building your own security controls catalog by incorporating countermeasures from Annex 5.

REG 155 does not mandate a specific CSMS and leaves it up to the OEMs to choose a framework that can achieve the objectives of the regulation. However, REG 155 does point out that ISO/SAE 21434 is one such framework capable of fulfilling the requirements of the CSMS. Due to the availability and prevalence of the ISO/SAE 21434 standard, most OEMs and suppliers choose it as the CSMS for demonstrating compliance with REG 155.

ISO/SAE 21434:2021, road vehicles – cybersecurity engineering

Building vehicles that are secure by design requires a cybersecurity-aware product life cycle that begins early in the concept and design stages and proceeds through production and post-production until a vehicle is decommissioned. Understanding the vehicle's life cycle is an important prerequisite to understanding the scope of ISO/SAE 21434, so let's walk through it *[15]*:

Figure 4.4 – Life cycle flow

In the **concept** stage, a product has a preliminary architecture and a candidate list of features or functions. This is the first opportunity to consider the cybersecurity relevance of the product to eliminate risky functions and adapt the architecture to reduce cybersecurity risk. By the end of this stage, threats in the scope of the product must be analyzed and a risk treatment plan must be prepared.

1. In the **development** stage, cybersecurity is considered by defining security requirements and reflecting those in the actual product architecture. Additionally, cybersecurity testing is incorporated into the overall product test plan.

2. Once in the **production** stage, aspects related to securely setting up, initializing, and installing the product must be considered, such as cryptographic key provisioning, code signing, firmware installation, and transitioning the product into a secure state, thereby marking a clear transition from production mode.

3. Upon entering **operation** mode, the product is now expected to function securely in the environment presumed in the design phase. During this stage, the product is monitored for new cybersecurity threats and vulnerabilities to ensure an adequate response in case of the occurrence of a cybersecurity incident.

4. When **maintenance** is needed, for example, to address a vulnerability through a software update, or to perform troubleshooting or repairs, cybersecurity controls are needed to transition the product into the maintenance phase.

5. Finally, when the product has reached its **end of life**, it is expected to enter a life cycle state in which users' private data, intellectual property, and product secrets are safely destroyed or made inaccessible.

> **Tip**
> Be aware of the life cycle stage that you are most concerned with and familiarize yourself with cybersecurity activities that relate to that stage.

ISO/SAE 21434 provides a comprehensive framework for addressing cybersecurity threats across these life cycle stages, both through organizational-level actions and project-level activities. It is equally applicable to automotive manufacturers and component suppliers who must collaborate to demonstrate that the vehicle has adequately addressed cybersecurity risks:

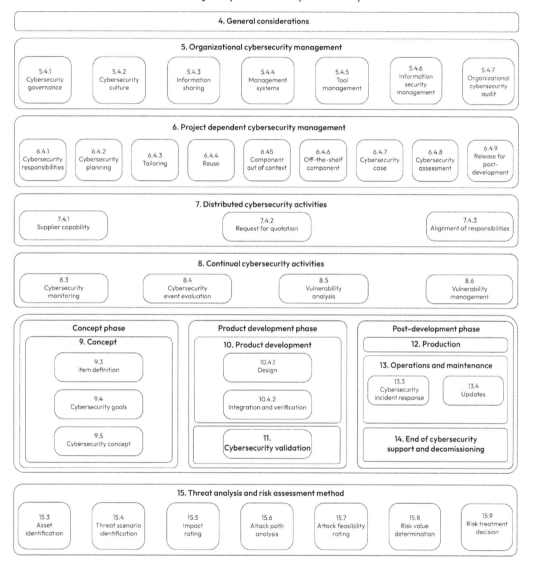

Figure 4.5 – Process areas covered by ISO/SAE 21434

A deep look into the various clauses of ISO/SAE 21434 shown in *Figure 4.5* will be offered in the next chapter, but for now, we will simply provide a high-level view of all the process areas covered within the standard to motivate their relationship with other standards presented in this chapter:

- **Clause 5** focuses on organizational cybersecurity management, which is reflected through establishing a cybersecurity culture, processes for information sharing regarding cybersecurity risk, and enabling supporting systems such as configuration, change, and documentation management. This section also focuses on the importance of managing tools by classifying ones that are exposed to cybersecurity risks and ensuring such tools are under security management to prevent risk propagation in the automotive products with an eventual impact on the vehicle.

- **Clause 6** shifts the focus from the organization to the product by highlighting the need for competence management and cybersecurity planning. Furthermore, it sets the expectations for developing components out of context and integrating off-the-shelf components. The cybersecurity case is introduced in this clause along with expectations for assessing a condition for product release readiness.

- **Clause 7** addresses the importance of assessing the supplier's cybersecurity capabilities during supplier selection and incorporating cybersecurity requirements in requests for quotation to ensure cybersecurity is not overlooked in the sourcing stage. It also addresses the need for a clear definition of cybersecurity responsibilities during distributed development between automotive OEMs, suppliers, and partners.

- **Clause 8** focuses on continuous cybersecurity activities such as those that are performed during the development stage as well as when the product has entered the operational state. These activities include cybersecurity monitoring to detect emerging threats and weaknesses, cybersecurity event evaluation for triaging risk reports, vulnerability analysis for assessing the impact of a confirmed event, and vulnerability management for resolving a confirmed vulnerability and informing the affected parties.

- With **Clause 9**, the engineering clauses come into the picture, starting with the concept phase. The goal of this phase is to produce a cybersecurity concept that provides the high-level cybersecurity controls and requirements needed to ensure all identified product cybersecurity risks are within a tolerable level. The requirements trace up to cybersecurity goals that are defined when risk reduction is required for a specific asset. These goals are derived through a **threat analysis and risk assessment** (**TARA**) process based on the item definition. The latter defines the scope of the analysis, including the components within the item and the operational environment.

- **Clause 10** uses the results of clause 9 to reflect the cybersecurity activities that are applied in the product development phase. This is captured through cybersecurity specifications that describe the decomposed cybersecurity requirements and the associated architecture at the component level to achieve the higher-level cybersecurity requirements and controls from the concept phase. The activities of the product development phase include applying secure design principles to the refined architecture and providing secure coding practices for software implementation. Then, for verification, the standard requires that security testing is incorporated through integration and verification tests such as requirement-based tests, fuzzing, and penetration testing.

- **Clause 11** sets the expectations for cybersecurity validation at the vehicle level by validating cybersecurity goals from the concept phase and the assumptions of accepted risk that the suppliers have produced.

- **Clause 12** requires a production plan to be prepared that incorporates cybersecurity requirements for post-development to ensure that secure installation and setup methods are correctly applied during production.

- **Clause 13** requires an incident response plan to be prepared to address confirmed incidents, as well as to issue patches through a secure update mechanism.

- **Clause 14** addresses the expectations for the end-of-life stage by protecting assets during vehicle decommissioning through access disablement or asset destruction.

- Finally, **clause 15** describes the TARA methods and practices that can be considered the hallmark of the ISO/SAE 21434 standard. The TARA approach is based on asset-driven threat analysis. Threats and attack paths are mapped to damage scenarios to calculate the overall risk and determine risk treatment decisions.

ISO/PAS 5112:2022 – road vehicles – guidelines for auditing cybersecurity engineering

Due to the wide acceptance of the ISO/SAE 21434 standard, a common challenge emerged for automotive organizations in how to demonstrate compliance with the standard. In response to this challenge, ISO/PAS 5112:2022 was published to guide audit teams performing audits of an organization's cybersecurity process. As defined by ISO/PAS 5112, an audit is an examination of a process to determine the extent to which the process objectives are achieved. To demonstrate the achievement of process objectives, a project developed according to that process (ISO/SAE 21434) must be used as a reference for the audit team *[14]*. For organizations that have never executed a project according to ISO/SAE 21434, the audit can be performed in stages using work products from the reference project as they become available.

The standard builds upon ISO 19011 (guidelines for auditing management systems) and applies it to the automotive sector, specifically concerning ISO/SAE 21434. The guidelines provided by the standard cover managing an audit program, planning and executing cybersecurity management system audits, and evaluating audit team competencies. Furthermore, it provides a set of audit criteria based on the objectives of ISO/SAE 21434 and includes an example questionnaire in Annex A to be adapted by audit teams. The audit questions are meant to be derived directly from the ISO/SAE 21434 process objectives. Here is an example audit question based on the Annex A questionnaire regarding clause 6 of the ISO standard:

Is a process established, implemented, and maintained to manage project-dependent cybersecurity?

The auditor should verify the following:

- A process has been established for the creation of a cybersecurity plan. Here, the evidence is [WP-06-01]: **cybersecurity plan**.

- A process has been established for the creation of a cybersecurity case. Here, the evidence is [WP-06-02]: **cybersecurity case**.

- A process has been established for a cybersecurity assessment. Here, the evidence is [WP-06-03]: **cybersecurity assessment report**.

While any automotive supplier is subject to the audit, a supplier may exclude certain phases of the cybersecurity life cycle if their component is not implicated in those phases. For example, a supplier who provides software libraries does not need to demonstrate a process that defines vehicle-level validation activities, as described in clause 11 of ISO/SAE 21434.

In preparation for the audit, the audit team will reach out to process experts to provide information related to the cybersecurity management system within the organization. They will also reach out to a project team whose cybersecurity work products can be used as evidence of the effectiveness of the cybersecurity management system. The findings are classified according to the following table:

Criteria	Grade
All objectives of a process area are achieved based on objective evidence	Conformity
Minor deviations observed	Minor nonconformity
Major deviations observed with one or more objectives not achieved	Major nonconformity

An audit will pass if there are no major or minor nonconformities. If one or more minor nonconformities do not demonstrate a lack of effectiveness of the CSMS, a conditional pass is given. However, if one or more major nonconformities or several minor nonconformities are found, indicating an evident lack of effectiveness of the CSMS, the audit will be given a failed outcome. Both a failed and conditionally passing audit must result in corrective actions.

> **Hint**
>
> Audits in the scope of ISO/PAS 5112 are for the adherence of an organization's process to ISO/SAE 21434. Product-level assessment is not in the scope of this standard. A successful audit of an organization's process is a prerequisite to performing a product-level cybersecurity assessment for measuring the compliance of the product to the audited process.

Next, we will turn our attention to the second primary standard, which governs a critical aspect of ensuring OEMs can react to successful attacks to keep vehicles safe.

REG 156: SUMS

While being able to issue OTA updates to keep automotive systems patched with the latest security fixes is a strong security measure, it is also a major source of threats against the integrity of the software and firmware of vehicle systems. Recognizing the criticality of the remote update mechanism, the UNECE WP.29 established a second automotive cybersecurity regulation to ensure that OEMs implement sound SUMS to prevent the misuse of this ability. The regulation addresses four main areas of concern that must be addressed by a conforming SUMS *[6]*.

Software version management

An essential aspect of deploying the correct software update is having a process in place for identifying all initial and updated software versions and relevant hardware components in the target system. This enables the OEM to trace software versions to a specific vehicle type and series. This becomes critical when a vulnerability is identified that impacts one or more vehicle components. On the one hand, OEMs are eager to find out which ECUs are affected to determine when the patch can be issued, and on the other hand, suppliers are racing to determine whether any of their components contain the vulnerability so that they may inform their customers and work on a resolution. Given the large number of ECUs and the diversity of the automotive supply chain, maintaining this information is a daunting task. It is very common for an automotive supplier to be using libraries or drivers without tracking the true origin, which leaves them and their customers exposed to potential vulnerabilities in those components. A common practice for tackling this challenge is to track software content and versions through a **software bill of materials (SBOM)** that can be shared with other stakeholders in the supply chain. An SBOM can be captured in multiple formats, such as **Software Package Data Exchange (SPDX)** or CycloneDX. Both are open standards for communicating software components, licenses, and copyright information. In addition to giving an organization the ability to trace software components that may be affected by a vulnerability, the SBOM helps in detecting open source license violations.

Safety compatibility

Deriving from the SUMS support for identifying the target vehicle software, a conforming SUMS must ensure the safe deployment of software updates. Knowing the software components and their respective versions allows the OEM to confirm the compatibility of the software update with the target vehicle configuration. Moreover, in cases where the software may have interdependencies on other systems, the SUMS must prevent software from being deployed that will adversely affect other ECUs. For example, if the software update results in a new communication matrix that is not supported by one of the target vehicle ECUs, excluding that ECU from the update will result in communication errors and a potential malfunction of a safety-critical system.

> **Note**
>
> A communication matrix is simply a table that describes message identifiers, message length information, and other parameters that are necessary for an ECU to perform signal-based communication over a serial bus such as CAN. Code generators use the communication matrix as an input to produce source and header files, which then get included in the ECU software build.

Having a process that assesses the impact of a software update is essential to prevent unintended consequences for the safe and continued operation of the vehicle. Adequately testing the update with the intended vehicle configuration is one way to prevent the deployment of an incompatible update that will produce unintended consequences to vehicle safety and operation. Similarly, accounting for the impact of enabling new functions that were not tested with the original vehicle software set is required to avoid an adverse impact of the newly enabled function.

Cybersecurity of the update

The regulation requires that the SUMS enforces security measures to protect software updates from manipulation, as well as to protect the update process from being compromised. Here, the SUMS would work hand in hand with the CSMS to apply a risk-based approach to identifying the relevant threats and determining the appropriate risk treatment plan. If an update fails, a process is needed to support rolling back to a safe version without the possibility of abuse by an attacker aiming to force a rollback to an unpatched software version. In certain cases, the update itself may also introduce new risks or vulnerabilities, so the SUMS must support a process to evaluate the cybersecurity risks of the change and apply adequate security reviews and tests.

User awareness

The regulation requires that a process is in place for informing the user when a vehicle update is about to be installed. This allows users to decide whether they are ready to receive the update or whether they must postpone the update until it is more appropriate to do so.

Next, we will turn our attention to ISO 24089, which is the standard that aims to satisfy the requirements of the SUMS that were laid out through REG 156.

ISO 24089

Note that at the time of writing, the ISO 24089 standard is still under development. The goal of the ISO 24089 document is to standardize a SUMS, similar to how ISO/SAE 21434 standardizes the implementation of a CSMS. As such, ISO 24089 is expected to be used by automotive manufacturers and suppliers to meet the requirements of UNECE REG 156 to obtain approval for automotive software update support. The purpose of the ISO standard is to provide a set of guidelines and requirements for the development, implementation, and maintenance of software updates for vehicles. Consequently, it ensures the safety, security, and reliability of software updates in vehicles by requiring a consistent approach to software updates across the automotive industry. To do so, it covers all aspects of software updates, including planning, design, implementation, testing, deployment, and maintenance, and provides recommendations for managing the life cycle of software updates *[16]*.

Chinese regulation and standardization

Following in the footsteps of other nations and international bodies, the **Cyberspace Administration of China** (**CAC**) has published several cybersecurity standards that impact OEMs and suppliers involved in the design, development, production, sales, and maintenance of vehicles in China. Learning about these standards is important for international suppliers who are planning to sell automotive products in that market. These standards range from defining process-related requirements to prescribing technical requirements for automotive systems and infrastructure. At the time of writing, several of these standards are still being drafted, so we will only focus on the published standards:

- **GB/T 38628-2020**: This is the first and most prominent standard and is known as the *Information security technology – Cybersecurity guide for automotive electronics systems [19]*. This standard covers areas overlapping with ISO/SAE 21434 but provides more context regarding software and hardware security best practices and test methods.

- **GB/T 40861-2021**: This standard, known as *General technical requirements for vehicle cybersecurity [20]*, is concerned with highlighting vehicle assets and providing the technical requirements, techniques, and principles to ensure their protection. Example areas covered by the standard are the protection of in-vehicle and off-vehicle communication, as well as ECU software. The standard is a useful reference for understanding cybersecurity principles and controls derived from those principles to address vehicle cybersecurity threats.

- **GB/T 40856-2021**: This standard, known as *Technical requirements and test methods for cybersecurity of on-board information interactive system [67]*, provides more specific technical requirements to critical areas of the vehicle, such as hardware components, network protocols, operating systems, and application software. The technical requirements are complemented with security test methods to ensure those requirements are implemented correctly.

- **GB/T 40857-2021**: This standard, known as *Technical requirements and test methods for cybersecurity of vehicle gateway [68]*, follows a similar structure as GB/T 40856-2021 but with a focus on CAN, Ethernet, and hybrid gateways. It specifies requirements such as the removal of backdoors, enforcement of message filtering, and anomaly detection by monitoring message identifiers and message frequency. Similarly, it specifies test requirements to verify the correct and secure implementation of gateway security functions.

- **GB/T 40855-2021**: This standard, known as *Technical requirements and test methods for cybersecurity of remote service and management system for electric vehicles [69]*, specifies requirements for securing onboard terminals in electric and hybrid vehicles when used in conjunction with enterprise and public service and management platforms. The requirements and their corresponding test methods cover areas such as secure communication, secure updates, and access management.

Recall that in *Chapter 2*, we discussed Chinese cryptographic algorithms. These are standardized through the following:

- **GB/T 32907.2-2016**: Digital Signature Algorithm SM2
- **GB/T 32907.3-2016**: Hash Algorithm SM3
- **GB/T 32907.9-2016**: Identity-Based Cryptography Algorithm SM9

These standards specify the technical requirements, test methods, and evaluation criteria for the implementation of the SM2, SM3, and SM9 algorithms. They aim to ensure the security, reliability, and interoperability of cryptographic systems and applications that use these algorithms. Automotive suppliers intending to sell their products in China are expected to provide support for these algorithms through hardware IP and software cryptographic libraries, for example.

Periodically monitoring the publication of standards by the CAC is recommended to ensure adequate preparation is planned for supporting new standards in product roadmaps.

As we saw in this section, building compliant automotive systems requires constant awareness of cybersecurity standards and regulations, which is a prerequisite to releasing vehicles in certain markets. In the next section, we will switch our focus to prominent cybersecurity standards and references that should be considered to ease compliance with the primary security standards and ensure that security best practices are being followed.

Secondary standards

While the primary standards may provide a holistic framework for engineering secure automotive products, they rely on secondary and supporting standards to address specific technical areas of the engineering life cycle. Awareness of such standards is necessary to judge whether they apply to your organization or product offering.

IATF 16949:2016

Developing automotive products within the framework of a **quality management system** (**QMS**) serves as a prerequisite to achieving product security. ISO/SAE 21434 makes adherence to a QMS a requirement, which is reasonable considering the difficulty of arguing that a product is secure while not being able to demonstrate its quality *[9]*. For example, software developed outside a QMS is expected to contain more bugs due to the lack of formal quality checks, such as code reviews and software tests. A percentage of those software bugs are likely exploitable by an attacker. Without the help of a QMS, we are unable to manage the number of software bugs efficiently, making it even harder to manage the number of vulnerabilities.

The IATF 16949 standard is designed to provide a common framework for quality management across the entire automotive supply chain to promote consistent quality, improved customer satisfaction, and increased efficiency. By following the requirements of IATF 16949, organizations can ensure that their automotive products meet customer requirements and are produced consistently and efficiently. The primary intended audience for the IATF 16949 standard is automotive suppliers, **original equipment manufacturers** (**OEMs**), and related service providers. The IATF 16949 standard is comprised of 10 clauses, with the first three being introductory and the remaining seven clauses structured according to the **Plan, Do, Check, Act** (**PDCA**) cycle, as shown in *Figure 4.6*:

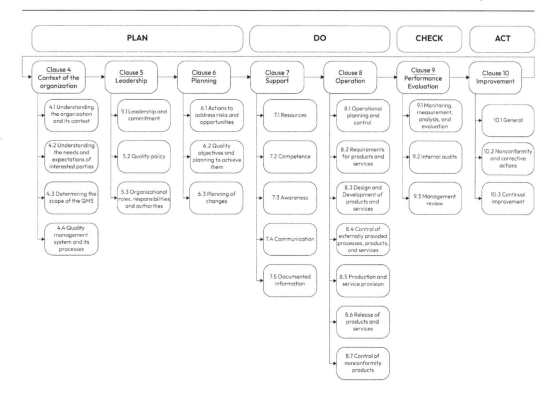

Figure 4.6 – IATF 16949 clauses arranged according to the PDCA cycle

As we explore the clauses of the IATF standard, it is useful to think of parallels between the requirements of the QMS and the CSMS to identify synergies between the two. For example, aspects of change management, configuration management, and documentation management are all useful processes that the CSMS requires that can be leveraged by the QMS with minor modifications to account for cybersecurity concerns. Similarly, QMS methods for requirements tracking and traceability can be leveraged for the creation and traceability of cybersecurity requirements to lower-level cybersecurity specifications. Let's briefly walk through the IATF clauses:

- In **clause 1**, the standard lays the ground for establishing a QMS that provides a framework for continuous improvement and the need for defect prevention while reducing waste in the automotive supply chain.

- **Clause 2** simply provides normative references, which are necessary for the application of the standard, including ISO 9001 *[71]*.

- **Clause 3** lists the terms and definitions to ensure a consistent interpretation and application of the standard.

- **Clauses 4, 5**, and **6** fall within the **Plan** cycle, with **clause 4** first stressing the need for the organization to identify the needs and expectations of the stakeholders as they relate to the QMS. Determining the scope of the system is essential to establishing the right quality objectives and identifying the risks that need to be managed.

- **Clause 5** is concerned with the leadership role in establishing and maintaining adherence to the QMS. This is achieved in several ways, such as communicating the importance of risk reduction and continuous process improvement. Also, establishing quality objectives as measurable goals for the QMS, and assigning roles and responsibilities to ensure the QMS can be implemented and maintained, are mandatory measures. This parallels clause 5 of ISO/SAE 21434 for the role of the organization in establishing an effective cybersecurity management system.

- **Clause 6** defines the requirements for planning to address quality objectives, such as the area of improving product quality, reducing defects, and increasing customer satisfaction. The organization is expected to identify and assess risks as they relate to the quality objectives and establish a process to mitigate those risks. A prominent aspect of clause 6 is change management, which requires the organization to establish a process for controlling changes to products and processes. In the context of cybersecurity, change management is critical as change is often correlated with exposure to new cybersecurity risks. Planning aspects also extend to product design and development, which includes planning for requirements elicitation, establishing product specifications, and verifying the product meets its intended objectives.

- **Clauses 7** and **8** fall within the **Do** cycle. As with any process, effectively applying the process requires establishing the right resources, competencies, and awareness, which is the scope of **clause 7**. The standard requires the organization to have the necessary human and infrastructure resources in place. It covers aspects such as training and professional development to ensure the staff is aware and capable of applying the process. Effective communication and documentation management are two aspects covered by this clause to ensure that all stakeholders have the information they need to understand the quality management system and their roles within it.

- On the other hand, **clause 8** focuses on the processes needed to produce products and services that meet customer requirements. Through operational planning and control, the organization must plan and control product design, production, and service delivery by establishing work instructions and quality checklists. Areas such as design review processes and design validation are in the scope of this clause to ensure that the product design is under quality control. Where components are acquired from suppliers, the standard requires supplier management processes to be enforced for selecting, evaluating, and monitoring suppliers to ensure their products meet the organization's needs. Furthermore, production aspects are also covered by this clause through the establishment of production plans, production control processes, and service delivery. Having the ability to identify and trace products and materials throughout the production and service delivery is an additional requirement of this clause. Finally, the management of customer property such as prototypes or product samples is covered to prevent property loss or damage.

- **Clause 9** covers the **Check** cycle by focusing on monitoring and measuring the QMS, as well as handling metrics to drive improvements. Establishing **key performance indicators** (**KPIs**) is one way to enable the measurement and evaluation of QMS effectiveness. Having internal audits of the QMS at planned intervals is required to identify nonconformities and take the necessary corrective actions. For continuous improvement, the organization must have methods to collect data on areas that require improvement and establish processes by which improvement can be realized.

- Finally, **clause 10** covers the **Act** cycle by focusing on actual improvement measures. This is achieved through establishing a culture of continuous improvement and engaging all stakeholders to not only identify trouble areas but also apply problem-solving methodologies to address those issues. Processes for error-proofing are an important aspect of this area as error prevention is more desirable than error correction. Having methods for root cause analysis is one effective way to avoid repeating the same errors in the future.

As we have seen, IATF 16949 provides the basis for many of the processes that are needed when establishing a cybersecurity management system. A QMS can be seen as a building block that can significantly reduce the burden of adopting the CSMS by leveraging common practices for both quality and cybersecurity. The standard can serve as a crucial tool for organizations in the automotive industry to demonstrate their commitment to quality and their ability to meet the needs of their customers.

> Tip
> Complying with IATF 16949 or an equivalent quality management system is a prerequisite for achieving compliance with ISO/SAE 21434.

Automotive SPICE (ASPICE)

Continuing with the theme of quality management, we will now consider a widely recognized industry standard called Automotive SPICE *[1]*, which helps organizations establish software development processes for automotive ECUs. The standard is tailored for the automotive industry from ISO/IEC 15504-5, also known as the standard for **Software Process Improvement and Capability Determination** (**SPICE**). ASPICE defines a process reference model that provides a set of best practices to be applied during the development of software across the various product life cycles. ASPICE divides the process areas into three main groups: primary life cycle processes, supporting life cycle processes, and organizational life cycle processes. Additionally, the standard contains a set of methods for evaluating the fulfillment of these processes, through a process assessment model. The results of an assessment determine the organization's maturity capability level, which ranges from zero to five. OEMs often demand that suppliers demonstrate their process capability during the quotation phase. These assessments help ensure that suppliers can meet the high standards set by the automotive industry for the development of safe, secure, and reliable software systems.

The benefit of compliance with ASPICE is that several process groups can be leveraged as supporting processes for achieving the requirements of the CSMS. What makes ASPICE even more attractive is that upon the publication of ISO/SAE 21434, ASPICE was extended with six additional process groups specific to cybersecurity, as defined in *Automotive SPICE for Cybersecurity [7]*. This is an assessment model that was created to support the implementation of UNECE R155 and ISO/SAE 21434 (road vehicles – cybersecurity engineering). The purpose of ASPICE for Cybersecurity is to identify and address product risks in cybersecurity-relevant projects. *Figure 4.7* shows the process groups as they overlay the V-model, with the security-impacted groups marked in green:

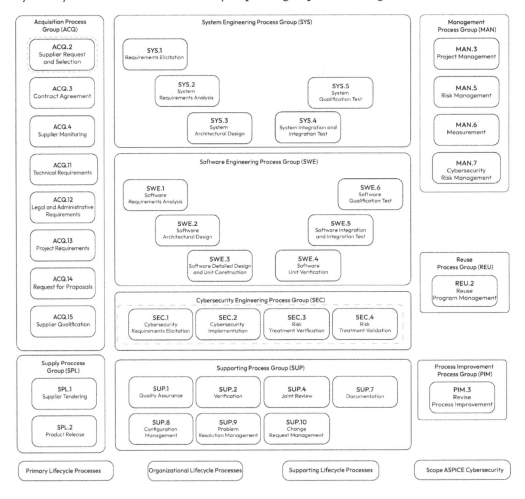

Figure 4.7 – Cybersecurity-specific process areas within ASPICE

The following table shows the mapping of ASPICE for cybersecurity process groups *[7]* both to
ISO/SAE 21434 clauses and the standard ASPICE process groups *[1]*:

ASPICE for Cybersecurity	ISO/SAE 21434 Section	ASPICE
ACQ.2: Supplier Request and Selection	7.4.1 Supplier Capability 7.4.2 Request for Quotation 7.4.3 Alignment of responsibilities	ACQ.3: Contract Agreement ACQ.4: Supplier Monitoring
-	5.4.4 Management Systems	SUP.1: Quality Assurance SUP.7: Documentation SUP.8: Configuration Management SUP.10: Change Request Management
SEC.1: Cybersecurity Requirements Elicitation	9.3: Item Definition 9.4: Cybersecurity Goals 9.5: Cybersecurity Concept	SYS.1: Requirements Elicitation SYS.2: System Requirements Analysis SWE.1: Software Requirements Analysis
SEC.2: Cybersecurity Implementation	10.4.1: Design	SYS.3: System Architectural Design SWE.2: Software Architectural Design SWE.3: Software Detailed Design and Unit Construction
SEC.3: Risk Treatment Verification	10.4.2: Integration and Verification	SWE.4: Software Unit Verification SWE.5: Software Integration and Integration Test SWE.6: Software Qualification Test SYS.4: System Integration and Integration Test SYS.5: System Qualification Test

ASPICE for Cybersecurity	ISO/SAE 21434 Section	ASPICE
SEC.4: Risk Treatment Validation	11: Cybersecurity Validation	SWE.6: Software Qualification Test SYS.5: System Qualification Test
MAN.7: Cybersecurity Risk Management	15: Threat Analysis and Risk Assessment Methods	MAN.5: Risk Management

Table 4.1 – Mapping of the ASPICE cybersecurity process groups to ISO/ SAE 21434 sections and the general ASPICE process groups

> **Tip**
> When updating your software development process to account for cybersecurity, you are encouraged to map requirements from ISO/SAE 21434 to the corresponding process area within ASPICE to demonstrate process coverage.

Trusted Information Security Assessment Exchange (TISAX)

Due to the highly distributed nature of the automotive supply chain, a breach in one of the supplier's information security systems can have cascading impacts on other members of the supply chain, with ramifications for users' private data, security sensitive data, trade secrets, and intellectual property. In response to this risk, TISAX *[23]* was created by the German Association of the Automotive Industry (VDA) and is now widely used by automotive companies worldwide. The standard provides a framework for assessing and certifying an organization's information security measures, with a focus on protecting sensitive data throughout the automotive supply chain. This allows partners to trust that once their data has been shared with other members of the supply chain, adequate measures are in place for safeguarding that information. An automotive organization can require evidence of TISAX certification before engaging with another partner within the supply chain.

> **Tip**
> ISO/SAE 21434 requires you to evaluate the supplier's cybersecurity capability during the supplier selection phase. TISAX can address the ISMS capability aspect.

A prerequisite to TISAX certification is having an ISMS in place to govern the management of security-sensitive information within the organization. The process of achieving TISAX certification consists of a registration step, in which information about the company is gathered, an assessment, in which a TISAX audit provider checks for compliance, and the exchange step, in which the company shares the results with partners.

TISAX defines eight assessment objectives, all of which may be in scope for the audit. These objectives range from handling information with high protection needs to protecting prototype parts, components, and vehicles, as well as protecting personal data, as specified in the European Union's **General Data Protection Regulation (GDPR)** *[21]*. The higher the protection needs, the more rigorous the assessment method that must be applied by the auditors. Therefore, TISAX defines three assessment levels determined by the requesting organization. Questions from the **Information Security Assessment (ISA)** questionnaire *[22]* are available for organizations to perform a self-assessment before undergoing an external audit. The ISA expects a maturity level between zero and five to be given per question. *Figure 4.8* shows an excerpt from the ISA:

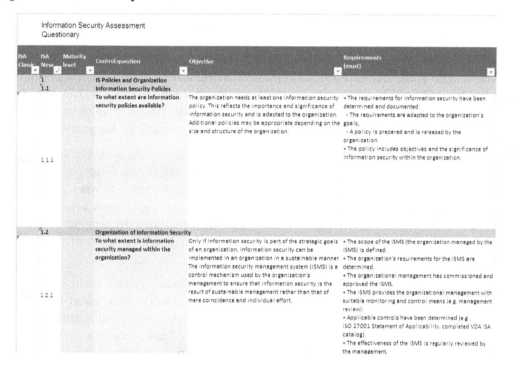

Figure 4.8 – Excerpt of the ISA questionnaire

Each question covers an area of concern, such as physical security or identity and access management. The questions are accompanied by the objective that must be fulfilled, along with specific requirements that allow the auditor to determine the level of satisfaction of the corresponding objective.

Once the self-assessment yields a result within the acceptable range for an external assessment to be carried out, the organization can reach out to the TISAX audit vendor to schedule an external assessment. The result of the audit will be captured in a TISAX assessment report, which classifies the result as conform, major non-conform, or minor non-conform. A corrective action plan is prepared to address the findings by capturing the root cause, planned action, the implementation date of the corrective action, and compensating measures for non-conformities that cannot be immediately addressed. When the assessment has been completed, the assessment results can be shared with the partners using an exchange portal.

Finally, TISAX labels are granted as a visible indication that an organization has completed a rigorous assessment of its information security measures and can protect the confidential data of its customers and partners. The TISAX label provides a standardized and recognized way to verify that a partner has the necessary security controls in place to protect data against cyber threats.

SAE J3101 – hardware-protected security for ground vehicles

Unlike standards that define the process, SAE J3101 *[24]* focuses on a specific technology area that is considered an enabler for ECU cybersecurity. The standard defines a set of security requirements for embedded **hardware security modules (HSMs)** commonly used in support of automotive security use cases such as secure onboard communication and **Over-the-Air (OTA)** updates. The standard refers to the HSM as the **hardware-protected security environment (HPSE)** and advocates for its use to enable security mechanisms that are critical for building security resiliency in ECUs. Without the support of an HPSE, ECUs would have to rely on software-only solutions, which have limited capabilities to support security controls such as secure boot and cryptographic key protection.

The security requirements in SAE J3101 cover eight main areas: cryptographic key protection, cryptographic algorithms, random number generation, secure non-volatile data, cryptographic agility, interface control, secure execution environments, and self-testing. For example, when addressing cryptographic key protection, the standard defines requirements for key generation, key ownership, wrapping, provisioning, and zeroization. The standard provides an automotive perspective on why and when such requirements are mandatory, which makes SAE J3101 especially useful for the automotive industry.

The use of the HPSE as the hardware root of trust alongside a secure execution environment and protected memory are the essential components to safeguard the security-critical assets of an ECU. Using an HPSE, it is possible to build secure protocols to protect the confidentiality, integrity, and authenticity of ECU data throughout the product life cycle stages. Example use cases in which the HPSE can play an essential role are authenticating diagnostic clients using digital signatures through immutable public keys, encrypting users' private data using hardware-protected cryptographic keys, and authenticating in-vehicle communication using message authentication codes.

Moreover, the growing security cases and increasing demands for cryptographic performance have resulted in the need for more powerful HPSEs with a higher number of cryptographic accelerators, larger internal system memory, and faster interfaces to the host CPUs. The latter is needed to facilitate the cryptographic processing of data at high throughput in applications such as sensor data authentication and cloud-based communication. OEMs and chip vendors who need a common reference for defining HPSE technology roadmaps can leverage SAE J3101 to define a baseline for what an HPSE is and what it needs to achieve. The standard is equally useful for chip vendors who are designing the HPSE hardware in silicon, as well as firmware vendors developing the software functionalities of the HSPE.

Coding and software standards

Software implementation errors are a common source of vulnerabilities. Eliminating software bugs that can be exploited by attackers is a challenging task, especially when using inherently unsafe languages such as C or C++. To help reduce the occurrence of software bugs with safety or security impact, developers rely on coding standards that prohibit risky features of the programming language through language subsets and the enforcement of defensive coding techniques. Applying coding rules is automated through **static code analysis tools**, also known as **SAST**. These are usually enabled upon each software commit, or when achieving a certain release milestone. Coding rule violations are returned by the tool in the form of warnings to be addressed by the software developer in case the warning cannot be justified. It is common for organizations to suppress specific rule violation warnings when these can be explained as non-critical deviations. However, blind reliance on SAST can be counterproductive if the developers are not adequately trained to differentiate between a warning that is pointing to a real issue and one that is simply a false positive. Another pitfall in using SAST is waiting too late in the program to run the tools to fix the violations. Teams who engage in this practice may have to rewrite large sections of code after significant testing has been performed, which is both expensive and risky to the project schedule and customer commitments. As with all security findings, it is important to prioritize rule violations based on the risk severity to avoid missing some severe violations in favor of fixing ones that are related to cosmetic or insignificant issues. Several coding standards apply to automotive software, so we will survey the most common ones next.

MISRA

The purpose of the **Motor Industry Software Reliability Association (MISRA)** is to provide coding standards for the development of safety-critical systems for both C and C++ programming languages. While MISRA rules' primary focus is generating reliable and safe code, they can be leveraged to prevent software vulnerabilities through proper code hygiene and defensive coding techniques [10]. For teams that have been developing safety-critical code, being MISRA-compliant is a good first step before expanding to more security-centric coding standards.

AUTOSAR C++

Due to the reliance of AUTOSAR Adaptive on C++ and the anticipated wide usage of the language in domain controllers and vehicle computers (introduced in *Chapter 1*), AUTOSAR and MISRA joined forces to develop safe and secure coding guidelines for the C++14 language variant. The result was the release of the *Guidelines for the use of the C++14 language in critical and safety-related systems [25]*. This subset was created through the addition of rules that address areas of the language that have been proven to pose a risk to memory safety, impact runtime determinism, or result in implementation-specific behavior. Organizations that use C++ in their automotive applications can follow AUTOSAR C++14 guidelines, even if they do not develop software within the framework of AUTOSAR Adaptive.

CERT C/C++

Like MISRA, CERT C and CERT C++ were created to provide a language subset to eliminate known security weaknesses. But unlike MISRA, CERT focuses on security and thus has a greater coverage for software implementation vulnerabilities. The rules are maintained by the Software Engineering Institute at Carnegie Mellon [26]. Each **rule** represents a grouping of software weaknesses that can be mitigated if the coding checks in the rule set are followed.

For example, Rule 06 addresses weaknesses in arrays and lists six coding checks to consider:

```
ARR30-C. Do not form or use out-of-bounds pointers or array subscripts
ARR32-C. Ensure size arguments for variable length arrays are in a
valid range
ARR36-C. Do not subtract or compare two pointers that do not refer to
the same array
ARR37-C. Do not add or subtract an integer to a pointer to a non-array
object
ARR38-C. Guarantee that library functions do not form invalid pointers
ARR39-C. Do not add or subtract a scaled integer to a pointer
```

Moreover, CERT C/C++ classifies rules in terms of criticality as L1, L2, and L3, where L1 is the most critical. Organizations aiming to eliminate software security weaknesses from a large code base should aim to resolve L1 violations before moving on to L2 and L3 as a general best practice.

NIST cryptographic standards

When implementing cryptographic functions, consulting the NIST standards is a must to ensure correct implementation and avoid common security pitfalls. NIST provides a large body of standards that describe how a cryptographic function shall be implemented, and what constraints must be followed to ensure the mechanism is deployed securely. In addition to cryptographic functions, some NIST standards provide valuable recommendations regarding areas such as key management and platform firmware resiliency. Ignoring these recommendations or constraints weakens the security of the cryptographic mechanisms and exposes systems to an increased risk of tampering and illegal access. Let's survey some common NIST cryptographic standards with a brief description of each:

- **FIPS 180-4**: The **Secure Hash Standard** (SHS) specifies a set of cryptographic hash functions that can be used to generate a fixed-length output from an input of any length. The output is referred to as a *hash value* and is used for a variety of applications, including digital signatures and data integrity checks [27].

- **FIPS 197**: The **Advanced Encryption Standard** (AES) is a federal information processing standard for encrypting electronic data. AES is widely used for data encryption in various applications, including secure communication and data storage [28].

- **FIPS 186-4**: The **Digital Signature Standard** (**DSS**) is a federal information processing standard for digital signatures. DSS provides a secure method for verifying the authenticity and integrity of digital data *[29]*.

- **SP 800-131A**: The standard titled *Transitioning the Use of Cryptographic Algorithms and Key Lengths* provides guidelines for transitioning from weaker to stronger cryptographic algorithms and key lengths. It provides recommendations for organizations to maintain the security of their systems and data by disallowing certain cryptographic algorithms and specifying the minimum allowed key strength *[30]*.

- **SP 800-57 Part 1**: The *Recommendation for Key Management* offers recommendations for managing cryptographic keys in various applications, including secure communication, digital signatures, and data encryption *[31]*.

- **SP 800-38A**: The standard titled *Recommendation for Block Cipher Modes of Operation* provides recommendations for the use of block cipher encryption modes, including format-preserving encryption *[32]*.

- **SP 800-38B**: The standard titled *Recommendation for Block Cipher Modes of Operation: The CMAC Mode for Authentication* provides recommendations for the use of the **Cipher-based Message Authentication Code** (**CMAC**) mode of operation, which is a block cipher mode that can be used for message authentication *[33]*.

- **SP 800-56A**: The standard titled *Recommendation for Pair-Wise Key Establishment Schemes Using Discrete Logarithm Cryptography* provides recommendations for the use of pair-wise key establishment schemes, which are used to establish secure communication between two parties *[34]*.

- **SP 800-56B**: The standard titled *Recommendation for Pair-Wise Key-Establishment Schemes Using Integer Factorization Cryptography* provides recommendations for the use of pair-wise key establishment schemes that use integer factorization cryptography *[35]*.

- **SP 800-133**: The standard titled *Recommendation for Cryptographic Key Management* provides guidelines for securely managing cryptographic keys, including key generation, key storage, key distribution, and key destruction *[36]*.

- **SP 800-90A**: The standard titled *Recommendation for Random Number Generation Using Deterministic Random Bit Generators* provides guidelines for generating random numbers using deterministic random bit generators. It covers a wide range of topics, including entropy sources, random number generators, and entropy testing methods *[37]*.

- **SP 800-90B**: The standard titled *Recommendation for the Entropy Sources Used for Random Bit Generation* provides guidelines for using entropy sources to generate random bits, which can then be used to generate random numbers through a DRBG. It covers a wide range of topics, including entropy sources, random bit generators, and testing methods *[38]*.

- **SP 800-90C**: The standard titled *Recommendation for the Use of Cryptographic Key Generation Techniques* provides guidelines for using cryptographic key generation techniques. It covers a wide range of topics, including key generation algorithms, key strengths, and key management practices *[39]*.

- **SP 800-108**: The standard titled *Recommendation for Key Derivation Using Pseudorandom Functions* provides guidelines for deriving cryptographic keys using pseudorandom functions. It covers a wide range of topics, including key derivation functions, pseudorandom functions, and key establishment protocols *[40]*.

- **SP 800-193**: The standard titled *NIST Platform Firmware Resiliency Guidelines* provides a comprehensive set of recommendations for improving the security and resiliency of platform firmware to reduce the risk of unauthorized access and malicious attacks to an embedded computer system. The standard includes recommendations for manufacturers, developers, and users of platform firmware, and covers topics such as firmware update and recovery, secure boot, and protection against unauthorized access. The guidelines emphasize the importance of protecting platform firmware from malicious attacks and ensuring that firmware updates are secure and trustworthy. It covers areas of firmware protection, detection, and recovery through **root of trust** (**RoT**) and **chain of trust** (**CoT**). The standard requires that firmware is only updateable through an authenticated mechanism. It also requires that in the case of firmware or critical data, corruption, detection, and recovery should be possible. It provides guidelines on how to securely store and manage cryptographic keys and certificates used in the protection of firmware. It can be applied to any ECU that offers flash reprogramming capabilities or OTA updates *[30]*.

Awareness of the secondary standards translates into a richer security process while providing organizations with valuable references to include when defining security requirements and exploring security solutions. In the next section, we will walk through some of the prominent supporting standards and resources that are useful for any cybersecurity professional. While this is only a sample of references, each organization is encouraged to create a database of supporting standards and keep it up to date to ensure that the latest and greatest in security technology is being followed.

Supporting standards and resources

The remaining part of this chapter focuses on standards and resources that are useful but not mandatory. Organizations are encouraged to maintain a list of such resources to raise awareness among security practitioners and stay up to date on the latest publications of security best practices.

MITRE Common Weakness Enumeration (CWE)

MITRE compiles a list of software and hardware security weaknesses based on vulnerabilities that are periodically filed in the **National Vulnerability Database** (**NVD**) *[72]*. These weaknesses are grouped into classes for ease of searching. Every year, MITRE publishes the Top 25 CWEs *[42]* based on the vulnerabilities reported throughout the year:

Rank	ID	Name	Score
1	CWE-787	Out-of-bounds Write	64.20
2	CWE-79	Improper Neutralization of Input During Web Page Generation ('Cross-site Scripting')	45.97
3	CWE-89	Improper Neutralization of Special Elements used in an SQL Command ('SQL Injection')	22.11
4	CWE-20	Improper Input Validation	20.63
5	CWE-125	Out-of-bounds Read	17.67
6	CWE-78	Improper Neutralization of Special Elements used in an OS Command ('OS Command Injection')	17.53
7	CWE-416	Use After Free	15.50
8	CWE-22	Improper Limitation of a Pathname to a Restricted Directory ('Path Traversal')	14.08
9	CWE-352	Cross-Site Request Forgery (CSRF)	11.53
10	CWE-434	Unrestricted Upload of File with Dangerous Type	9.56
11	CWE-476	NULL Pointer Dereference	7.15
12	CWE-502	Deserialization of Untrusted Data	6.68
13	CWE-190	Integer Overflow or Wraparound	6.53
14	CWE-287	Improper Authentication	6.35
15	CWE-798	Use of Hard-coded Credentials	5.66
16	CWE-862	Missing Authorization	5.53
17	CWE-77	Improper Neutralization of Special Elements used in a Command ('Command Injection')	5.42
18	CWE-306	Missing Authentication for Critical Function	5.15
19	CWE-119	Improper Restriction of Operations within the Bounds of a Memory Buffer	4.85
20	CWE-276	Incorrect Default Permissions	4.84
21	CWE-918	Server-Side Request Forgery (SSRF)	4.27
22	CWE-362	Concurrent Execution using Shared Resource with Improper Synchronization ('Race Condition')	3.57
23	CWE-400	Uncontrolled Resource Consumption	3.56
24	CWE-611	Improper Restriction of XML External Entity Reference	3.38
25	CWE-94	Improper Control of Generation of Code ('Code Injection')	3.32

Figure 4.9 – Snapshot of the Top 25 CWEs from 2022

As shown in *Figure 4.9*, CWE-787 remains in the Top 25 CWEs as the most common root cause of memory safety vulnerabilities that produce out-of-bound writes. Being aware of the Top 25 CWEs as well as CWE classes is a powerful method to ensure your system has considered and avoided common pitfalls. When performing threat analysis, it is useful to consult the CWE website to identify weaknesses that may exist in the system under analysis and help enrich the threat identification phase. Similarly, during security reviews, being aware of common weaknesses against a specific component can help the reviewer focus on trouble spots.

US DoT NHTSA Cybersecurity Best Practices for the Safety of Modern Vehicles

To help OEMs and automotive suppliers cope with the emerging threats against connected vehicles, the **National Highway Traffic Safety Administration** (**NHTSA**) published a guide for enhancing motor vehicle cybersecurity through the application of cybersecurity best practices. These practices are divided into two main categories: general cybersecurity best practices, which address process and management-related activities, and technical cybersecurity best practices, which address countermeasures applied at the vehicle and ECU level *[2]*:

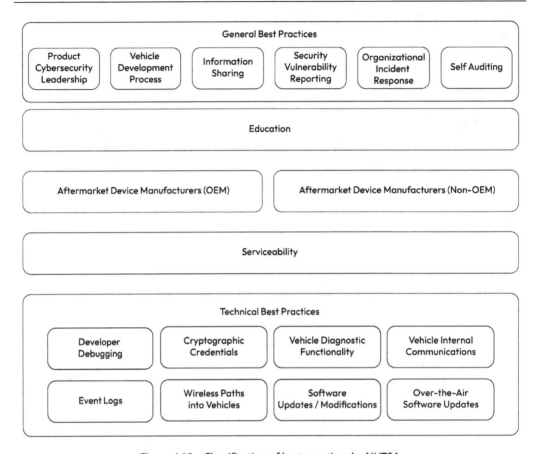

Figure 4.10 – Classification of best practices by NHTSA

NHTSA defines 45 general cybersecurity best practices across the key areas shown in *Figure 4.10*. Here is an abridged version of the general best practices:

- Apply a systematic approach based on the NIST Cybersecurity Framework to develop layered cybersecurity protections for vehicles

- Commit leadership to allocating resources, facilitating communication related to cybersecurity matters, and incorporating cybersecurity voices within the vehicle safety design process

- Build a robust process based on a secure engineering approach

- Apply risk assessment methods that prioritize the safety of vehicle occupants and road users

- Consider threats against sensors such as GPS spoofing, LiDAR/Radar jamming, and camera blinding

- Remove or mitigate safety-critical risks

- Create layers of protection with clear security requirement definitions communicated to suppliers of those protections

- Maintain inventories of software and hardware components within a vehicle to track the impact of a newly discovered vulnerability

- Apply cybersecurity testing, including penetration tests, and perform vulnerability analysis for each known vulnerability

- Implement monitoring, containment, and remediation to mitigate safety risks to vehicle occupants and road users when a cyberattack is detected

- Apply robust documentation management and information sharing with industry bodies such as Auto-ISAC

- Periodically evaluate risks due to changes in the cybersecurity landscape

- Participate actively in industry standardization bodies and collaborate with industry partners to address new risks

- Establish an automotive-centric vulnerability reporting program

- Support the creation of incident response planning and tracking

- Apply internal reviews and audits for cybersecurity-related activities

- Increase the cybersecurity awareness of staff through education and training

- Consider the risk of aftermarket devices when connected to vehicle systems, especially ones that provide external connectivity through Wi-Fi and Bluetooth

- Include aftermarket device manufacturers in the scope of parties that must apply cybersecurity protections to their products

- Balance cybersecurity needs to restrict ECU access with vehicle serviceability by third-party repair services

Additionally, 25 technical best practices are distributed across several key areas related to debugging access, cryptographic methods, vehicle diagnostics/tools, internal communication, logging, wireless interfaces, network segmentation, communication with the backend, and software updates. Here is an abridged version of the technical best practices:

- Limit or eliminate developer-level debug access after an ECU is deployed

- Use robust cryptographic methods and protect cryptographic credentials that are bound to a vehicle platform

- Limit or eliminate diagnostic functions that can be abused

- Enforce access control when diagnostic tools request diagnostic services or reprogramming operations

- Address the threats of spoofing and replaying safety-critical messages across internal vehicle channels

- Create support for event logging in the case of a cyberattack to aid in data forensics

- Secure external network interfaces and wireless paths

- Apply network segmentation and isolation to prevent the corruption of one channel from cascading to safety-critical domains

- Apply whitelist-based filtering across the vehicle gateway to restrict traffic flow across vehicle domains

- Eliminate unnecessary network protocols that could be abused by attackers and apply port-level protections

- Establish secure communication channels with backends through encryption and authentication

- Protect firmware and software from unauthorized modification and prevent rollback attacks

- Secure OTA servers and address MITM attacks against OTA updates

> **Tip**
> When preparing cybersecurity requirements for an ECU, cross-check the NHTSA best practices to identify potential gaps in your cybersecurity requirements coverage.

ENISA good practices for the security of smart cars

ENISA, which is a European agency focused on cybersecurity, has published several automotive security reports to raise security awareness in the automotive industry and provide guidance on practices and technical measures to address cyber threats. The *ENISA good practices for security of Smart Cars [43]* report is one such publication that contains pertinent information for all members of the automotive supply chain. The asset taxonomy presented in the report provides a holistic view of tangible assets that are critical for the safe operation of vehicles, such as sensor data, in-vehicle networks, vehicle functions, decision-making algorithms, supporting backend servers, and external network protection systems. On the other hand, the threat taxonomy enumerates threats of various types, such as session hijacking, data replay, denial of service of communication systems, software manipulation, and more. A list of attack scenarios is provided to clarify common attack steps, impacted stakeholders, and potential countermeasures. The ENISA assets, threats, and attack scenarios can be useful to pre-populate or enhance a vehicle-level TARA. The report also lists security measures through policies, organizational practices, and technical countermeasures. The latter is quite useful for building a cybersecurity controls catalog that aids security practitioners when creating the cybersecurity concept of a specific vehicle system.

SAE J3061 – cybersecurity guidebook for cyber-physical vehicle systems

Although superseded by ISO/SAE 21434, J3061 still serves as a good resource on general methods and practices that can improve the security of automotive systems. The purpose of the SAE J3061 guidebook is to provide a comprehensive framework for ensuring the cybersecurity of connected vehicles *[8]*. When used with ISO/SAE 21434, it can provide useful reference material, for example, in the area of safety and security cross-analysis, as well as risk assessment frameworks such as EVITA and HEAVENS. The guidebook also includes information on common tools and methods that are used in designing and verifying cyber-physical vehicle systems.

ISO/IEC 27001

ISO/IEC 27001 is an international standard that outlines requirements for an **information security management system** (**ISMS**) *[45]*. It provides a comprehensive framework for protecting sensitive information, such as financial data, intellectual property, and personal information through the development and implementation of policies and procedures to manage information security risks. This is achieved through a systematic approach to risk assessment, treatment, and continuous monitoring and improvement. The standard emphasizes the role of leadership in establishing and maintaining a management framework to support the ISMS. It describes the role of risk assessment methods in identifying and assessing risks to data confidentiality, integrity, and availability. Furthermore, it requires security controls to be implemented to manage the identified risks. Protection is complemented through incident management to establish procedures for reporting, investigating, and responding to information security incidents. Continuous improvement and compliance management are also two important aspects of the ISMS.

It is expected that engineering teams developing secure automotive products will cross paths with IT teams handling information security due to the reliance of the former on IT systems throughout the product life cycles. Therefore, high-level knowledge of ISO/IEC 27001 is useful to harmonize expectations wherever conflicts arise.

NIST SP 800-160

NIST SP800-160 provides a generalized understanding of what a secure engineering process is. Something especially useful for automotive cybersecurity is the enumeration of security controls. Since ISO/SAE 21434 requires that organizations build cybersecurity control catalogs to assist engineers in choosing well-established security countermeasures to mitigate a specific threat, the catalog from the NIST standard can serve as a good starting point for building a product-specific catalog.

Similarly, ISO/SAE 21434 requires that organizations establish security design principles to guide engineers during the architecture design phase. NIST provides a comprehensive list of security principles, as introduced in *Chapter 2*, as the principles of trustworthy secure design *[13]*. Adapting those principles to supplement them with examples from the product area in scope is a good practice that can aid teams in making security-aware design decisions.

Uptane

Uptane *[12]* was initially started as a collaborative effort between academia and industry experts to provide a secure architecture for OTA updates in vehicles. The goal of Uptane is to address threats against OTA update infrastructure as well as the target ECUs to improve the security and reliability of this critical vehicle function. Uptane can be applied to all parties involved in the design and implementation of OTA systems, such as OEMs, backend solution providers, and ECU developers. The Uptane standard enforces the separation of roles in managing the OTA updates to ensure that no single breach can result in a complete loss of integrity regarding the OTA function. To do so, it separates the software repositories into the image repository, which contains binary images, and the director repository, which deploys the software binaries. Furthermore, the PKI is separated into four roles. The root signing role is the certificate authority of the Uptane environment, and it distributes public keys for all the other roles. The timestamp signing role indicates when there is new metadata or software binaries to update. The snapshot signing role creates signed metadata about images released by the repository at a point in time for a specific target. Finally, the targets role provides target metadata such as binary hashes and file sizes. The Uptane standard is designed to protect against various types of attacks, including replay attacks, rollback attacks, and MITM attacks. Protections use a combination of techniques, such as digital signatures, secure hashes, and timestamping. The Uptane security model ensures the integrity and authenticity of software updates, and the Uptane metadata format provides information about the contents and properties of software updates, including the cryptographic keys used to sign and verify software updates.

Summary

In conclusion, understanding and implementing automotive cybersecurity standards is not merely a regulatory requirement but a cornerstone of building cyber-resilient automotive systems. In this chapter, we classified standards into three main categories: primary, secondary, and supporting, to provide a holistic view of the compliance layers. While primary standards form the backbone and are often mandated, secondary and supporting standards play an important role in implementing a robust cybersecurity management system. They also serve as useful resources in understanding security weaknesses and security best practices and offer general guidance for developing secure automotive systems and their supporting infrastructure. Furthermore, compliance with these standards ensures an orderly, process-driven approach that fortifies each stage of the vehicle life cycle, from development to operation. Given the fact that the landscape of automotive cybersecurity is in constant flux, staying updated and adapting to new norms ensures that industry-wide cybersecurity practices are adopted in a consistent manner that strengthens the individual members of the supply chain. Therefore, this chapter should serve as a starting point for standardization awareness, offering a snapshot of the key standards today, while motivating you to stay up to date on relevant standards that are critical to your domain of expertise.

In the next chapter, we will take a deep dive into the ISO/SAE 21434 standard, which establishes methods and guidelines for a comprehensive cybersecurity lifecycle for road vehicles, including their components and interfaces.

References

Besides the standards and references we discussed in this chapter, the following list contains additional resources that are worthy of consideration for further reading:

- *[1] Automotive SPICE® Process Reference Model Process Assessment Model Version 3.1*: `http://www.automotivespice.com/fileadmin/software-download/AutomotiveSPICE_PAM_31.pdf`

- *[2] Cybersecurity Best Practices | 2020 Update*: `https://www.nhtsa.gov/document/cybersecurity-best-practices`

- *[3] UN Regulation No. 155 - Cyber security and cyber security management system*: `https://unece.org/sites/default/files/2021-03/R155e.pdf`

- *[4] SEI CERT C Coding Standard*: `https://wiki.sei.cmu.edu/confluence/display/c`

- *[5] UN Regulation on uniform provisions concerning the approval of vehicles with regard to cyber security and of their cybersecurity management systems*: `http://www.unece.org/DAM/trans/doc/2020/wp29grva/ECE-TRANS-WP29-2020-079-Revised.pdf`

- *[6] UN Regulation No. 156 – Software update and software update management system*: `https://unece.org/sites/default/files/2021-03/R156e.pdf`

- *[7] Automotive SPICE® Process Reference and Assessment Model for Cybersecurity Engineering*: `https://www.automotivespice.com/fileadmin/software-download/AutomotiveSPICE_for_Cybersecurity_PAM_1st_edition_2021.pdf`

- *[8] Cybersecurity Guidebook for Cyber-Physical Vehicle Systems J3061_201601*: `https://www.sae.org/standards/content/j3061_201601/`

- *[9] IATF 16949:2016*: `https://www.aiag.org/quality/iatf-16949-2016`

- *[10] MISRA-C*

- *[11] Automotive Industry SBOM Project*: `https://www.ntia.doc.gov/files/ntia/publications/ntia_sbom_energy_automotive.pdf`

- *[12] IEEE-ISTO 6100.1.0.0 Uptane Standard for Design and Implementation*: `https://uptane.github.io/papers/ieee-isto-6100.1.0.0.uptane-standard.html`

- *[13] NIST Special Publication 800-160*: `https://nsarchive.gwu.edu/sites/default/files/documents/5989591/National-Security-Archive-National-Institute-of.pdf`

- *[14] ISO/PAS 5112:2022 road vehicles – guidelines for auditing cybersecurity engineering*: `https://www.iso.org/standard/80840.html`

- *[15] ISO/SAE 21434:2021 road vehicles – cybersecurity engineering*: `https://www.iso.org/standard/70918.html`

- *[16] ISO 24089:2023 road vehicles – software update engineering*: `https://www.iso.org/standard/77796.html`

- *[17] WP.29 – Introduction*: `https://unece.org/wp29-introduction`

- *[18] GB/T 32960.2-2016*: `https://www.chinesestandard.net/PDF.aspx/GBT32960.2-2016`

- *[19]* `https://www.chinesestandard.net/PDF.aspx/GBT38628-2020`

- *[20]* `https://www.chinesestandard.net/PDF/English.aspx/GBT40861-2021`

- *[21]* `https://gdpr.eu/`

- *[22]* `https://portal.enx.com/TISAX/downloads/vda-isa-archive`

- *[23]* `https://enx.com/en-US/TISAX/`

- *[24]* `https://www.sae.org/standards/content/j3101_202002/?src=iso/sae21434.d1`

- *[25]* `https://www.autosar.org/fileadmin/standards/adaptive/18-03/AUTOSAR_RS_CPP14Guidelines.pdf`

- *[26]* `https://resources.sei.cmu.edu/downloads/secure-coding/assets/sei-cert-cpp-coding-standard-2016-v01.pdf`

- *[27]* `https://csrc.nist.gov/publications/detail/fips/180/4/final`

- *[28]* `https://csrc.nist.gov/publications/detail/fips/197/final`

- *[29]* `https://csrc.nist.gov/publications/detail/fips/186/4/final`

- *[30]* `https://csrc.nist.gov/publications/detail/sp/800-131a/rev-2/final`

- *[31]* `https://csrc.nist.gov/publications/detail/sp/800-57-part-1/rev-5/final`

- *[32]* `https://csrc.nist.gov/publications/detail/sp/800-38a/final`

- *[33]* `https://csrc.nist.gov/publications/detail/sp/800-38b/archive/2005-05-01`

- *[34]* https://csrc.nist.gov/publications/detail/sp/800-56a/rev-3/final

- *[35]* https://csrc.nist.gov/publications/detail/sp/800-56b/rev-2/final

- *[36]* https://csrc.nist.gov/publications/detail/sp/800-133/rev-2/final

- *[37]* https://csrc.nist.gov/publications/detail/sp/800-90a/rev-1/final

- *[38]* https://csrc.nist.gov/publications/detail/sp/800-90b/final

- *[39]* https://csrc.nist.gov/publications/detail/sp/800-90c/draft

- *[40]* https://csrc.nist.gov/publications/detail/sp/800-108/rev-1/final

- *[42]* https://cwe.mitre.org/

- *[43]* https://www.enisa.europa.eu/publications/smart-cars

- *[44]* https://www.sae.org/standards/content/j3061_201601/

- *[45]* https://www.iso.org/standard/82875.html

- *[46]* https://www.intertek.com/automotive/ul-4600/

- *[47]* https://www.csagroup.org/testing-certification/testing/cybersecurity/

- *[48]* https://webstore.iec.ch/preview/info_iec62443-3-3%7Bed1.0%7Den.pdf

- *[49]* https://standards.ieee.org/ieee/21451-1-6/7315/

- *[50]* https://www.etsi.org/deliver/etsi_en/303600_303699/303645/02.01.01_60/en_303645v020101p.pdf

- *[51]* https://www.sit.fraunhofer.de/fileadmin/dokumente/studien_und_technical_reports/China-electric-vehicle-study_2021.pdf?_=1631783328

- *[52]* https://www.aiag.org/about/news/2018/05/02/automotive-industry-collaborates-on-new-cybersecurity-guidelines

- *[53]* https://www.astm.org/get-involved/technical-committees/work-items-full-list

- *[54]* https://blackberry.qnx.com/content/dam/qnx/whitepapers/2017/7-pillar-auto-cybersecurity-white-paper.pdf

- *[55]* https://nvlpubs.nist.gov/nistpubs/ir/2014/nist.ir.7628r1.pdf
- *[56]* https://www.iso.org/standard/59689.html
- *[57]* https://www.sae.org/publications/technical-papers/content/2020-01-0142/
- *[58]* https://www.iso.org/standard/72891.html
- *[59]* https://www.cisecurity.org/controls
- *[60]* https://www.iso.org/standard/77490.html
- *[62]* https://www.en-standard.eu/pas-11281-2018-connected-automotive-ecosystems-impact-of-security-on-safety-code-of-practice/
- *[63]* https://www.singaporestandardseshop.sg/Product/SSPdtDetail/81ad7d3f-2e04-4497-a72b-dd0bd0875148
- *[64]* https://www.congress.gov/bill/115th-congress/house-bill/701/text
- *[65]* https://research.chalmers.se/publication/527752
- *[66]* www.chinesestandard.net
- *[67]* https://www.chinesestandard.net/PDF.aspx/GBT40856-2021
- *[68]* https://www.chinesestandard.net/Related.aspx/GBT40857-2021
- *[69]* https://www.chinesestandard.net/PDF/English.aspx/GBT40855-2021
- *[70]* https://www.iso.org/obp/ui/#!iso:std:68383:en
- *[71]* https://www.iso.org/iso-9001-quality-management.htm
- *[72]* https://www.nvd.nist.gov
- *[73] ISO/IEC 15408-1:2022 Information security, cybersecurity, and privacy protection*
- *[74] ISO/IEC 27002:2022 Information security, cybersecurity, and privacy protection — Information security controls*

5

Taking a Deep Dive into ISO/SAE21434

ISO/SAE21434 is the de facto standard for ensuring cybersecurity in automotive engineering. It provides a comprehensive framework for managing cybersecurity risks throughout the product development life cycle, from planning and design to production and beyond. In *Chapter 4*, we introduced the ISO/SAE 21434 standard and asserted the importance of taking a systematic approach to engineering secure products. In this chapter, we will delve deeper into the various aspects of this approach and demonstrate why it is crucial for overcoming the technical and process-related challenges of developing a secure product. Rather than focusing on each requirement of the standard, we will instead provide a detailed summary of the objectives of each clause, along with best practices and practical examples to achieve those objectives. We will cover a broad range of topics, including the following:

- Organizational cybersecurity management
- Acquisition and supplier management
- The concept phase
- Design and implementation
- Verification testing
- Validation testing
- Product release
- Production planning
- Operation and maintenance
- End-of-life support

Notations

As you read this chapter, we expect that you will frequently be consulting the ISO/SAE 21434 standard to better understand a process requirement or work product. When doing so, it helps to understand a few conventions that the **International Organization for Standardization** (**ISO**) standard uses. First, the standard denotes mandatory process requirements with **[RQ-xx-yy]**, where *xx* is the section number and *yy* is the requirement number within that section. Failure to meet a process requirement will trigger a finding by an auditor, so it is important to pay attention to those requirements. On the other hand, recommended practices are denoted as **[RC-xx-yy]**. It is good practice to include all the recommendations within your cybersecurity engineering process. Note that assessors will question why a recommendation was ignored by a specific project. **[PM-xx-yy]** refers to project management-related process statements that can be considered when you're conforming to a specific standard requirement. On the other hand, cybersecurity activities are captured through work products denoted as **[WP-xx-yy]**. Work products are the evidence that certain process requirements related to a cybersecurity activity have been performed and they are used to build the overall cybersecurity case.

Now that we have covered the notations, let's look at the overall scope of the standard before diving into its detailed sections.

At a glance – the ISO 21434 standard

The ultimate goal of any cybersecurity engineering management system is to produce secure systems that are suitable for their intended use. This is achieved by accurately identifying and assessing cybersecurity risks that emerge throughout the product life cycle and providing mechanisms to reduce those risks to reasonable levels. Without the structured systematic engineering approach, engineers resort to an ad hoc approach to identifying risks as they become known and applying cybersecurity controls using a mixture of security best practices and expert knowledge. This commonly leads to three outcomes:

- Certain risks remain unknown as the program cannot claim with certainty that all risk sources have been accounted for or that all technical risks have been analyzed

- Inadequate cybersecurity controls are chosen, leaving residual risk that is not quantified or understood

- Cybersecurity controls are over-engineered, resulting in the misdirection of resources with increased cost and schedule delays

Contrary to the ad hoc approach, the risk-based systematic approach to cybersecurity engineering is intended to provide organizations with a clear view of their cybersecurity risk exposure. This helps in properly setting the priorities of applying security measures while avoiding the haphazard application of security controls. By providing tools to enumerate and quantify residual risk, the organization is better prepared to address those risks methodically. Similarly, having processes that guide the proper selection of cybersecurity controls can ensure that mitigations are applied at the right level of the design to maximize their effectiveness. Before delving into more detail, let's take a look at the overall picture of the cybersecurity engineering approach and how it applies to the full product life cycle:

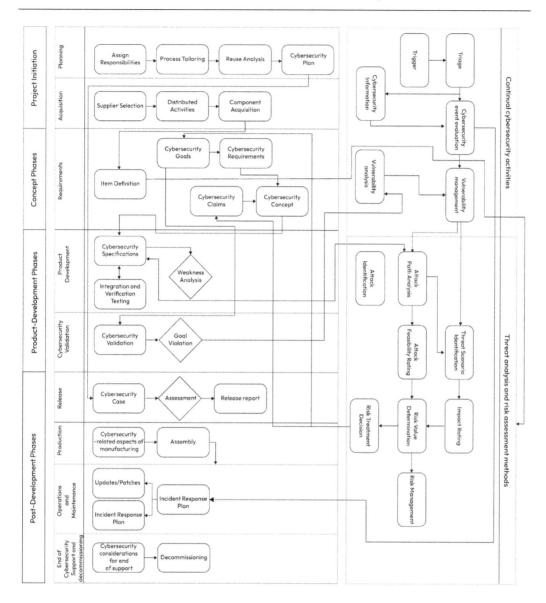

Figure 5.1 – Project-specific process flow

Figure 5.1 subdivides the life cycle into four main project phases:

1. **Project initiation**: This phase lays the foundation for the cybersecurity activities that must be planned, as well as capturing risks related to component acquisition.

2. **Concept phase**: This phase captures the system-level security goals and requirements through the application of threat analysis and risk assessment methods.

3. **Product development:** This phase incorporates cybersecurity controls throughout the design and implementation while minimizing security weaknesses. This ensures the security controls have been correctly implemented and deployed through security verification and validation testing.

4. **Post development:** This phase defines the security prerequisites to prepare the product for release, and the cybersecurity implications to production, operation, maintenance, and end of life.

As shown in *Figure 5.1*, process dependencies exist between the different phases. Specifically, the vulnerability management and threat and risk assessment process areas span multiple phases, so they are shown as process verticals. In later sections, we will continuously refer back to this flow to highlight the interdependencies between project phases and process areas. Next, we'll explore the role of the organization in establishing a **cybersecurity management system** (**CSMS**) and providing the right resources to ensure its successful deployment.

Organizational cybersecurity management

Like any good cybersecurity engineering process, **ISO21434** starts with organizational-level expectations. Because the cybersecurity engineering approach is about managing risk, and because different organizations have different risk appetites, discussions about cybersecurity must start at the management level of any organization. This is captured through the cybersecurity policy, which sets the stage for managing the cybersecurity risk by defining processes and responsibilities and allocating resources. Typically, organizations are used to the security policy, which governs **information security management systems** (**ISMSs**). This policy can be leveraged to expand existing policies to govern **operational technology** (**OT**) through the **CSMS**:

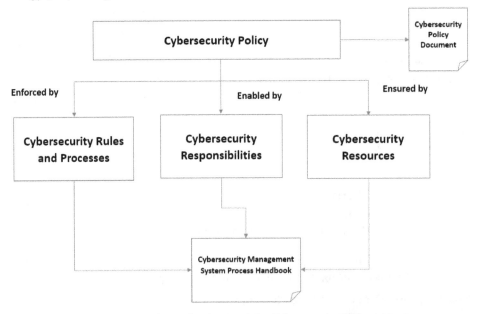

Figure 5.2 – Relationship between the Cybersecurity Policy and
Cybersecurity Management System Process Handbook

Briefly, the policy is the basis for requiring a cybersecurity management system that will be captured through a process handbook. This can be a simple document or an interactive process definition tool. A very important aspect of the policy is aligning the risk matrix of product engineering with the overall risk matrix of the organization. Even though the risk scoring methods can differ between **Information Technology (IT)** and OT systems, having a policy that dictates which risk levels must be mitigated versus which ones can be shared or accepted is one-way executive management can help engineering teams establish a baseline for the level of security the products must strive for.

> **Note**
>
> Risk scoring methods combine the attack feasibility with the corresponding impact level to produce a risk score that guides the risk treatment decision. This is described in more detail in the concept phase later in the chapter..

To jumpstart the adoption of a CSMS an organization should consider the following roadmap:

1. **Perform a gap analysis**: Assuming that the organization has not yet accounted for a CSMS, the first step is to perform a gap analysis to estimate the time and resources needed to achieve compliance. Rather than building a parallel engineering process, cybersecurity engineering must be integrated with existing quality management and safety management systems. Similarly, the supporting management systems must be extended to address security risks. This requires the confluence of experts from multiple domains to ensure that process adaptations to account for cybersecurity do not result in conflicts or duplications with existing processes and procedures. More on management systems will be covered in the next section.

> **Hint**
>
> A gap analysis must be performed against each requirement in the ISO/SAE 21434 standard to ensure that all process requirements are accounted for (not only the work products).

2. **Establish a cybersecurity-aware culture**: Besides the policy, the organization is responsible for establishing a cybersecurity-aware culture by instituting frequent training and establishing processes for information sharing and risk escalation. But before you can have a cybersecurity-aware organization, you need to provide adequate staffing for the cybersecurity roles. Having the right security professionals is a prerequisite to ensuring that inputs from the product cybersecurity domain are routed to the proper management channels. Such input is essential to aid the cybersecurity roles in eliminating unreasonable risk, which, if left untreated, will manifest as expensive security breaches in the future. With the proper staff in place, the organization can establish a cybersecurity culture by emphasizing that cybersecurity is not treated as an afterthought or as a marketing ploy. Instead, it should result in cybersecurity vigilance at all levels of the product life cycle, treating cybersecurity incidents as imminent events and planning ahead to respond to them. To achieve this, employees must be aware that all products have

vulnerabilities and are at risk of compromise. Mentoring by experienced cybersecurity engineers is also essential. This allows employees to receive guidance and learn best practices, which can be incorporated into their work. An open exchange of ideas and questions is encouraged to create a collaborative culture. Consequently, employees will understand that it is their responsibility to be aware of and incorporate cybersecurity into their designs. This can be achieved by integrating cybersecurity awareness into existing processes and forums, as appropriate. .

3. **Develop a continuous learning environment**: The organization should make investments in continuous education, while encouraging participation in industry cybersecurity bodies (for example, AutoISAC), and monitoring various security channels (including the dark web) in anticipation of cybersecurity events. Along the lines of information sharing is the institution of rules and processes for vulnerability disclosure. The organization must have a policy regarding the timeliness of when vulnerabilities are disclosed, who can perform the disclosure, the communication channels for such disclosures, and how to handle sensitive information. Such processes must be aligned across various departments to prevent common mishaps such as disclosing vulnerabilities on behalf of suppliers who did not yet authorize such disclosure, or waiting too long before informing customers about critical vulnerabilities that will impact their products.

4. **Ensure optimum tooling**: Providing the right tooling is essential to achieve wide acceptance among the engineering staff. If, for example, the toolchain is cumbersome and difficult to deploy, engineers will choose to bypass the process or come up with shortcuts that will defeat the original intent. Additionally, incorporating lessons from vulnerabilities in previous products into new and future products is recommended as people are bound to repeat the mistakes of the past.

An essential part of integrating the cybersecurity process at the organization level is extending the supporting systems so that they include security aspects. We'll look at this next by considering the impact on management systems.

Management systems

Management systems are enablers for cybersecurity management. Companies that do not have such systems will find it difficult to achieve the requirements of ISO21434, especially when submitting for a process audit. The following are mandatory management systems that must be adapted to incorporate cybersecurity.

Quality management

As mentioned in *Chapter 4*, quality management is a prerequisite to cybersecurity management. A **quality management system (QMS)** ensures that product development is carried out in a controlled and measurable fashion which naturally helps in reducing defects that can turn into vulnerabilities. Not only is the QMS needed, but the right level of quality maturity is essential to meet the expectations of the secure engineering process. For example, if the QMS allows creating software without the need for producing requirements or design artifacts, then it would not be suitable for cybersecurity management as those are prerequisites for producing the product development work products such as cybersecurity specifications. Moreover, quality management can help enforce quality gates by requiring that a minimum set of cybersecurity work products be available before passing the quality gate. Including cybersecurity metrics alongside quality metrics can draw a more comprehensive view of the system's maturity and allow management to prioritize problem resolution by weighing cost-benefit trade-offs.

Configuration management

A configuration management system ensures that work products and design artifacts are stored in a traceable and reproducible manner. This is done by controlling the version, date, and ownership information of each work product so that it is possible to view the change history. During a cybersecurity product assessment, it is expected that all security work products are versioned and traceable.

Requirements management

The primary objective of requirements management is twofold:

- Firstly, to ensure that requirements are accurately defined in terms of their attributes and characteristics

- Secondly, to maintain consistency in managing those requirements throughout the life cycle of a system

The requirements management system enables the proper classification of requirements as security requirements and establishes traceability to other work products. This includes tracing functional security requirements to more refined technical security requirements, architectural elements, and interfaces, as well as test specifications.

Change management

The objective of **change management** is to ensure that changes made to a system or a product are systematically analyzed, controlled, monitored, implemented, and documented throughout the product life cycle. During this analysis, impacts on cost, project schedule, and required resources are analyzed. Typically, a **Change Control Board** (**CCB**) is expected to weigh these factors before accepting or rejecting the change. From a cybersecurity angle, each feature or change request has the potential to upset the security posture of the system. One of the main job roles of cybersecurity engineers is to continuously monitor change requests to ensure they are not introducing a risk that will be hard to mitigate after the feature is accepted. Therefore, the CCB must evaluate the impacts of cybersecurity and include cybersecurity engineers in the decision-making and sign-off processes to avoid accepting changes that expose the product to significant security risks. Maintaining a change history log is an important feature of any change management system to ensure change requests capture the origin of the change, including the date, reason for the requested change, and a description of the impact analysis.

Documentation management

Cybersecurity plans, manuals, cases, and more need to be managed in a documentation management system that can trace document versions, document owners, intended audience, and so on. The documentation management system must support document reviews and tracking of document changes. Additionally, documents should be classified based on security criticality to enforce data-sharing policies.

Intersection of cybersecurity with other disciplines

Automotive cybersecurity crosses paths with several organization-level disciplines such as the ISMS, functional safety, and quality management. Defining processes and communication channels between these separate groups helps you avoid conflicts and oversights. For example, the cybersecurity management system will rely on the ISMS to provide evidence that infrastructure tools are secure against intrusion and security breaches. Additionally, there can be scenarios in which the CSMS wants to leverage ISMS procedures to gain evidence that the cloud and backend services are protected. Instituting and encouraging communication between these departments prevents duplication of work and lengthy delays in collecting the required information, such as during an audit. Similarly, functional safety processes have significant overlaps with the CSMS, such as during the concept, product development, and testing phases. Establishing periodic meetings between safety and security experts to identify overlaps, conflicts, and synergies is crucial to prevent a major rework when conflicts are found late in the development life cycle.

> **Note**
> The next chapter is dedicated to safety and security overlap. For now, be aware that your process must not overlook this area.

Tool management

Tools are used in every aspect of the product engineering life cycle. Whether it is a tool to model the system design, configure the software, or generate signed binaries and flash them in the field, each tool carries the potential to introduce cybersecurity risk for the product. For example, a third-party tool that is used for code signing may contain a vulnerability that results in injecting malicious code into software binaries before applying the digital signature. In other cases, the tool itself may be compromised due to the usage of vulnerable open source code, making it a launch pad for more nefarious attacks on the product.

To manage the risk related to tools, first, a process for classifying tools as cybersecurity-relevant is needed to account for all tools that should be under cybersecurity management. For each such tool, a process is needed to evaluate the tool's security level, enable security controls specified by the tool vendor, and apply any missing controls to mitigate risks identified during the tool's security evaluation. Maintaining a database of all cybersecurity-relevant tools is an essential step so that you can track tool-related vulnerability reports to ensure that the latest patches are deployed to across all teams using the tools. Evidence of tool management can be captured through a report that shows that all cybersecurity-relevant tools have been correctly identified and that measures are in place to track and maintain the security of these tools.

To show compliance with clause 5, all work products in *Table 5.1* must be completed. This will be necessary during a cybersecurity audit that measures the compliance and effectiveness of cybersecurity processes and determines whether procedures are in place for continuous improvement. The results are captured in the audit report, also known as *WP-05-05*:

Standard Section	Work Products in Scope
5.4.1 Cybersecurity governance	[WP-05-01] Cybersecurity policy, rules, and processes
5.4.2 Cybersecurity culture	[WP-05-01] Cybersecurity policy, rules, and processes [WP-05-02] Evidence of competence management, awareness management, and continuous improvement
5.4.3 Information sharing	[WP-05-01] Cybersecurity policy, rules, and processes
5.4.4 Management systems	[WP-05-03] Evidence of the organization's management systems
5.4.5 Tool management	[WP-05-04] Evidence of tool management
5.4.6 Information security management	[WP-05-03] Evidence of the organization's management systems
5.4.7 Organization cybersecurity audit	[WP-05-05] Organizational cybersecurity audit report

Table 5.1 – Work products in scope for the organizational management clause, as defined by ISO 21434

Now that we have seen the organizational aspects of automotive cybersecurity, we are ready to explore how the cybersecurity standard impacts each phase of the product engineering life cycle, starting with the planning phase.

Planning

It may sound trivial, but preparing a cybersecurity plan is essential to guide teams on the overall required work that must be executed before the product is considered ready for release. The cybersecurity plan covers assigning cybersecurity roles and responsibilities, cross-relations to the project and safety plans, the cybersecurity activities that must be completed, tailoring any activities, rationale for reuse, and handling off-the-shelf components, as well as components out of context. Teams can leverage existing project plans and simply extend them to account for cybersecurity activities. Alternatively, a dedicated cybersecurity plan can be prepared to capture the cybersecurity activities. ISO/SAE 21434 requires that at least the concept phase, product development phase, validation phase, and **Threat Analysis and Risk Assessment (TARA)** activities are described in the cybersecurity plan. However, it can be useful to cover additional aspects, such as planning cybersecurity assessments and release activities.

> **Note**
>
> The TARA activity, as well as other cybersecurity activities relating to the concept, product development, and validation phases, will be described in detail throughout this chapter.

As shown in *Figure 5.1*, the cybersecurity plan is an input for preparing the cybersecurity case. By examining the cybersecurity plan, the assessment team can judge whether the evidence compiled in the cybersecurity case conforms with the cybersecurity plan and whether any gaps exist between the two.

For each cybersecurity activity, the following aspects must be covered in the plan:

- The objective of the cybersecurity activity.

- The assigned resources that shall execute, review, and approve the activity.

- The required inputs to perform the activity. For example, cybersecurity validation requires that the cybersecurity goals have been defined and are available from the concept phase.

- Tailoring the activity based on the project's needs.

- Reuse arguments regarding whether the activity can leverage prior work.

- The expected output of the activity – for example, validation test reports.

Defining the objective of the activity ensures that team members who are tasked with executing the plan are aware of what needs to be performed to consider the activity complete. Assigning roles and responsibilities helps prevent miscommunication across teams on who will do what, and whom to ask for the right level of approvals to mark the activity done. It is recommended that roles and responsibilities be predefined in a project-level resource assignment sheet that is referenced from the cybersecurity plan so that it is easy to look up the names and roles of resources. Evidence of competence for each role can be found in the resource assignment management document, which will be handy when you're answering the assessor's questions on whether the positions have been filled with the right personnel.

> **Note**
>
> A project-specific resource assignment management document is typically used to capture all the roles required for a given project, the individuals that have been assigned to each role, and evidence that the assigned person has sufficient skills to perform the role's functions.

The plan can also include tailoring sections for each activity where applicable. A project team may argue that certain activities are not fully applicable and thereby can either be completely or partially tailored. For example, an argument for excluding cybersecurity validation testing can be provided if the product is a component that is not directly integrated at the vehicle level, making it impossible for the product supplier to validate the cybersecurity goals. In that case, the cybersecurity plan describes what portions of the activity have been tailored and why.

Since most projects do not start from scratch, in many cases, reusing components makes it possible to reuse their respective cybersecurity work products if the conditions of reuse are met. To determine that reuse is possible, a reuse analysis is either documented within the cybersecurity plan or as a standalone document that's referred to by the cybersecurity plan. The analysis should enumerate components that have been reused from a previous product version, along with a characterization of the conditions for reuse – for example, whether the component is being reused without any modification, whether the operational environment in which the component is integrated is still the same, or whether the assumptions under which it was initially designed are still valid. Depending on the answers to such questions, an argument can be made for reusing some or all of the cybersecurity work products of the component. For example, a library that has been integrated with a new microcontroller under the same vehicle environment and use cases can reuse the same security requirements and design artifacts but may require security tests to be re-executed to ensure the library still achieves its security requirements on the new target. In reality, most reuse cases involve a change, resulting in the cybersecurity work products being updated. Typically, a TARA must be performed to ensure that additional cybersecurity risks can still be addressed by existing security work products, and if not, that the additional work has been accounted for.

Finally, a cybersecurity activity must document the expected output, along with any specific instructions on how teams shall prepare this output. For example, when defining the plan for preparing the cybersecurity concept, the output should capture the format in which the concept is captured, and where it will be stored.

In addition to planning cybersecurity activities for the product under development, the plan must consider externally supplied components that are in the scope of integration with the product. Such components come in two types: off-the-shelf and **components developed out of context (CooC)**.

The plan must account for all such components and specify the cybersecurity activities needed to mitigate additional risks that are introduced by the use of these components. As shown in *Table 5.2*, all planning-related cybersecurity activities are covered by a single work product – the cybersecurity plan:

Standard Section	Work Products in Scope
6.4.1 Cybersecurity responsibilities	[WP-06-01] Cybersecurity plan
6.4.2 Cybersecurity planning	[WP-06-01] Cybersecurity plan
6.4.3 Tailoring	[WP-06-01] Cybersecurity plan
6.4.4 Reuse	[WP-06-01] Cybersecurity plan

Table 5.2 – Work products in scope for the cybersecurity plan

In the next section, we'll learn how to address risks introduced by third-party components by following the acquisition and supplier management processes.

Acquisition and integration of supplier components

You've started planning project and cybersecurity activities and in the process of doing so, you've identified several components that you must source for your project. You have two choices: use an off-the-shelf component that has been developed for a wide range of use cases without consideration of your exact product or work with a third party on developing or adapting an existing component to fit your product needs. In both cases, you want to demonstrate that your integrated product is still compliant with ISO/SAE 21434, regardless of the security maturity level of such components. By integrating a new component, you are essentially exposed to the inherited cybersecurity risks of that component. To address those risks, you have to achieve the following objectives:

- Identify ISO/SAE 21434 compliance gaps in the component

- Assess whether the component is capable of fulfilling your allocated cybersecurity requirements

- Validate the assumptions of intended use, external interfaces, and the operational environment, as well as any risks that were transferred or accepted by the component supplier

In terms of process gaps, you can seek the assistance of the supplier to provide evidence of process compliance. In terms of assessing the suitability of the component for your intended use, you must first perform a **TARA** to identify risks and the corresponding cybersecurity mitigations that must be fulfilled by the component.

> **Note**
>
> The TARA approach identifies assets managed or influenced by the component, as well as potential threats impacting those assets. By performing the TARA, we can derive cybersecurity requirements that the component must fulfill and determine if the component is capable of achieving them. More details about TARA methods will be provided in the *Item-level concept* section.

For example, assume that you need to integrate an off-the-shelf microcontroller into your secure gateway's **electronic control unit** (ECU), which requires the usage of cryptographic accelerators and a key store to handle the in-vehicle communication security requirements. If the **microcontroller unit** (MCU) does not support a **hardware-protected security environment** (HPSE) or the capability to manage keys, then it should not be considered for integration with the smart gateway. If the MCU does support an HPSE, then you can engage with the component supplier to further confirm that it can fulfill your process-level expectations. Similarly, if you are planning to integrate a CooC, you must confirm that in addition to the ability of the component to fulfill your requirements, the assumptions of use considered during the component development are acceptable for you. If not, additional security countermeasures are needed in the integrating product to bridge those gaps. To facilitate the communication with suppliers and the distribution of roles regarding shared cybersecurity activities, ISO/SAE 21434 defines a process for supplier selection and sharing distributed activities through the **Cybersecurity Interface Agreement** (**CSIA**). This is best integrated into existing processes that govern acquisition and supplier management.

Supplier capability assessment and the role of the CSIA

ISO/SAE 21434 expects that the organization institutes a process for evaluating the cybersecurity capabilities of suppliers during supplier selection before they are added to an approved supplier list. This ensures that only suppliers who are capable of meeting process-level security requirements set forth by the organization can be considered for **requests for quotations** (**RFQs**). Supplier capability assessment can be carried out through a questionnaire that scores the supplier's security maturity in areas such as information management systems security and product security. While the standard does not specify a work product for capturing evidence of supplier capability, it is good practice to compile documentation that tracks each supplier's cybersecurity capability through a scoring system. Suppliers with significant gaps should be actively monitored to ensure they are taking measures to close such gaps. Suppliers that refuse or fail to address cybersecurity findings should be excluded from future bids as a way to eliminate supply chain risks.

Once a supplier has been approved for responding to RFQs, it is recommended to establish a cybersecurity interface agreement that delineates responsibilities between the customer and the supplier. Sharing cybersecurity goals and requirements at the RFQ phase is essential to help the suppliers assess whether they can achieve these requirements and whether they need to adjust their costs to account for additional work. In some cases, the supplier may not be planning for ISO/SAE 21434 compliance and, as such, might push back on the need to fill a CSIA. It is in those cases that a CSIA is useful to identify gaps in the supplier's deliverables and help the project team plan for addressing these gaps by performing cybersecurity activities. For example, the project team may plan for additional security testing or may decide to perform a TARA on the supplied component to address unmitigated risks by the supplier.

Aspects such as who will perform each cybersecurity work product, whether the results can be shared and in which form, the length of the cybersecurity support period, the frequency of sharing information such as vulnerability reports, **Software Bill of Materials** (**SBOM**) sharing, assessment expectations and the level of detail of each deliverable are all captured in the CSIA. The CSIA must be treated like a legally binding contract to ensure that a supplier will not renege on prior commitments. This agreement must be frequently consulted when milestones are reached to ensure that the information exchange is taking place regarding cybersecurity deliverables. It is common for suppliers to resist sharing detailed work products such as the TARA documents and prefer instead to share the results in the form of a summary. It is up to the vendor and supplier to negotiate the adequate level of details to be shared while considering the legitimate concerns of intellectual property protection against the need to verify the correctness and rigor applied while preparing the work products. In these cases, relying on an external assessment to prove compliance with the standard can be useful in addressing some of those concerns:

Standard Section	Work Products in Scope
6.4.5 Component out-of-context	[WP-06-01] Cybersecurity plan
6.4.6 Off-the-shelf-component	[WP-06-01] Cybersecurity plan
7.4.1 Supplier capability	No work product, but requirements apply
7.4.2 Request for quotation	No work product, but requirements apply
7.4.3 Alignment of responsibilities	[WP-07-01] Cybersecurity interface agreement

Table 5.3 – Work products in scope for supplier management and distributed cybersecurity activities

Now that we have understood the cybersecurity planning and supplier management activities, it is time to transition into the first phase of cybersecurity product engineering, namely, the concept phase.

The concept phase

You are in the concept phase if you are developing a new vehicle function in an item or a single component out of context and need to determine the cybersecurity goals and requirements that must be fulfilled by your item or component. As shown in *Figure 5.3*, you are on the top left-hand side of the V-development cycle and your objective is to identify and treat the risks related to your system:

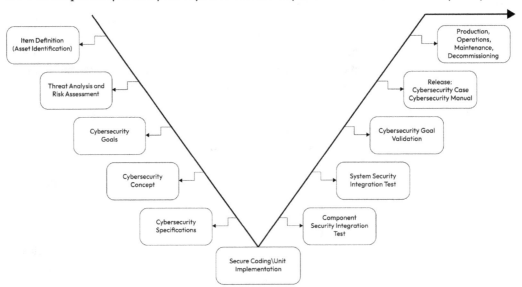

Figure 5.3 – V diagram with a security overlay

To achieve this objective, you must rely on the TARA methods shown in *Figure 5.1*. In practice, this process is initiated whenever a new security-relevant feature is introduced into the system to ensure that any new cybersecurity risk is understood and the overall cybersecurity concept is adapted to handle this new risk. This is known as the **secure by design approach** and it promises to reduce the likelihood of expensive rework when issues are discovered late in the product life cycle.

Before delving into the details of this section, you are encouraged to refer to *section 3* of the *ISO/SAE 21434* standard for a refresher on terms and definitions.

Item-level concept

The item is simply the set of ECUs, sensors, actuators, and network channels that work together to achieve a function at the vehicle level. The practice of performing analysis at the item level is inherited from the functional safety standard, which also requires vehicle functions to be partitioned into items to identify hazards and safety goals. In cybersecurity, the item definition must expose the operational environment and its external interfaces, which is critical for identifying threat sources. To properly capture the item definition, you must identify the vehicle functions that are in the scope of the analysis, then draw the item boundary around the components that participate in achieving that vehicle function, making sure to include external interfaces at the vehicle boundary. Providing a correct description of the item boundary and operational environment is a critical step to identify assets that must be protected and the threats that are in the scope of those assets. Overexpanding the item boundary will result in the inclusion of assets that may belong to a different item, resulting in duplicate threat analysis. On the other hand, choosing an item boundary that is too restrictive will result in excluding assets that are relevant to the threat analysis activity. Let's look at an example of an item that achieves SAE Level 3 autonomous driving functions such as **automatic emergency braking (AEB)**. To perform the AEB function, the item must process vehicle sensor data, fuse the sensor data, and provide actuation commands over the vehicle network to the braking ECU:

Standard Section	Work Products in Scope
9.3 Item definition	[WP-09-01] Item definition
9.4 Cybersecurity goals	[WP-09-02] TARA
	[WP-09-03] Cybersecurity goals
	[WP-09-04] Cybersecurity claims
	[WP-09-05] Verification report for cybersecurity goals
9.5 Cybersecurity concept	[WP-09-06] Cybersecurity concept
	[WP-09-07] Verification report of cybersecurity concept

Table 5.4 – Concept phase work products

The first step is to determine the item boundary. We will call this the ADAS system boundary, as shown in *Figure 5.4*. All the components that are required to fulfill the AEB function are within the item boundary, starting with the **system on chip (SoC)**, which executes the AEB sensing, control, and actuation algorithms, and the memory storage unit, which stores the AEB software, firmware, and machine learning models, the various sensors and their data, and the communication channels required to transmit the sensing and actuation data. A microcontroller that acts as a safety monitor and fail-over system is included as it ensures that our AEB function is available, even if the SoC experiences a critical fault. The MCU also provides in-vehicle communication support to send and receive vehicle state data. Note that we also include the backend services because the system can report emergency braking events to a telemetry service through its Wi-Fi and cellular channels:

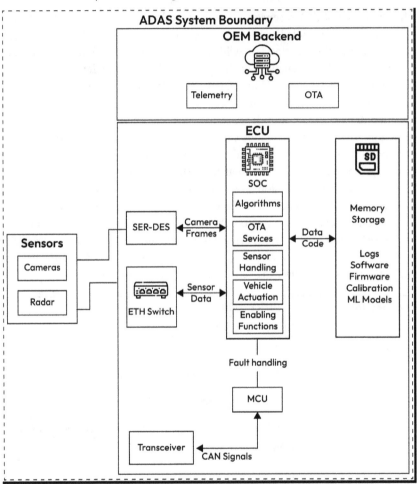

Figure 5.4 – Item definition without the full operational environment

Next, we need to include the operational environment, which contains components that are directly interfaced with our item and can affect the security of the item. Note that the security analysis must account for all vehicle interfaces that make up the vehicle attack surface, even if they are not safety-relevant. The emphasis on analyzing external interfaces of the item stems from the fact that threats originate from outside the vehicle through malicious attacks, while hazards (in the scope of functional safety) originate from inside the vehicle due to system failures. Let's see how adding the operational environment extends the item definition:

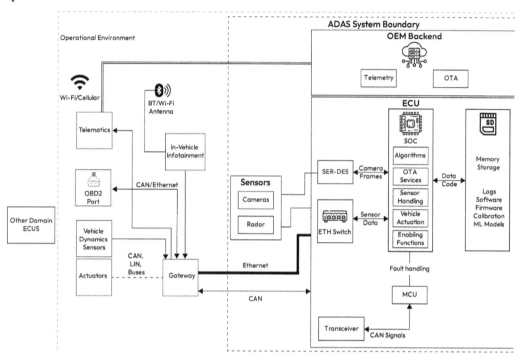

Figure 5.5 – Item definition showing the operational environment

To support our AEB function and report the emergency braking event to the backend, we must include the central gateway, which allows the CAN, LIN, and Ethernet frames to be sent and received to/from the vehicle side; this includes the actuators and vehicle dynamics sensors. The telematics unit is included to show how telemetry data is transmitted to the backend over the Wi-Fi and cellular link. The OBD2 port is shown as it enables UDS-based flash programming of the ADAS SoC. Other ECUs that do not interact with the AEB function are denoted in the figure as outside the operational environment and are included simply to signify that they are intentionally being excluded.

To improve the analysis, a final step is to expose any additional external interfaces to the item that may or may not be relevant to the item's functionality but would be relevant for threat analysis. For example, the **in-vehicle infotainment (IVI)** system is shown as it interfaces with Bluetooth and Wi-Fi, and it is connected to the central gateway ECU. Including this interface in the item definition will help us later as we try to identify threats and attack paths that can impact the assets in the scope of this item.

Once you are satisfied with the item definition, and assuming that all the stakeholders have reviewed and approved your scope of analysis, it is now time to move on to preparing the TARA:

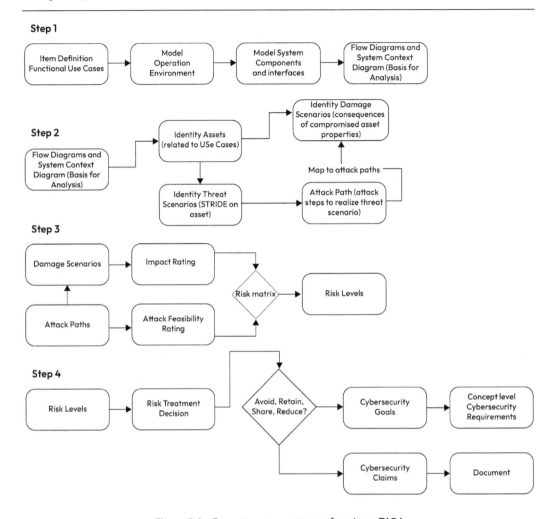

Figure 5.6 – Four-step process to performing a TARA

As shown in *Figure 5.6*, there are four main steps to performing the TARA in compliance with ISO/SAE 21434:

> **Note**
>
> In this chapter, we will briefly describe each step and leave the full details for *Chapter 7* where we will focus on optimizing the approach and incorporating aspects of functional safety.

1. *Step 1* was already covered by defining the item; however, additionally, we collect data flow diagrams that can describe how the system interacts with the operational environment to aid in identifying threats and attack paths.

2. In *Step 2*, we use the diagrams describing the item, the context, and its hardware and software components to identify objects of value as assets. By examining the effects of compromising the cybersecurity properties of these assets, we can determine the adverse consequences at the vehicle level, also known as damage scenarios.

    Using these assets, we can apply a threat modeling framework such as STRIDE to enumerate threats that impact the assets. Each threat scenario is further expanded into a list of attack steps that must be carried out to realize the threat. The impact of each attack path is mapped to a damage scenario.

3. With all assets identified, threats enumerated, and attack paths defined and mapped to damage scenarios, it is now possible to assess the attack feasibility and damage impacts. Thus, in *Step 3*, damage scenarios are given an impact rating based on the impacts on safety, vehicle operation, financial damage, and user privacy, while attack paths are given an attack feasibility rating based on attack parameters such as elapsed time, expertise needed, knowledge about the item or component, a window of opportunity to mount the attack, and equipment needed. With the help of a risk management framework, the impact rating and attack feasibility are transformed to a risk value between 1 and 5.

4. In *Step 4*, all risk values are analyzed to determine the risk treatment decisions. Risks can either be avoided by eliminating the source of the risk (for example, by modifying the system architecture), reducing the risk by defining cybersecurity controls, retaining the risk by providing a rationale for risk acceptance, or sharing the risk by transferring it to another party such as the system integrator or buying cybersecurity insurance. Risks that have been reduced result in the creation of a cybersecurity goal, while risks that have been retained or shared result in a cybersecurity claim. The cybersecurity goals are further refined into system-level cybersecurity requirements while the cybersecurity claims articulate why retaining or sharing the risk is acceptable.

    The cybersecurity goal is the highest level of abstraction of a cybersecurity requirement. It simply states the objective of what asset properties need protection.

Assuming that our ADAS system has been adequately analyzed, we expect to produce a set of cybersecurity goals that must be achieved to ensure that the ADAS system is free from unreasonable risks. Some example goals are shown here:

```
1- The ADAS system shall protect the integrity of software,
calibration and ML models against physical and logical threats
2- The ADAS system shall protect the integrity and authenticity of
sensor communication data received over CAN and Ethernet against
physical and network threats
```

It is possible to write goals by incorporating the vehicle function directly:

```
The ADAS system shall prevent the loss of AEB function caused by
network or physical threats.
```

While this may technically be a valid cybersecurity goal, it may result in many redundant goals as the system has many functions that will be exposed to the same threats. Therefore, we prefer the asset-based goal definition.

Another output of the concept phase is the definition of cybersecurity claims. The latter is simply a statement about the rationale behind retaining or sharing a risk. The statement must be documented to allow the integrator of the component to validate such statements. For example, the ADAS system owner may have decided to accept the risk that the heartbeat message between the SoC and the MCU is exposed to physical tampering, which can result in the unnecessary shutdown of the ADAS system.

This results in the following claim:

```
The ADAS system accepts the risk of 'physical tampering of the
heartbeat signal (between the SoC and MCU)' due to the localized
impact of such an attack and the low feasibility of performing the
attack while the vehicle is in motion. The user is advised to apply
tamper resistant enclosures to reduce the likelihood of this attack.
```

Following the creation of the cybersecurity goals and claims, a review is necessary to verify the correctness and completeness of the TARA. This is done by inspecting the asset coverage of the item, the correctness of the damage scenarios in exposing the consequences to the vehicle, the breadth of coverage of the threat scenarios, and the attack path detail levels to enable attack feasibility ratings to be evaluated. The reviewer can also check whether impact ratings have been captured reasonably to cover the impacted stakeholders and whether the attack feasibility ratings follow the conventions set forth by ISO/SAE 21434. Finally, the correctness of the risk treatment decisions must be checked to ensure that risks that need to be reduced have been assigned valid cybersecurity goals and cybersecurity claims have been raised where applicable. Since a typical TARA can have tens if not hundreds of threats and attack paths, it is important to verify the consistency of all the cybersecurity goals and claims when considered together.

Cybersecurity concept

Now that you've finished the TARA and got it reviewed and approved, it is time to articulate the security problem you are trying to solve and the overall cybersecurity strategy for doing so. The problem can be defined by stating the item functions in scope, including the system context diagram, system-level assets that require protection, and the risks that were considered for reduction or elimination during the TARA. On the other hand, the strategy for solving the problem is defined through the specification of cybersecurity controls and requirements and allocating them to the item and its components. Establishing traceability between the controls, requirements, and cybersecurity goals is essential to demonstrate that goals have been adequately covered.

When selecting cybersecurity controls, it is recommended to consider the following categories:

- **Protection**
- **Detection**
- **Recovery**
- **Logging**

In our example system, the goal of **protecting** the software binaries in media storage can be realized by applying controls that prevent unauthorized binaries replacement by using secure update mechanisms and enforcing strong access controls for flash programming tools such as UDS clients. If an attacker succeeds in tampering with the binaries, such tampering must be **detected** by the usage of secure boot mechanisms during startup. Controls for **recovering** the system software may also be prescribed to ensure the system's availability is protected – for example, by requiring the usage of backup storage partitions that can be booted in case one partition fails to boot. Finally, controls for **logging** security anomalies can be prescribed to allow security events to be analyzed and identified after the system has been deployed in production. Each control can be further refined through the definition of system-level cybersecurity requirements that capture the intended system behavior in response to each threat scenario that must be mitigated. Here, you will find that the attack paths in the TARA can be quite useful to help derive cybersecurity requirements as your objective is essentially to prevent or at least significantly reduce the likelihood of those attacks. In some cases, the cybersecurity requirements are allocated to components within the operational environment outside the item boundary. Such requirements must be documented and shared with the system integrator, who must ensure that the requirements are fulfilled. Coming back to our example, enforcing access control mechanisms on the diagnostic client will produce an operational environment requirement for the client to support a **public key infrastructure** (**PKI**)-based routine for authenticating itself to the ADAS system. This requirement would require both the ADAS system provider and the diagnostic client owner to agree on a scheme for authenticating the client before enabling flash programming. The ISO/SAE 21434 standard requires that the cybersecurity concept be verified to ensure the correctness and completeness of the cybersecurity requirements and controls in fulfilling the cybersecurity goals.

The reader of the cybersecurity concept should be convinced that you have produced a reasonable cybersecurity strategy that is sufficient to guide the rest of the product design. As such, the cybersecurity concept serves as the highest level of functional security requirements since it acts as the basis for deriving component-level security controls and requirements by the project teams. All the teams must be able to refer back to the cybersecurity concept to understand which threat types must be considered as they develop their refined components. This will be explored in more detail in the *Design and implementation* section.

Implications to component-level development

ISO/SAE 21434 presents the concept phase from the perspective of an item at the vehicle level. It provides a hint (in requirement *RQ-09-01, Note 6*) that developing a component out of context can be based on an assumed or generic item, along with assumptions on the operational environment and external interfaces. Applying the concept phase to a component is less obvious than the item, so we will walk through an example to clarify the differences.

In our ADAS item shown in *Figure 5.4*, several components are developed out of context, such as the Ethernet switch, the MCU software monitoring the SoC AEB function, and the camera sensor, which feeds the ADAS system with camera frames. If you are developing any of these components, you cannot simply explore every possible item in which your component can be integrated, so you must make some assumptions about the item in which your component will be used, its operational environment, and the likely interfaces that will exist. Component suppliers are encouraged to assume the most hostile environment before preparing their cybersecurity concept. Even though you may not be able to mitigate or eliminate all the threats of that environment as a component supplier, you will at least be able to document the cybersecurity requirements that the operational environment must fulfill to enable the secure usage of your component. Take, for example, the camera sensor as a component. If you assume the camera sensor is well isolated from the rest of the vehicle and has a very small attack surface, you may develop a sensor with no cybersecurity controls to mitigate threats such as camera frame spoofing, tampering, or replay. For customers who want to use the camera sensor in an environment where camera sensors can easily be replaced, such a sensor will not be suitable for use and the customer may be forced to switch to a different sensor. On the other hand, assuming a hostile environment will help you, as a sensor supplier, to account for all threats in which camera frames may be intercepted by a **man-in-the-middle** (**MiTM**) attack to fake, tamper with, or replay those frames. As such, the cybersecurity concept of that sensor would provide adequate cybersecurity controls to protect the sensor's assets.

Once the assumed context has been captured, it is possible to prepare an assumed item to facilitate the security analysis. While the activity may seem redundant to what the OEM has done, in this case, the focus of the TARA is on the component itself. In other words, while performing the TARA, you want to zoom into your component interfaces to ensure that you are producing actionable cybersecurity goals and cybersecurity requirements for your component. This approach can be scaled to any component supplier, whether they're providing a software stack in an embedded system or an MCU that can be used in many use cases. To help enrich the threat analysis of components that are far removed from the item boundary, it is recommended to consider common weaknesses that are in scope for your component. By simply considering all applicable weaknesses, it is possible to derive meaningful threats and attack paths, as well as reverse-engineer the component assets that require protection. Take, for example, an MCU supplier who must prepare a TARA. In addition to capturing common security-relevant use cases to prepare a top-down threat analysis, the supplier can account for weaknesses in a bottom-up fashion, such as poor access control for JTAG ports, improper locking of embedded flash memory commands, weak memory management mechanisms for isolating mixed-criticality software, and a lack of IP block-level isolation controls. These can each produce a set of threats that can be defined by considering how such weaknesses are exploited. The result is a more complete TARA that ensures the component is delivered with adequate security rigor.

Now that we have covered the expectations of the concept phase both for an item and a component developed out of context, it is time to turn to the product development phase, where the results of the concept phase are applied to both the design and implementation.

Design and implementation

Revisiting the V-diagram from *Figure 5.3*, we can see that requirements from the cybersecurity concept are further refined into cybersecurity specifications, which are allocated to the architecture and its sub-components. The primary objective of the cybersecurity specifications is to ensure that the architecture fulfills cybersecurity requirements from the higher level (such as the concept or parent components). Here, existing architectural specifications may be leveraged to satisfy this work product by simply providing traceability to the parent cybersecurity requirements.

Next, you must refine the high-level security requirements and architectural details into component-level security requirements and architectural fragments. The set of security requirements and architectural fragments at the component level comprise the component cybersecurity specification. Let's assume that you are developing software that provides key management services to the rest of the software application. The cybersecurity concept will contain requirements regarding cryptographic key protection against illegal access and exfiltration. The cybersecurity specification must derive security requirements that detail exact mechanisms to fulfill these requirements, such as using discretionary access controls and enabling hardware countermeasures to side-channel attacks. Furthermore, the component architecture should at least provide a security overlay that shows how these requirements are satisfied through the architecture. There are two main impacts to the architecture when considering cybersecurity. For security requirements that result in new system functionalities, there can be new architectural elements and interfaces describing them. For example, a security requirement that mandates the use of MACsec to protect the integrity and confidentiality of Ethernet frames will result in new sequence diagrams, and static architecture diagrams that outline how MACsec is supported in software and hardware. Rather than capture these details in a standalone architecture document, it is preferred to integrate these fragments with the common system architecture documents to ease the traceability and cross-links with other supporting functionalities from the architecture. In some cases, the security requirements only constrain existing functionalities. For example, a security requirement may specify that all processes drop root privilege before they can transition from initialization to operational mode. This can be expressed in the architecture by first identifying the architectural elements and interfaces that describe how processes are launched and adding the constraints regarding how root privileges are dropped. The result is a security overlay that augments existing architectural diagrams.

Post-development requirements

As part of deriving security requirements, several requirements will emerge that will impact the component integrator. These are captured as post-development requirements that inform the user on how to install, initialize, or operate the component securely.

These requirements can be captured as security procedures so that you can apply cybersecurity controls after the component has been deployed. This includes procedures for securely setting up, initializing, producing, and decommissioning the system. Examples include procedures for provisioning cryptographic keys in the factory, burning fuses to transition the chip into a secure life cycle state, locking debug ports, and clearing private data before transitioning the device into a decommissioned state. Note that these procedures must be tagged for sharing with the system integrator through a customer-facing document such as a cybersecurity manual.

Configuration and calibration

The required configuration and calibration settings associated with the component related to enabling cybersecurity controls or fulfilling cybersecurity requirements must also be documented in the cybersecurity specifications – for example, defining the configuration options for enforcing secure boot once the chip has transitioned to a specific life cycle state.

Depending on the complexity of the system, cybersecurity specifications may be refined at multiple layers of the design until they reach the unit level to ensure that the security behavior has been adequately specified to enable unit implementation.

Weakness analysis

While the cybersecurity specification is being developed and the architecture starts taking shape, it is expected that new risks will emerge. Simply put, the introduction of cybersecurity controls adds new assets to the system, which, in turn, are exposed to new threats that may not have been considered in the system-level TARA. It is recommended that a residual risk analysis is prepared to examine threats that can violate cybersecurity requirements from the higher level. This results in an iterative process for treating residual risk until the risk level has reached an acceptable level.

For example, while attempting to protect an asset in persistent storage against tampering, you decide to derive a new key that is dedicated to producing an HMAC (*keyed-hash message authentication code*) of the storage record. But that key may be abused by an unauthorized application that can use the key to produce a new HMAC and write it along with the tampered storage record. This risk will need to be mitigated by applying additional security controls, such as restricting the key's usage to a single owner through a software-based access control mechanism. This process of analyzing residual threats and refining security requirements can be referred to as a design-level TARA, or a residual risk assessment. While ISO/SAE 21434 does not mandate that the TARA gets repeated in each layer of the design, it is good practice to account for residual risk through an iterative TARA process that further decomposes threats from the system level into the component and sub-component level. This ensures that as the design evolves, the high-level cybersecurity goals remain satisfied.

An alternative to a full-blown design TARA would be architectural weakness analysis. ISO/SAE 21434 makes this type of analysis a requirement and points to attack path analysis as one way to perform it. Depending on the criticality of the component, it may be sufficient to rely on common weakness checklists that are consulted with the help of a security expert to ensure that best practices have been followed and known weaknesses have been eliminated.

> **Reminder**
>
> In *Chapter 3*, we explored threats and vulnerabilities at all layers of the vehicle. Being aware of common weaknesses is an important prerequisite to addressing vulnerabilities in a real design.

The vulnerability analysis process that is normally employed when an incident is reported can also be used to analyze potential weaknesses during the design phase. For example, a weakness in handling update software authentication can be analyzed to identify attack paths by which the weakness is exploited. If a viable attack path is identified, the weakness should be treated as a vulnerability and a CVSS score can be calculated to determine the priority of the fix. The weakness can be eliminated by revising the architecture or introducing a new countermeasure.

Unit implementation

The product development section of the ISO standard also points to the need to apply security design principles and secure coding guidelines. The former can be prepared with the help of well-established trusted design principles, which were introduced in *Chapter 2*. Principles such as performing input validation, input sanitization, applying least privilege, and domain separation must be considered whenever new design choices are being made. To support the secure unit implementation, static code analysis tools and secure code reviews must be employed. If you are developing hardware components, information flow analysis, and formal verification tools can be leveraged to eliminate weaknesses in which a hardware security asset can be exposed under specific circumstances.

With the design and implementation covered, it is time to turn to the cybersecurity activities that are performed during the test phase to verify that our security requirements have been fulfilled and that our implementation is free from security vulnerabilities.

Verification testing

Cybersecurity tests that cover all hardware and software cybersecurity requirements are necessary to determine if the hardware and software design matches the cybersecurity specifications. Traceability between security requirements and security test cases is an essential step to ensure that the security measures are implemented as intended.

Similarly, formal verification techniques can be employed to verify that a specific hardware module can achieve its security objectives. At the unit level, ISO/SAE 21434 does not make specific process requirements, besides standard unit verification. Following a common quality management system will ensure that software units are tested with the right level of coverage before they're integrated into larger components. A good practice for unit testing is to apply tests that exercise unit inputs, outputs, data, and control flows. The tests should cover error handling, fault injection, and methods for recovery to ensure the unit is behaving as intended. From a security angle, a unit-level bug in those areas can introduce an exploitable vulnerability. So, correcting unit test failures increases the confidence in the software or hardware being absent of unknown vulnerabilities. It is also important to apply regression testing to eliminate the possibility of a unit change adversely impacting other software units. When designing test cases for unit testing, a representative sample of test cases should be taken from general test data, edge cases, error handling, and failure/recovery handling. It is worth noting that a good source of vulnerabilities is edge cases, which can be ignored by testers under the assumption of a normal environment, even though they are quite plausible in the presence of a malicious actor.

When it comes to cybersecurity verification testing, the ISO standard specifies several methods, including **fuzz testing**, **vulnerability scanning**, **requirements-based testing**, **inspection**, and even **penetration testing**.

> **Note**
>
> Requirements-based testing and inspection are common testing methods that are shared with functional safety and quality management practices. In the case of cybersecurity, the purpose of requirements-based testing is to verify that security requirements have indeed been fulfilled by the product while considering test scenarios that evaluate whether the security functionality is adequate to handle the respective attack scenarios. Similarly, inspection intends to verify that the design and code truly capture the requirement's intent by considering scenarios in which the requirement can be violated by an attacker. In both cases, the differentiating factor is considering the attacker's mindset during verification.

Fuzz testing is a software testing method that injects malformed inputs to expose software defects that may constitute system vulnerabilities. A fuzzing tool injects these inputs into the system and then monitors for exceptions such as crashes or information leakage. In addition to having the ability to produce the right test input set, a fuzzer must also be able to detect adverse impacts on the system, such as a system crash or an exception.

The simplest fuzz test cases rely on random data generated based on a fixed seed to ensure the random set is repeatable. Template-based fuzzing introduces invalid inputs and then adjusts subsequent tests based on the system's behavior feedback to make the tests more effective. Generational fuzz testing requires an understanding of the protocol, API, or data sources under test to ensure that the tests will systematically violate the underlying rules in the hope of triggering an unexpected exploitable behavior.

Note that fuzzing does not directly test the security measures but rather exposes bugs that may result in the security measures failing to achieve their objective.

Fuzz testing has demonstrated its effectiveness as a cost-efficient approach to identifying potential cybersecurity vulnerabilities within software systems. Such vulnerabilities include buffer overflows, resource exhaustion, and parsing bugs, which all hold the potential to be exploited by malicious attackers so that they can gain unauthorized access to an ECU.

For example, a cryptographic function may be able to produce correct results under normal circumstances that fulfill a security objective. However, a buffer overflow bug that results in secret keys being leaked may only be discoverable using a fuzz test tool, which would provide the malformed input to expose the bug and, consequently, the security vulnerability of the cryptographic function. Incidentally, fuzzing is both a test tool and a hacking tool that can be leveraged by attackers who wish to identify easy-to-find exploitable bugs. An added benefit to uncovering security bugs is gaining assurance of the robustness of the system against unusual or random inputs. A challenge for fuzz testers is that if a crash is triggered, the time to restore the system may be long, as is the case with complex ECUs. This makes reproducing and analyzing the bug harder to achieve. To help with root cause analysis, code instrumentation is necessary to identify the exact event that triggered the crash.

It is good practice for software components that provide an interface at a trust boundary to be fuzzed. Fuzzing is especially useful for components that perform complex operations over input data, such as parsing or data translation. This ensures that the component can handle malformed inputs and will not degrade the system's security as a result of an invalid input. Penetration testing at the component level through an independent analysis or probing is optional according to ISO/SAE 21434. Typically, a component vendor may choose specific parts of the system to be externally analyzed or tested due to their security criticality. For example, a chip vendor may want their boot ROM code to be analyzed by an independent security reviewer before tape-out to avoid expensive fixes:

Standard Section	Work Products in Scope
10.4.1 Design	[WP-10-01] Cybersecurity specifications
	[WP-10-02] Cybersecurity requirements for post-development
	[WP-10-03] Documentation of the modeling, design, or programming languages and coding guidelines
	[WP-10-04] Verification report for the cybersecurity specifications
	[WP-10-05] Weaknesses found during product development
10.4.2 Integration and verification	[WP-10-05] Weaknesses found during product development
	[WP-10-06] Integration and verification specification
	[WP-10-07] Integration and verification report

Table 5.5 – Work products in scope for the product development phase

Note that reviews must be instituted for each work product to ensure the quality of the work product is achieved.

With the integration and verification testing done, we must validate the fulfillment of the cybersecurity goals.

Validation testing

ISO/SAE 21434 defines validation as an activity to be performed at the vehicle level. The objective of this clause is to validate that the cybersecurity goals that were identified during the concept phase have truly been fulfilled now that the item has been integrated within the actual vehicle environment. A component supplier may perform cybersecurity goal validation by applying tests to an environment that emulates the vehicle. While it is not mandatory to do so, it is generally a good practice to validate that the cybersecurity goals that you've placed on your product are satisfied before the OEM discovers that they aren't. Validation is usually carried out through penetration testing by attempting to violate cybersecurity goals through the discovery of unknown vulnerabilities. An OEM who is trying to prioritize ECUs for penetration testing may want all externally facing ECUs, such as telematics or infotainment, to be tested by a third party before other more deeply embedded ECUs are tested:

Standard Section	Work Products in Scope
11 Cybersecurity validation	[WP-11-01] Validation report

Table 5.6 – Work products in scope for the cybersecurity validation testing phase

Penetration testing aims to uncover the residual risk after cybersecurity controls have been incorporated. Penetration testing can be performed at multiple levels. For example, network penetration testing can be performed to identify insecure ports, usage of development protocols, and more. Interface penetration tests can be performed to identify open interfaces or services, such as SSH and Telnet. ECU-level penetration testing can perform semi and fully-invasive tests to extract cryptographic keys using glitching and side-channel analysis. Let's take a closer look at the objectives that can be achieved by performing penetration testing:

- **Identify security vulnerabilities**: Penetration testing helps identify security vulnerabilities that could be exploited by attackers. These vulnerabilities could include outdated software, weak passwords, unsecured network configurations, and other issues that could put sensitive data at risk.

- **Reduce the risk of a data breach**: By identifying and addressing security vulnerabilities, the organization can reduce the risk of a data breach. Data breaches can be costly and damaging to a company's reputation, so it's important to take proactive steps to prevent them.

- **Enhance the overall security posture**: Regular penetration testing can help organizations enhance their overall security posture by identifying areas for improvement and implementing best practices for security.

With the product development-related cybersecurity activities completed, it is time to prepare for the release phase. The next section goes into the details of the required steps to deem a product worthy of release after specific security checks and assurances have been completed.

Product release

At this point, you've performed all the cybersecurity activities defined in your cybersecurity plan. Now, you are ready to make an official product release. But before doing so, you must prove that the work products have been prepared as per the organization's CSMS and that the objectives of the CSMS have been fully achieved by your product. Gaining release approval requires that you prepare a cybersecurity case and undergo a cybersecurity assessment.

Cybersecurity case

Fast forwarding to the end of the project, the argument for why the product has achieved an adequate level of cybersecurity for its intended use case must be captured within the cybersecurity case. Typically, the case relies on two types of arguments: a process argument and a technical argument. The process argument demonstrates that the product has followed the cybersecurity engineering process and presents any deviations, along with arguments for why those deviation-based risks are acceptable. The entire body of cybersecurity work products is compiled into a repository to serve as evidence that all planned activities have been adequately fulfilled. The technical argument explains the cybersecurity goals that were planned, along with all the technical countermeasures that were incorporated across the entire life cycle to ensure those goals have been fulfilled. Again, any residual risks are included with an argument for why the residual risk is within a reasonable level to allow the product to be released for production.

Cybersecurity assessment

Using the plan as the roadmap, an assessment is performed to measure the product's level of compliance relative to the organization's cybersecurity engineering process. An assessment is typically done in phases as the work products become available. This is the preferred approach to ensure that nonconformities are detected while there is time to apply corrections rather than waiting until the project has neared production to start making adjustments. An assessor will typically request the work products to be delivered to an independent group, either external or internal to the organization, for assessing compliance. Besides process compliance, assessment teams might also rely on independent technical reviewers to judge the quality of the work product – for example, whether TARA has adequately considered all threats relevant to the product or whether technical countermeasures were selected and implemented correctly. A successful assessment will result in the release for the post-development report being signed off, indicating that the product has achieved all its intended process and technical goals:

Standard Section	Work Products in Scope
6.4.7 Cybersecurity case	[WP-06-02] Cybersecurity case
6.4.8 Cybersecurity assessment	[WP-06-03] Cybersecurity assessment report
6.4.9 Release for post-development	[WP-06-04] Release for post-development report

Table 5.7 – Work products in scope for product release

> **Note**
>
> Products can be released at multiple levels of maturity (for example, alpha, beta, and production intent). It is important to choose which cybersecurity activities must be performed for each product release level. For example, vulnerability scanning should be performed even if a software product is being released for road testing only. Similarly, certain cybersecurity controls should be applied regardless of the release type if the underlying asset is common between release versions. For example, if certain machine learning models have been deemed confidential, then their encryption should be applied, even if the release is for bench testing only, to prevent information disclosure by an attacker who gets hold of an early product release.

Having a product deemed worthy of production intent release paves the way for the next phase, which encompasses manufacturing and production. In the next phase, we will consider production aspects that relate to cybersecurity that must be considered for items and components that undergo a production cycle.

Production planning

You've released the product, indicating that it is ready for production. At this point, it has to be physically produced in a manufacturing environment. Whether you are producing a single component or a completely integrated vehicle, applying cybersecurity measures during the manufacturing process is an essential part of protecting the system during normal operation. The post-development requirements that were identified during the design phase are applied during the production phase by the system integrator. All such activities must be captured through a production plan. For example, an MCU/SoC vendor may specify procedures for injecting secret keys during manufacturing or locking specific interfaces. These procedures must be captured within the production plan of the chip vendor if they are responsible for performing this step or in the corresponding integrator's plan, such as the ECU vendor. Similarly, post-development requirements related to the ECU and vehicle assembly must be captured within the respective production plans. Note that if the TARA has adequately analyzed the manufacturing flow, then cybersecurity countermeasures are expected to be integrated with the manufacturing process. For example, specifications for the usage of **hardware security modules** (**HSMs**) within the manufacturing line to perform code signing and generate wrapped keys to be injected within the ECU before transitioning to a production state must already be in place.

In the case of software components, production planning normally entails binary encryption and code-signing aspects. If the component is delivered in encrypted form and the supplier intentionally wants to prohibit the modification of the software, then they may choose to sign it with their own private key before delivery. Planning how the code is signed and how the keys will be managed can be documented in a software cybersecurity production plan:

Standard Section	Work Products in Scope
12 Production	[WP-12-01] Production control plan

Table 5.8 – Work products in scope for the production phase

> **Note**
>
> It is expected that an ECU or a hardware component will have a production plan, though certain software components may be exempted. For example, a software library that is integrated into a larger system does not need a formal production plan. Instead, simply documenting how the library can be securely integrated within the larger system in the user manual is adequate.

If manufacturing is not considered early in the design process, it is very unlikely that changes can be made when components are well into production, so it is a must to include manufacturing engineers in the early stages of threat and risk analysis to avoid unpleasant surprises later:

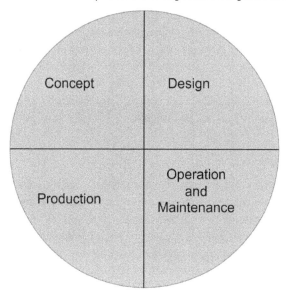

Figure 5.7 – The different phases mapped to cybersecurity risk management

With the product exiting the production phase, it is now entering the operational and maintenance phase. In the next section, we will see how ensuring the cybersecurity of the product within this phase is critical to completing the life cycle.

Operations and maintenance

You produced your part and it is now on the road. Congratulations – you can celebrate! Oh, but not so fast – your job of cyber defense has now transitioned to incident response. During the first three phases, as shown in *Figure 5.7*, we aimed to eliminate or reduce risks wherever possible. Where risks could not be reduced, a rationale was provided to either accept the risk or transfer it to other parties. Once in the operations and maintenance phase, our goal is to respond to emerging risks by following a process that identifies and addresses those risks effectively and promptly.

When the system is in its real environment, it is exposed to all the hypothetical threats that you considered during the concept and design phases. Now, attackers from all domains may be actively attempting to subvert your systems, and therefore planning to maintain cybersecurity during operational mode is a must. This can be achieved through two main methods:

- Cybersecurity monitoring
- Incident response and remediation

The operations phase also includes service, which must be accounted for during the threat analysis to ensure cybersecurity is maintained during that event. For example, if an ECU must be replaced at the dealer shop, cybersecurity procedures must be defined so that the new ECU can be provisioned securely. Similarly, if diagnostic routines are executed to troubleshoot vehicle issues or reflash a part, proper diagnostic client authentication must be accounted for. This can extend to all vehicle components to ensure that failure analysis is performed without the security of operational systems being jeopardized. For example, enabling JTAG to debug a failed part should not result in the exposure of global secrets that would render production intent systems insecure.

Monitoring

First, it is important to be aware of the threats that are emerging against your product in the field. By monitoring domains adjacent to your product, you can stay up to date on vulnerabilities that may apply to you. For example, if you are building a telematics unit, keeping track of attacks on mobile phones and the cellular infrastructure is essential to identify relevant vulnerabilities. This requires a process to be in place for ingesting risks, triaging events, and reacting through incident response. *Figure 5.8* shows typical information sources that can be monitored to identify potential cybersecurity events:

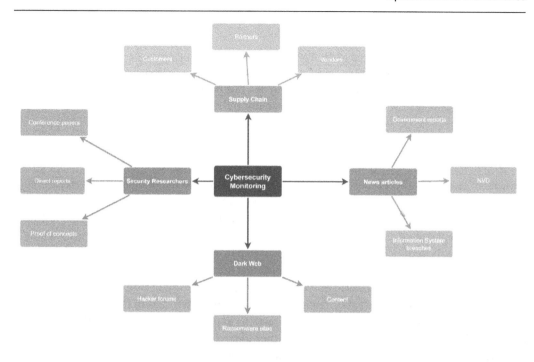

Figure 5.8 – Information sources considered during cybersecurity monitoring

Vulnerability analysis

During product development, vulnerability analysis is a critical tool to identify and eliminate exploitable security weaknesses. We touched upon this in the *Design and implementation* section, where we highlighted the need for security checklists coupled with a design-level threat analysis to analyze potential vulnerabilities.

Once the product has been shipped, vulnerability analysis becomes a process by which events can be analyzed to determine whether the system is impacted and to what degree. Let's assume a researcher contacted your company, claiming that your ECU contains a vulnerability that allows the vehicle odometer to be rolled back through a diagnostic service. This event is first triaged to determine whether the issue applies to your vehicle and who the impacted groups within the organization are since they must be included. If the event is confirmed as plausible, the team performs an attack path analysis to determine the attack steps needed to exploit the vulnerability. Its feasibility can be scored through an attack potential-based approach or a CVSS-based approach. The former relies on a risk scoring method such as HEAVENS, while the latter relies on exploitability metrics, as defined by the **Forum of Incident Response and Security Teams (FIRST)**. Coupled with attack path analysis, the impact is evaluated to determine the overall cybersecurity risk level. If the overall risk level is shown to be above the tolerable level for the organization, the vulnerability is transitioned from the analysis phase to the management phase.

> **Note**
>
> Attack path analysis is not limited to the TARA that's performed during the development phase. It is also an important tool that is applied during the vulnerability analysis phase of a released product. The objective of attack path analysis is to describe how a vulnerability can be exploited to accurately evaluate the severity of the vulnerability and determine whether a fix is needed.

Vulnerability management

The incident response process must ensure the prompt analysis and handling of reports regarding cybersecurity vulnerabilities/incidents. Having the procedures for incident reporting at hand is essential to give the affected parties ample time to create a mitigation plan that covers preparing and testing patches before deployment. Giving the vulnerability an issue ID, such as a JIRA ticket, and assigning the right individuals to track the resolution is the first step in ensuring the vulnerability is managed. Next, the team must prepare an incident response plan that includes identifying the impacted parties, the message that shall be communicated to those parties regarding the mitigation, and the action plan to execute the mitigation. In the background, a **root cause corrective action** (**RCCA**) is triggered to find the causes of the event and apply corrective actions to prevent its recurrence in the future. In some cases, the OEM may choose not to mitigate the vulnerability and accept the risk if the cost of the mitigation is higher than the cost of the resolution. In our odometer mileage scenario, the OEM may argue that the impact of fake warranty claims due to a rolled-back odometer value is significantly less than modifying the software and issuing an update (assuming the software is no longer under maintenance and an OTA mechanism does not exist). In all cases, the rationale for mitigation or risk acceptance must be documented:

Standard Section	Work Products in Scope
8.3 Cybersecurity monitoring	[WP-08-01] Sources for cybersecurity information [WP-08-02] Triggers [WP-08-03] Cybersecurity events
8.4 Cybersecurity event evaluation	[WP-08-04] Weaknesses from cybersecurity events
8.5 Vulnerability analysis	[WP-08-05] Vulnerability analysis
8.6 Vulnerability management	[WP-08-06] Evidence of managed vulnerabilities
13.3 Cybersecurity incident response	[WP-13-01] Cybersecurity incident response plan

Table 5.9 – Work products in scope for vulnerability management

Updates

One crucial method by which emerging cybersecurity risks can be mitigated is through the ability to promptly patch vulnerable vehicle systems. In recent years, this has meant that adding **Over-the-Air** (**OTA**) update capabilities has become mandatory to prevent vehicle systems from remaining in an insecure and potentially unsafe state. In addition to software updates, vehicle systems must be capable of receiving hardware updates if absolutely necessary. Due to the significant cost of hardware changes, it is incumbent that automotive companies invest in cybersecurity engineering systems to avoid the scenario where a component has to be physically changed. This can happen, for example, if the hardware contains un-patchable vulnerabilities such as boot ROM bugs, which can result in secure boot being bypassed.

With the operation and maintenance phase covered, the last phase to consider from a cybersecurity perspective is that of end of life. In the next section, we will look into how protecting this final aspect of the life cycle contributes to the security of products that are still in use and safeguards the assets of various stakeholders.

End of life

The product has reached its end of life. Now, you can rest assured that no one can attack your system, right? No – even when you are ready to bury that product in its final resting place, you must take care of active assets that may be "exhumed" by a determined attacker who wishes to launch attacks against the other still alive and functioning products. For example, intellectual property, or user private data, may still be accessible in a vehicle that is slated for the junkyard. It is common for hobbyists to buy such parts on eBay, so products must have procedures for transitioning such systems into a secure state in which the assets cannot be exposed. This can be achieved by invoking routines that randomize secret keys or wipe user secrets. End-of-life preparation must also include change of ownership events. An OEM must provide procedures for the removal of **personally identifiable information** (**PII**) when a change of ownership occurs:

Standard Section	Work Products in Scope
14.3 End of cybersecurity support	[WP-14-01] Procedures to communicate the end of cybersecurity support
14.4 Decommissioning	None

Table 5.10 – Work products in scope for the end of life and decommissioning phase

In addition to addressing decommissioning, ISO/SAE 21434 requires that end of cybersecurity support be well defined by all parties involved to ensure that systems can receive adequate support until their planned expiry date. Given that vehicles may be on the road more than fifteen years after being produced, it is very important to negotiate cybersecurity support with your component suppliers to ensure that in the event that a supplier is no longer in business, you still have a way to maintain and patch a critical product in the supply chain.

Summary

This chapter has provided a comprehensive overview of the ISO/SAE 21434 standard and the crucial role it plays in implementing a systematic cybersecurity engineering approach to developing automotive systems. By delving into the intricacies of the V-model life cycle stages and demonstrating how they are interdependent, we have highlighted the importance of following the secure-by-design approach at every step of the product engineering process. As we have shown, cybersecurity activities must be embedded into that process from start to finish, rather than being bolted on as an afterthought. Our discussion has emphasized the significance of understanding the various work products associated with the standard and how they can be leveraged to achieve a secure system. Furthermore, we have illustrated how the standard's cybersecurity activities are relevant throughout the system's lifespan, from planning to end of life.

In summary, the insights provided in this chapter underscore the need for a systematic approach to cybersecurity engineering that follows the ISO/SAE 21434 standard. Adopting this approach will ensure that cybersecurity risks are managed effectively, creating safer and more secure automotive systems for all. In the next chapter, we will explore the areas of difference and intersection between cybersecurity and functional safety. By integrating the procedures and technical work products from both domains, we can create a more comprehensive and robust approach to automotive system development that addresses both functional safety and cybersecurity risks.

Now that we have become intimately familiar with the ISO/SAE 21434 standard, we will turn our attention to areas of overlap and conflicts between the security standard and its counterpart from automotive functional safety – the ISO 26262 standard.

6
Interactions Between Functional Safety and Cybersecurity

Even a cursory survey of **electronic control units** (ECUs) in a typical vehicle will reveal that the majority of these ECUs are safety-relevant. Whether it is braking, steering, propulsion, or battery management, there is barely a vehicle system where maintaining safety is not a primary objective. Whenever a system is subjected to safety hazards, a whole suite of engineering practices and methods is employed to achieve the required level of safety integrity. These practices aim to eliminate unreasonable safety risks that would lead to harming a human being while the system was in use. Engineering safety-critical systems that are also resilient to cyberattacks adds a new dimension to automotive engineering and are one of the main differentiating factors between automotive cybersecurity and information security. In addition to its focus on securing vehicle and user data, automotive cybersecurity is also concerned with eliminating unreasonable security risks that have a physical impact on the vehicle and its environment. For many automotive companies, functional safety practices are well established, so when cybersecurity comes into the picture, there is a natural tendency to adapt existing engineering processes and practices to account for cybersecurity with the least impact on existing management systems. The alternative to an integrated safety, security, and quality management system is a disjointed approach that continuously produces inconsistencies and duplication of effort, resulting in high costs and serious schedule delays. In this chapter, we will explore ways in which safety and security management systems can be integrated not only to eliminate conflicts but also to uncover synergies throughout the full development life cycle.

This will be demonstrated through the exploration of the following main topics:

- A tale of two standards

- A unified versus integrated approach

- Establishing the foundational understanding of functional safety and cybersecurity

- Extending the safety- and quality-supporting processes

- Creating synergies in the concept phase

- Finding synergies and conflicts in the design phase

- Secure coding practices versus safe coding techniques

- Finding synergies in the testing phase

A tale of two standards

ISO 26262 is the de facto safety standard for systematically eliminating unreasonable safety risks in automotive systems. It establishes a structured and uniform approach to managing safety risks throughout the development process, from the concept phase to decommissioning. The standard defines the required processes and guidelines over 12 parts and covers various aspects of the safety life cycle, such as management, development, production, and operation. The parts are organized into a hierarchical structure, with each part building upon the previous one to create a comprehensive safety framework.

Like its sibling standard from functional safety, the **ISO/SAE 21434** standard was set up to guide automotive **original equipment manufacturers** (**OEMs**) and suppliers into adapting their existing engineering processes to ensure their products are free from unreasonable cybersecurity risk through a systematic approach. Comparing the two standards reveals a high degree of parallelism that stems from the common root foundation being the V-model. Furthermore, by structuring the standard in a way that mirrors the functional safety standard, automotive engineers with a background in functional safety are better equipped to transition into the cybersecurity domain. Consequently, ISO/SAE 21434 borrows many terms from functional safety and aligns the activities between the two domains across the V-model, as shown in *Figure 6.1*:

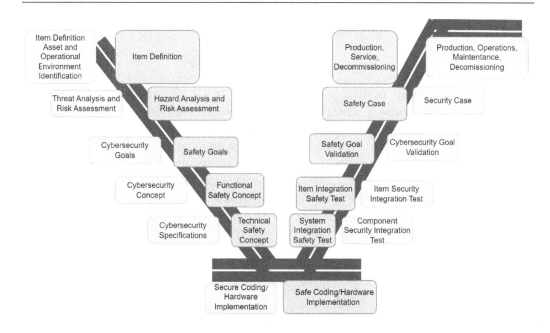

Figure 6.1 – Mapping activities between the safety and security standards

Starting from the concept phase, the **hazard analysis and risk assessment (HARA)** is analogous to the **threat analysis and risk assessment (TARA)**. The definition of safety goals and functional safety requirements mirrors the definition of cybersecurity goals and deriving cybersecurity requirements. Analogies also extend to analysis methods, for example, **fault tree analysis (FTA)** is mirrored by attack trees, while **failure mode effect analysis (FMEA)** is mirrored by vulnerability analysis. The parallelism continues into architecture definition and coding, as well as integration and verification testing. While these analogies imply a high level of synergy between the two system engineering approaches, there are unique aspects that must be carefully examined to resolve conflicts as they emerge throughout the development life cycle. Throughout this chapter, we will explore areas of synergy as well as differentiation during each phase, but first, let's explore the type of approach that must be followed when combining the two engineering frameworks.

A unified versus integrated approach

Both safety and security engineering approaches analyze risks, impose limitations on the system through design and implementation constraints, and produce protective measures. However, they do so by leveraging a unique set of methods, guidelines, and tools. While it is self-evident that a disjointed approach to safety and security engineering is inefficient and results in significant reworks, the choice between a unified and an integrated approach is not so obvious. *Briefly, a* **unified approach** *is one in which the methods and work products become unified to address both aspects of safety and security.* For example, the HARA would be extended to incorporate hazards originating from malicious events, the FMEA would be expanded to consider malicious causes of failure modes, and so on. Similarly, rather than producing a separate set of safety and security requirements, those would be unified to address both aspects of the system. This would continue throughout the development life cycle in a unified and harmonized fashion. Since safety and security teams typically belong to different departments and have different sets of expertise, it is not trivial to have these experts converge on a common process to execute both safety and security activities. Even when experts converge, disturbing well-established safety work products by injecting security (and vice versa) can be quite challenging due to legacy considerations.

Moreover, the safety and security analysis methods and tools are well established and have significant differences. A unified approach would require the unification of the methods and tools, which creates a challenge for legacy toolchains. Furthermore, the approach requires a unification of expertise for both safety and security professionals so that they can work on both aspects simultaneously. In practice, safety and security professionals have unique skill sets and are constantly moving into further specialization in their respective fields, making a unified approach an unnatural one.

On the other hand, an **integrated approach** *aims to align safety and security processes to identify flows between the two approaches and establish checkpoints that aim to find and eliminate conflicts.* For example, the HARA results would feed into the TARA when evaluating the safety impact of damage scenarios and accounting for safety-related damage scenarios. Similarly, safety requirements would be incorporated into security analysis to identify ways by which safety mechanisms can be tampered with or disabled through a malicious agent. Checkpoints are established at each development milestone to perform cross-disciplinary reviews to ensure that conflicts are detected – for example, in case of an error handling policy contradicting a security policy and vice versa. As such, the integrated approach maintains experts in two different domains but ensures that they are not working in complete isolation from one another by defining interactions between the two and enforcing cross-checks. This is further reflected in an integrated engineering management process. To an engineer, the process framework should be common, but each person refers to the parts of the process that affect their area while viewing the overall process flow, which incorporates both safety and security activities:

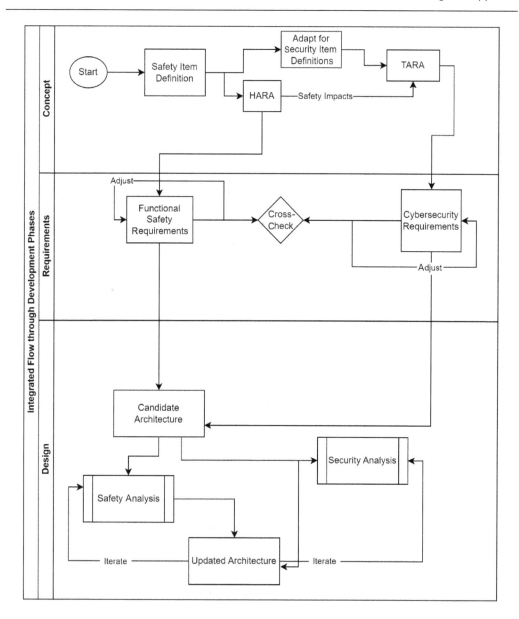

Figure 6.2 – Integrated process flow during concept, requirements, and design phases

Figure 6.2 shows an example flow in which inputs from safety processes are routed to the security process and cross-checks result in changes to work products from each domain. In the concept phase, the item definition from safety is shown to be leveraged for the TARA, which reuses aspects of the item definition but can adjust the item boundary and include additional interfaces and operational environment actors that are especially relevant to security. In addition, the safety impacts from the hazard analysis are ingested by the damage scenario's impact rating for the concept-level TARA. The resulting functional safety and cybersecurity requirements are reviewed by experts from each domain to eliminate conflicts before being fed into the candidate architecture. Both safety and security analyses are done in parallel, resulting in updates to the candidate architecture. With each change, further iterations of safety and security analysis are needed until the architecture reaches a stable state where all safety and security risks have been addressed adequately. In this example of an integrated process approach, an engineer should have no ambiguity regarding the dependencies of each process and doesn't need to be an expert in each process area. Furthermore, keeping the work product templates synchronized and consistent results in no rework of legacy work products and can help teams easily adapt to new processes. Therefore, while aiming for a unified process that fully accounts for all safety and security activities in a harmonized fashion is the ideal scenario, it is more practical to aim for unifying processes with high overlap and to integrate processes with fundamental differences by creating process flow points and cross-functional checkpoints to ensure the consistency and completeness of their output.

> **Note**
>
> It is easy for teams to get carried away with the number of design iterations leading to substantial schedule delays. While well intentioned, it is important to set a clear limit on design iterations to avoid analysis paralysis. A prerequisite for cross-domain collaboration is achieving a minimum level of functional safety and cybersecurity literacy.

For effective cross-domain collaboration, you must first attain a foundational understanding of functional safety and cybersecurity. We'll delve into this topic in the next section.

Establishing a foundational understanding of functional safety and cybersecurity

Implementing an integrated approach to safety and security engineering results in frequent interactions between safety and security teams. These teams analyze risk from different perspectives and are spread across different product life cycles, such as manufacturing, development, and testing. While the expectation is that neither team will become a full expert in the other's domain, it is valuable for practitioners from each domain to be familiar with the terms, concepts, and general methods and tools available in each approach. This eases the conversation to help understand the areas of concern and why they are important from each perspective. Let's look at an example where lack of a common understanding produces a real problem for a safety and security-critical system. During a safety analysis of a feature that controls how the system is booted, safety engineers discover that a rare corruption in a specific configuration structure describing the boot chain would result in a failure to boot the system. Since the risk is limited to the initialization phase, leading to, at worst, an inoperable system, they decide that this risk has no safety impact. A system that would not boot is technically safe since it cannot do anything else either! They even go one step further and claim that the risk does not need to be mitigated, even if the corruption were triggered by a malicious cause – again, this would not result in a hazardous event based on the argument that an inoperable system cannot do any harm. While the impact analysis is correct from a safety perspective, an attack that can corrupt this configuration structure and consequently result in a boot failure will have significant financial and operational impacts (for example, it may render the vehicle inoperable), making it a significant security risk. Imagine a scenario where this hypothetical attack leaves thousands or even millions of ECUs in a bricked state. This would result in a massive recall that would lead to severe financial damage to the automotive manufacturer and significant disruption to the vehicle owners. While having cross-checks in place to detect such scenarios should prevent the risk from being ignored, relying on cross-checks alone means that in some cases, a check might be missed, and this type of risk may escape into the product. Therefore, it is essential to equip both safety and security practitioners with basic knowledge about what makes each domain unique, making them literate in each other's fields of expertise. Furthermore, by mandating specific introductory training for all engineers, regardless of their field of specialization, a security engineer would become familiar with basic terms from functional safety, such as the meaning of an **automotive safety integrity level** (**ASIL**), the various fault metrics, the types of safety mechanisms, and different safety methods and tools.

> **Note**
>
> ASIL is a risk classification framework outlined in the ISO 26262 functional safety standard. It reflects the necessary rigor in the development process to ensure that specific automotive functions satisfy the required safety measures. The levels range from ASIL A, denoting the lowest safety requirements with minimal consequences upon failure, to ASIL D, which signifies the most stringent safety requirements and process rigor due to the potential for fatal outcomes in case of a malfunction. The determination of these levels is rooted in evaluating the possible severity of a failure, its likelihood of occurrence (exposure), and its controllability (the driver's ability to manage the situation if the system fails).

Similarly, a safety engineer would be familiar with basic terms from cybersecurity, such as asset definition, various impacts considered for security, classes of security weaknesses, types of security controls, as well as unique security methods and tools. This literacy will prove crucial in enabling practitioners from both domains to speak in a common language without necessarily overstepping their areas of expertise. To introduce this common understanding, let's explore some fundamental aspects that make cybersecurity and functional safety unique by examining the differences and interdependencies between the two domains.

Understanding the unique aspects and interdependencies between the two domains

If you ever sit at a joint meeting between safety and security experts, it is very common to see experienced engineers mixing discussions about system faults and hazards with ones about security attacks and damages. Without the proper perspective, it is easy to start confusing terms and inadvertently amplifying risks that should be considered purely from either a safety lens or a security angle and vice versa. To avoid this confusion, we will take a look at the differences and interdependencies between these domains next.

Differences between safety and security scope

One of the fundamental areas of difference is between *safety and security scope*. From a failure perspective, functional safety is concerned with reducing the risk that failures due to systematic or random hardware faults can produce a hazard. This is a search in a finite set that stabilizes over time. On the other hand, cybersecurity is concerned with reducing the risk that attacks not only result in a hazardous event but also cause the loss of system operability, financial losses, and privacy violations:

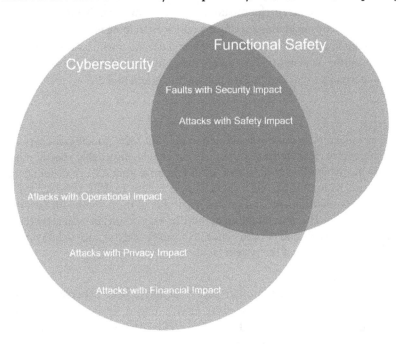

Figure 6.3 – Difference in scope regarding the analysis and intersection areas

Intuitively, this is a larger search space than that of functional safety. Moreover, once all the safety failure causes have been accounted for, they remain well known and fixed for a given system. As you build millions of vehicles and drive them thousands of miles, you will quickly identify safety-critical defects. As a result, the likelihood of finding a safety defect that was missed during development starts low and eventually approaches zero as time progresses. In contrast, cybersecurity engineering deals with an evolving space of intelligent attacks where the malicious causes are continuously changing. This means that a system may start at a high state of security where security-critical defects are unknown, and as time passes, the system experiences an erosion of its security strength due to the advancements in attackers' abilities while the built-in cybersecurity defenses remain the same. Take, for example, software that was written for a given CPU instruction set containing both safety and security functions. After years of operating on that CPU architecture without defects, the safety hardware functions are assumed to be reliable. However, during that period, researchers discover a new category of CPU architecture weaknesses based on speculative execution, which results in new methods by which the security functions are exposed to timing-based side-channel attacks. Suddenly, what was once a safe and secure system has now become insecure, potentially impacting the system's safety as well. Furthermore, this dimension of intelligent attackers means that cybersecurity engineers will rarely have a full grasp of the entirety of the search space for malicious causes since new security weaknesses and attacks emerge constantly. As a result, assessing a security threat is radically different from assessing a safety hazard. Sources of these threats cover an extremely broad range of possible scenarios, making it quite difficult to have a single expert who can account for all threats and potential mitigations. While safety experts do specialize in certain areas, such as hardware and software safety, cybersecurity demands a more granular level of specialization as the skill set of someone who works on network security, for example, is quite different from a person who specializes in CPU and microarchitecture security. That is because even though the security principles are the same, the types of vulnerabilities that exist in each specialized field and the required mitigations are diverse and ever-evolving.

Differences in the level of interdependence

Another fundamental difference is in the *level of interdependence* between the two domains. While safety engineering is necessary to ensure a system is free from unreasonable safety risks, it cannot eliminate all safety risks originating from malicious causes. In a sense, cybersecurity engineering is a prerequisite for functional safety as it safeguards the system's ability to meet its safety requirements. Let's take, for example, a system that has been designed to eliminate interference between software elements that have been developed at a lower ASIL level (for example, QM) against software of a higher ASIL level (for example, ASIL D). By enforcing **spatial isolation mechanisms**, the system can be shown to be resilient to transient and systematic faults that can impact the ASIL D software. Now, let's assume that the QM software happens to be responsible for sending and receiving network messages, putting it at risk of network-based attacks. Due to a successful code injection attack into the QM software, attackers find a way to disable the spatial isolation mechanisms defined by safety, causing that software to interfere with the ASIL D software. This is possible because the safety analysis has only considered faults with non-malicious causes in which the QM software may, for example, accidentally attempt to write into the memory of the ASIL D software. As a result, the safety analysis did not consider that the QM software was given a high privilege level, allowing it to reconfigure the **memory management unit** (**MMU**) to disable the memory isolation. It is only when security analysis is performed that the malicious causes are analyzed while considering the potential of multiple successful attack steps. This results in additional security controls to mitigate the associated threats – for example, by removing unnecessary privileges from both the QM and ASIL D software to prevent either one from violating the spatial isolation rules. As a result, cybersecurity methods can be viewed as an important enabler for the system to maintain its safety objectives, especially when the fault is triggered by a malicious cause.

> **Multi-point faults versus multi-attack steps**
>
> Even if functional safety considers multi-point faults, the order of faults analyzed rarely reaches three or more. This is reasonable in functional safety because the probability of three or more independent events occurring at the same time to exhibit a fault is quite low. On the contrary, faults triggered through attacks can easily exceed the order of three as attackers build sophisticated attack chains to breach the system.

On the other hand, developing a system that is proven to be safe is helpful but not sufficient to prove that the system is secure. A system developed according to the safety standard implicitly indicates that it is also compliant with a solid quality management system (ISO26262 references ASPICE, ISO 9001, and IATF 16949). This naturally strengthens the quality argument, which is a prerequisite for cybersecurity. While a safe and reliable system is less likely to contain defects that would otherwise become vulnerabilities, it is not necessarily free from design flaws that can be exploited in a cyberattack. Later in this chapter, we'll see how a system developed as per the safety standard brings in many methods and tools that can prove useful to satisfy cybersecurity expectations in a symbiotic fashion.

Differences in the risk analysis techniques

Yet another major difference is in the *risk analysis techniques*. This is evident in the attack feasibility rating, which considers evolving factors such as the attacker's knowledge of the system, their expertise level, and the equipment they need to mount an attack. For safety, given a fixed set of hazardous scenarios and a constant operational environment, the safety risk levels should remain stable over time. For cybersecurity, even if the system remains the same and the operational environment is not changed, the attack feasibility of previously defined threats can increase over time. Take, for example, the security strength of a cryptographic function and its associated cryptographic keys. Over time, the attackers' computational abilities evolve, making the security key strength insufficient to withstand more sophisticated cryptanalysis attacks. Therefore, TARA results are periodically revised to account for newly discovered vulnerabilities and attack methods that can increase the risk level of previously accepted risks. In addition to these risk assessment methods, there are significant differences in the analysis methods employed by each domain. Let's explore a few of the commonly used safety analysis methods and show how they differ from security analysis methods:

- The **HAZard and OPerability (HAZOP)** study is a risk assessment methodology that is used to identify potential hazards and operational issues in the design and operation of automotive systems. During a HAZOP analysis of an automotive system, a team of experts systematically reviews the system and identifies any deviations from the intended design or operational parameters that could potentially lead to hazardous situations using a set of standardized guide words. The analysis considers the possible causes of each deviation and assesses the likelihood and severity of potential incidents. Examples of hazards that may be identified in a HAZOP analysis of an automotive system include malfunctioning brakes, steering failure, engine stalling, and electrical system malfunctions. The analysis may also consider potential hazards arising from external factors, such as adverse weather conditions or road conditions.

- **FTA** is a top-down safety analysis approach that's used in safety engineering to identify potential causes of system failures or accidents. FTA works by identifying and analyzing the various possible combinations of faults or events that could lead to the failure of a system or component. In an FTA, a fault tree is created to outline the different possible scenarios that could lead to a system failure. The fault tree is constructed by breaking down the system into its various components and subsystems and then identifying the possible faults or events that could cause each component or subsystem to fail. Each identified fault or event is represented as a node in the fault tree, with the various possible combinations of events leading to the system failure represented by the branches and links in the tree. The analysis considers the probabilities of each event occurring and assesses the overall likelihood of a system failure.

- **FMEA** is a bottom-up approach that's used in engineering and manufacturing to identify potential failures in a system or process and to develop strategies to prevent or mitigate those failures. The FMEA technique involves breaking down a system or process into components or steps, identifying potential failure modes for each component or step, and analyzing the potential consequences of those failures. During an FMEA analysis, a team of experts systematically evaluates the likelihood and severity of each potential failure mode, as well as the detectability of those failures. This information is then used to assign a **risk priority number** (**RPN**) to each failure mode, which represents a relative, qualitative measure of risk rather than an absolute, quantitative measure. Once the potential failure modes have been identified and analyzed, the FMEA team can develop strategies to prevent or mitigate those failures. This may include redesigning components or processes to reduce the likelihood of the failure mode, implementing additional testing or inspection procedures to detect potential failures, or developing contingency plans to minimize the impact of failures that cannot be prevented.

- **Critical path analysis** (**CPA**) is a deductive approach based on the sequential call flow between system elements forming what is known as the "critical path." The analysis starts by creating a critical path for a specific use case, starting with the output of a safety goal or safety requirement, and identifying the path through all the impacted element interfaces to identify possible failure causes in a top-down manner. The analysis results in additional safety measures to treat failure modes that can result in safety goal violations.

Security, on the other hand, relies on a different set of methods that runs in parallel to the safety analysis methods:

- **Asset and interaction-based threat modeling** is a risk analysis method for identifying threats that apply to a system by either focusing on the assets or studying interactions that cross a trust boundary. Similar to HAZOP in identifying hazards, threat modeling aims to identify threats. In the case of an asset-based approach, a threat model such as STRIDE can be used to uncover threats targeting each of an asset's cybersecurity properties. Enumerating all threats that are in the scope of a system is a fundamental step in the exploring attack methods by which those threats can be materialized. In the case of interaction-based threat modeling, the system is modeled to expose interactions between its elements crossing a trust boundary. Depending on the type of interaction and the source and destination of the interaction, a set of predefined threats can be explored.

- **Attack path analysis**, which is similar in structure to the FTA, decomposes a high-level threat into a tree of attack steps to reveal the necessary actions to realize the top-level event. The result is an attack tree that provides a visual representation of how a system can be attacked, starting with the root being the threat and damage scenario and then traversing through the tree to identify the attack methods and the corresponding attack steps. Attack paths are given attack feasibility ratings to enable risk assessment.

- **Weakness analysis** is similar to FMEA in that it is performed in a bottom-up fashion to explore common weaknesses in existing functionalities and determine whether they are present in the system. While the FMEA considers components failing due to random and systematic faults, weakness analysis aims to uncover one or more component defects that can give a malicious adversary an advantage in achieving their attack objective. When a weakness is found, an attack path can be constructed to evaluate the attack feasibility and decide on the proper mitigation.

- **Information flow analysis** is a security technique that involves examining how information flows within a system or network to identify potential vulnerabilities or security breaches. It is used to understand the paths that information takes as it moves through a system and to identify any possible points of weakness that could be exploited by an attacker. By analyzing the flow of information, security experts can gain insights into how data is processed and whether security assets are exposed to an untreated threat. Information flow analysis is particularly useful for identifying risks related to data leakage, unauthorized access, and other security threats that can arise when sensitive information is shared across multiple systems or networks.

Being aware of the different analysis methods allows safety and security practitioners to discover ways to share analysis artifacts. For example, system diagrams used for FTA and CPA can be useful to jumpstart the creation of data flow diagrams, which are needed for asset-based threat modeling and information flow analysis. Similarly, functionalities used in the FMEA can be leveraged to uncover weaknesses and attack scenarios that can induce the same failure mode effect.

Differences in the level of interdependence between safety and security requirements

Understanding the taxonomy of the relationships between safety and security requirements and countermeasures helps optimize resources, reduce costs, and improve the overall system reliability and security. There are four possible relationships that we must consider between safety and security requirements – interdependent, synergistic, adverse, and independent:

- **Interdependent:** This relationship exists when the fulfillment of safety or security requirements is dependent on the fulfillment of the other domain's requirements. For instance, a safety requirement to prevent temporal interference between QM software and a higher ASIL software depends on security measures that prevent malicious attacks against both the QM and ASIL software from violating the timing performance of the ASIL software. Conversely, a security requirement for the detection of **Denial of Service** (**DoS**) attacks can depend on safety monitoring measures that detect when a resource has stopped responding due to either a fault or an attack. Clearly, in these cases, one cannot be fully satisfied without the other.

- **Synergistic**: This relationship arises when fulfilling safety requirements or measures contributes to security, or vice versa, resulting in resource optimization and cost reduction. While similar to the interdependent relationship, the primary difference is that safety and security measures reinforce each other's objectives. Theoretically, the objectives could be achieved independently but due to the overlap in the output of the measures, we say that there is a synergistic relationship. A famous example of a synergistic measure is the use of **message authentication codes (MACs)** or hash values to protect the integrity of messages in place of **cyclic redundancy checks (CRCs)**. Since a MAC or a signed hash value offers stronger data integrity guarantees, and since it provides added security benefits (prevent message forging), it can be used to achieve message safety integrity protection.

- **Adverse**: This relationship exists when safety and security requirements or measures lead to conflicting outcomes. Another famous example is when safety analysis of the hazard of being trapped, in the case of an accident, produces a requirement that windows must be open when an accident is detected. Conversely, security analysis of the threat of unauthorized vehicle unlocking will require that windows remain closed unless an authorized action is triggered by the vehicle operator. These two requirements conflict, so it is essential to harmonize the objectives to account for all scenarios.

- **Independent**: This relationship exists when safety and security requirements or measures do not interact. It is crucial to mark requirements as independent to avoid false assumptions of synergistic relationships. For instance, using dual CAN channels to transmit the same messages can help ensure safety availability, but attackers who can flood one CAN bus may also be able to flood the second, albeit with more effort. Assuming that the dual CAN channels mitigate DoS attacks without careful consideration of attack feasibility is a common mistake. This can be prevented by explicitly marking requirements or controls as common only after performing cross-functional safety and security analysis to avoid false assumptions.

Now that we have seen the various areas of differences, it is natural to expect that conflicts between the safety and cybersecurity domains will arise at various points of the development life cycle. Therefore, preparing for such conflict is essential to defining a strategy for conflict resolution.

Conflict resolution

Even when checkpoints are in place to catch and resolve interdependencies between safety and security, in practice, halting safety engineering to allow for conflict resolution and vice versa can prove very challenging, especially in fast-paced projects where different teams are operating on different schedules. Unless teams are truly integrated with a well-synchronized process, conflict resolution will only be possible at specific checkpoints or gates, which also means that there is a risk of detecting issues later in the development cycle, resulting in unnecessary rework.

To help with conflict resolution, teams should chart policies that codify the rules for order of precedence when the two domains conflict. Let's look at some examples of rules that an organization can define for conflict resolution:

- If a security requirement or a design decision hurts a safety objective, then give precedence to the safety objective by amending the security requirement or design

- If a security requirement addresses a financial impact that conflicts with a safety requirement addressing the loss of life, then give precedence to the safety requirement

- If safety requires security-sensitive information to be captured to aid in fault analysis, then give precedence to security requirements that prohibit this type of logging

As the organization matures and more areas of conflict are identified, the rulebook on conflict resolution is expected to evolve as well. Besides knowing how to resolve conflicts, having a process that flags conflict and provides a path for resolution is just as important.

For the rest of this chapter, we will explore how areas of synergies and conflict play out across various phases of the development life cycle, starting with management processes.

Extending the safety and quality supporting processes

A common challenge when introducing a cybersecurity management process is identifying how it can be integrated with existing processes.

To tackle this challenge, we must first assume that a quality management team exists that maintains the overall development life cycle – for example, by defining and maintaining a common engineering development handbook. There is usually also a safety engineering team that maintains a layer of safety practices on top of standard engineering practices. For example, there can be a process for managing requirements with safety overlays that describe expectations based on the ASIL of the system. The first hurdle is to determine how to adapt the quality and safety engineering process to account for cybersecurity activities. The natural step is to perform a **gap analysis** of ISO/SAE 21434 against the existing safety and quality engineering practices to determine how to integrate cybersecurity process requirements. A deep understanding of the ISO/SAE 21434 process requirements and a familiarity with the ISO26262 process are mandatory to accurately map process areas between the different domains. This calls for an additional team that's familiar with the incumbent engineering process to efficiently identify gap areas. It is important to understand that while safety and reliability practices are necessary to develop secure systems, they are not sufficient for building a security-resilient system. Therefore, it is necessary to add another security process layer that augments safety and quality practices to address the requirements of all the applicable engineering standards. In the case of quality management systems, synergies can be found in supporting processes, such as the requirements management process, configuration management, and documentation management. When adapting such processes, it is essential to consider the cybersecurity risks to these management systems. For example, configuration management accounts for managing cybersecurity work products that need special handling due to the sensitive nature of their content. Similarly, for documentation management, the process accounts for marking documents with the right confidentiality level and ensuring processes are in place to approve access.

Table 6.1 shows a mapping between safety and security work products that should be targeted for harmonization and alignment. Let's walk through the listed activities to introduce areas of synergies and touchpoints; then, in the following section, we will take a deep dive into each specific topic of interest.

Planning

First, we encounter the safety plan, which mirrors the cybersecurity plan. As mentioned in *Chapter 5*, a cybersecurity plan is required to demonstrate the security relevance of the system, the planned cybersecurity activities, and additional aspects, such as the reuse of previous components and handling off-the-shelf components and components out of context. Adhering to a common cybersecurity plan template ensures that teams will produce complete and consistent cybersecurity plans. Rather than starting from scratch to prepare the cybersecurity plan template, you can consult the safety plan template and borrow aspects that are common or that can be adapted for cybersecurity. By performing this exercise, you will quickly realize that ISO/SAE 21434 was largely modeled to mirror the functional safety standard for this exact reason, which is to ease the adoption of cybersecurity within automotive organizations that have made significant investments in defining safety-compliant engineering processes. One aspect of the safety and security plans is capturing the roles and responsibilities to show role assignments as evidence that the project has been adequately staffed to execute the planned safety and security activities. Using a common resource management document for both safety and security roles ensures that the lists are always consistent and eases the process of engineers looking up resources, who need to identify, for example, their project security or safety managers. Similarly, the safety plan documents **components off the shelf** (**COTS**), which can be useful for jump-starting the list of off-the-shelf components that must be considered for cybersecurity evaluation. Rather than creating separate communication channels with COTS suppliers, it is recommended to use a single interface so that all the safety and security questions are answered efficiently. Moving to the reuse analysis, the list of components that are planned for reuse, as mentioned in the safety plan, can be shared to prepare the arguments for reuse in the cybersecurity plan. For example, the level of changes in the component, the operational environment changes, and whether any use cases have been altered can all be inherited from the safety reuse analysis to evaluate the impact of cybersecurity activities. It is important to note that while the context of use can be shared, the arguments for which cybersecurity activities can be reused must be performed strictly from a security angle. For example, a network driver that is planned to be reused between one project variant and another may have no safety-related changes; however, the threat model may be different as the system is now exposed to additional threat vectors due to a change in the vehicle architecture. This calls for a separate guideline for when cybersecurity work products can be carried over from another project variant or version and when they have to be updated or completely redone.

Supplier management

When it comes to supplier management, the **cybersecurity interface agreement** (**CSIA**) can share a similar structure and format with the **design interface agreement** (**DIA**) for safety. It is recommended that you adapt the DIA template and simply replace safety work products with cybersecurity work products instead. To ease adoption, fields such as responsibility distribution and approval procedures can be shared between the two documents. Since several supplier products may be considered both safety- and security-relevant, it is important to align the processes to ensure the CSIA and DIA are triggered within the same project milestones, including the same supplier management team, or at least by keeping those responsible for safety and security aware of how each agreement is progressing. Even when planning to receive certain safety work products, it is useful to align the security work product delivery to avoid multiple rounds of product integrations. While there is a significant overlap between the safety DIA and the CSIA, a major differentiator is handling maintenance and end-of-life support. The likelihood of finding a significant safety-relevant software defect after 20 years in the field is essentially zero. On the contrary, the likelihood of finding a security-relevant vulnerability after 20 years will likely be one. Therefore, when crafting the maintenance and end-of-life support terms, it is important to consider cybersecurity aspects with the expectation that software, hardware, and tools may need to remain supported for a very long period beyond what is normally expected for a safety product.

Concept

As we transition from project management activities into engineering activities, we find that the item definition between safety and security is the first candidate for integration and harmonization. Leveraging the item definition from safety, such as the item functions, the operational environment, and the item interfaces, can jump-start the process of preparing the item definition from a security perspective. Security engineers must adapt the safety item definition to expose security-relevant entities in the operational environment that may be missing from the safety item definition, as well as to account for security-relevant interfaces that may have no safety impact. For example, in the safety item definition, external vehicle interfaces such as Bluetooth or Wi-Fi may be ignored because they are seen as channels for delivering driver convenience features rather than contributing to safety-related functions such as ADAS. However, from a security perspective, accounting for such interfaces is critical to accurately defining attack paths and evaluating attack feasibility. Similarly, some tools such as diagnostic clients or debug equipment introduce new security threats and may be missing from the safety item definition when they are not safety-relevant. These must be included to account for all threats originating from the operational environment. Finally, adjusting the item boundary to incorporate additional system components that are relevant to the security analysis may be necessary.

As we transition into the definition of the cybersecurity concept, it is important to establish procedures for cross-reviews between safety and security goals on the one hand and safety and security requirements on the other. It is especially useful for security practitioners to be aware of safety goals as these are the objectives that security must safeguard against malicious attacks. Similarly, cross-functional reviews of safety and security requirements allow you to identify inconsistencies and even potential conflicts. When capturing safety and security requirements, it is natural to use a common requirements management system. Adapting the requirements management plans from safety to account for cybersecurity requirements management is also a good practice to avoid divergence in processes. Furthermore, having a way to identify requirements as safety-related, security-related, or dual-purpose is useful for traceability to the higher-level goals and requirements.

Design

Similarly, for the architecture definition, it is not practical to rely on separate architecture documents to capture safety and security aspects. Instead, a common architecture specification should be leveraged that supports the traceability of safety and security requirements to the architecture specification. Having a common architecture specification is also necessary to ease the analysis of both safety and security aspects and avoid teams becoming oblivious to certain aspects of the architecture that are overlapping, resulting in incomplete analysis from both sides.

Implementation

During implementation, both safety and security domains expect coding and design guidelines to be followed to prevent the introduction of software and design defects. Safety design principles share many aspects with security design principles due to the common objective of building reliable and efficient systems. It is recommended to unify such design guidelines because an engineer is expected to follow a consistent set of principles rather than constantly switch between the two domains. While this area is obvious, familiarity with safety and security design principles requires a conscious effort to establish a common level of understanding. This is one area where cross-literacy is essential to ensure that design choices consider safety and security with equal focus and intent.

Similarly, for coding practices, being aware of safety and security coding rules is essential if you wish to write defect- and weakness-free code. Furthermore, using a common toolset to apply safety and security static code checks helps identify rule violations and update the code. Here, again, executing these code checks cannot happen in silos; otherwise, the same software is likely to go through several iterations until all safety and security coding violations are fixed. Instead, organizations should institute common processes that enforce coding rule checks on certain events, such as code commits, or when a specific release milestone is reached.

Safety Work Product	Security Work Product	Scope of Harmonization
Safety Plan	Cybersecurity plan	Model the cybersecurity plan after the safety plan while meeting the requirements of ISO/SAE 21434 for planning. Create cross-functional links between the two plans. Leverage common aspects such as competency management, reused components, and off-the-shelf component lists.
Design Interface Agreement	Cybersecurity interface agreement	Model the CSIA after the design interface agreement while capturing the specific cybersecurity work products in the CSIA. Leverage a common method for approval and signoff across the documents. Align when these documents are initiated for common products that are both developed to achieve safety and security requirements.
Safety Item Definition	Cybersecurity item definition	Reuse the item definition from safety but specify the different aspects that must be captured regarding external interfaces and the operational environment. Expect to have two versions of the item definition with linkage to keep them synchronized.
Safety Goals	Cybersecurity goals	Establish cross-functional reviews.
Safety Concept	Cybersecurity concept	Establish cross-functional reviews.
Safety Requirements and Architecture Specifications	Cybersecurity specifications	It is recommended to use common requirements and architecture documents with safety and security tags and overlays for ease of traceability.
Safety Coding and Design Guidelines	Security coding and design guidelines	Harmonize the processes and guidelines to ensure that engineers can follow a common set of tools to enforce the guides. Unify safety and security design principles, if possible, to emphasize the need for engineers to consider both aspects at design time.
Safety Testing	Security testing	Model security test plans after the safety test plans. Define new test methods to address security while aiming to leverage common test infrastructures.

Safety Work Product	Security Work Product	Scope of Harmonization
Safety Validation	Security validation	Model security validation plans after safety validation plans while focusing on the differences in the methods and tools.
Safety Case	Cybersecurity case	Model the cybersecurity case after the safety case to produce a familiar and consistent format. Aim for a unified dependability case that can capture the overall evidence that the system is both safe and secure.
Safety Manual	Cybersecurity manual	Model the cybersecurity manual after the safety manual to avoid disrupting existing processes for capturing requirements allocated to the user for the safe and secure integration of the product. Establish links between the manuals and align the release cadence for ease of use by customers.
Safety Assessment Report	Cybersecurity assessment report	Align the processes to ensure assessments are planned in sequence to minimize the rework that can result from out-of-sync assessments.
Release for Post-Development Report	Release for post-development report	Model the cybersecurity report after the safety report while capturing the unique aspects of cybersecurity release conditions. Leverage a common format for approvals and signoff.
Safety Production Control Plan	Security production control plan	Model the security production control plan after the safety production control plan while focusing on the different aspects of applying cybersecurity controls during production. Perform cross-functional reviews to eliminate potential conflicting production requirements.
End of Safety Support	End of security support	Align the processes for end of support.

Table 6.1 – Mapping work products from the safety and security domains

Testing and validation

Entering the testing and validation phase, we realize that safety testing and validation plans can be leveraged to define security testing and security validation plans. Similarly, the test environment should be leveraged to the best extent possible between the two domains. While the test methods can differ, wherever possible, test cases that provide coverage of security requirements should be leveraged from functional and safety requirements and vice versa.

Release

Getting closer to the release phase, we first see the potential for synergies in the safety and security manuals. These manuals, which are intended to be shared with the system integrator contain requirements that must be followed to ensure the system is safely and securely integrated. As a result, these manuals should have a high degree of similarity in structure and scope. The process by which the content of these manuals is created should be harmonized as much as possible. For example, hazards or threats that are identified during the concept phase, and for which mitigation is allocated to one or more vehicle components, should flow into the safety and security manuals, respectively. Similarly, there can be common requirements allocated to the operational environment of the vehicle that should be incorporated in both the safety and security manuals. This calls for the ability to easily cross-reference content between the two documents to avoid divergence.

When preparing the security case, you should refer to the safety case as a model of how to capture the evidence regarding the level of security assurance in the product as a condition for production release. Ideally, a common safety and security case work product should be targeted as the arguments for safety and security can strengthen one another. However, when that is not possible, the two documents should leverage a common format and structure as they both rely on similar processes and input sources. Similarly, the safety and security assessment reports can be modeled to mirror one another. More importantly, aligning the execution of safety and security assessments throughout the project milestones ensures that safety and security findings can be addressed in a synchronized fashion and avoids triggering unnecessary re-assessment work. The product release approval process for both safety and security is a good candidate for harmonization to ensure that all product risks are presented to the approving authority in a consistent way to provide a holistic picture of release readiness.

Production

Moving to the production phase, the safety and security production control plans should be harmonized in a way that eases the execution of the plan in a production environment. Care must be taken to ensure that production steps that are necessary for safety such as end of line testing do not result in residual cybersecurity risks by exposing assets or leaving behind exploitable test routines after the production phase is complete. To eliminate the potential for conflicts between the plans, cross-reviews are necessary.

End of life

The definition of end-of-life support for safety and security needs alignment to address the aspect of monitoring and support. While ISO 26262 requires product monitoring in the field to detect previously unknown faults that can pose an unreasonable risk, the cybersecurity standard places an even greater emphasis on the need to continuously monitor cybersecurity events due to emerging threats and the discovery of new vulnerabilities. This monitoring activity requires dedicated resources that will periodically search through vulnerability reports from various sources to determine if there are any impacts to the product.

Moreover, when it comes to the monitoring and end-of-life support period, cybersecurity requires a longer period than safety due to the potential of continuous security patches as new threats and attack methods emerge.

Whenever a security update is deemed necessary, the safety impact has to be evaluated to avoid a scenario in which patching a security vulnerability creates a safety-relevant defect. As a result of these dependencies, organizations must adapt their end-of-life support plans to incorporate cybersecurity aspects.

In the remaining sections, we will take a deeper look at how synergies, conflict, and harmonization may be possible at the work product level of the processes mentioned here. This should give us a more practical feel for how these domains interact.

Creating synergies in the concept phase

The concept phase is where the security analysis begins. The aim is to map out the threats and choose the correct risk treatment decisions. As a result, a set of cybersecurity goals, claims, and requirements is produced. In this section, we will see how various security work products in the scope of the concept phase can be enhanced by considering inputs from the safety analysis, as well as the safety concept.

Item functions

As we saw earlier, the first step in performing a TARA in the concept phase is to define the item by listing its functions, the boundary at which those functions interact with the rest of the vehicle, and the environment in which the item operates. When performing a TARA for a safety-relevant system, many of the safety artifacts can be easily leveraged or adapted for security analysis.

The functions of the item serve as a valuable resource for grasping its objectives. Understanding the objectives of the system is the first step to uncovering misuse cases that result from security threats. Let's consider two main functions of a fictitious steering system: providing the driver with steering assist ability by reducing the exerted torque to steer the vehicle, and keeping the vehicle centered within the two lanes by continuously correcting the steering angle to match the center of the road. From a security point of view, it is the job of the security team to ensure that these functions are available and executed correctly, even when the system is under attack. To analyze the security resilience of the system when the system is under attack, we must account for all supporting functions that contribute to the vehicle-level functions. It is only after all these supporting functions are adequately protected that we can claim that the vehicle functions can be protected as well. For example, in our steering system, the ability of the system to provide steering assistance and lane centering hinges upon the following functions being performed correctly:

- The ability to sense data
- The ability to perform the control functions
- The ability to send actuation commands to the steering motors and other vehicle ECUs

Decomposing these abilities further, we uncover a host of supporting functions that must be protected to support the availability and correctness of the steering system. The correctness and availability of the sensing and actuation functions rely on the correctness and availability of communication services with steering system sensors and vehicle input messages. The correctness and availability of steering control functions rely on the correctness and availability of the runtime execution environment and its associated software. When evaluating supporting functions that are exposed to security threats and that contribute to these properties, we can identify several system features, such as software installation and reprogramming, diagnostic services, communication services, and system calibration services. Enumerating all such functions is the first step to ensure the security analysis will adequately cover all threats that can violate our high-level vehicle functions, namely steering assist and lane centering. As features get added, we are continuously evaluating whether the new feature is expanding the attack surface and producing new security risks. For example, let's assume that the OEM decides to add a new feature that allows the steering system to support hands-free steering through Ethernet frames received from the ADAS system. This feature will call for a new state management function to enable transitioning from human driver mode to an autonomous driving mode. The state management and Ethernet-based connectivity will now add a new set of threats that did not exist in the previous analysis, so the functions that are associated with this feature must be added to the list of functions that are subject to security analysis. Including the security team in the review of new functions is essential to intercept risky features before they are accepted by the program without proper evaluation of the security risk.

> **Pro tip**
> Having a toolchain that allows you to transfer information between the safety and security item definitions is recommended to ensure work products remain synchronized and the security and safety analysis remains consistent.

Item boundaries and operational environments

Besides item functions, the system context diagram can be reused for security analysis by copying over the common interfaces and components within the item boundary and operational environment. Here, it is important to pay attention to additional interfaces that may not be considered in the safety analysis but that are critical for security analysis. For example, debug interfaces will likely not be exposed in the operational environment of the safety item definition but will need to be added to the security analysis. Similarly, ECUs that provide external connectivity may be absent from the operational environment of the safety analysis but are mandatory to include for security analysis to understand the attack paths that originate from outside of the vehicle:

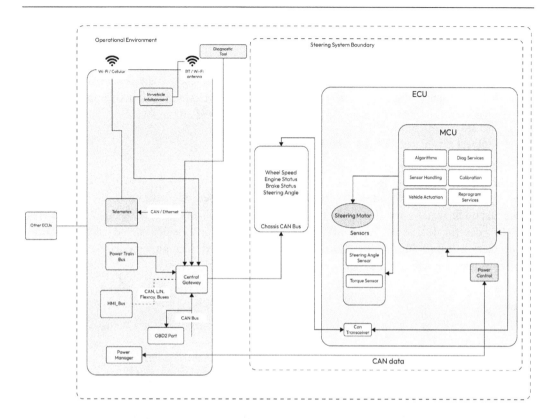

Figure 6.4 – Adapted item model from a safety item definition

Figure 6.4 shows an example item model of our steering system. The item boundary includes the MCU, which runs the sensing, control, and actuation functions. The calibration data that defines how the steering function behaves, as well as the diagnostic and reprogramming functions that can alter the steering system software and behavior at runtime, are all resident in the MCU embedded flash. Also, within the item boundary lies the specific sensors that are used for steering, along with the steering motor, which provides steering torque assist. All the CAN messages that are transmitted and consumed by the steering system are grouped within the chassis CAN bus within the item boundary. Similarly, the power control and CAN transceiver are considered elements of the item boundary as they impact the power of the system and its connectivity to the vehicle network. All these elements are inherited from the safety item boundary with the exception that diagnostic and reprogramming services are exposed due to security relevance. These functions must be included in the security analysis due to their critical impact on the integrity of the software and the correctness of its operation. Outside the item boundary, we can see that the telematics, **in-vehicle-infotainment** (**IVI**), OBD-2 port, and diagnostic tool are included in the operational environment (for the sake of demonstration). Such components are not normally included in the safety item model because they do not impact a safety-related function. However, from a cybersecurity point of view, these components contribute to the construction of attack paths originating from external vehicle interfaces.

Damage scenarios and hazards

With the item functions and item boundary well defined, we can proceed to asset identification and damage scenario creation. The former can leverage the results of the safety analysis to identify objects of value that contribute to the system's safety. For example, fault detection functions, sensor data, and vehicle actuation commands all are considered security assets based on the following criteria:

- The object is valuable for achieving a safety goal

- The object is exposed to a security threat

Of course, we cannot fully rely on safety-driven assets as other assets that have value can exist due to their impact on financial, operational, or privacy loss. For example, in our steering system, there are proprietary control algorithms that need confidentiality protection as well as driver crash logs that need protection against falsification. These can only be identified through a security analysis that considers all the functions of the system, regardless of their safety relevance.

> **Note**
> The TARA work products that were introduced here for safety relevance will be discussed in depth in *Chapter 7*.

When creating damage scenarios that impact safety, we can start by examining the hazards from the safety analysis and consolidate them into a set of damages. While it is possible to simply copy over the hazards and call them damage scenarios, typically, those hazards share an underlying asset and have common threats and attack paths. Therefore, consolidating overlapping damage scenarios into a smaller set of damages caused by the compromise of common unique assets will reduce redundant analysis in the TARA. For example, in our steering system example, there will be hazardous events such as the following:

- Unintended steering assist at high speed

- Loss of steering assist while entering the freeway

- Oversteering during a curve driving maneuver

- Understeering during the exit from a curve

All these hazards can occur if the firmware or sensor data is tampered with, or the network messages are spoofed. Therefore, we can consolidate the hazardous events into the following damage scenarios:

- Unintended, excessive, or erratic steering

- Loss of steering assistance

Note that we decided to keep the loss of steering as a unique damage scenario because looking ahead, we realize that system availability depends on different assets and attack paths.

When assessing the safety impact of the damage scenario, we must consult the HARA to find the safety severity level. One challenge here is that the safety severity level is defined for specific driving scenarios, such as driving during rain, over gravel, at night, and so on. For cybersecurity, these conditions are not significant because attackers who have successfully breached our steering system can trigger the attack during any driving scenario. Therefore, we must assume the most severe safety impact from all these hazardous events when deriving the damage scenario safety impact:

S0	S1	S2	S3
No injuries	Light and moderate injuries	Severe and life-threatening injuries	Life-threatening injuries, fatal injuries

Table 6.2 – ISO 26262 safety severity levels that are inherited by a damage scenario safety impact level

If the HARA is not available, such as due to the element being developed out of context, it is possible to derive damage scenarios from the system's FMEA. The latter captures the external system effect of each failure mode. By examining the FMEA, we can identify the safety severity of system-level impacts that can be leveraged for the damage scenario safety impact level when the damage is triggered through a cyberattack.

Next, we will learn how the output of the TARA interplays with the output of the HARA through safety and security goals.

Safety and security goals

After completing the TARA, we arrive at a set of cybersecurity goals that is tightly linked to the assets that need to be protected. If we have decomposed the functions that have an impact on the system's safety adequately, we should arrive at a set of security goals that, by default, ensures that the safety goals can be maintained when the system is under attack. For example, by deriving security goals to protect the integrity and authenticity of sensor and actuation data, as well as the integrity and availability of the steering control functions, we are supporting the safety goal of preventing unintended steering, oversteering, and understeering. To verify that the security goals provide adequate coverage for the safety goals, a cross-review of the safety and security goals is essential to align the final objectives of the system. For example, safety may have dictated that the system functions must remain available, even in the case of the loss of a certain steering sensor. As a result, safety analysis specifies redundant network communication channels to ensure that the system can remain functional even if one channel is experiencing faults that prevent sensor messages from being received. If the security analysis only specifies that corrupt messages are discarded but that DoS attacks are tolerated, then when both network channels are attacked simultaneously, the safety goal of system availability cannot be maintained. This requires careful consideration to agree on whether the system's behavior in response to the security risk is acceptable from a safety perspective. A cross-functional review can result in a decision that the risk of both channels being successfully attacked is low enough to accept that risk. If not, a design change may be needed to introduce additional security controls that block network interference before such corruption can become feasible.

Safety and security requirements

Assume that you have prepared your cybersecurity concept and you are ready to start refining requirements at the component and sub-component levels. Before you start, it is important to perform a cross-review between the cybersecurity and safety requirements of the item. Without this cross-review, the refined requirements will expose inconsistencies and even conflicts that will be more expensive to remedy later in the design process.

Let's assume that the security concept prescribes the use of a **hardware-protected security environment** (**HPSE**) to verify the cryptographic integrity of network communication messages. In doing so, the security concept expects all messages to be routed to the HPSE, where the MAC value of the message will be verified against the message payload. The initial security analysis ascertained that the HPSE hardware and firmware should be developed as QM components. A cross-review with the safety team reveals that this approach is inconsistent with the ASIL strategy for network message integrity protection. Relying on a QM component to achieve a safety requirement without any additional safety measures is not acceptable from a safety perspective. Upon further discussions between the teams, it is decided that network messages will need an additional safety integrity CRC value (rated with the required ASIL) that is checked by the application after the MAC has been correctly verified. This ensures that even if the MAC verification fails due to an HPSE hardware transient or random fault, the application can still detect that the message is corrupted by using the CRC mechanism that's computed with the help of the safety-certified MCU. This change was only possible because a process was in place to ensure that safety and security teams performed this cross-check.

> **Note**
> Having a way to identify interdependent safety and security requirements can be facilitated, for example, using traceability mechanisms in the requirements management system to uncover potential inconsistencies or even conflicts.

In addition to identifying conflicts or inconsistencies, the cross-review can identify requirement duplication, especially in the areas of integrity protection and freedom of interference. Since both domains are concerned with these properties, it is quite common to see safety and security requirements that address remarkably similar objectives. For example, a safety requirement can specify that ASIL D software partitions are spatially isolated from QM software partitions. Similarly, a security requirement can specify that software entities that are not intended to exchange data are isolated through memory management and protection mechanisms. While these requirements have a common objective, the security requirement has a larger scope as it is not concerned with the ASIL level of the software partition. From a security point of view, process and memory isolation is a strong condition to prevent a successful compromise of one software entity from corrupting other software entities in the system. Attempting to unify these requirements will increase the ASIL level scope of the unified requirement, effectively raising the ASIL level of the system components that must fulfill this requirement, even if they are not safety-relevant. Therefore, it is necessary to let the two requirements co-exist while creating a traceability relationship between them, as shown in *Figure 6.5*.

This helps the architecture sub-components realize this overlap when refining their requirements without the need to duplicate their component-level requirements to satisfy both objectives. As such, a refined sub-component requirement can be traced to both upstream requirements if the mechanism to fulfill both objectives is the same:

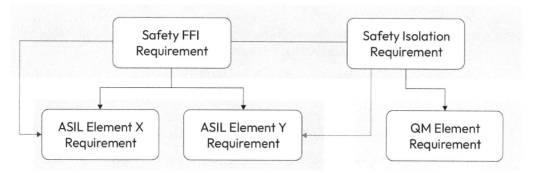

Figure 6.5 – Tracing a common requirement to both the safety and security requirements

Finding synergies and conflicts in the design phase

During the design phase, cybersecurity controls and requirements from the concept level are refined into technical security requirements and architectural elements and interfaces at the software and hardware levels. The refined security and safety requirements need another round of harmonization so that synergies can be identified and conflicts can be eliminated. In this stage, synergies are easier to identify as the mechanisms become more concrete due to requirements being allocated to the components of the architecture. When safety and security objectives overlap, a common strategy is to leverage security mechanisms to satisfy a safety objective and vice versa.

Leveraging safety and security mechanisms

As mentioned previously, safety and security objectives overlap in three main areas:

- Achieving freedom from interference
- Protecting data integrity
- Detecting and recovering from availability faults or attacks

During the design phase, it is desirable to reuse common mechanisms from the safety and security domains to achieve an overlapping objective. Doing so produces an efficient design as you can choose the optimal solution that satisfies the system's safety and security objectives.

Let's look at a system designed to detect communication message-related faults. In AUTOSAR classic, the end-to-end library enables a safety application to detect any one of the following faults with received messages:

- **Corruption**: A message can be corrupted as it traverses software and hardware layers from the source to the destination. This can occur, for example, due to a transient hardware fault in the communication controller, a bit-flip over the network channel, or an incorrect copy operation from the network controller to the software network stack.

- **Incorrect source**: The message's content can be accidentally swapped with that of another message due to a systematic software fault or a failure in the communication controller.

- **Stale messages**: A message can get delayed or become stuck due to a myriad of transient or systematic faults, such as loss of network message priority or a hardware failure in the sender.

- **Out-of-sequence messages**: A message may be received in the wrong order due to a network congestion issue.

- **Timeout**: A message may be lost temporarily or permanently due to a link fault.

Here are some of the safety mechanisms that the end-to-end library will use:

- Append a CRC to the message payload to detect message corruption errors

- Include the message identifier in the CRC calculation to detect the inadvertent swapping of message identifiers and the message payload

- Embed a message counter to ensure that the correct order and freshness of the message are easily determined

- Use the message counter to detect out-of-order messages

- Implement a timeout monitor that will report an error if the message is not received by the configured deadline period

Now, let's consider the same problem from a security angle. Through message spoofing, tampering, and DoS attacks, it is possible to trigger each one of the aforementioned fault conditions. For example, an attacker with network access can construct a message with tampered data, modify the message identifier, replay old messages, and block or delay transmission.

As we saw in *Chapter 2*, cryptography provides message integrity and authenticity protection through the use of MACs. The MAC value can include the message payload and source identifier to mitigate both payload corruption as well as malicious and inadvertent identifier swapping. Appending a freshness counter to the message and including it in the MAC generation makes it possible to detect replayed messages. Incorporating network intrusion detection systems can help in detecting DoS attacks that aim to block or congest the network traffic. Since the MAC provides stronger integrity protection than the CRC, it is desirable to leverage the MAC instead of the CRC to address the first two faults. The message freshness and order check can be unified between safety and security by applying a common detection policy. With security, the use of hardware-protected monotonic counters ensures that freshness is guaranteed even across ignition cycles. Finally, the timeout monitoring mechanism can be leveraged from safety to monitor when messages are not received within the expected deadline. Alternatively, the network intrusion detection software could also implement deadline monitoring to detect anomalies in the message reception rates. The decision to use security mechanisms to satisfy safety objectives introduces a new potential conflict relating to the safety integrity level at which that mechanism must be implemented. Once the security mechanism has been designated as a dual-purpose safety and security mechanism, it becomes governed by both the ISO 26262 process as well as the ISO/SAE 21434 process. This means that a safety analysis is needed to determine whether the mechanism can achieve the assigned ASIL level related to the safety goal that it is tracing. For example, safety analysis can uncover issues in how the MAC is verified with potential faults in the crypto engines, resulting in the verification step producing the wrong result. Even after ASIL alignment, there is a need for additional reviews to eliminate any potential conflicts that may arise from the additional safety modifications. For example, to make sure the MAC value is checked correctly, the safety team might suggest giving both the expected and received MAC values to the safety application, allowing it to compare them directly. Since the safety application is developed to the appropriate ASIL level and is executed within an ASIL-qualified runtime execution environment, this is considered an adequate countermeasure from a safety perspective. However, exposing the expected MAC value to the application exposes the system to the risk that an attacker can trick the system into divulging the expected MAC value by supplying invalidly authenticated messages and waiting for the system to report the expected MAC value. If the attacker has access to the application receiving this MAC, then they can construct a message with a valid MAC at a later point. Upon performing another round of cross-functional reviews, the security team adds another constraint that MAC values cannot be repeated due to the usage of a monotonic counter that prevents an old message from being replayed without detection. If an unauthentic message is received with a future freshness value, then the expected MAC will not be calculated to prevent oracle type attacks.

> **Note**
>
> Note that this process can sometimes be lengthy, so establishing periodic cross-functional reviews can help avoid endless circular discussions between the safety and security teams.

Another example where safety can leverage a security mechanism is with the secure boot check. Safety involves detecting software corruption before the system transitions into operational mode to prevent a software error that can result in a hazard. Rather than rely on a CRC to verify the integrity of the software image at startup, safety can leverage the digital signature algorithm applied during secure boot to verify both the integrity and authenticity of the software image. However, since secure boot is now aiming to achieve a safety goal, it must undergo a safety analysis to ensure faults that can occur during the secure boot sequence do not result in the designation of a corrupted image as valid. Here, a safety analysis method such as FMEA can be leveraged to ensure that the secure boot check has adequate safety countermeasures to eliminate faults with a high **risk priority number** (**RPN**):

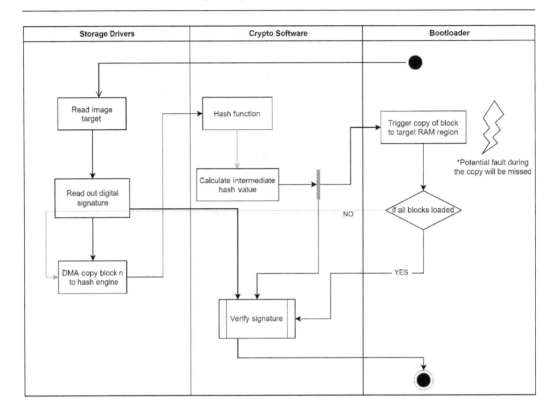

Figure 6.6 – Unsafe handling of boot check

As shown in *Figure 6.6*, assume that during the boot check, each block of code is copied from flash memory into the hash engine, and then loaded into the target RAM region. Once all the blocks have been hashed and copied to RAM, a hash check is performed by comparing the hash of the blocks copied from flash memory with the signed hash that was fetched from the image itself. This way, it is possible to determine whether the image loaded from flash memory has any corruption (either due to fault scenarios or tampering attacks). However, the safety analysis uncovers a scenario where the RAM block itself may become corrupted due to a hardware memory fault while the block is being copied from flash memory into the RAM region. As a result, the final loaded image will still contain corrupted data, even though the source image in flash memory has been verified to be authentic and free from corruption. Thanks to the safety analysis, we can choose to modify the secure boot sequence to load the blocks into RAM first, and then feed the data into the hash engine, as shown in *Figure 6.7*. If a corruption occurs while the image is being loaded into RAM, the final hash check will fail, resulting in the fault being detected, regardless of whether the fault originated from a malicious or a non-malicious cause:

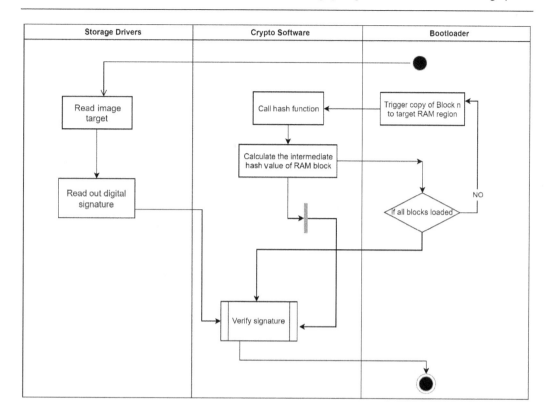

Figure 6.7 – Safe handling of boot check

As shown in the timeout monitoring case of the end-to-end safety library, security can leverage safety mechanisms in the case of attack detection. Since safety specifies rigorous requirements for fault detection, in many cases, security analysis may rely on such monitors to detect security-related attacks on one condition: the monitoring mechanism itself must be hardened against tampering or disablement. Let's assume that security wants to mitigate a scenario where an image processing engine can enter a frozen state due to malicious inputs from the user. A quick check on the safety error handling of hardware engine failures uncovers a monitoring algorithm that detects a hanging condition and issues a recovery sequence. By verifying that the monitoring condition can handle the malformed input, the security analysis can leverage this monitor to detect DoS attacks that aim to make the hardware engine unavailable. Next, the security of the monitoring mechanism is evaluated by analyzing potential attack paths that can disable or tamper with the safety monitor. The analysis may result in additional constraints on how the monitor is set up and who can configure its parameters, ensuring that the safety mechanism is both effective and resilient in the face of both cyberattacks and system faults.

Table 6.3 shows additional mechanisms and techniques that can be considered for harmonization between safety and security domains:

Safety	Security
Plausibility checks on calibration data	Sanity checks on calibration data
Redundant storage and comparison of calibration data	Redundant storage of critical security parameters
Calibration data checks using error-detecting codes	Integrity check values for critical security parameters
Robustness against erroneous inputs	Input validation against malformed inputs
Independence or freedom of interference between different functionalities	Isolation and sandboxing to maintain spatial integrity

Table 6.3 – Mapping safety mechanisms that overlap security mechanisms

Self-tests across safety and security

Self-tests are an established safety technique for detecting active and latent faults. The latter consists of hidden or dormant defects that have not yet caused any malfunction but may cause a malfunction if certain conditions are met. These conditions could include changes in the system environment, component aging, or interaction with other faults. Self-tests such as **built-in self-tests (BISTs)** ensure that such faults are detected before they can be hazardous to the system. These tests are typically performed during initialization but may also be executed at runtime with careful consideration so that they don't interfere with ongoing operations.

On the other hand, security relies on self-tests for security-critical functions such as entropy tests of hardware random number generators and known answer tests for cryptographic functions. These types of tests are meant to detect faults that prevent the system from generating the right level of entropy of random numbers and to prevent faulty cryptographic accelerators or implementations from being used to perform security-critical operations. While the focus area of the safety and security self-tests is different, the security domain benefits from the safety-driven self-tests when they are applied to security elements such as the HSPE or cryptographic accelerators. Detecting active faults increases the confidence in the correctness of the underlying hardware to perform its function, which contributes to the overall reliability of the system.

Leveraging error detection safety mechanisms

Understanding how a safety-critical system can detect and respond to a safety-related error is useful when you're looking for ways to detect an attack. This further lays the foundation for what is an acceptable security policy when a security anomaly is detected.

The following list demonstrates mechanisms that are employed by safety for error prevention and detection:

- **Homogenous redundancy** to control transient or random faults in hardware involves using redundant hardware components to detect and control transient or random faults

- **Diverse redundancy** involves using multiple, diverse components or systems to prevent and control systematic failures

- **Error-correcting codes** (**ECCs**) are used to detect and correct errors that may occur in memory or data transmission

- **Enforce access permission checks** over software or hardware to prevent unauthorized access to shared safety-related resources

These strategies are well in line with the security objectives for attack detection, protecting the system in case of an attack, and possible recovery. Some of these mechanisms can even aid in mitigating special types of attacks. For example, dual lock step cores, a type of homogenous redundancy mechanism, can, under certain conditions, enable the detection of glitch attacks due to the difference in the state of the programming element (for example, the CPU). Another mechanism that can be leveraged for security is ECC protection, which involves adding extra bits to each memory word to detect and correct bit errors. When an error is detected, the ECC protection can correct the error automatically, preventing data corruption and maintaining data integrity. Rowhammer attacks flip adjacent bits in RAM cells by writing a specific sequence in the attacker's memory space. Rowhammer's ability to flip bits in the target memory block is severely hampered when ECC is supported. Enforcing access permissions is a common security strategy, with the latter providing a larger scope of access permission enforcement through security policies for shared files, libraries, and resources. Here, security provides a wider scope of access permissions as it is not limited by whether the shared resource is safety-relevant or not. It is noteworthy that safety mechanisms alone are not guaranteed to be fully effective against security attacks because they were not designed to treat such attack scenarios. Careful consideration must be applied when you're planning to leverage such mechanisms for security.

When it comes to error handling, safety employs a few strategies when an error is detected:

- **Deactivation of failing functions** involves detecting when a function has failed and taking appropriate action, such as deactivating the function, to maintain a safe state

- **Static recovery** involves returning the system to a safe state after a fault has been detected, without the need for active intervention

- **Graceful degradation** involves prioritizing critical functions and allowing non-critical functions to degrade gracefully in the event of a fault

The security domain must be aware of the designed safety error-handling strategy to avoid defining conflicting security policies. Furthermore, having a central system element that handles both error reports as well as security anomaly logs can be an effective method to ensure a harmonized approach between the two domains.

Eliminating inconsistencies in the error response

Inconsistencies can occur when defining safety and security error-handling strategies. As we saw previously, from a safety point of view, deactivating failing functions up to a full graceful shutdown as a result of a severe safety failure is considered an acceptable safe state. On the other hand, enabling such a graceful shutdown in response to a system failure serves as a potential attack vector where an attacker mounts a DoS attack by maliciously triggering the fault condition(s) that results in the safe state. Let's assume that an attacker discovers that replaying five consecutive messages with the same counter value results in the system reporting a stale message fault and thereby disabling certain safety functions that depend on that message. As part of the safety error handling response, the system will attempt to restore functionality after receiving a set number of fresh messages. Now, the attacker who has gained network access will easily mount such an attack by periodically sending stale messages and then repeating the pattern after the function is restored, causing the system to continuously degrade the safety function and then restore cyclically. At a minimum, this causes driver inconvenience due to the fault being displayed on the instrument cluster requiring the driver to take their car to the service shop. This, in turn, can result in financial damage to the automotive manufacturer due to increased warranty costs. Due to the nature of this pattern, it is desirable to log these events for further analysis. Using an IDS that reports anomalies to a **security operation center** (SOC) via the telematics unit, the OEM can detect such attack patterns and start the vulnerability analysis process to determine how the attacker managed to gain access to the system. Instating reviews of safety error-handling strategies by security engineers allows the two teams to agree on an effective error-handling strategy that is hardened against security manipulation. In some cases, it is not possible to mitigate the exploitation of the safe state by attackers due to the ease of mounting such an attack. However, it should be possible to detect such patterns to ensure that an active attack is not falsely logged as a normal system failure.

Similarly, with a security error policy, there is a need to harmonize the security and safety behavior when the system detects an attack. A normal security action in response to an attack consists of immediately making assets inaccessible and issuing a reset or halting the system to prevent further damaging attacks. However, this behavior can be dangerous if the vehicle is in motion, where a sudden reset would result in the interruption of safety functions. Therefore, the security team, in collaboration with the safety team, must define the acceptable secure state that would lead to the graceful shutdown and restoration of the system while protecting the system assets. For example, the security policy can include disabling access to cryptographic keys so that the system can still operate but cannot authenticate any messages from the vehicle side. This will eventually result in the degradation of safety functions that rely on such messages by mimicking the scenario where a network error has occurred.

Another important aspect of aligning error handling and security policies is considering the failure response and handling time. Safety provides well-defined metrics for fault handling through **Fault Tolerant Time Interval** (FTTI) and **Fault Handling Time Interval** (FHTI). FTTI refers to the time interval from the occurrence of a fault to the point at which the hazard occurs. Therefore, any safety mitigation must be active before the FTTI time is reached. As shown in *Figure 6.8*, FTTI is the maximum duration for which the system can operate safely before a hazard occurs if the safe state is not reached before the **diagnostic test interval** (DTI) and **fault reaction time** (FRTI) expire:

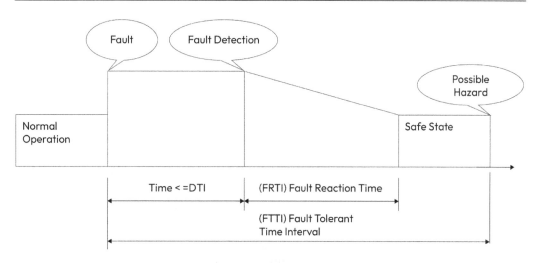

Figure 6.8 – Breakdown of the FTTI

FHTI, on the other hand, is the time interval within which a fault must be detected, diagnosed, and handled to prevent a hazardous event from occurring. FHTI is the maximum time allowed for the system to recover from a fault before it poses a safety risk. FHTI is used to define the safety mechanisms and procedures for fault detection, diagnosis, and handling. When performing security analysis, security must be aware of these metrics to ensure that a security error policy does not violate these times for safety-critical functions. For example, if a cryptographic function is used to detect a safety message corruption through a MAC verification operation, the function must be able to indicate the integrity status within the FHTI to allow the application enough time to react to this corrupted value.

Parallels in design principles

If you work in functional safety, then you are probably familiar with the term **safe by design**. Cybersecurity engineering promotes a similar practice called **secure by design** to ensure that while designing a system, security is a primary consideration and not merely an afterthought or an add-on. This practice is enforced in both disciplines through the adherence to a well-defined set of design principles. These principles aim to reduce safety and security risks by building system architectures that are easier to analyze and are less prone to defects and design weaknesses. By simplifying the design and implementation of the software, we can ease the verification and validation of the software for safety- and security-critical applications.

Table 6.4 shows the software design principles that are defined in *Part 6* of **ISO 26262** side by side with common security design principles as defined in *NIST SP800-53*, showing areas of overlap and correlation:

Number	Safety Principle	Security Principle
1	Organize software components into a clear and well-defined hierarchical structure. This ensures that the components are properly interconnected and that each component is responsible for a specific function or task.	The principle of clear abstractions requires that a system has simple, well-defined interfaces and functions that provide a consistent and intuitive view of the data and how it is managed.
2	Restrict the size and complexity of software components. This ensures that each component is designed and tested for a specific function or task and that the interactions between components can be well defined and tested. This naturally eases safety analysis and component testing.	Modularity enables the isolation of functions and related data structures into well-defined logical units. Layering allows the relationships of these units to be better understood so that dependencies are clear and undesired complexity can be avoided.
3	Restrict the size of interfaces to ensure that only the required interfaces are exposed to other system components to minimize the opportunities for misuse and ease integration testing.	The principle of reduced complexity states that the system design should be as simple and small as possible. A small and simple design is more understandable, more analyzable, and less prone to errors.
4	Strong cohesion within each software component by focusing the component's scope on a single functionality or behavior.	Partially ordered dependencies and system layering involve organizing system components into layers based on their level of dependence on other components. This means that components with fewer dependencies are placed in lower layers, while components with more dependencies are placed in higher layers. This contributes to the simplicity and coherency of the system design.
5	Loose coupling between software components involves designing software components that are independent and loosely coupled. When components are loosely coupled, changes to one component are less likely to affect other components, which can make it easier to maintain and modify the system over time without compromising safety.	The least common mechanism principle states that the amount of mechanisms common to more than one user and depended on by all users is minimized. This reduces the potential impact of security breaches by minimizing the sharing of components or resources between different users or processes.

Number	Safety Principle	Security Principle
6	The appropriate scheduling properties principle ensures that safety-critical tasks are scheduled and executed within their expected time slice. This can involve techniques such as real-time scheduling, priority-based scheduling, and deadline-driven scheduling, which help ensure that safety-critical functions are prioritized and executed on time while minimizing the risk of interference from non-critical tasks.	The principle of least privilege is based on the idea that users or processes should only have access to the minimum set of resources or privileges that is required to perform their specific tasks or functions. This helps minimize the potential impact of security breaches or attacks to strengthen the scheduling properties of system tasks.
7	Restricted use of interrupts aims to produce a deterministic system that is less likely to experience unexpected high workload peaks. It also lowers the risk that a malfunctioning component can render the system unavailable through a deluge of interrupts.	The principle of attack surface reduction aims to reduce the number of potential entry points that can be exploited by attackers to gain unauthorized access to a system or its resources. Reducing interrupt mechanisms is one way to minimize the potential misuse of these interrupts, effectively shrinking the attack surface.
8	Appropriate spatial isolation of software components. This principle aims to prevent faults or failures in one component from affecting other components or systems, by enforcing memory and resource isolation between different components.	Isolation of security functions from non-security functions using a separation boundary through partitioning and domain separation. Systems can implement code separation through the support of exception levels, filesystem access permissions, and address space memory access management by implementing least privilege.
9	Appropriate management of shared resources involves managing and controlling the use of shared resources such as memory, network bandwidth, or I/O devices in a way that minimizes the risk of conflicts or errors that could lead to system failures.	The minimized sharing principle aims to protect user domain resources from arbitrary active entities by ensuring that no resource is shared unless that sharing has been explicitly requested and granted.

Table 6.4 – Comparing safety and security design principles based on NIST SP800-53 revision 5

It is recommended that an organization develops a unified set of design principles that addresses both safety and security design concerns in a harmonized fashion. During the architecture design phase, engineers are expected to be intimately familiar with both sets of principles to ensure that the architecture is consistently free from safety and security risks. Even if the system has no safety relevance, the safety design principles can be useful to reinforce the quality aspects of the system, which is a prerequisite property for system security. This ensures the design is comprehensible, simple, verifiable, modular, and maintainable. These principles further ease the security analysis, minimize the opportunity for misuse, and decrease the likelihood of design errors, which, in turn, can be abused as vulnerabilities by a determined attacker.

Next, we'll look at the differences and similarities between secure coding practices and safe coding techniques.

Secure coding practices versus safe coding techniques

Similar to the design principles, coding guidelines between safety and security have a high degree of correlation. Both safety and security engineering approaches aim to reduce code complexity to prevent defects and vulnerabilities. They both require the usage of language subsets to avoid risky features of the programming language that can introduce unexpected or unwanted behavior. This can be enforced by using static code analysis tools based on MISRA C, CERT C/C++, and AUTOSAR C++. Normally, the toolchains support the safety and security guidelines, allowing the developers to check for all coding rule violations in a single run. When it comes to defensive coding techniques, there is a high degree of overlap between several such techniques:

- Input validation requires all inputs from external sources to be validated to ensure they conform to the expected formats, ranges, and data types. This can help prevent working on implausible inputs and causing buffer overflows of code and data segments.

- Boundary checking ensures that all variables and data structures are used within their defined boundaries, such as array sizes, maximum values, and other limits. This can help prevent memory overflows, buffer overruns, and other types of errors.

- Error handling requires the use of appropriate error-handling techniques to gracefully handle unexpected conditions, such as invalid inputs, system errors, or resource usage violations. This can help prevent crashes or other system failures that could lead to safety hazards or leave the system in a vulnerable state.

- Proper management of concurrency and elimination of race conditions prevent the system from reaching a deadlock state, crashing, or working on malicious inputs (for example, in the case of TOCTU bugs).

- Structural constraints ensure that a program operates predictably, such as requiring that a function has only one exit point. This makes the control flow of the function easier to understand and test. Similarly, defining explicit conditions to terminate loops reduces the risk of infinite loops, which can lead to unresponsiveness or system crashes.

While there are significant areas of overlap, some differences exist in the way certain defensive coding techniques are applied and the aspects they cover. An example unique safety defensive coding technique is the "write-read-back" sequence when handling safety-critical registers. By reading back the register value after the write operation, the software ensures that a hardware fault that prevented the write operation from completing successfully does not go undetected, leaving the system or a component in an improperly configured state:

```
void process_register(uint8_t* register_ptr, uint8_t data) {
    // Initialize the register
    register_value = 0x00;

    // Write to the register
    write_register(register_ptr, data);

    // Read back the register
    read_register(register_ptr, register_value);

    if (register_value == data) {
        // Proceed
    } else {
        Log_fault(register_ptr, register_value, data);
    }
}
```

This type of technique is not normally enforced in the security domain due to the focus on malicious causes rather than transient or random hardware faults.

Similarly, security defines unique defensive coding techniques against glitching and fault injection attacks. Such techniques include the usage of constants with large hamming distances when performing conditional checks and performing duplicate negated if statements. The first coding technique prevents the case that a glitch of the conditional check could flip the test bit from a zero to a one, causing the check to pass. By using a specially constructed constant (for example, 0x3CA5965A), even if the test bit is glitched, it is not going to match the expected constant, as shown here:

```
if (signatureVerificationResult == 0x3CA5965A)
{
    // Hamming distance check passed, now perform a second check using
    // the inverse of the variable
    if (~signatureVerificationResult != 0xC35A69A5)
    {
        Log_fault(error_type);
    }
    else
    {
        Allow_application_to_run(); // Attacker wants to get here
                                    // through glitching
    }
}
```

The second check prevents a glitch that causes a CPU instruction to be skipped from bypassing a critical security function, such as the signature verification result check. In the preceding example, the `if` statement is repeated twice, first with a positive test, and the second with a negated test, making it very difficult to glitch both checks to launch an application that is failing the signature verification check.

> **Why are the two checks needed?**
>
> The first check (`signatureVerificationResult == 0x3CA5965A`) determines whether `signatureVerificationResult` has the correct and expected value. The second check verifies the inverse (bitwise negation) of `signatureVerificationResult`. This step ensures that the value hasn't been tampered with in a way that might evade the primary check. If an attacker tries to induce an error (for example, through voltage or clock glitching) that changes the value of `signatureVerificationResult`, both the original value and its inverse would likely change. Therefore, even if a glitch causes the first check to pass erroneously, it's improbable that the inverse of the glitched value will also pass the second check. The significance of this dual check is to increase the resilience of the system against fault injection attacks.

It should be evident now that safety engineering provides the security engineering approach with many reinforcing properties for system quality and reliability. When safety is not in scope for an automotive system, it is important to supplement such measures with quality management processes that ensure the system's dependability in the absence of normal software defects.

Now that we have seen similarities and differences in the coding techniques, we will do the same for the test strategies during the integration and verification development phase.

Synergies and differences in the testing phase

Verification testing takes place at multiple stages of the development process, starting with the unit level, then the component level, and ending at the system level. A system developed according to ISO 26262 is expected to achieve a high level of quality assurance through testing rigor in proportion to the system safety integrity level. These test methods reinforce the quality argument of the system by verifying the correctness of the unit design and implementation, and the ability of the integrated system components to achieve the system objectives. One example test method defined by safety engineering is **boundary value and equivalence class-based (BVEC)** testing. BVEC testing involves testing the software system with values that are at the boundaries of the input domain or just outside of it to detect improper software responses. BVEC testing aims to identify any errors or exceptions that occur at the boundary values of input domains. It also feeds the software with sample input values from input equivalence classes as a replacement for exhaustive input testing. Fuzz testing, on the other hand, involves inputting a large number of random or semi-random data inputs into a system to test its response to unexpected or malformed inputs. Fuzz testing aims to identify software vulnerabilities by bombarding a system with a wide range of inputs, including inputs that were not anticipated by the software developers. BVEC testing is best used in cases where the input domain can be easily defined and the potential failure modes at the boundaries of that domain can be anticipated. However, it may not be effective in detecting vulnerabilities that are outside the input domain, such as those that arise from unexpected user inputs. Fuzz testing, on the other hand, is ideal for identifying vulnerabilities due to unexpected inputs. It can be especially useful for identifying buffer overflow and memory corruption vulnerabilities. However, fuzz testing may not be as effective in identifying errors or exceptions at the boundary values of input domains, which is where BVEC testing excels. While fuzz testing is a recommended method for verifying the system's resilience to malformed inputs, in some narrow cases, BVEC testing may be leveraged as a replacement for fuzzing if the software interfaces have well-defined input ranges (for example, Boolean input values). Furthermore, when coupled with code coverage testing tools, fuzz testing can be an effective method to verify that a high degree of test coverage has been established using a large space of malformed inputs. This increases the confidence in the code being able to handle malformed inputs without crashing or exposing system secrets.

Requirements-based testing can be commonly used to verify the correct implementation and integration of safety and security mechanisms. By designing test cases that exercise the condition that triggers a mechanism, the test can uncover any related defects in both positive and negative cases. For example, a requirement for enforcing digital signature verification over boot images can be tested by programming an image with a corrupted block and verifying that the signature verification check resulted in a boot failure and system halt. While in essence, this is the same as any functional test that involves negative and positive testing, the security test cases must account for security constraints that may not be apparent to the tester. Therefore, all the security constraints related to the requirement must be well known if you wish to write complete and consistent test cases. For example, with the digital signature verification test, the test case can include constraints on how small the corruption should be to verify that the mechanism is properly implemented and deployed to capture the corruption of even a single bit.

One area of differentiation between safety and security testing is **fault injection testing**. This test method is essential to ensuring that the hardware and software can safely handle fault conditions that may exist naturally throughout the lifetime of the product. Fault injection testing of software involves corrupting variables, register values, or even code segments. Verifying that the system detects and responds gracefully indicates that the system has been adequately designed to handle such fault conditions.

Fault injection testing can be adapted for security by focusing on faults that can be maliciously triggered by an attacker beyond what a safety fault injection test may detect. For example, a safety fault injection test of a stack overflow overwrites a process stack buffer to mimic a software failure. Stack overflow detection mechanisms will trigger an exception when specific markers on the stack are modified, resulting in the system logging the fault and terminating the offending process. However, from a security point of view, additional tests are needed to mimic a security attack in which parts of the stack are corrupted without the overwrite of the stack overflow marker. These tests will need to target the return address on the stack to change the software control flow. If a security mechanism is correctly implemented to detect stack corruption, the system will trigger an exception and an error policy will be executed.

> **Fault injection versus penetration testing**
>
> Penetration testing and fault injection testing from **Functional Safety (FuSa)** focus on intentionally introducing irregularities or anomalies into a system to observe its response and identify defects. While fault injection in FuSa primarily aims to ensure that safety mechanisms can detect and handle hardware or software faults, thus preventing unintended operations, penetration testing extends this framework by simulating deliberate attacks on a system. Its goal is not just to uncover unintentional weaknesses but also to assess the system's resilience against malicious exploits, ensuring that data remains secure and unauthorized access is prevented.

Similar to fault injection testing, penetration testing is a unique cybersecurity test method that is performed to identify unknown vulnerabilities in the system by emulating the actions taken by an attacker. Penetration testing requires a combination of test tools that are mostly unique for security. These can be network fuzzes, reverse engineering tools, and specialized scripts that aim to identify unprotected assets such as hardcoded keys or passwords.

It is important to note that although safety tests can reinforce cybersecurity properties, a safety-critical system does not apply the same level of test rigor to all its components. Due to the ASIL level partitioning, only the high ASIL software partitions and hardware components will be rigorously tested. While a QM-level software or hardware component is not safety-relevant, it can still exhibit high security relevance, thus requiring a high degree of test rigor to ensure that defects in such components do not materialize as security vulnerabilities that can impact the rest of the system. Furthermore, when developing test cases, it is useful for security testers to be familiar with the full test environment and test tools available from safety to identify areas of overlap and minimize duplication.

Summary

This chapter explored the similarities and differences between safety and security engineering approaches, highlighting the importance of taking an integrated approach to these two disciplines. First, this chapter focused on the process impacts and the need to extend existing safety and quality processes to satisfy the cybersecurity engineering approach. We then discussed the unique areas of each domain, emphasizing the need to increase safety and security literacy to understand how safety engineering focuses on identifying and managing risks that prevent accidents, while security engineering focuses on identifying and mitigating threats that prevent intentional harm. Conflicts between safety and security can arise, and this chapter presented strategies for resolving these conflicts. Similarly, many areas of synergies were explored throughout the concept, design, implementation, and testing phases. Several examples were shown in which safety reinforces the security properties of the system and vice versa. Importantly, this chapter emphasized that safety practices can be a necessary but not sufficient condition for security. In conclusion, safety and security engineering approaches share many commonalities, but it is critical to recognize and address the differences between the two disciplines in a systematic approach.

In the next chapter, we will take a deep dive into a practical approach to threat modeling, which will leverage our awareness of the functional safety domain to enrich the security analysis with safety-related inputs.

References

To learn more about the topics that were covered in this chapter, take a look at the following resources:

- *[1]* T. Novak, A. Treytl, and A. Gerstinger, *Embedded security in safety-critical automation systems*, in Proceedings of the 26th International System Safety Conference (ISSC 2008), Vancouver, Canada, 2008, pp. S.1–11.

- *[2]* L. Piètre-Cambacédès, *Des relations entre sûreté et sécurité*, Télécom ParisTech, 2010.

- *[3]* G. Stoneburner, *Toward a Unified Security-Safety Model*, Computer, vol. 39, no. 8, pp. 96-97, 2006.

- *[4]* D. P. Eames and J. D. Moffett, *The Integration of Safety and Security Requirements*, in Proceedings of the 18th International Conference on Computer Computer Safety, Reliability and Security, London, UK, UK, 1999, pp. 468-480.

- *[5]* B. Hunter, *Integrating Safety And Security Into The System Lifecycle*, in Improving Systems and Software Engineering Conference (ISSEC), Canberra, Australia, 2009, p. 147.

- *[6]* M. Sun, S. Mohan, L. Sha, and C. Gunter, *Addressing Safety and Security Contradictions in Cyber-Physical Systems*, in 1st Workshop on Future Directions in Cyber-Physical Systems Security (CPSSW'09), Newark, United States, 2009.

- *[7]* A. Derock, *Convergence of the latest standards addressing safety and security for information technology*, in Proceedings of Embedded Real Time Software and Systems (ERTS2 2010), Toulouse, France, 2010.

- *[8]* Force, Joint Task. *Assessing security and privacy controls in information systems and organizations*. NIST Special Publication 800 (2022): 53A.

- *[9]* J. Delange, L. Pautet and P. Feiler, *Validating Safety and Security Requirements for Partitioned Architectures*, in Reliable Software Technologies – Ada-Europe 2009, F. Kordon and Y. Kermarrec, Eds. Springer Berlin Heidelberg, 2009, pp. 30–43.

- *[10]* S. Zafar and R. G. Dromey, *Integrating safety and security requirements into the design of an embedded system*, in Software Engineering Conference, 2005. APSEC '05. 12th Asia-Pacific, 2005.

- *[11]* D. K. Holstein and B. Singer, *Quantitative Security Measures for Cyber and Safety Security*, in ISA Safety & Security Symposium, 2010.

- *[12]* W. Pieters, Z. Lukszo, D. Hadziosmanovic, and J. van den Berg, *Reconciling Malicious and Accidental Risk in Cyber Security*, J. Internet Serv. Inf. Secur. JISIS, vol. 4, no. 2, pp. 4-26, 2014.

- *[13]* W. Young and N. G. Leveson, *An integrated approach to safety and security based on systems theory*, Commun. ACM, vol. 57, no. 2, pp. 31-35, Feb. 2014.

- *[14]* W. Young and N. G. Leveson, *Systems Thinking for Safety and Security*, in Annual Computer Security Applications Conference, New Orleans, LA, pp. 9-13, December.

- *[15]* Kriaa, Siwar. *Joint safety and security modeling for risk assessment in cyber-physical systems.* Diss. Université Paris Saclay (COmUE), 2016.

- *[16]* Kreiner, Christian Josef, and Richard Messnarz. *Integrated Assessment of AutomotiveSPICE 3.0, Functional Safety ISO 26262, Cybersecurity SAE J3061.* IIR Konferenz: ISO. Vol. 26,262. 2017.

Part 3:
Executing the Process to Engineer a Secure Automotive Product

In this part, we shift into the practical aspects by building on top of what we have learned in the prior chapters to make the vehicle secure. First, we go through the threat modeling approach to understand how to perform an effective TARA that uncovers all threats relevant to our product. Then, we explore technical cybersecurity controls that can be applied at the vehicle architectural layers. Finally, we dive into the ECU hardware and software architecture to highlight technical cybersecurity controls that can be applied at those layers as well.

This part has the following chapters:

- *Chapter 7, A Practical Threat Modeling Approach for Automotive Systems*
- *Chapter 8, Vehicle-Level Security Controls*
- *Chapter 9, ECU-Level Security Controls*

A Practical Threat Modeling Approach for Automotive Systems

Threat modeling is at the core of any secure engineering process. It is the driver for understanding and prioritizing threats against the system and deriving cybersecurity goals, security controls, and security requirements necessary to treat those threats. Before performing a **threat analysis and risk assessment** (**TARA**), teams are essentially blind to most risks that their system is exposed to. They also have no clear vision of which risks are the most urgent to treat. Even when a rudimentary security analysis has taken place through brainstorming or consulting a security expert, there is no guarantee that risks have been analyzed comprehensively. The TARA solves this problem by providing engineering teams with a systematic approach to exposing and prioritizing threats based on a risk management approach. Due to the safety and operational aspects of automotive systems, simply borrowing threat modeling methods from IT is not adequate. ISO/SAE 21434 addresses this gap by providing an automotive-centric threat modeling approach. The approach breaks down a complex automotive system into its most security-relevant functions, leverages existing system models for analysis, and produces a finite set of threats within a reasonable time frame to allow the project teams to make informed decisions about risk prioritization. Building on the ISO 21434-defined TARA method, this chapter delves into practical aspects of that approach by shedding light on common pitfalls and highlighting best practices. The goal of this chapter is to provide you with the tools and methods needed to avoid common pitfalls and produce value-adding security analysis that achieves the right security level of the system without severely impacting the project schedule and delivery commitments.

In this chapter, we shall cover the following topics:

- The fundamentals of performing an effective TARA
- Common pitfalls to avoid when preparing a TARA
- Defining the appropriate TARA scope

- The practical TARA approach
- Case study using a **digital video recorder** (**DVR**)

The fundamentals of performing an effective TARA

In *Chapter 5*, we introduced some of the basic tenets of the ISO/SAE 21434 threat modeling approach. But even when following the ISO methodology, it is not uncommon to execute the TARA poorly, producing sub-optimal analysis results while exceeding the allotted time for analysis. It is not uncommon for teams to spend so much time performing the TARA that it makes it impossible to incorporate the risk mitigations within a given project schedule. As we dive deeper into the practical aspects of a TARA, we will keep this in mind to ensure that we are not simply going through the motions of performing the TARA but rather producing a valuable output within a reasonable time frame to elevate the security bar of our automotive systems. But first, let's review some of the basic terms and definitions that will be repeatedly referenced throughout this chapter.

Assets

ISO/SAE 21434 defines an asset as "*an object that has value or contributes to value.*" It also hints that an asset has cybersecurity properties, which are attributes requiring protection such as **confidentiality, integrity, and availability** (or the famous **CIA** triad for short). This set of attributes can be extended to include authenticity, authorization, and accountability. These granular properties can be helpful when deriving threats, but granularity also means a more rigorous and lengthy security analysis. Assets in the automotive context can either be tangible or non-tangible. While some organizations may include non-tangible assets such as safety or performance, we stress the need to focus on tangible assets as they are the easiest to produce concrete and finite threats.

> **Tangible versus intangible assets**
>
> Intangible assets describe an ephemeral concept of the system, such as system safety or the system's ability to achieve its operational and performance targets. Teams that use intangible assets end up defining abstract cybersecurity goals that are very hard to validate, such as "*The system should ensure that all performance metrics are not violated.*" Tangible assets, on the other hand, refer to a concrete system object of value that can be contained within a physical boundary. For example, an actuation command that is transported over a physical network link, a software calibration table that is loaded in a volatile memory region, or a software binary stored in an external flash memory region are all tangible assets that can have concrete cybersecurity goals associated with them, such as "*The system should protect the integrity and authenticity of software binaries stored in external flash memory.*"

Additionally, accurately identifying assets is a fundamental prerequisite to producing a meaningful security analysis. This can be achieved by calling out the asset's name and description and whether it is in transit, at rest, or in use. An example vehicle asset with an accurate description would be camera sensor frames transmitted over a camera link. The asset *is* consumed by an ADAS function, for example, to keep the vehicle centered between the lanes. We will spend more time on asset identification later in this chapter, but for now, keep a mental note that proper asset identification is key for effective TARA outputs.

Damage scenarios

ISO/SAE 21434 defines a damage scenario as an *"adverse consequence involving a vehicle or vehicle function and affecting a road user."* The latter is a pedestrian, cyclist, motorist, or vehicle occupant. In the simplest terms, damage scenarios are the effects of a successful attack against a vehicle stakeholder. While ISO 21434 only refers to effects on the road user, an organization should explore damages from the perspective of all vehicle stakeholders to uncover assets and threats that are not limited only to the road user. For example, an OEM engine calibration dataset may be treated as intellectual property whose exposure would result in financial damages to the OEM. This damage scenario will be missed if only the road user's perspective is considered. Furthermore, an accurate description of the primary system stakeholders and their assets ensures that a comprehensive set of damage scenarios will be produced. A good damage scenario should answer the question, *"What is the effect on the vehicle stakeholders if an asset property is compromised?"* By producing a comprehensive list of damage scenarios, we can assess whether enough threats have been defined and analyzed to cover all the respective damage scenarios, especially ones that are considered of high impact to the vehicle stakeholders.

Threat scenarios

ISO/SAE 21434 defines a threat scenario as the *"potential cause of compromise of cybersecurity properties of one or more assets to realize a damage scenario."* Threat scenarios can easily be confused with damage scenarios because of the tight coupling between causes (threats) and effects (damages). To avoid this confusion, threats should answer the question, *"What high-level action is needed to compromise an asset property and produce a specific damage scenario?"* Furthermore, threats are enumerated with the help of threat modeling approaches such as Microsoft's STRIDE and simple brainstorming exercises involving domain experts and security specialists.

Given a set of assets and a selection of their corresponding properties that are of importance to the vehicle stakeholders, threats can be enumerated with the help of **STRIDE** by exploring the following actions:

1. **Spoofing**: An action to forge the identity of the asset.
2. **Tampering**: An action to modify the value of the asset.
3. **Repudiation**: An action to deny accountability for a change in the asset.
4. **Information Disclosure**: An action to disclose the content of the asset.
5. **Denial of Service (DoS)**: An action to disrupt the availability of the asset.
6. **Elevation of Privilege**: An action to gain unauthorized access to the asset.

Here, it's important to focus on the threat itself against the asset property and not the attack steps or the consequence of the threat. Failure to do so will result in a confused classification of threat types. For example, tampering with the **Cyclic Redundancy Check (CRC)** field of a camera sensor frame during transmission will result in an **Advanced Driver Assistance System (ADAS)** discarding the frame and eventually degrading the ADAS function that depends on this frame if the tampering is persistent. Even though the impact (or damage scenario) is the loss of availability of the ADAS function, the threat type is still considered tampering with the camera frame's contents. Similarly, a **Denial of Service (DoS)** threat against the camera frame can be achieved by gaining unauthorized control of the camera sensor's power input. Even though the attack steps involve tampering with the camera sensor's power control, the threat is still considered a DoS threat. By defining all asset properties that matter to the stakeholders and applying STRIDE, we get a comprehensive list of potential threats that require further analysis. This is a summary of what is known as the asset-driven approach to threat modeling. An alternative threat modeling method identifies threats by accounting for all component interactions within the system that cross a corruption boundary and then assigning a threat type from the STRIDE model. To ease interaction-based threat generation, special tools can be employed with the help of predefined threat generation rules that consider the interaction type and the components involved in the interaction. For example, a write transaction to a storage device will always produce a threat of tampering with the storage device contents, while a read transaction will produce an information disclosure threat. An example toolchain that supports this method is the Microsoft Threat Modeling tool, which allows components to be modeled through stencils and interactions through data flows between the stencils.

While both the asset and interaction-driven approaches result in a high number of threats, interaction-based threats tend to produce more false positives because the threat is based purely on the interaction type and the two parties involved in the interaction. This results in a large effort to verify which threats are valid and justify ones that are not applicable. This incurs a great deal of additional analysis to eliminate invalid threats. Since the asset-driven threat modeling approach is mandated by ISO/SAE 21434, we will focus on it for the remainder of this chapter.

Attacker model and threat types

A prerequisite for an effective threat analysis phase is accurately defining the attacker model and the threat types in scope for a given system. Without this, teams repeatedly fall into the trap of debating whether a given threat is even worthy of consideration while performing the TARA. By arguing up front why certain threat types are out of scope, we can debate the topic once and use the rationale throughout the TARA. Take, for example, physical threats against an ECU while the vehicle is in motion. You may argue that such threats are equivalent to physical sabotage and can only be mounted against targeted victims in a way not different from tampering with the vehicle's brake lines. Excluding this type of threat from analysis with valid rationale allows teams to focus on other more feasible threat types without the need for repeated justification of threat exclusion. Such arguments can be updated in the future if certain threat types increase in feasibility and scope of impact. Let's look at one more example that frequently comes up when evaluating the security of MCU-based ECUs. In this example, the **hardware-protected security environment** (**HPSE**) is required to protect the confidentiality, integrity, and availability of cryptographic keys from physical, network, and logical attacks. At the onset, we define an assumption that since only a single application will be running in the ECU environment, all software components of this application are treated with an equal level of trust from the perspective of the HPSE. As a result, the HPSE firmware will be designed to protect its keys from exposure to any software component within the application; however, it will not differentiate between these components when they submit a job request requiring the usage of a specific cryptographic key. By documenting the rationale of this assumption, we can justify why it is acceptable to exclude threats of one software component becoming malicious and using the keys of another software component. The rationale in this case must be agreed upon with the security experts and the residual risk must be captured. During system integration, the OEM must validate this assumption and agree that it is consistent with their threat model as well. Furthermore, if someone comes along later and flags this security risk as a weakness, then they can be referred to the predefined assumptions to avoid unnecessary debates on whether the system suffers from a vulnerability or not. Note that the same assumption in a multi-virtual machine SoC-based ECU will not hold. Since applications in such a system are built and deployed separately with varying degrees of security and safety criticality, we must adapt our assumptions to ensure the threat of malicious applications in the same system is in scope. As a result, the HPSE firmware must be designed to enforce key usage access separation based on the access permissions granted to specific applications.

Attack paths

ISO/SAE 21434 defines an attack or an attack path as a *"set of deliberate actions to realize a threat scenario."* Assuming you have enumerated all threats in the scope of the assets under analysis, an attack path is simply the steps needed to achieve the threat objective. At this stage of the analysis, you are aiming to answer the question, *"What is the most efficient way by which an attacker can realize the threat?"* The reason why we stress the need for efficient attack paths is to focus on the most feasible and plausible ways to compromise a system. Such attack paths must always be prioritized over theoretical and highly implausible attack steps. Moreover, the more detailed the attack path is, the more accurate the mitigation definition will be. In fact, during the TARA verification process, you must evaluate whether the cybersecurity controls adequately cover the attack paths, which can only be achieved if the attack is described with sufficient detail. Let's take the example threat scenario of physically tampering with the camera sensor link and derive an attack path consisting of four steps:

1. Gain physical access to the camera link through an exposed access point that's normally used for troubleshooting.

2. Record valid camera frame messages from a prior camera session with the ADAS system.

3. Disconnect the camera sensor.

4. Replay the recorded camera frames from a different driving scenario to produce an unsafe reaction by the ADAS system.

Of course, discussing attack paths in a vacuum is not recommended, so this example is purely for illustration purposes. In a real TARA, you need to have a good understanding of the system and vehicle architecture to accurately describe where the threat originates from and how it will be carried out to determine the attack feasibility. One way to handle the complexity of attack paths is to rely on threat modeling tools that help visualize the attack steps and their relationship with the parent threat scenario through attack trees, as we will see later in this chapter.

Risk assessment methods

Once all damages, threats, and attack paths have been adequately described, there is a need to quantify the associated risk to achieve two objectives:

- Determine the risk treatment decision
- Determine the priority of risk mitigation

Let's take the scenario where an organization has a process for threat analysis but no process for risk assessment. If you are "fortunate" to work in such an organization, then at any given point in time, someone can identify a security risk, decide that this risk must urgently be mitigated, and proceed to make system changes to mitigate the risk. The major downside of this approach is the continuous disruption to the project schedule and the lack of any sense of overall cybersecurity risk that a given program is carrying. In these organizations, risks can easily be over-amplified purely based on opinion rather than based on a quantitative measure such as a risk score. Eventually, either the exhausted teams will revolt, or customers will seek legal restitution due to missed project delivery commitments. Ironically, this approach can still result in accepting major cybersecurity risks because teams may not get to mitigate all risks in the pipeline due to the absence of risk prioritization.

On the flip side of this narrative, organizations may exist where the engineering teams and program managers have the sole discretion to determine which threats to mitigate. For the sake of maximizing profit and adapting to customer needs, these teams tend to deem most threats as hypothetical and therefore choose to do nothing. In these organizations, teams will argue that there is no time to make any design changes to mitigate a security risk or that a change will incur costs and therefore push for risk acceptance!

The common thread between these two narratives is that both types of organizations lack insights into the level of risk that they and their stakeholders are exposed to, which will inevitably lead to unhappy endings in the future. Thankfully, ISO/SAE 21434 requires that once all threats and attack paths have been defined, a risk management framework is applied to quantify the associated risks. These calculated risk values are then used to drive the rationale for risk treatment decisions, which can range from risk mitigation or risk transfer to risk acceptance.

Cybersecurity risks are composed of two components: the attack feasibility rating and the impact rating. The first component aims to capture the likelihood that an attack path of a given threat scenario can be realized. This is done by assessing factors such as the required knowledge about the system under attack, the type of access needed, the level of sophistication of the equipment needed, and the level of expertise to pull off the attack. The second component aims to capture the impact level according to impact areas such as financial, safety, operational, and privacy under the assumption that the attack is successful. Intuitively, a lower attack feasibility and impact rating means that the risk is low, while a high attack feasibility and impact rating means the risk is high.

While ISO provides examples of how to calculate the attack feasibility, impact rating, and risk value, it does not mandate a specific method. It is left up to the automotive organization to use an existing risk management framework such as **HEAling Vulnerabilities to ENhance Software, Security, and Safety (HEAVENS)** or **E-safety vehicle intrusion protected applications (EVITA)**, for example, or to define their own framework. When it comes to the damage impact rating, the ISO standard requires that if the damage scenario can be mapped to a safety hazard, the safety severity level is considered when defining the safety impact rating unless an argument can be made about controllability and exposure (see ISO21434 Appendix F.2). In terms of risk scoring, ISO does not define the risk matrix that translates the risk components into the actual risk score. Instead, it requires that the risk score be a value between 1 and 5:

Security Level (SL)	Impact Level (IL)				
		0	1	2	3	4
Threat Level (TL)	0	QM	QM	QM	QM	Low
	1	QM	Low	Low	Low	Medium
	2	QM	Low	Medium	Medium	High
	3	QM	Low	Medium	High	High
	4	Low	Medium	High	High	Critical

Figure 7.1 – HEAVENS risk matrix [5], [6]. Threat Level is the
corollary to the ISO21434 attack feasibility rating

Organizations can define the risk matrix tuned to their own level of risk tolerance or borrow an existing one, such as the one from HEAVENS 2.0 shown in *Figure 7.1*. When defining its risk matrix, an organization may give more weight to impact ratings over attack feasibility ratings, pushing risk scores higher if the impacts are severe, even if the attack is highly unlikely to materialize. Alternatively, an organization may follow a more balanced view that tempers risk levels by giving the impact rating an equal weight to the attack feasibility rating. This prevents the organization from chasing risks that are likely to never materialize and focuses instead on the more practical risks that have severe impacts. Overall, the risk management framework is a highly tunable machine, and it can be adapted for the product type and the overall risk tolerance of the organization. Discussions regarding the risk management framework should involve stakeholders from the executive, project management, and engineering sides to ensure all stakeholders' interests and needs are reflected without tipping the balance completely in one direction. These decisions must be documented in the cybersecurity management system of the organization and included in the cybersecurity case of the product.

Risk treatment

Before defining the risk treatment decision, the organization must define a security policy for which risk scores can be accepted and which ones require reduction. Typically, a risk score of 1 can be considered acceptable to retain, while 2 and higher will require reduction or justification. Assuming a policy has been defined and a risk value is calculated for a given threat, the ISO standard offers four risk treatment options:

- **Avoid**: This decision is the most effective in treating the risk as it translates to completely avoiding the risk by eliminating the feature that is the source of the risk. For example, the risk of code injection into the ADAS system through the Wi-Fi link can be avoided by eliminating the option to support Wi-Fi connectivity within the ADAS system. While this option is the most secure choice, often, the vehicle stakeholders cannot tolerate the elimination of features and therefore will require some mitigations to be applied to reduce the risk level.

- **Reduce**: This is the most common decision when the risk score is above a certain threshold and risk avoidance is not an option. Risk reduction is achieved by applying one or more cybersecurity controls. The control has to be strong enough to lower the risk below the risk threshold to consider the risk adequately treated. If not, then the residual risk must be captured, along with the respective treatment decision (for example, the residual risk may be shared with the system integrator, who can apply system-level cybersecurity controls).

- **Share**: In many cases, the action for risk mitigation can only be done by another vehicle stakeholder. This may be the full risk or the residual risk after the system under analysis applies a cybersecurity control. When choosing to share a risk, the integrating system stakeholder must be given adequate instructions on what they are expected to do. These are essentially user requirements that must pass a minimum feasibility check to avoid placing an undue burden on the user. For example, as a base software developer, you may decide that your software cannot encrypt all files in a filesystem due to performance issues and decide to share the risk with the ECU supplier who is integrating your base software with their application. The supplier can choose which files in the filesystem to encrypt based on the level of confidentiality needed for each file. Explaining the risk and how encryption can be performed is important to enable the ECU supplier to properly mitigate the risk. Typically, shared risks are documented in a cybersecurity manual that is delivered along with the product.

- **Accept**: Risks can be automatically accepted if they are below a predefined risk tolerance level. However, in some cases, even though the risk level is above the acceptable risk threshold, the target system can neither mitigate nor transfer the risk, making risk acceptance the only viable option. In that case, documenting the risk acceptance rationale is mandatory, and escalating the risk to a management body is necessary to evaluate the impact of the risk acceptance decision on the organization. A confirmed accepted risk may also need to be communicated to the final system integrator to allow them to validate the risk acceptance decision and consider making changes at their system level if necessary. For example, an ECU supplier may accept the risk that someone could physically tamper with internal sensor interfaces within the ECU enclosure. This is guided by a risk management framework, which may score such attacks lower due to the physical attack vector and the fact that the impact is localized to a single target ECU. By sharing the accepted risk, the OEM can determine whether the risk is also acceptable within their risk model or not. Note that this is the point where the definition of the threat and attacker model comes into view again. If the OEM has not defined a threat and attacker model, then the ensuing discussions will be painful as the stakeholders argue about why certain risks can be accepted. It is highly advisable to compare attacker and threat models to force the discussion to be grounded in the stated assumptions rather than be driven by subjective views on what risks cannot be tolerated.

With the fundamentals out of the way, it's time to look at some common pitfalls that are faced while preparing a TARA.

Common pitfalls when preparing a TARA

Before discussing the details of the practical TARA methods in this chapter, let's take a moment to give an honorable mention to the telltale signs that the TARA being prepared will have bad outcomes. By understanding the common pitfalls, we will gain some perspective as to why a better approach is needed.

As we introduced earlier, the lack of agreement on the attacker and threat model is a guaranteed source of heartburn throughout the TARA process. If you are the reviewer of a TARA where the authors cannot articulate which attackers and threat types they are aiming to defend against, then this should raise a red flag. Along the same lines, a lack of correct assumptions about the operational environment is a sign of a likely incomplete analysis or an over-engineered system. In many cases, you do not have the full details about your target system. You may be developing an ECU, a software application, a microcontroller, or even just a library and do not have a full view of all the possible use cases in which your component will be used. However, even then, some basic assumptions are needed regarding the operational environment and vehicle architecture. Both the lack of assumptions as well as the highly optimistic assumptions can be problematic. In the former case, the team assumes everything to be corrupt and malicious, resulting in a very lengthy analysis with some unrealistic requirements. A typical example is handling physical threats under the assumption that any hardware component within an ECU could be tampered with or replaced. By foregoing any assumptions regarding the vehicle's physical security, the analysis will reveal highly implausible threats that could have been excluded if we provided solid arguments as to why certain hardware component tampering should be outside the scope of the analysis.

On the flip side, the system architects who assume a perfect vehicle environment will justify the majority of the risks their system is exposed to by defining assumptions that the vehicle side did everything correctly and adequately! This will certainly result in missed security controls that should have been implemented at the component level. As a result, mitigation becomes the responsibility of the component integrator, who may be ill-equipped to do so. Take, for example, the assumption that the ECU will always be positioned behind a central gateway that will filter all unwanted CAN traffic. As a result, the ECU supplier decides that they will not filter any implausible CAN message identifiers, nor will they assume that the CAN channel will ever be abused. If this assumption is not valid, then the mitigation has to be placed elsewhere, causing expensive architectural changes that may not be feasible at the vehicle level. Therefore, the system assumptions must always err on the side of a sub-optimal vehicle security architecture that's in line with the defense-in-depth security principle.

Like bad assumptions, an improper description of the security target under analysis is a common source of inadequate or improper analysis. Invite a component engineer to the TARA and they will describe the target in its most intricate details. Doing so means that you will get tens if not hundreds of assets to analyze and thousands of threats to enumerate. Invite a system architect and they may draw a single box with three inputs and one output. Analyzing this system will result in both naïve threats and mitigations that barely move the needle on the security posture of the vehicle. Selecting the right level of system abstraction is therefore critical to uncover meaningful assets and impactful threat scenarios that will efficiently produce value-adding mitigations.

Even when the correct asset abstraction has been chosen, a common pitfall with asset identification is repeating the same asset type over and over again. As a result, we are left with an explosion of damage scenarios that will essentially have the same impact ratings and an intractable set of threat scenarios that will map to the same attack paths and leverage the same mitigations. Noticing when a group of assets shares a high degree of similarity is a key method to improve the efficiency of the TARA without sacrificing its completeness and correctness. Rather than analyze each asset individually, it is possible to bucketize such assets and analyze them once.

> **Bucketizing assets**
>
> A word of caution when bucketing assets is to pay attention to temporal aspects relating to such assets. An asset within the grouping may be subject to a unique attack path due to when the asset becomes exposed to the threat (for example, only during system shutdown). Keep an eye out for such assets and make sure you exclude them from the grouping to avoid missing a valid threat and attack path.

Another sign of trouble when reviewing a TARA is if you start noticing threats being described in the language of damage scenarios or if attack steps are defined as abstract compromises of an asset. The problem with the ambiguous and confused usage of these terms is that it obscures the author's intention and makes it difficult to assess the effectiveness of the mitigation or the correctness of the risk-related values. Later in this chapter, we will introduce the threat and damage scenario writing templates to help you write consistent and coherent TARA work products that can be easily checked and verified.

Even if you managed to avoid all these pitfalls, when performing the risk assessment, you are likely to get stuck with subjective debates over selecting risk parameters. It is a natural human tendency to disagree over risk parameters such as the knowledge needed to pull off an attack, the equipment needed, the safety severity impacts, and so on. While these values are important to prioritize the risk properly, giving this step precedence over threat enumeration and attack description can deplete most of the bandwidth allocated to the security analysis, leaving you with a thin but highly debated threat list. Instead, it is better to decouple risk assessment from threat analysis to allow engineers to focus on the technical aspects at first and then switch to the risk assessment mindset. When converging on risk values is difficult, an averaging method can be followed to allow multiple opinions to be factored in. Having said that, in cases where the risks are slated for acceptance or sharing, it is acceptable to allow for extended arguments when experts are unable to agree on the risk values as these decisions impact what the end user must either live with or mitigate on their own. Guides on how to select risk values for a given product can go a long way toward providing the team with a common reference for interpreting how such risk parameters relate to their product.

Assuming that your team has overcome the hurdle of risk assessment, another common pitfall is ignoring the residual risk after applying risk mitigation actions. It should come as no surprise that not all mitigation actions are equal in effectiveness when treating a risk. Taking the time to evaluate whether the risk is adequately mitigated is essential to ensure that no significant residual risk is implicitly accepted. Some toolchains allow the user to calculate the differential attack feasibility after the cybersecurity control is applied. This produces a secondary risk score that shows the residual risk level. If the risk score is still higher than the minimum risk threshold, then additional mitigations may be needed or the residual risk may need to be transferred to the system integrator. A final pitfall we will share in this section is not performing the TARA for all the relevant life cycles of a product. This pitfall will be discussed in the next section as we explore how to properly scope our TARA.

Defining the appropriate TARA scope

ISO/SAE 21434 mandates that the TARA is performed during the concept phase while considering all product life cycles (production, operation, maintenance, and decommissioning). A common pitfall is to focus purely on the operational phase because that is the phase where vehicle safety is directly exposed to cybersecurity threats. The result is an inadequate cybersecurity concept that misses security goals covering how the vehicle is produced, maintained, and taken out of service. That is why it is important to involve all engineering teams across all the product life cycles and assign clear responsibilities when planning out the TARA(s). When there is resistance to expanding the scope of the TARA to cover these life cycle stages, development teams must capture all the assumptions on risks of the other life cycles to ensure that at least the system integrator is aware of those risks. For example, if the manufacturing phase is not adequately analyzed, then the operational phase TARA can make assumptions that the production phase is not adequately secure and derive security requirements to mitigate risks that impact the operational phase, such as controls for how cryptographic keys are provisioned in the factory, or how a chip life cycle's state is managed:

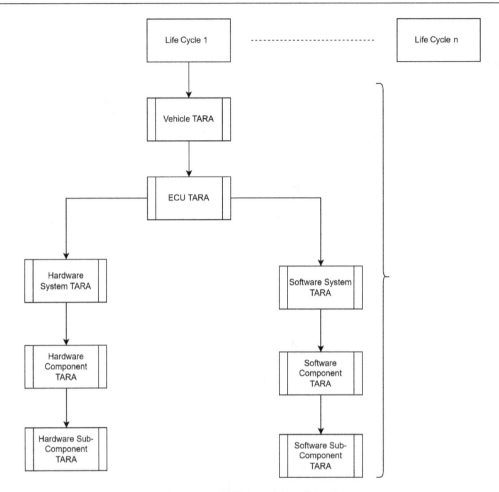

Figure 7.2 – TARA breadth and depth

As shown in *Figure 7.2*, both the breadth and depth of the security analysis must be adequate to consider the analysis results complete. The former is achieved by covering security-relevant life cycles, while the latter is achieved by covering the vehicle architecture layers down to the sub-component level, where security weaknesses are expected to have a significant impact on the overall vehicle security. Indeed, relying solely on the OEM vehicle TARA to discover all risks and required mitigations of the ECU and its subcomponents is both naïve and unrealistic. Instead, the TARA must be seen as an iterative process that is performed at multiple layers of the design to identify and eliminate risks that are not obvious at higher layers of the architecture. While performing the TARA at the concept level is essential to uncover the overall set of cybersecurity goals that a given system must achieve and the high-level cybersecurity concept, refining the TARA at various levels of the architecture is necessary to uncover security weaknesses that become apparent only as the architecture details are concretized. One way to look at this iterative TARA process is to apply the closed box versus open box approach.

A vehicle TARA can model an ECU as a closed box to focus on interface-level threats relating to network channels, sensors, actuators, common hardware components, and vehicle-level protocols. The OEM performing this TARA then hands over to the ECU supplier a set of cybersecurity goals and high-level security requirements that must be fulfilled to comply with the overall vehicle cybersecurity concept. Additionally, the OEM can perform a detailed TARA over vehicle protocols that the supplier cannot cover fully on their own. For example, key management protocols, software update procedures, diagnostic services, and in-vehicle network protocols should all be within the scope of the analysis of the vehicle TARA to allow the OEM to produce a set of technical cybersecurity specifications that all ECUs comply with. The ECU supplier considers these inputs and performs a system-level TARA, where the ECU is modeled as an open box while the software and hardware components are treated as a closed box. Modeling system-level architectural details allows you to enumerate more refined threats and attack paths at the system level. This analysis will yield an ECU-level cybersecurity concept that will serve as the source for refining software and hardware security requirements. Similarly, software and hardware teams are expected to repeat the security analysis at their respective levels by going from a closed box to an open box view until all security-critical aspects of the design have been adequately covered.

> **Note**
>
> The closed box versus open box classification is used here to refer to cybersecurity analysis as opposed to the black box and white box concept that is used in testing methods. Although these concepts are similar on the surface, we have chosen the closed box, open box terminology to stress the need to intentionally choose what level of system detail is in the scope of the analysis, even though more knowledge about the system's internal architecture may be already known.

Let's look at a brief example of how the vehicle-level versus ECU-level TARAs complement one another. A vehicle-level TARA can expose risks that relate to the abuse of the diagnostic protocol and the various services it supports. This will result in cybersecurity goals and requirements to reduce these risks, which get allocated to the diagnostic clients, target ECUs, and diagnostic gateways. The derived cybersecurity requirements include enforcing diagnostic client authentication and performing diagnostic frame filtering at select points in the network architecture. Based on how diagnostic data persists in non-volatile memory, the ECU TARA exposes threats of tampering that were not considered in the vehicle-level TARA. This is because the target of analysis at the vehicle level intentionally abstracted ECU-level details about how diagnostic data is stored and accessed (closed box view). This process can be repeated in the diagnostic software and hardware storage layers to identify and eliminate security weaknesses that relate to diagnostic data tampering. In this example, the TARAs at the vehicle level and the ECU level each exposed a different set of threats and corresponding security requirements. This would not have been possible if the TARA's scope was limited incorrectly to one or the other.

Furthermore, a design-level TARA can be highly effective in identifying security weaknesses, but it comes with a high cost of effort due to the granularity of assets and the large number of attack paths that can emerge when the detailed design is analyzed. Therefore, teams must be cognizant of the point after which the TARA starts yielding diminishing returns relative to the effort invested. That is the point where further refinement of the TARA should not happen to avoid a never-ending analysis phase. This does not necessarily mean that if risks emerge later in the design phase the TARA cannot be updated. Instead, there should be a clear cutoff point after which changes to the TARA are purely driven by new emerging risks rather than a deliberate unbounded analysis phase.

> **Complementing the design of a TARA with weakness checklists**
>
> Organizations are encouraged to define architecture weakness checklists that can complement or supplement a design-level TARA when identifying residual risks. A thorough architecture weakness checklist can produce equivalent results to a detailed design TARA without the high cost in time and effort. The decision to rely on the checklist is normally driven by the security criticality of the component under analysis and the level of its complexity.

The practical approach

Armed with the TARA fundamentals and the common pitfalls, we are now ready to walk through the practical approach of threat modeling automotive systems. Throughout this approach, we will focus on three objectives:

- Producing the highest threat coverage possible for our target system
- Choosing the correct risk treatment decisions
- Finishing the TARA within a reasonable time frame that fits within the project's allotted time

Know your system

TARA is most effective and streamlined when the security analyst is intimately familiar with the system under analysis. However, given the breadth of knowledge required for accurately analyzing automotive systems, in most cases, the security analyst must collaborate with the domain experts to understand the system functions, uncover damage scenarios, and accurately capture assets that need protection. This can be done in an interview-style setting, where the security analyst asks a series of questions to understand the nominal objectives of the system, explore its use cases, and start uncovering the common set of misuse cases. When analyzing a complex system that involves multiple domain experts, it helps to first decompose the system to the most security-relevant use cases while deliberately exploring each product life cycle stage.

If the system is not yet fully defined, the analysis can be done using a preliminary architecture, along with the set of known use cases. The TARA can be refined later in the design phase when more details become available to evaluate the true attack path feasibility and damage scenarios.

> **Best practice – identify the domain experts who will provide details about the system**
>
> The safety item definition is a great resource to quickly understand what the system aims to achieve and what needs to be protected. If the safety item definition is not present, then you can consult functional specifications that describe the system, or even design documents that capture the requirements and architecture of the component under analysis. For non-safety-relevant systems such as the Telematics Unit, consulting functional specifications and high-level architecture documents can be a good start for security analysis.

Make your assumptions known

Before diving into the threat analysis process, one step that sets the stage for all ensuing analysis is the set of assumptions about who the system stakeholders are, what asset properties they care to protect, and what threat types they aim to mitigate. These assumptions are typically implicit and normally start emerging as the TARA process hits some contentious topics. Articulating the assumptions from the start is one of the most critical steps you can take to ensure the TARA is performed efficiently. Although the cybersecurity concept work product is not expected to be available before the concept TARA is complete, it is a good practice to start documenting assumptions in the cybersecurity concept as you make progress with your TARA.

Use case-driven analysis

The very first time you perform the TARA on an existing system, you will be faced with the challenge of choosing the starting point of analysis. A typical ECU may have tens if not hundreds of use cases that vary in the level of detail and complexity. Therefore, it is recommended to filter for the most security-relevant use cases to expose those assets that are in most need of protection. This step requires the collaboration of domain experts and security experts to prioritize use case analysis based on the use case's exposure to security risks and its importance for the system to function as expected. For example, an ADAS system relies on functionalities that provide sensor data processing, map data services, and OTA updates. Understanding how the system fulfills each type of use case through modeling interactions and data flows is the first building block for comprehensive security analysis. It is a good practice to even decompose a use case into smaller user stories to expose more data flows and system interactions that need analysis.

Best practice – prioritize use cases for analysis based on security relevance

If all system interactions, both internal and external, were visualized as a loaf of bread, then your job in this phase would be to slice this loaf of bread to expose those interactions that are most at risk of security compromise. This is both an art and a science. Let's assume you are performing the TARA for a telematics ECU. First, you explore all the use cases offered by this highly security-critical system looking for use cases that expose the vehicle and its data to external threats. You uncover a use case for delivering software updates, extracting telemetry data, and providing the vehicle cabin with external temperature readings. The use cases of software updates and telemetry data reporting are more security-relevant than providing the driver with an accurate reading of the outside temperature, something they can confirm if they just extend their arm out of the window! These use cases are then broken down into user stories and user scenarios that expose interactions between external and internal vehicle components.

As these details emerge, it should be possible to quickly identify assets and damage scenarios associated with each use case as you initiate the analysis:

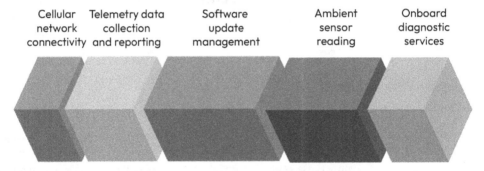

Figure 7.3 – Slicing a telematics ECU use case based on security relevance

After the base set of use cases has been analyzed, future updates to the system should follow a TARA process that is integrated with normal feature development. This way, risk can be intercepted at the source before it propagates through the design and requires expensive changes. We like to view this as a micro-TARA approach. This can be aided by the existing change management system to forward feature requests to the TARA process whenever the feature passes a certain risk threshold. Consequently, additional security requirements can be derived to accompany the functional requirements related to the new feature request. Similarly, in the design phase, a micro-TARA should be tightly coupled with the functional design to identify security weaknesses and eliminate them, as shown in *Figure 7.4*. This calls for an integrated toolchain that makes TARA a natural part of the development cycle:

Tip

Engineers are normally apprehensive about performing the TARA due to the perceived overhead it introduces. Having a streamlined TARA process can help reduce that apprehension. The TARA should be viewed as a natural step of the process, not an add-on.

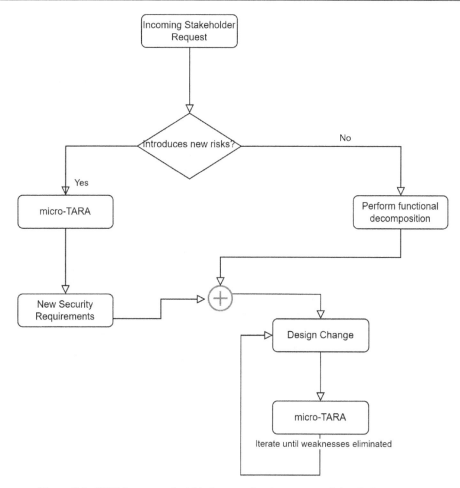

Figure 7.4 – TARA integrated within feature development and the design process

Prepare context and data flow diagrams

Before committing to analyzing the set of use cases and user stories, it's important to review that set with the domain experts to ensure that these use cases are both accurate and sufficient to model assets and threats. During these discussions, normally, new use cases emerge, in which case you must decide whether they meet the priority bar for analysis. On one hand, we want to maximize threat coverage but on the other, we want to bind the analysis in a way that does not derail the project's schedule. We recommend checking whether the new use cases introduce completely new assets and unique threat scenarios that will likely be missed if the use case is not included. If not, then de-prioritizing the analysis can be acceptable in favor of a more thorough and timelier TARA.

Once the set of use cases and user stories has been narrowed down and refined, it is time to model the system context and the corresponding data flows. Here, we need to leverage the item definition discussed in *Chapter 5* to expose details from the operational environment and identify the system boundary. This will prove handy when constructing attack paths, which would otherwise remain theoretical unless the full vehicle environment is modeled.

> **Best practice – choose the right level of diagram detail**
>
> Besides context diagrams, we need to model the interactions within the system as they relate to a specific use case. Choosing the right level of detail for modeling the system sets the stage for how thorough the analysis can be. Here, it is important to pick just the right balance of detail to avoid producing an intractable threat model that contains hundreds of redundant threats. This is one of the critical factors that determines whether a TARA will be carried out efficiently or not. During the concept TARA phase, security experts must insist on abstracting details from the design to limit the number of assets and flows that should be analyzed. Here, again, the open box, closed box approach comes in handy. Since the objective of the TARA is to derive cybersecurity goals and high-level cybersecurity requirements, choosing the open-box view of system components and sub-components will produce detailed technical security requirements, which are supposed to be derived at a later phase. To avoid a very lengthy and expensive TARA, we should scope the analysis to ensure it is conducive to deriving the high-level security requirements and allocating them to various components of the system. This way, we can use the remaining time to define a security architecture that will act as a reference when deriving detailed technical security requirements. Additional TARA iterations performed at the component and sub-component levels can then focus on specific aspects of the refined design to uncover tangible security weaknesses.

In many cases, data flow diagrams are not readily available, and teams may resist creating dedicated diagrams due to the additional effort needed. While drawing such diagrams is preferred, it is possible to leverage existing sequence and state diagrams to expose the various interactions within the system. In that case, the diagrams must be extended to showcase the system context to help clarify where a given threat may originate from.

Damages versus assets – where to start

A common question when preparing a TARA is what should be identified first: damage scenarios or assets? Understanding the system functions and objectives can give quick hints about the effects on the system if these objectives were maliciously violated, making damage scenarios a natural first work product to derive. For example, when analyzing a steering system that provides steering assist functionality and without knowledge of the assets of such a system, the damages become apparent when we consider that an attack on the steering system will result in the loss of steering assist, oversteering, understeering, or erratic steering behavior. However, when a system's primary objective is security-related, identifying damage scenarios directly from the assets can easily be achieved as the assets are more self-evident. With the assets known, the damage scenarios are derived by exploring the impacts on the system when each asset property is affected. For example, a central gateway that provides network routing and translation across the vehicle is responsible for protecting assets such as network messages flowing through the gateway, the network's configuration, and the corresponding filter rules. By analyzing these assets, we can determine that the compromise of their respective properties can lead to damages such as unsafe actuation of safety-critical functions, and the inability of safety-critical ECUs that rely on the gateway to receive their messages and perform their function. Overall, the decision of where to start is the preference of the person performing the TARA. In practice, the process of defining damage scenarios and assets is iterative, with one step feeding the other until all damages and assets have been adequately identified.

Best practice – leverage the Hazard Analysis and Risk Assessment (HARA) to derive safety-relevant damage scenarios

With safety-critical systems, especially when the TARA is done at the item level, a rich source of damage scenarios with safety impacts is the **Hazard Analysis and Risk Assessment (HARA)**. By inspecting the hazardous events, you can easily identify hazards that are producible through attacks rather than system faults. Here, rather than copy each hazard into a damage scenario, it is possible to generalize the hazards into a smaller set of damage scenarios, so long as the assets and threats contributing to these damage scenarios are common. For example, a HARA of a steering function may call out hazards such as oversteering during the entrance to a ramp, understeering during the exit from a ramp, erratic steering, loss of steering, and more. From a security point of view, understeering, oversteering, and erratic steering can all be caused by common attacks against network messages, software images, or sensor input data, and they all have a similar safety impact when triggered maliciously. Therefore, they can be combined into a single generalized damage scenario to ease the mapping of individual threat scenarios. Loss of steering, on the other hand, can be separated as a standalone damage scenario because it is mapped to different asset properties, such as the availability of the power source. In addition to using the HARA as a source of damage scenarios, the safety impact rating of the damage scenario should be correlated to the corresponding hazard's safety severity level. In some cases, it is possible to argue that the safety impact of the damage scenario should be considered lower than that of the corresponding hazard safety severity level due to the event being controllable by the driver. For example, the loss of **Lane Keep Assist (LKA)**, which aims to warn the driver when they are veering over the lane boundary, has a high safety impact, but the driver can always act, even if the LKA were disabled maliciously. Consulting the safety architects during this process can help solidify the arguments for why a certain safety impact rating has been chosen.

As we mentioned in the *The fundamentals of performing an effective TARA* section, there is a need to ensure consistency in damage scenario definition by using a damage scenario template. An example template takes the following form:

```
<adverse consequence> to <system stakeholder> due to <compromise of
asset(s) property(s)>.
```

Based on this template, we can write the following example damage scenarios:

- The inability of road users to steer the vehicle safely due to the steering system software being tampered with

- Exposure of OEM intellectual property through illegal access to machine learning models stored on the ADAS system

Note that including the cause of the damage scenario in the description results in a large number of damage scenarios that have a common adverse effect. This results in more impact ratings to calculate and more options to choose from when mapping the threat scenario to the closest damage scenario that applies. Therefore, you may choose to abstract the cause description from the damage scenario when the damage scenario has sufficient information that allows for an accurate impact rating.

Identifying assets with the help of asset categories

The assets are first identified and refined with the help of the system architecture model and the item model. As you scan through these models and become familiar with functions under analysis, you may recognize certain asset properties that are exposed to a security-related threat. Usually, it helps to interview the domain expert about how their system works to uncover vulnerable assets. Having damage scenarios pre-identified can also aid in asset identification as we ask the question, "*Which tangible objects of the system need to be compromised to realize a given damage scenario?*"

Take the example of our steering system, which has the following identified damage scenario:

```
Erratic, under or over steering caused by the misbehavior of control
algorithm
```

Through discussions with the steering system domain expert and careful inspection of the system diagrams, we can identify that the steering control algorithms can misbehave if any of the following objects are maliciously tampered with:

- The steering software binaries in flash

- The steering calibration data in flash

- Sensor inputs over CAN, **Single Edge Nibble Transmission (SENT)**

- Vehicle status messages over CAN

- Actuation requests received by the steering system over CAN

It also helps to perform asset identification by assuming the role of each of the system's stakeholders and articulating what they truly care about. From the OEM perspective, having the ability to identify the root cause of a system malfunction is an important objective, and therefore the availability and integrity of the diagnostic fault data are asset properties that need to be protected. However, from the supplier's perspective, the confidentiality of software algorithms is important as they are considered valuable intellectual property.

Best practice – prepare an asset catalog

Since each system is bound to have a set of unique asset types based on its intended function and its underlying architecture, a great way to aid teams in producing consistent and coherent asset definitions is for the security architect to decompose a system into asset categories. These categories would then act as a reference to ensure that team members are identifying assets from a finite set of buckets with just the right level of abstraction. This approach will produce an asset catalog that can be useful to quickly uncover the existence of a new asset when a product change is made. When a candidate asset is identified, it is first compared against the asset catalog to determine whether the asset fits in an existing bucket or whether perhaps there is a need for a new category of assets to be added to the catalog.

Furthermore, mapping asset categories to threat classes, as shown in *Table 7.1*, enables new TARAs to leverage threats from a common catalog simply by bucketizing the asset. This maximizes threat coverage and avoids inconsistencies in threat definition from one team to another. Note that the more granular the assets, the more refined the attack paths and the corresponding security controls and requirements will be:

Number	Asset Grouping	Asset Properties	Threat Type
1	Binaries in persistent storage	Confidentiality, Integrity	Physical tampering in storage
2	Cryptographic keys	Confidentiality, Integrity, Availability	Side channel analysis
3	Communication channels	Integrity, Availability	Spoofing and tampering over the network link

Table 7.1 – An example asset catalog to ease the asset identification and threat mapping processes

Building threat catalogs

Using STRIDE coupled with the threat type and threat agent can help construct meaningful threats, even if the details of how the threat can be realized are not initially known. Let's consider this threat enumeration template:

```
<Threat agent> performs <STRIDE action> <against asset property> <via
attack method> to produce <damage scenario>.
```

Starting with the threat agent is a useful way to shine the spotlight on the attack surface by which the threat is carried out. For example, the threat agent can be an attacker with physical access to the ECU, a network endpoint, or a vulnerable application running within the system software. The STRIDE action follows closely from the asset property that is in the scope of analysis. For example, tampering threats affect asset integrity, DoS for availability, and so on. Although not mandatory, including the attack method in the threat description helps motivate the attack path's generation. To calculate the attack feasibility rating, the threat in conjunction with the attack path must be considered together so that, one way or another, the information will be revealed during the risk assessment phase. Additionally, linking to the damage scenario within the description is not mandatory but can be useful to clarify why the threat is important to analyze. Regardless of whether it is included in the description or not, the traceability to the damage scenario will be established during the risk assessment phase when calculating the overall risk value.

Now, let's assume we are analyzing threats against the LiDAR sensor data transmitted over Ethernet and considering the integrity and availability of the sensor data to be the most important cybersecurity properties to protect. Using our threat enumeration template, we can define the following example list of threats:

- The Ethernet network endpoint forges the identity of the LiDAR sensor using a counterfeit sensor that sends unreliable data, causing false object detection in the ADAS system

- The Ethernet network endpoint tampers with the LiDAR sensor data by compromising the Ethernet switch to cause invalid object detection in the ADAS system

- The Ethernet network endpoint blocks the LiDAR sensor data by compromising the Ethernet switch to degrade the ADAS system's functions

---

Best practice – invest time in a threat catalog

Typically, people who are great at threat enumeration and deriving attack paths have spent a significant portion of their careers reading security papers, attending security conferences, building exploits, and keeping up with security news. For everyone else, it is a painful brainstorming exercise that often produces a small set of rudimentary threats and attack methods. One way to overcome this challenge is by encouraging security experts to generalize their threats and attack method descriptions for use in a common threat catalog. Similar to building an asset catalog, as we uncover threat scenarios, it becomes possible to group these threat scenarios in a threat catalog to aid in future TARA preparation. The generalized threats in the catalog can then be mapped to asset categories and asset properties from the asset catalog. Including the asset category and the asset type in the threat catalog allows automation tools to identify unique threats based on the mapping of a new asset to a predefined asset category. For example, software images in non-volatile memory are mapped to tampering and exfiltration threats through JTAG and flash programming tools, while the RAM instance of the same asset can be mapped to tampering threats through DRAM interposers. Such a threat catalog ensures that teams will build rich TARAs when analyzing a new product rather than having to start the brainstorming exercise from scratch.

To jump-start the process of creating the threat catalog, several resources can be used, such as *Annex 5 from REG155 [1]* and the *ENISA automotive threat report [2]*.

> **Note**
>
> Assessors will normally ask for evidence that the REG 155 threats have been considered in your TARA when compliance with REG155 is required. The threat catalog can come in handy in that case.

Creating attack paths using a system flow diagram

As with threat enumeration, defining an attack path requires a mixture of domain knowledge and security expertise. For an attack to be possible, a weakness in the system must be exploited, so it is necessary to be familiar with weakness classes relating to the item or component under analysis. For example, if you are deriving attack paths against an Ethernet link, it helps to be familiar with protocol-level weaknesses at the physical and network layers, as well as Ethernet switch configuration weaknesses.

> **Best practice – keep an eye on known weaknesses to uncover threats**
>
> Weaknesses and threats come hand in hand. In many cases, you may be aware of the weaknesses that a certain part of the architecture is likely to contain, but not the exact threats. Knowing the weaknesses can stimulate the threat enumeration by extrapolating actions that can exploit the weakness.

While relying on security experts is essential in producing meaningful attack paths, it is recommended that domain experts continuously enrich their knowledge about vulnerabilities and attacks that apply to their components so that they may be better equipped to carry out a rich and comprehensive attack path analysis. When building attack paths, your objective is to uncover the least difficult attack paths that realize the threat while exploiting all possible weaknesses in the system under analysis. This allows us to prioritize the elimination of plausible attack paths over the highly improbable ones. Once we have spotted an applicable weakness, we must assume the perspective of the attacker and derive the sequence of steps to realize the threat. Using a threat modeling tool that supports the creation of attack trees makes it possible to better visualize the threat coverage to judge when the analysis is complete, as shown in *Figure 7.5*:

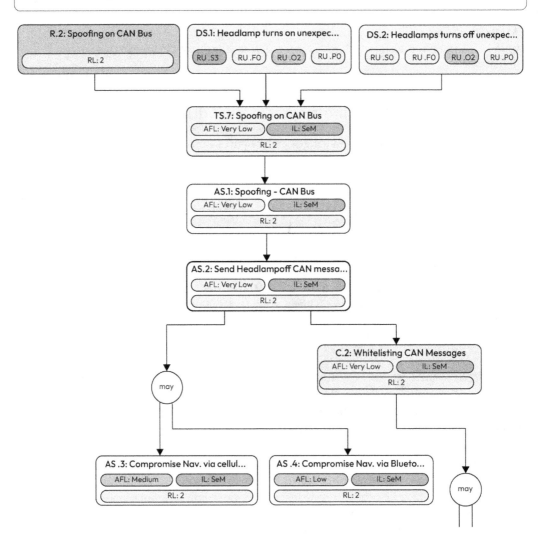

> **Note**
>
> RL = risk level, AFL = attack feasibility level, IL = impact level, DS = damage scenario, AS = attack step, TS = threat scenario, C = control.

Figure 7.5 – Example attack tree using the Yakindu threat modeling tool

This example shows a threat scenario for spoofing the CAN bus. This is traced to two attack paths, starting with compromising the navigation system through either cellular or Bluetooth to masquerading as a CAN node. The navigation system sends a `Headlamp_Off` CAN message, which amounts to a successful spoofing attack on the CAN bus. It also shows links to two damage scenarios, along with a risk object, which is how the tool captures the risk assessment aspect.

Best practice – jump-start the analysis with an attack database

Being able to spot weaknesses in a diverse set of software and hardware components is a skill that takes years to master, so it is useful to rely on attack and weakness databases. Having such a database tailored for your product can be a powerful tool that helps domain experts derive meaningful attack paths. These databases can be built using open source information from reputable sources such as the MITRE **Common Enumeration Weaknesses** (**CWEs**) *[3]* and **Common Attack Pattern Enumeration and Classification** (**CAPEC**) databases *[4]*. Rather than sifting through hundreds of weaknesses, a product-tailored database can give engineers the list of weaknesses and attacks that they should focus on for their product. As weaknesses are discovered over time within the product itself, such a database can be extended to ensure that old mistakes are not repeated.

A word of caution with attack path analysis is to beware of **tunnel-visioned analysis**. It is common for security experts and domain experts alike to be attracted to parts of the design that they see as highly security relevant and therefore worthy of extra attention during analysis. But by doing so, they lose perspective of the full system view, ignoring obvious attack surfaces in less security-critical parts of the system. This can result in a successful entry point into the system and an opportunity for lateral movement. These are typically low-hanging fruits that can easily be addressed, making the job of securing the more security-critical aspects of the system easier. Let's take the example of a new concept for supporting the IPSec protocol to allow an ECU to communicate with the OEM backend. A security specialist will gravitate toward handling cryptographic keys and whether the protocol design contains weaknesses. In doing so, the security specialist will focus on analyzing MITM attacks, replay attacks, configuration and implementation flaws, and cryptographic key management weaknesses. Being tunnel-visioned on the cryptographic and security protocol implementation, they may ignore the fact that all applications in the system can create an IPSec tunnel with an external endpoint, even if they were not authorized to do so. This makes our security mitigations against the session key establishment and key exposure ineffective as the attacker can simply access the IPSec service and spoof the endpoint without possessing the actual key. Keeping an open mind about attack sources helps us avoid scenarios where emphasis is placed on difficult security problems while ignoring easier attack paths that circumvent our strong security controls.

Risk prioritization

Once all the threats, attack paths, and damage scenarios have been linked, it is possible to start the attack feasibility and damage scenario impact rating. Whether you're using a professional threat modeling tool or a worksheet-based approach, the risk scoring process must be automated based on the risk management framework chosen by the organization. Here, it is important to standardize the definition of each parameter used in the risk assessment to avoid circular discussions about attack feasibility or impact rating meaning. A guideline that clearly explains each rating value and provides examples of when to choose each can help reduce the level of inconsistency between TARAs performed by different teams. But even when everything is written down, this step can still be highly contentious due to its qualitative nature. For example, analyzing the level of expertise needed to mount glitch attacks may be viewed by some as requiring a proficient level of expertise while others may deem it to require expert knowledge. To help promote convergence, the organization can employ an averaging approach to allow multiple experts to weigh in individually and simply choose the mean risk value. Alternatively, multiple risk scoring methods can be employed with an averaging method to provide a more accurate representation of risk. For example, using the **Common Vulnerability Scoring System** (**CVSS**), it is possible to get an additional score that can be factored into the overall calculation of the attack feasibility rating. Whichever method is chosen, teams must be discouraged from burning through precious time when discussing risk values and be cognizant that in some cases, mitigating the attack may take less effort than scoring its risk level!

An organization can choose to prioritize damage impact over attack feasibility when performing risk scoring. Doing so, however, may result in a large set of inflated risk levels without the possibility to prioritize them. As a result, highly infeasible attacks will be considered with the same level of priority as ones that are quite easy to pull off. Given the limited bandwidth and schedule limitations of automotive projects, treating all risks with the same level of priority means that some risks will not be treated even though they have a higher urgency if the attack feasibility rating is given adequate weight. Therefore, it is important to choose a risk management framework that allows you to accurately prioritize risks to avoid a product that has strong security controls in one area but glaring vulnerabilities in another.

> **Best practice – rely on the security policy to determine risk tolerance**
>
> Deciding on the risk tolerance level is another area that requires organizational support. It should not be up to the engineering teams to define the risk tolerance level for which a cybersecurity risk can be accepted or mitigated. Ultimately, it is a decision for the organization because if a threat is not treated for a given risk score, then the organization must make a conscious decision that it is acceptable to do so. Having a policy in place that specifies which risk levels can be tolerated and which ones must have a treatment action is essential. Also, defining a risk escalation process can help when teams reach a deadlock on risk treatment decision-making. These deadlocks can occur when certain team members insist on implementing mitigations that other team members want to transfer to another party or postpone to a future product version. By defining a risk escalation and resolution process, we can ensure that the decisions are being considered objectively rather than having a single opinion dominate regardless of the risk exposure of the organization.

Defining cybersecurity goals

When all the dust of risk scoring has settled, the outcome is either a set of cybersecurity goals to reduce the risks or cybersecurity claims to capture the risk being shared or accepted.

> **Quick note**
>
> When performed outside the concept phase, the TARA does not produce goals or claims but rather a set of refined cybersecurity requirements, design changes, and user-allocated requirements.

A cybersecurity goal can be viewed as the highest level of abstraction of a security requirement for the system. It states the desired protection for a given asset and the respective set of threat scenarios that must be mitigated. When writing cybersecurity goals, we have to keep in mind how these goals will be used. First, the goals provide a high-level view of what the cybersecurity concept must achieve. When teams familiarize themselves with the cybersecurity goals of the system, they are more apt to recognize security risks in their design that are violating a cybersecurity goal at the system level. Second, goals serve as the basis for validation activities both by the development teams and through independent penetration testing. Validation can be achieved by performing inspection reviews of all the downstream cybersecurity work products, as well as penetration testing being performed by an independent team to prove that the goals are not violated in real-world attack scenarios.

> **Best practice – aim for an optimal set of goals to ease awareness and validation**
>
> When performing extensive TARAs, numerous cybersecurity goals will be defined that must be validated and maintained. Each goal needs to be traced to downstream cybersecurity requirements and controls showing how the goal is realized. Aiming for a consolidated set of cybersecurity goals reduces the traceability effort and ensures that validation can be completed efficiently. Consolidation is possible by grouping similar assets, their properties, and the respective threat classes in the definition of the cybersecurity goal. Note that consolidation is a common practice that is shared with ISO26262, which also encourages the consolidation of safety goals.

There are two styles for writing effective yet concise cybersecurity goals:

*   The first method describes the asset properties that need protection and the respective set of threat classes:

    ```
    The system should protect the integrity and authenticity of
    camera sensor data and sensor identity against physical and
    network-based threats.
    ```

*   The second method describes the required prevention against attack methods without explicitly referring to the asset properties:

    ```
    The system should prevent camera sensor counterfeiting and data
    spoofing or tampering through sensor replacement or MiTM attacks
    over the sensor communication link.
    ```

In this style, the focus is on attack prevention. In both styles, validation teams should investigate how an attacker could violate the cybersecurity goals by at least launching attacks from the list defined in the scope of the goal. The benefit of the first style of goal definition is that a smaller set of goals can be created, allowing the author to focus more on creating refined security requirements at the concept and product levels. The second style has the benefit of being more explicit in stating the exact attacks that must be prevented. However, it can easily become unwieldy as the set of attacks expands over time and it becomes necessary to group and abstract such attacks into threat classes.

Choosing security controls and operational environment (OE) requirements

Security controls vary based on the use case and the level of analysis. At the concept level, the controls are high level in nature, such as using an HPSE, enforcing MACsec over an Ethernet communication, or using secure memory for key storage. By refining the architecture, the controls also become more refined as we leverage parts of the hardware and software architecture to mitigate threats and treat security weaknesses. At these levels, we are going to encounter detailed controls such as configuring the MMU/MPU to isolate memory regions or assigning CPU core priority to prevent runtime exhaustion attacks.

Like the unique skillset that's required for spotting weaknesses and deriving attack paths, selecting security controls and applying them correctly to the architecture is an equally challenging task that requires years of experience both in the cybersecurity and functional domains. As we will see in *Chapters 8* and *9*, this task requires a deep understanding of the underlying hardware and software architecture to determine where the control can be applied and how to deploy it effectively.

> **Best practice – maintain a common security controls catalog**
>
> Having a security controls catalog can ease the process of risk reduction by giving engineering teams validated choices that are known to treat specific security risks. Additionally, creating common security design patterns that have been analyzed and verified can ensure that security solutions are applied consistently throughout the product. For example, in a large SoC-based ECU, there can be common attack paths against purpose-specific microcontroller units within the SoC that are interacting with the normal application environment. Rather than analyzing the threats related to this type of communication model individually and prescribing security controls in an uncoordinated way, a common security design pattern can describe a well-trusted method for establishing and maintaining secure communication for this design pattern. This reference security design pattern can define how mutual authentication can be applied between the communicating parties over a shared memory region, along with message integrity protection, such as through logical channel isolation. This further reduces the review effort because now, the reviewer's task is to verify that the security design pattern has been applied correctly. After applying the cybersecurity control, the threat modeling infrastructure needs to support being able to automatically update risk values to reflect the residual risk. When evaluating the residual risk, the control can be seen as lowering the attack feasibility and, consequently, the overall risk level. In many cases, the control itself introduces new assets that require further threat analysis and additional security controls. This iterative process of applying controls and evaluating residual risk is necessary until the system has reached a state where all residual risk has been reduced to a tolerable level.

Once controls have been chosen, it is possible to define security requirements that are allocated to either the system under analysis, the operational environment, or the end user. It is at this stage of the analysis that two important outputs are produced: the cybersecurity requirements that make up the cybersecurity concept and the user requirements that must be shared with the system integrator to ensure the system is integrated securely. When the TARA is performed at deeper layers of the design, the resulting requirements will feed directly into the cybersecurity specifications of the component under analysis, as well as the security manual, which explains to the system integrator how the component can be integrated securely.

> **Best practice – share reasonable requirements with the user**
>
> When allocating security requirements to the system user, it is important to be aware of what is reasonable to expect from the user. For example, requiring the OEM to deploy a state-of-the-art firewall and deep packet inspection solution to shield the vehicle from network attacks may be an unreasonable way to justify why your ECU performs zero network packet filtering.

Tracking shared and accepted risks

During the risk assessment phase, there can be several risks that are either not severe enough to meet the bar for mitigation or that are out of scope for the system under analysis and therefore should either be shared with the end user or accepted by the system stakeholders. Risks that are accepted due to a low-risk level may be considered candidates for future improvements and therefore should be tracked in a common database for monitoring and evaluation in the next product version. The latter might offer new hardware security mechanisms or an enhanced software architecture that makes it possible to mitigate such risks practically. If the risk is accepted due to the infeasibility of mitigation at the system or component level, then the claim must be documented to describe the risk being shared or accepted, along with the stated rationale to enable the end user to validate the risk treatment decisions. When sharing risks with the end user, it helps to document the user action that can be taken to reduce the risk. For example, rather than documenting the acceptance of the risk of quantum computing compromising public key cryptosystems, the claim can instruct the user to consider implementing quantum-resistant cryptographic algorithms and deploying them through application-level software updates. Having a central work product such as a cybersecurity manual to capture and communicate these risks is a must to ensure the end user can integrate the system securely.

Review and signoff

After completing the TARA and producing the related cybersecurity work products, a verification step is needed both for the TARA itself and the generated work products that resulted from the TARA. Normally, a checklist can be defined to capture the criteria for passing the verification step by evaluating the following aspects:

- Adequate asset coverage
- Adequate threat coverage
- Meaningful attack description
- Properly mapping damage scenarios to assets and threat scenarios

- The completeness of the asset properties is considered

- The correctness of the residual risk scoring

- The correctness of the risk treatment decisions

- The correctness and adequacy of the chosen security controls and requirements

- The completeness of the user requirements and cybersecurity claim definition

With the review phase completed, the TARA enters the maintenance phase. During this phase, the TARA can be updated periodically when new functions are added to the system, or when new risks emerge after the product enters the operational phase. Throughout this process, security practitioners should avoid performing informal security analysis outside the TARA unless the issue at hand is fairly simple or has previously been analyzed in a separate TARA. For all other cases, capturing the evidence of analysis and the risk treatment decisions formally in the TARA ensures that all risks can be centrally accounted for and that a systematic risk-driven approach is applied consistently.

For the remainder of this chapter, we will illustrate the practical TARA approach using a fictitious **digital video recorder** (**DVR**) integrated with an ADAS system. The case study intentionally leaves some details out, but you are encouraged to work out the missing assets, threats, damages, and attack paths that we have skipped.

Case study using a digital video recorder (DVR)

Let's assume that you have been given the task of performing a TARA for a video recording function in an ADAS system that continuously records video data to capture a 20-second window around the time an **automatic emergency braking** (**AEB**) event is triggered. The recording is then made available for an external client to download either through the USB interface or the telematics unit. This is needed to analyze the event details and determine responsibility in the case of a crash. Your task is to identify high-risk threat scenarios related to this feature and define the necessary risk treatment decisions. Let's walk through the steps of applying the practical TARA approach to this use case.

> **Note**
> The following analysis is an abridged version of a full TARA and is not meant to be comprehensive.

Before we begin, it helps to capture the use case details in a table format, as shown here. The more details we capture about the use case, the more likely we are to uncover assets, threats, and attack surfaces:

Use Case Name	Video Recorder of AEB Event
Description	The system captures image data from the front camera to encode a video stream in a 20-second circular buffer. If an AEB event is detected, the buffer is persisted in eMMC to analyze AEB effectiveness and, if applicable, determine crash responsibility. The video is uploaded through the Telematics Unit upon the request of the OEM or downloaded via USB.
Actors	Crash analyst engineer
Inputs	• Camera sensor data • AEB event trigger • Video upload request
Outputs	A 20-second video is stored in MP4 format
Termination Condition	The video is stored in eMMC and a request to upload the video is fulfilled

Table 7.2 – Representing the Video recorder functionality as a use case to ease the threat analysis

Before diving into the threat analysis process, we also need to capture some assumptions about the operational environment and the objectives of the system stakeholders.

Assumptions

The camera sensor is connected to the DVR directly through a private link, so network-based threats against the camera sensor data are excluded from the TARA. Furthermore, the OEM cares about the non-repudiation of the video content to establish responsibility if the AEB is not triggered under the expected conditions. In terms of our threat model, we are considering network-based threats as well as the threat of a malicious application that is already running within the ADAS SoC and may attempt to interfere with the video recording.

Context diagram

Now that we've understood the use case and its assumptions, we need to prepare a context diagram that shows the system under analysis within the vehicle's environment. This is critical for understanding the full attack surface and defining attack paths:

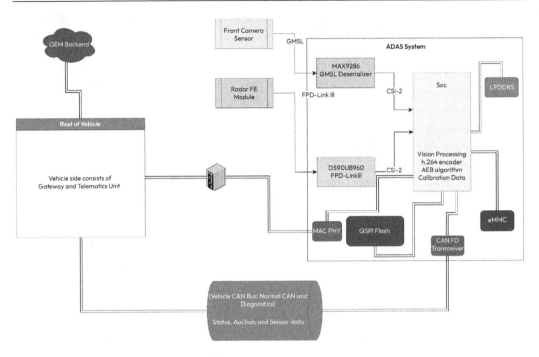

Figure 7.6 – Assumed context of the ADAS system and vehicle operational environment

Identifying the assets

By inspecting the system diagram and specifically our DVR function, we can identify several objects of interest that can be considered assets:

- Camera sensor input
- Video encoding software in QSPI Flash
- AEB event trigger input signal
- Calibration data used to configure video length
- Buffered video in LPDDR5 memory
- Persisted video in eMMC
- CAN messages that provide commands to upload the video
- Ethernet packets to transmit the stored video

> **Note**
>
> We are intentionally ignoring the assets of the AEB function because our scope of analysis here is the DVR. The AEB must still be analyzed as part of a separate TARA that is not shown in this case study.

At this stage, we have decided that enough assets have been identified and it is time to identify the damage scenarios.

Damage scenarios

Considering the stakeholders are primarily the OEM and the driver, both of which want to determine crash responsibility, we can uncover the following damage scenarios:

Asset	Property	Damage Scenario
Buffered video Persisted video Ethernet streaming data	Integrity Accountability	Invalid assignment of crash responsibility due to the crash recording data being tampered with
Buffered video Persisted video Ethernet streaming data	Availability	The inability of OEM to demonstrate that the AEB function did not contribute to the crash event due to the loss of video data
Ethernet streaming data	Confidentiality	Violation of road user privacy due to video data being uploaded by unauthorized parties

Table 7.3 – Derived damage scenarios using the assets and their corresponding asset properties

Now, it's time to consider how these damages can be triggered through malicious causes by enumerating the threats against the asset properties under analysis.

Threat enumeration and damage scenario mapping

For the sake of simplicity, we will combine the attack and threat scenarios in the threat description. In a real system, we should draw the attack trees to show how each attack path contributes to the threat scenario:

Threat ID	Asset	Threat Type	Threat Attack Description	Damage Scenario
T1	Ethernet streaming data	Information disclosure	The compromised Telematics Unit requests the DVR data to be uploaded and relays the video to the attacker's backend	Violation of road user privacy due to video data being uploaded by unauthorized parties
T2	Persisted video	Repudiation	An unauthorized diagnostic tool issues a request to replace the video recording with a recording from a prior event that contains no crash	Invalid assignment of crash responsibility due to the crash recording data being tampered with
T3	Persisted video	Tampering	A malicious diagnostic tool erases the video recording after a crash occurs	The inability of the OEM to demonstrate that the AEB function did not contribute to the crash event due to the loss of video data
T4	Buffered video	Tampering	A malicious application within the ADAS system wipes buffered video data periodically to prevent access to the recording in case of an accident	The inability of the OEM to demonstrate that the AEB function did not contribute to the crash event due to the loss of video data

Table 7.4 – Snapshot of the threat analysis of the DVR function

Assuming that all threats against the asset properties have been identified and the attack paths have been drawn, we move on to the risk assessment phase. We will assign the attack feasibility rating for each attack step, and the impact rating for each damage scenario. Consequently, we will produce a set of risk values. Considering the ease of manipulation through a compromised telematics unit and OBD diagnostic tool, we decide that threats T1 to T3 must be mitigated while T4 can be accepted.

As a result, we can derive the following cybersecurity goals and cybersecurity claim:

- **Cybersecurity goals**:

    - The ADAS system should protect the integrity and availability of the persistent video recording against network-based attacks

    - The ADAS system should prevent the non-repudiation of the video recording

    - The ADAS system should protect the confidentiality of the streamed video recording against network-based attacks

- **Cybersecurity claim**: The risk of buffered video data being erased by a malicious application is accepted due to the demonstrated difficulty of installing a malicious application within the ADAS system and the subsequent low-risk value

Now that we have our cybersecurity goals, we need to derive cybersecurity controls and concept-level cybersecurity requirements. Due to their high degree of coupling, we prefer to integrate cybersecurity controls as part of the cybersecurity requirement definition. Doing so allows us to quickly identify the cybersecurity control being used by simply reading the cybersecurity requirement.

Cybersecurity requirements and controls

By examining each attack path in our TARA that requires risk reduction and the impacted assets, we can derive cybersecurity requirements, along with the corresponding controls:

- The ADAS system shall apply a digital signature over the video data recording that includes a non-forgeable timestamp or monotonic counter before storing it in non-volatile memory

  Control family: Data authentication, anti-replay protection

- The ADAS system shall encrypt the video recording using a NIST-approved cryptographic algorithm before storing the video data in non-volatile memory

  Control family: Data encryption

- The ADAS system shall support a device-unique private key for signing crash records to prevent repudiation

  Control family: Non-repudiation through digital signatures

- The ADAS system shall restrict access to video recordings when queried over a network link to a predefined set of authorized clients through a cryptographic authorization mechanism

  Control family: Cryptographic challenge and response, role-based access controls

- The ADAS system shall reject video recording erase requests after a secure production state has been enabled

  Control family: Secure storage

- The ADAS system shall apply a tamper-evident enclosure to prevent the destruction and physical tampering of the video storage media

  Control family: Anti-tamper

At this stage, the respective hardware and software teams are expected to decompose the concept-level requirements into hardware and software security requirements. Remember that further refinement of the TARA is needed at each layer of the design to identify and eliminate architectural weaknesses. When decomposing security requirements, it helps to review the attack paths that were considered in the TARA to ensure that the lower-level security mitigations are providing adequate security coverage.

Summary

In this chapter, we introduced a practical approach to performing an efficient TARA. Our goal was to explain the fundamentals behind the ISO/SAE 21434 TARA methods while highlighting steps that can improve the results of the TARA and reduce the overall TARA preparation effort. We showed numerous pitfalls that engineering teams can fall into when performing the TARA process and provided tips and best practices to avoid them. The practical approach was broken into several phases, with the first phase starting with knowing the system by defining assumptions, understanding the use case under analysis, and modeling the system context and data flow. In the second phase, assets, damage scenarios, threats, and attack paths are identified and traced to one another. This paves the way for the third phase of attack feasibility and impact rating, which are necessary steps to calculate the risk levels and enable the risk treatment decision-making process. Once the risks have been prioritized, the cybersecurity goals are defined, and requirements can be derived both for the system under analysis and for other vehicle components in the operational environment. This is concluded by a TARA review and signoff. To demonstrate this approach, we gave an example of a DVR system that captures crash-related video in an ADAS system. The sample TARA products shown in the case study should provide a useful reference when you're preparing a real product TARA. Armed with this knowledge, you are now ready to perform security analysis to uncover threats and attacks that need treatment within your system.

In the next chapter, we will dive into the field of specifying cybersecurity controls to ensure that our security analysis is not only uncovering risks but also enabling us to define effective mitigations.

References

To learn more about the topics that were covered in this chapter, take a look at the following resources:

- [1] UN Regulation No. 155 - Cyber security and cyber security management system

  `https://unece.org/transport/documents/2021/03/standards/un-regulation-no-155-cyber-security-and-cyber-security`

- [2] Cyber Security and Resilience of smart cars

  `https://www.enisa.europa.eu/publications/cyber-security-and-resilience-of-smart-cars/@@download/fullReport`

- [3] Common Enumeration Weaknesses (CWEs) `https://cwe.mitre.org/`

- [4] Common Attack Pattern Enumeration and Classification `https://capec.mitre.org/`

- [5] HEAVENS first edition: `https://autosec.se/wp-content/uploads/2018/03/HEAVENS_D2_v2.0.pdf`

- [6] Proposing HEAVENS 2.0 – an automotive risk assessment model: `https://dl.acm.org/doi/pdf/10.1145/3488904.3493378?casa_token=CkQCLzI4xMkAAAAA:GO4IswB9yKy6lbLujicVslr94Av7MOKzOgt5sSrLX4x2Z4_vx9FpHlQLu06m9bcl-sN1mxNXqrw`

8

Vehicle-Level Security Controls

In *Chapter 3*, we discussed the different types of cybersecurity threats in automotive systems and how they relate to the vehicle's E/E architecture. Instead of jumping straight into technical solutions, we emphasized the importance of a systematic engineering approach to identifying and managing risks. Now, in this chapter, we will shift our focus to technical solutions to minimize cybersecurity risks through a defense-in-depth strategy. It is sometimes possible to eliminate a risk by removing a risky feature from the product's design. Most of the time, we must find ways to manage the risks using appropriate cybersecurity controls. As we will see in this chapter, introducing cybersecurity controls can lead to increased costs from added components as well as impact the system's performance. Furthermore, with each design modification, the vehicle risk profile is impacted, sometimes negatively, due to the potential for misconfiguration or mismanagement of the security control itself. In this chapter, we'll explore various security controls and techniques that can be applied to the layers of the E/E architecture to make the vehicle resilient to cyberattacks. We will delve into each technology area and discuss the most common methods for developing risk mitigations while considering the entire vehicle life cycle. We'll also cover common mistakes to avoid when implementing these controls and the challenges that may arise.

In this chapter, we will cover the following topics:

- Choosing cybersecurity controls
- Vehicle-level versus ECU-level controls
- Policy controls
- Secure manufacturing
- Secure manufacturing
- Secure off-board network communication
- Host-based intrusion detection
- Network intrusion detection and prevention
- Domain separation and filtering

- Sensor authentication
- Secure software updates
- In-vehicle network protection
- Securing diagnostic abilities
- Secure decommissioning

Choosing cybersecurity controls

If the job of cybersecurity professionals were to simply look up cybersecurity controls to mitigate threats, then it would have been a relatively easy job. In reality, knowing which cybersecurity control to apply is only the first step in implementing effective threat mitigation. After choosing the control, security analysis is needed to identify emerging threats that can result in the bypass or disablement of the control itself. Furthermore, knowledge about the security pitfalls and weaknesses associated with a given control is critical to ensure that the mitigation can truly be effective. This results in several rounds of security analysis to identify and examine the new assets that are introduced by the control and how they are subject to attack before the job of threat mitigation can be considered complete. Take, for example, secure boot, a well-known cybersecurity control that is expected to detect tampering in **electronic control unit** (ECU) code or calibration data and prevent the execution of malicious software not intended for a specific platform. The primary assets that are protected by secure boot are the ECU code and calibration data in non-volatile memory. When enabling secure boot, we introduce a whole suite of new assets whose compromise can lead to defeating the secure boot control and, again, exposing our primary assets (ECU code and calibration data) to the original threat of tampering.

> **Pause to think!**
> What new assets are introduced as a result of secure boot and how can they be protected?

It's exactly this question and the number of iterations you attempt to answer it that determines the target security rigor when designing and implementing the security control. Let's attempt to answer this question as a brief demonstration of the challenges that are faced when applying this security control.

First, enabling secure boot requires that the code and calibration data are either digitally signed using a private asymmetric key or authenticated using a secret symmetric key. The former is preferred since only the public key needs to be provisioned in the ECU; therefore, we will focus on that option. For starters, the private key that's used in signing the software and calibration data must remain confidential. Assuming the private key is accessed during manufacturing to sign the binaries, a **threat analysis and risk assessment** (TARA) is needed to identify attack paths that can lead to the disclosure or misuse of the private key by a malicious agent. This can produce additional security controls for the management of the private key in a **hardware security module** (HSM) and restrict access to the code signing ability in the manufacturing environment. Turning our attention to the target ECU, the matching public key must be provisioned in a way that ensures its authenticity and integrity. If done through an insecure channel, it could potentially be replaced, allowing an attacker to provide self-signed binaries without the possibility of tamper detection. To mitigate this risk, we need to add a new control that allows the public key to be transported through an authenticated channel. Now, assuming the public key has been provisioned securely, we must consider the risk of tampering inside the ECU's non-volatile memory by an attacker who can reprogram or physically replace that memory. To mitigate this residual threat, we must store the public key inside the **one-time-programmable (OTP)** memory or fuse arrays under the management of the **hardware-protected security environment (HPSE)**.

> **Quick hint**
> Storing a hash of the public key is a common practice to reduce the OTP or fuse array storage footprint without compromising the integrity protection of the public key itself. The latter can then be appended to the binary images being checked during secure boot.

So far, we have iterated over several countermeasures and residual risks in the hope of making the secure boot process truly effective. But if you stop at this point, then you have left several residual risks unmitigated, which will eventually result in the defeat of the secure boot process and nullifying all the good work you have done, so let's continue. When the secure boot check starts, there are critical code sections that perform the digital signature verification by comparing the decrypted hash with the computed hash value of the binaries. If the two do not match, the secure boot process is halted. An attacker with access to glitching equipment can first replace the software images in non-volatile memory with their own binaries, then apply **electromagnetic fault injection (EMFI)**-based glitches to cause the CPU to skip over the branch instruction where the verification check is performed, effectively bypassing secure boot to launch the tampered software image, as shown here:

```
if (decrypted_hash != computed_hash)
{
    Halt();
}
else
{
    StartApp();
}
```

You might argue that this attack will only result in malicious code execution on the target that that the attacker owns. But let's assume that the attacker's goal is to extract software binaries that contain valuable intellectual property that are stored in encrypted form. By successfully booting tampered software, the attacker can enable a UART shell that dumps the loaded software binaries after they have been loaded in plaintext form in volatile memory. In response to this risk, we harden our secure boot code against glitching by applying anti-glitch coding techniques such as using constants with a large hamming distance when performing the comparison, as well as using redundant nested if statements to raise the difficulty of the glitch attack (refer to *Chapter 6* for an example).

Are we done now? Not exactly! If the secure boot implementation relies on the multi-stage boot approach, then with each booted software stage, we have the residual risk that the booted software partition may interfere with an ongoing or previously completed boot stage. But wait – isn't secure boot meant to ensure that only authentic software is booted to establish a chain of trust?

This depends on your attacker model and system architecture. Assume that you have a system of heterogeneous cores that can be booted in parallel to one another with software that originates from different sources. If one of the booted software entities has write access to the memory of another core, then we cannot guarantee that the chain of trust remains intact. This can happen because the offending software entity might contain an unpatched exploit, so even though the software itself is signed, there is no guarantee that it does not misbehave. Therefore, we must enforce strong memory isolation over software partitions that are booted in separate runtime execution environments to avoid memory corruption attacks. At this point, you must feel quite good about your defenses. You are about to log off for the day and mark that JIRA ticket complete – but wait! In the voice of an infomercial marketer: "*There's more!*"

A frustrated attacker who cannot run malicious code on your platform can finally resort to DoS attacks because if they cannot run their code on your platform, neither should you!

Using a validly signed image from another ECU, they replace the target ECU binaries. At a minimum, this can result in booting incompatible software that results in erratic behavior or even a crash. To mitigate this, you must incorporate an ECU identifier and/or software versioning metadata into the digital signature generation process to ensure that only software intended for that specific platform will pass a signature verification check.

At this point and for the sake of this demonstration, we will assume that our job has truly been finished and we are satisfied that any residual risks are within a tolerable level. Notice how in each step of this analysis we were forced to analyze residual risks, forcing us to continue the analysis and add new security controls based on the premise that the residual risk was simply too high to be ignored. We can measure the residual risk using the ISO 21434 *[1]* risk assessment method by calculating the attack feasibility after the cybersecurity control has been applied. This should be the deciding factor to determine when the analysis is complete to avoid a never-ending TARA that can derail a program's schedule:

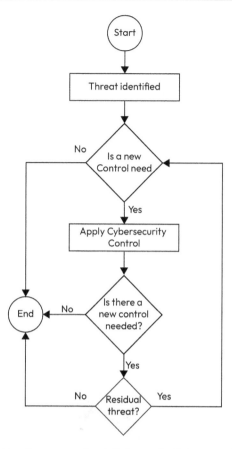

Figure 8.1 – Iterative process for defining and refining security controls

The role of security experts

This analysis could be developed iteratively as the architecture evolves with each adjustment. However, security experts help uncover such gaps from experience, so even after you follow this methodical approach to threat mitigation, having a security expert review your analysis ensures that your work has not missed any critical threats or weaknesses.

Challenging areas

Even after the right cybersecurity solution has been identified to mitigate a threat, adapting vehicle architectures, networking infrastructure, the backend, supporting tools, and manufacturing processes to accommodate such solutions remains a major challenge for OEMs. For one, the supply chain's depth means that the OEM must work closely with suppliers and standards committees to ensure new security solutions can be adapted. Similarly, adapting the vehicle's infrastructure to support procedures such as code signing and key provisioning has wide-ranging impacts on many processes, as well as a significant cost factor. Therefore, we recommend that OEMs who are starting to incorporate cybersecurity controls within their vehicles take a step-wise approach in which the high-priority threats are identified and addressed first. Moreover, management must commit the necessary resources and budget to see the deployment of such security controls in a reasonable time frame.

Now that we are familiar with both the technical and procedural challenges of defining and deploying cybersecurity controls, it's time to look at how these controls can be applied at the vehicle and ECU levels.

Vehicle-level versus ECU-level controls

Just as the **threat analysis and risk assessment (TARA)** is performed at multiple layers of the design, the security controls are applied hierarchically. As a result of this layered analysis, cybersecurity controls are applied in a layered fashion, which is essentially a **defense-in-depth cybersecurity strategy**. With each security layer, the likelihood of a successful breach is reduced as attackers must defeat or find gaps in multiple security layers before achieving their objective. *Figure 8.2* shows 11 security layers applied across the various vehicle life cycles:

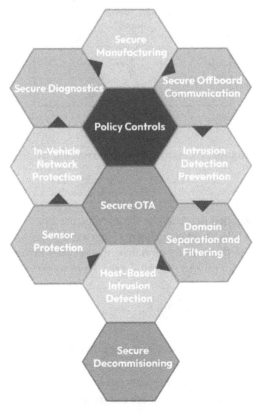

Figure 8.2 – Defense-in-depth security layers and controls

Each security layer shown in Figure 8.2, is considered a single cybersecurity control family, which, in turn, relies on several technical controls. In the remainder of this chapter, we will walk through the layers of the vehicle architecture to present common cybersecurity controls that are applied at each layer to realize this defense-in-depth security strategy. As with previous chapters, our objective is not to be exhaustive while covering the topic but rather to lay the foundation so that you may understand how to incorporate more control families that fit your vehicle architecture's needs. Even though some of these controls impact the ECU design, we will intentionally leave the ECU-level security controls to the next chapter. The same security layering approach will be applied at the ECU level, with a focus on both hardware and software technical measures to further reduce the risk of security breaches down to the lowest level of the ECU design. Now, let's turn our attention to the first family of **vehicle-level cybersecurity measures**, which is known as **policy controls**.

Policy controls

This first type of control is enforced through organizational-level procedures that define what is permissible from a security perspective. Policy controls are simply dos and don'ts that must be observed to eliminate certain risks that would otherwise be very expensive or difficult to mitigate through technical controls. An example of a policy control relates to the use of aftermarket telematics units and **onboard diagnostics** (**OBD**) dongles. Such devices are known to be abused by hackers to gain access to a vehicle's internal network and spoof its components. This can result in modifying the target ECU software or data, enabling the attacker to take control of the vehicle remotely.

To mitigate the risks associated with aftermarket **telematics control unit** (**TCU**) devices/OBD dongles, **original equipment manufacturers** (**OEMs**) can define a policy control that prohibits the vehicle owner from using such devices if they want to avoid voiding their vehicle's warranty. Detection of this policy violation can be supported through intrusion detection software running, for example, in the central gateway, which can monitor for typical messages that are transmitted by these devices. Another policy control that can be applied at the vehicle level is the requirement that drivers keep their vehicle software up to date by limiting how many times a driver can postpone an update. When this limit is reached, a forced update can be triggered at the first opportunity that the vehicle is parked and able to deploy a software update.

While these controls can help with improving the security of the vehicle, they are usually not fully effective in reducing risks due to the need for user compliance; the user will attempt to ignore or bypass such policies. Therefore, policy controls should be used sparingly and be strengthened by technical cybersecurity controls, which we will discuss next.

Secure manufacturing

The first set of technical cybersecurity controls deals with securing the manufacturing process both at the component and vehicle levels. This includes applying security controls for the process of installing firmware and software, provisioning **critical security parameters** (**CSPs**), and transitioning the component or vehicle into a secure production state. The goal of such controls is to ensure that the vehicle's assets are protected from the start of production until the vehicle rolls off the production line. The usage of a secure key management infrastructure is fundamental to achieving these goals. This is enabled by **hardware security modules (HSMs)** deployed within the factory environment to generate secret keys that need to be provisioned into each vehicle. The HSM can also be used to sign software images and calibration sets before flashing vehicle ECUs. Wherever possible, the HSM should be leveraged to generate private/public key pairs and shared symmetric keys that are unique for a given vehicle. This ensures that keys extracted from one vehicle cannot be used to spoof ECUs in another vehicle and that an ECU cannot be easily swapped across vehicles without proper authorization.

> **Unique private/public key pair usage**
>
> When creating root public keys to be provisioned in a vehicle, it is recommended to generate a new private/public key pair for a given vehicle class. Having a per-vehicle unique root public key localizes the impact of the private key getting compromised to a single vehicle rather than to the entire fleet.

The use of vehicle-unique private/public key pairs, such as for secure boot, helps in simplifying the key revocation strategy in case of a breach against the private key. By avoiding the use of a global root private key for all vehicles, we can ensure that an attacker who gains access to the private key will only be able to compromise a single vehicle rather than the entire fleet.

Moreover, implementing procedures for deleting development keys, wiping memory contents before software installation, and setting up fuse arrays are all essential controls to ensure the vehicle enters operation mode in a secure state. To that end, routines that are available in the factory for vehicle setup should be removed after the production phase is complete to prevent abuse by malicious actors after the vehicle is released to the consumer. Similarly, any special test mode for hardware or software that is enabled during manufacturing should be removed through irreversible locks, for example, to test ports and apply anti-tamper seals to the ECU test interfaces.

Challenges

Adapting manufacturing processes to incorporate cybersecurity controls is a challenging endeavor for several reasons. First, the manufacturing environment prioritizes procedures that ensure that vehicle systems are installed and configured correctly within the least amount of time possible. As a result, there is a need to support test procedures at various stages of the production process. This creates tension with cybersecurity best practices that advocate for the removal or adaptation of test procedures to avoid abuse by malicious actors. Similarly, the process of software installation requires access to serial programming interfaces. Cybersecurity practices advocate for obfuscation of such ports and disabling them as soon as access is no longer needed. Then, there is the time overhead of applying cybersecurity controls while the ECU or vehicle is being assembled. For example, creating digital signatures of software binaries and calibration sets as the ECU is being produced creates several communication rounds that involve transferring the code to a signing authority and receiving the digital signatures back before flashing can be completed. Similarly, provisioning keys and certificates can cause delays as such keys have to be produced for a specific ECU and procedures must be in place to verify that the key provisioning step has been finished successfully before proceeding to the next production stage. When cybersecurity controls rely on newer technologies, it is often discovered that manufacturing systems are lagging and cannot be easily updated to support new algorithms, such as quantum secure digital signature algorithms. Besides these challenges, even when the right tools and procedures are in place, manufacturing can introduce vulnerabilities, for example, mistakenly installing development keys in production intent ECUs, which renders the whole ECU security ineffective. For this and other reasons, it is extremely important to involve manufacturing engineers in cybersecurity activities through the cybersecurity production plan described in ISO 21434 [1]. All manufacturing procedures must be carefully considered to ensure that the threats to the manufacturing environment are well understood and that incorporating cybersecurity controls will not hinder the manufacturing process.

Only through the careful and correct application of the cybersecurity production plan can we ensure that the vehicle is ready to enter operational mode with the expected level of security.

Secure off-board network communication

Earlier in this book, we discussed how attackers can use Wi-Fi, cellular, Bluetooth, and other external connectivity interfaces to eavesdrop or tamper with vehicle data and control functions. Some ways to reduce security risks linked to off-board communication technologies include creating network firewalls, setting up intrusion detection and prevention systems, using network segmentation and isolation methods, restricting network access to vehicle ECUs, and establishing secure communication channels with backend servers.

When adopting such controls, automotive engineers must be aware of the impacts on computing resources, power consumption, real-time performance, and cost factors. In the remainder of this section, we will explore the controls at each communication interface layer and point to ways they can be tailored to fit within the vehicle's environment.

Wi-Fi

Wi-Fi can be used in vehicles to provide hotspot services, stream media, and, in some cases, enable OTA updates, such as when a car is parked at night and connected to a home router. When using Wi-Fi as a communication channel for off-board vehicle communication, it's important to secure each component of the **Wireless Local Area Network (WLAN)** throughout its life cycle, from initial design and deployment through ongoing maintenance and monitoring. At the vehicle level, securing Wi-Fi chipsets through careful supplier selection is the first step to prevent supply chain-style vulnerabilities. In addition, monitoring for vulnerabilities in the firmware of those chipsets is essential to quickly patch devices that are deemed at risk. Furthermore, mandating the use of **Wi-Fi Protected Access 3 (WPA3)** is essential to avoid common vulnerabilities with weaker Wi-Fi security protocols. A common source of Wi-Fi network breaches is the use of Wi-Fi passwords based on low-entropy data, making them vulnerable to brute-force attacks. Therefore, vehicle systems that offer Wi-Fi connectivity should reject the setup of weak passwords and preferably require **multi-factor authentication** (**MFA**) to prevent unauthorized access to the vehicle's Wi-Fi network.

Separating the user Wi-Fi network, which is used for entertainment and internet browsing, from the vehicle operational network, which handles OTA updates and reporting of vehicle telemetry data, is another essential control that reduces the likelihood of malicious interference. This can be done using **Virtual Local Area Networks** (**VLANs**) and **Service Set Identifiers** (**SSIDs**). For vehicles offering internet browsing features, the use of intrusion detection and prevention systems, firewalls, and URL filtering is essential to filter out malicious traffic and block access to known malicious sites.

It's also essential to disable any special network ports used for development purposes, such as SSH or Telnet, after the vehicle transitions to the production state. Failing to do so gives attackers powerful tools to manipulate vehicle networks, causing vehicle safety to be compromised. Finally, conducting a network penetration test can help you identify security weaknesses before a vehicle is released to consumers.

Bluetooth

In *Chapter 3*, we explored the widespread use of Bluetooth technology in vehicles for various applications, such as audio streaming and hands-free calling. However, the reliance on fixed PINs and the numerous vulnerabilities found in Bluetooth stacks make it an attractive target for attacks on vehicle communication services. To counter these threats, it is essential to employ Bluetooth Core Specification 5.3 or later as it addresses several weaknesses present in previous versions. Additionally, utilizing random PINs during mobile device pairing with the vehicle can significantly reduce the risk of connecting to untrustworthy devices. Given the history of implementation vulnerabilities, it is crucial to depend on solutions that have undergone rigorous security verification. The ability to promptly update Bluetooth software is also vital in addressing emerging security vulnerabilities. This can be accomplished by monitoring open source software implementations through **software composition analysis** (**SCA**). Lastly, ECUs with Bluetooth connectivity should incorporate sandboxing techniques for Bluetooth software, preventing the spread of software corruption to safety-critical or security-sensitive code sections.

Cellular

Vehicles rely on cellular-based communication as a reliable means of connectivity to receive OTA updates and report telemetry data through the telematics unit. Securing the vehicle's cellular link requires several layers of protection, starting with the carrier backend systems. For starters, split **Access Point Name** (**APN**) is a technique used by cellular carriers to segregate cellular traffic based on its source and only allow traffic from authorized sources to access the cellular network. By doing so, carriers can significantly reduce the risk of unauthorized access and data breaches. APNs are essentially identifiers that enable mobile devices to connect to a specific packet data network within a cellular network, such as the internet or a corporate intranet. By creating multiple APNs for different types of data traffic, different security policies, **Quality of Service** (**QoS**), and routing rules can be applied for each type of network traffic. In the context of automotive security, this can ensure that convenience features are routed differently from safety-related services such as OTA and map updates, which require a higher QoS.

Due to the deterministic nature of vehicle traffic, it is possible to limit the services that a vehicle can connect to using URL filtering. This technique allows a cellular carrier to control or restrict access to specific websites or web content over their cellular networks based on the OEM-defined filter rules. This is done by analyzing the URLs that have been requested through the telematics unit and then allowing or blocking access based on predefined rules or policies. This can protect the vehicle from malicious websites and content, such as phishing sites, malware, or spyware. By blocking access to known harmful sites, the OEM can further reduce the risk that a compromised telematics unit can download malicious content from blacklisted sites. The URL filtering process usually involves a combination of techniques, such as DNS filtering, IP blocking, and **deep packet inspection (DPI)**. When a user requests a URL, the carrier's filtering system checks the request against a database of blocked or allowed URLs. If the URL is found in the blocked list, the request is denied, and the user may receive a notification or error message indicating that access to the site is not allowed. Reducing the set of whitelisted trusted sites for a vehicle can greatly reduce the attack surface of internet-based attacks.

> **Note**
> When managing network filter rules, it is important to plan for periodic updates of such filters through a software update channel to ensure the filters are keeping up with emerging threats.

Since securing the cellular network hinges largely on the telematics unit's security posture, it is important to note that such units must leverage **embedded SIM (eSIM)** technology to protect network carrier shared credentials. An eSIM is a virtual SIM card that's embedded directly into telematics unit hardware, eliminating the need for a physical SIM card. eSIMs offer secure storage for cryptographic keys and unique identifiers, reducing the risk of an attacker masquerading as a vehicle's telematics unit to attack the backend. eSIMs can also be remotely provisioned and managed by the carrier, which allows for better control and monitoring of the SIM's life cycle. This can help prevent unauthorized changes to the eSIM's settings and ensure that security updates are applied promptly. Since eSIMs are embedded within the device, they cannot be physically removed or tampered with as easily as traditional SIM cards, making it harder for attackers to swap an approved telematics unit with off-the-shelf units whose security is questionable.

Preventing network downgrade attacks is essential to avoid the reintroduction of vulnerabilities related to older cellular network generations such as 2G/2.5G, which are vulnerable to MITM attacks via spoofed base stations. The telematics unit should be configured to reject any requests to use a networking protocol lower than 4G or LTE. Using 4G or later, it is possible to secure communication using mutual authentication between the telematics unit and a cellular network carrier. This begins with the telematics unit identifying its network carrier using unique identifiers such as a **Mobile Network Code (MNC)** and **Mobile Country Code (MCC)**. To authenticate the subscriber, the telematics unit uses its eSIM, which contains a unique **International Mobile Subscriber Identity (IMSI)** number and an **authentication key** (**Ki**). The network carrier sends a **random challenge** (**RAND**) to the telematics unit, which in turn processes the RAND using the Ki and an authentication algorithm (for example, A3) to generate a **signed response** (**SRES**) and a **session key** (**Kc**). The carrier calculates its own SRES and Kc and compares them to the values received from the telematics unit. If the values match, the subscriber is authenticated. The telematics unit then challenges the network carrier to authenticate itself. The carrier responds with a calculated result based on a shared secret key. The telematics unit then verifies the network's response and, if valid, the carrier is authenticated. Finally, both parties establish a secure communication channel using the Kc to encrypt and authenticate the exchanged messages from that point on.

Assuming the cellular link is now secure, it is important to protect the vehicle from protocols that rely on the cellular network, such as SMS. With SMS spoofing, an attacker can keep waking up the cellular modem in the telematic unit or attempt to deliver malware through malformed SMS messages.

SMS filtering methods

SMS filtering is one security control that can curtail the ability of attackers to abuse SMS to spoof the vehicle telematics unit using the following methods:

- **Sender-based filtering**: This relies on analyzing the sender's information (for example, phone number or alphanumeric sender ID) to determine if it is associated with known spammers or malicious sources

- **Content-based filtering**: This inspects the content of the message to identify keywords, phrases, or patterns associated with spam, phishing, or other malicious activities

- **Machine learning and AI**: These leverage AI to analyze SMS messages, identify anomalous messages, and adapt filtering rules accordingly

In addition to SMS filtering, disabling **Multimedia Messaging Service** (**MMS**) can be an effective method to prevent the use of malicious multimedia files to inject malware into the vehicle through the telematics unit. MMS messages can be used to exploit vulnerabilities in the telematics unit messaging app or the underlying operating system.

It is essential to implement rate-limiting mechanisms to control the number of SMS messages that can be processed by the network at any given time. Rate limiting is a technique that's used to restrict the rate of traffic that flows through a network. In the context of SMS, it involves setting a limit on the number of messages that can be processed by the telematics control unit at any given time. This limit is designed to prevent excessive traffic from overwhelming the telematics unit and causing performance degradation or service disruption.

To implement rate limiting for SMS, network operators can use various techniques, such as setting a maximum rate for outgoing messages, blocking messages that exceed a predefined threshold, or delaying messages that exceed a certain limit. These techniques can be configured based on different parameters, such as the source and destination of the messages, the content of the messages, or the time of the day. By enforcing rate limiting for SMS, network operators can also mitigate SMS flooding.

Host-based intrusion detection

Even with state-of-the-art security controls, the OEM has no visibility of how effective those controls are during normal operation. Indeed, some controls may start out being quite effective yet diminish in strength over time as attackers' abilities and tools increase in sophistication. Therefore, a security strategy that relies only on preventive security controls is incomplete unless complemented by attack detection mechanisms. Building anomaly detection systems in the vehicle accompanied by a backend **security operation center** (**SOC**) enables an OEM to bridge that gap and gain real-time perspective about the level of threats that the entire vehicle fleet is experiencing. This further enables the OEM to react promptly after an incident is detected when patching vulnerabilities is needed. With the distributed E/E architecture, no single ECU can know about all security events in the vehicle, so the host-based **intrusion detection system** (**IDS**) itself must be implemented as a distributed system. A distributed IDS has the added advantage that a single point of failure in one ECU that reports anomalies does not result in the loss of all anomaly detection capabilities. Furthermore, to avoid overloading the network with messages carrying anomaly events, the security events should be collected and qualified inside the ECU before being sent to a central event aggregator. The latter should be able to qualify security events under real-time constraints to ensure timely and appropriate responses to potential threats. Typically, a complete IDS solution consists of two main components: anomaly reporting and anomaly analysis. The reporting part is preferably implemented in specific ECUs that are deemed critical for vehicle security. Anomaly reports are typically aggregated by an ECU that supports external connectivity such as the telematics unit before transmitting the events to the SOC. The latter is then expected to implement security analytics to analyze reports from vehicles to detect attack patterns and initiate incident response, as shown in *Figure 8.3*. It is common for the SOC to rely on machine learning algorithms to detect anomalies across vehicles. Such algorithms must be regularly tested and updated as attackers discover new ways to evade detection. Also, collaboration and information sharing between different manufacturers and industry stakeholders is essential to combat emerging threats:

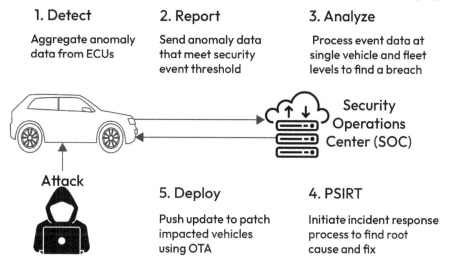

1. Detect

Aggregate anomaly data from ECUs

2. Report

Send anomaly data that meet security event threshold

3. Analyze

Process event data at single vehicle and fleet levels to find a breach

Security Operations Center (SOC)

Attack

5. Deploy

Push update to patch impacted vehicles using OTA

4. PSIRT

Initiate incident response process to find root cause and fix

Figure 8.3 – Incident response process driven by anomaly detection

The need for a consistent interface for collecting and reporting anomaly events in the vehicle is a motivator for the AUTOSAR-defined IDS solution. In that IDS, security sensors are software algorithms embedded in ECUs to detect and report security events to a dedicated software module within the ECU called the **intrusion detection system manager (IdsM)**. In the IdsM, the security events pass through qualification filters and become **qualified security events (QSEvs)** when specific criteria are met. An example QSEv can be detecting a failed MAC verification of a network message or detecting a failed image signature verification during flash programming. Setting criteria for what events to log and report provides automotive manufacturers with a much-needed advantage as they become aware of what attackers might be trying and how effective the existing cybersecurity controls are in thwarting such attacks. From a software perspective, the IdsM sends relevant QSEvs to the central **intrusion detection reporter (IdsR)** and stores them in the **security event memory (SEM)**. The SEM must be protected against tampering or deletion to ensure that events can be examined in the future in case of a forensic security analysis. Typically, the IdsR is implemented in the telematics unit or central gateway to support the forwarding of QSEvs to a **security operations center (SOC)** at the vehicle manufacturer. There, security experts work to check the plausibility of the data supplied. Based on their findings, countermeasures are implemented to treat the detected threats and improve protection against similar attacks in the future:

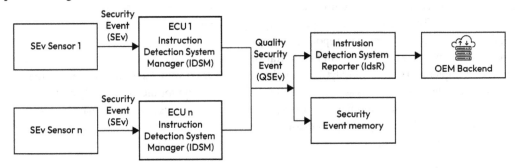

Figure 8.4 – Process flow of AUTOSAR-based IDS

What to do when an intrusion is detected

The dilemma of adding intrusion detection systems emerges when we ask about what to do in case an intrusion is confirmed to be active. One possible answer is to execute a minimum risk maneuver (for example, with an autonomous vehicle), but that can lead to the frustration of the driver if they are suddenly stranded in the middle of nowhere. Perhaps that was the attacker's motive all along! In recent years, some ideas have been floated, such as creating a kill switch that would stop all external connectivity to minimize the impacts of an active breach. The solution has to be more granular by ensuring that each impacted ECU can detect the attack's effects and can transition to a safe operational state to allow the vehicle to proceed to its destination. Meanwhile, a backend monitoring service should analyze the root cause of the breach based on anomaly reports sent by the vehicle so that it may react promptly through a software update.

Network intrusion detection and prevention (NIDP)

While host-based intrusion detection systems can be effective in alerting the OEM of potential active attacks, the time to respond makes them inadequate to fully mitigate active breaches. Naturally, there is a need to incorporate network intrusion prevention systems that can eliminate breaches before they become a persistent threat. However, any such solution must be carefully designed to account for the requirement of determinism in automotive systems. Unlike an IT environment, where a false positive that may lead to closing a network connection is tolerated, in a vehicle environment, falsely denying a network message that carries safety-related data can produce a high degree of indeterminism, which can eventually affect the availability of safety-related functions. Therefore, when picking network intrusion prevention solutions, eliminating false positives is a high-priority objective.

Some techniques for deploying NIDP in vehicles include designing network firewalls, deep packet inspection, and disabling potentially vulnerable network protocols. The first place to apply firewalls is the automotive-grade Ethernet switch, which is either a standalone device or integrated with the central gateway, as shown in *Figure 8.5*:

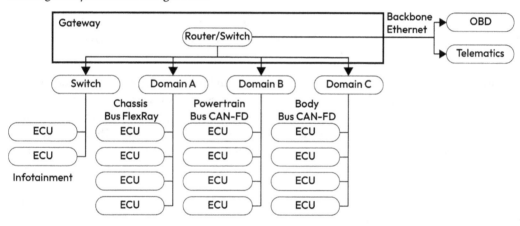

Figure 8.5 – Position of the firewall in the domain controller architecture

Some of these switches are capable of enforcing Layer 2 and Layer 3 level network filters, taking advantage of the static topology of the vehicle network design. Dropping network packets that do not meet the filter rules is an effective way to eliminate malicious intrusion attempts. These filters can be applied at ingress and egress ports to limit traffic flows based on a predetermined network architecture. Any network firewall must abide by the network timing requirements of automotive systems to avoid inserting latency and jitter that will adversely impact the safety of the vehicle. Having the ability to update firewall rules is another essential security control to allow OEMs to adapt the vehicle architecture when a network vulnerability is discovered.

Firewalls in vehicles are normally stateless, meaning each filter is applied over a given packet without considering prior packet receptions. Stateless firewalls make filtering decisions based on individual packets' header information, such as source and destination IP addresses, protocol types, and port numbers, but they do not keep track of the connection state or context. Stateless firewalls can prevent IP spoofing attacks by filtering out packets with known malicious IP addresses or blocking packets that originate from an external network but have a source IP address that belongs to the internal network. They can also prevent port scanning by filtering packets targeting unused or blocked ports to prevent attackers from discovering open ports on a system. On the other hand, stateful firewalls make filtering decisions based on the connection state and context, in addition to the packet header information. To do so, they maintain a state table to track the state of each connection. With stateful firewalls, attacks such as TCP SYN flooding can be prevented. A stateful firewall can mitigate this attack by monitoring the state of connections to limit the number of incomplete connections allowed. This prevents an attacker from forcing the system to exhaust its runtime resources when a large number of SYN packets are sent to a target system. Stateful firewalls can also prevent fragmentation attacks, where an attacker sends fragmented packets that, when reassembled, can bypass security controls or exploit vulnerabilities. Stateful firewalls reassemble these packets and apply filtering rules to the complete packet, thus detecting and blocking the attack before it takes effect. While adding stateful firewalls enables more complex filtering techniques, it comes at the expense of increased memory and computation resources.

In addition to network firewalls, incorporating hardware and software (for example, in the central gateway) that can perform deep packet inspection is desirable, especially when supporting applications that are directly exposed to the internet. Such solutions require high computational power and therefore must be accelerated in hardware to avoid consuming the CPU application runtime. The challenge with such systems is that false positives are still possible and therefore, they must be applied for network traffic that is not safety-critical. Like firewall rules, intrusion prevention systems that rely on known malicious packet signatures require frequent updates and large memory resources to promptly handle newly discovered malicious packets. Over time, enterprise-style network intrusion prevention solutions are expected to be incorporated into the vehicle environment with adaptations to account for the power consumption, cost, and computational capabilities of the vehicle.

Domain separation and filtering

Besides filtering unwanted traffic and detecting malicious network packets, enforcing domain isolation over the internal vehicle network is a critical security control to prevent the corruption of a single network segment from propagating to deeper layers of the vehicle network architecture. It is not uncommon to find vehicle network architectures with multiple gateways that route messages between different vehicle control domains. The challenge with multiple gateways is that it is easy to create unintended communication paths, which result in traffic flowing into network segments that must have a high degree of integrity and availability. To eliminate weak architecture design, central gateways and domain controllers provide a clean way of domain separation, which further eases the application of network filtering. Network segmentation can be used to separate connectivity domains such as telematics and infotainment from actuation domains such as the chassis and powertrain. In addition to network isolation, central gateways serve as the hubs that securely and reliably interconnect and transfer data across the different networks in a vehicle. They provide protocol translation (for example, Ethernet to CAN) to route signals between functional domains such as the powertrain, chassis and safety, body control, infotainment, telematics, and ADAS. Their central location makes them ideal to perform firewall and intrusion detection/prevention functions:

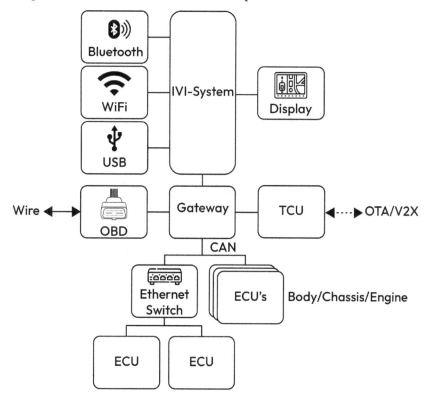

Figure 8.6 – Domain separation using a security gateway embedded in a vehicle

Network segmentation is also important to improve operational performance by reducing network congestion, especially if an attacker is mounting DoS attacks by flooding one network segment in the hope of affecting other layers of the network architecture. Applying VLAN filters, ingress/egress filters, and routing tables are all mechanisms that can strengthen the network security concept.

Another powerful technique of central gateways is network filtering across heterogeneous networks such as CAN-CAN, CAN-LIN, and Ethernet-CAN. The gateway applies network filter rules that prevent communication from crossing into a network domain if it is not required for the proper functionality of the vehicle. The gateway can easily drop CAN frames that are not mapped to a given channel or that do not match the expected **data length code** (**DLC**) to prevent them from being mirrored on other

CAN bus channels. Similarly, the gateway can detect implausible network patterns such as messages transmitted at a higher periodic rate than expected. In such a case, the gateway can choose to limit the rate of transfer to prevent the disruption of CAN network channels. This can be especially useful in blocking CAN flooding attacks:

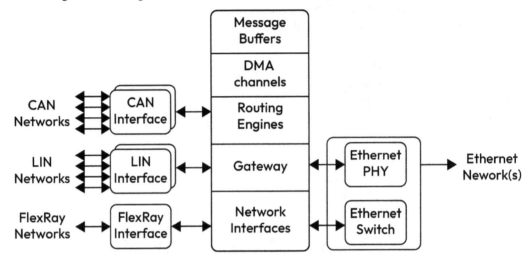

Figure 8.7 – Secure gateway message routing capabilities

If anomalies are detected, the gateway can report the anomaly to the telematics unit so that it can be sent to the SOC. More importantly, it can filter anomalous CAN messages before they reach the target network segment. One challenge with central gateways, when network authentication is enabled, is the need to re-authenticate frames, which can place a significant computational burden on the gateway for verifying and then re-generating new message authentication codes. This has to be considered to ensure that hardware cryptographic accelerators are designed to produce minimal latency in message transfer and minimal impact on CPU resources.

Sensor authentication

Sensor data integrity and identity protection were shown to be primary security objectives to ensure the correctness of the vehicle control functions. With the rise of ADAS use cases, the need for trusted sensors experienced a sharp rise. A secure sensor needs to support one or more of the following security controls:

- Identity authentication
- Cryptographic data integrity and confidentiality
- Physical attack mitigation

The first control ensures that before accepting any communication from a sensor, a secure session is established, where the sensor can prove the authenticity of its identity. This can be done using a pre-provisioned sensor root public key in the ECU communicating with the sensor. Then, the sensor can be challenged to prove possession of the private key by submitting a random challenge that the sensor must sign. This step can involve exchanging an ephemeral session key (for example, using ECDH(E)) to protect further communication. The cryptographic integrity of the sensor data can be protected using the shared session key. Each message is authenticated by the sensor and verified by the receiver. Note that typically, encryption is not enabled due to the nature of the sensor data not requiring confidentiality protection. However, in cases where the sensor is capturing PII, encryption should be considered, such as in the case of camera sensors. To standardize the establishment of a secure session and authentication of sensor messages, the **Secure Protocol for Device Management** (**SPDM**) standard was introduced. This eliminates the need for proprietary secure sensor protocols and improves the interoperability of sensors with different ECUs.

The SPDM standard provides a security framework to enable secure communication among automotive devices over widely used communication interfaces, including I2C, CSIE, and PCIe. SPDM offers a collection of cryptographic capabilities at line speed through inline encryption engines. The standard incorporates secure key exchange, device attestation, and encrypted data transmission thereby enhancing the security of automotive systems. Moreover, sensors, especially those exposed to the external environment, such as cameras, LiDAR, Radar, and GPS, are at risk of physical manipulation. Attacks that abuse the physical properties of the sensor cannot be eliminated through cryptographic measures alone and require physical and software techniques to detect implausible sensor readings. For example, LiDAR tampering through maliciously timed lasers can confuse the LiDAR sensor reading. Measures such as defensive AI/ML are necessary to detect implausible sensor input that can be the result of nefarious activities.

Secure software updates

Securing software updates over the air is a critical component in the overall strategy of keeping the vehicle software patched while preventing the tampering of ECU software. To achieve this objective, an end-to-end approach is needed, starting with the backend and terminating at the target ECU. This holistic approach requires a series of security controls to be applied at each stage of the **OTA** update process, including a robust update service architecture, strict access controls and privilege separation in the backend, secure data transfer to the vehicle, and authentication and encryption of software packages before software reprogramming. Let's examine these security controls closely throughout the software update chain.

First, a code-signing service is needed to protect the authenticity and integrity of software updates before they are deployed. Establishing a secure service that enables suppliers to submit their software packages for signing is an essential first step. Using a **hardware security module** (**HSM**), it is possible to protect the confidentiality of the signing keys and prevent illegal access. Equally important to leveraging the HSM is constructing the key hierarchy to reduce the risk that a single private key compromise causes a complete loss of security in the software update process. To this end, we recommend the role separation defined by **UPTANE** (a software update security system developed as a collaboration between academia and the automotive industry) due to its robust security model. By separating the key hierarchy, UPTANE ensures that a single compromise of a role (except for the root role) is not sufficient to break the security of the entire software update process. First, the root role signs public keys used to verify metadata produced by all other roles and can revoke keys if a role is compromised. The corresponding root private key must be stored in an HSM without online access. A **timestamp role** produces and signs metadata indicating the presence of new metadata or images in the repository. This addresses multiple timing-related threats such as replay, freeze, and endless data attacks. The **snapshot role** keeps track of the version numbers of all targets metadata to ensure that OTA clients receive the most recent and consistent metadata about their updates. This mechanism prevents mix-and-match attacks, where an attacker could try to trick the ECU into installing incompatible or malicious software updates. The **targets role** produces and signs metadata about binary images and delegations. This metadata contains essential information about the software updates, such as file sizes, hashes, and custom data, which helps ensure the authenticity and integrity of the updates. This makes it difficult for an attacker to tamper with or replace the update files without being detected. It can also delegate the responsibility of signing metadata to custom-defined roles called delegated targets, which can be useful in large software update ecosystems where multiple suppliers and stakeholders are involved in providing and managing software updates for different components or vehicle models. This distributed responsibility helps ensure that a compromise in one supplier or component does not jeopardize the entire software update process since the attacker would not have access to the signing keys for other components:

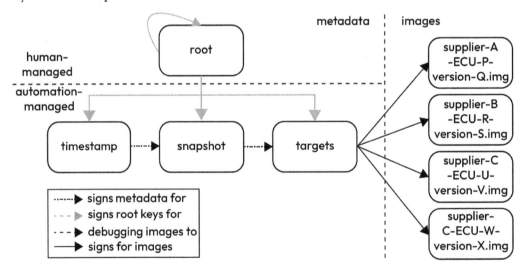

Figure 8.8 – Role separation, as proposed by UPTANE

Managing updates remotely requires the backend to query software manifests from vehicles to ensure the update package contains the correct software, calibration, and firmware versions for a given vehicle's make, model, hardware components, and installed software versions.

Using a pull-only mode to query vehicle software versions is a preferred approach as it allows the vehicle to remain in control of when and how it shares information with the OTA infrastructure. Once a package is ready for deployment, the update needs to be transferred over a secure channel. This can be achieved by using mutual authentication security protocols that ensure that communication between the vehicle and the backend is encrypted and authenticated. A popular secure communication protocol for OTA is TLS 1.3, which enables authenticated and confidential communication between the backend and the vehicle OTA master, such as the telematics unit. One of the significant changes in TLS 1.3 is the removal of vulnerable cryptographic algorithms and cipher suites, which reduces the risk of attacks such as MITM and downgrade attacks. Additionally, TLS 1.3 has improved key exchange mechanisms, which further enhance the security of communication. Additionally, restricting the ability to establish TLS sessions to a limited set of trusted servers can be an effective control to reduce the attack surface by limiting who an OTA master can communicate with:

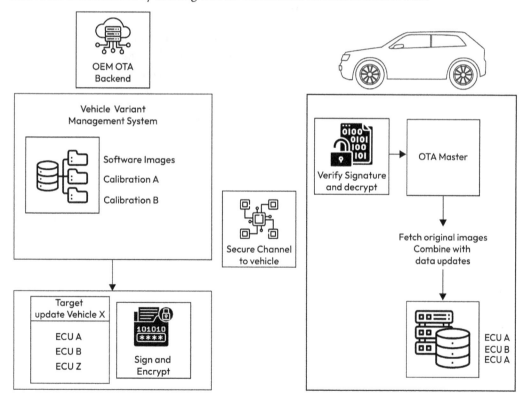

Figure 8.9 – Typical communication flow between the OTA backend and a vehicle

On the vehicle side, assigning a dedicated OTA master within the vehicle helps with centralizing the OTA update process to ensure that updates are handled securely and efficiently. Typically, an OTA master should have external connectivity and access to large storage to buffer OTA packages before initiating the update of individual ECUs. Leveraging backup storage both in the OTA master and target ECUs is required to recover from both faulty and maliciously interrupted updates. Without allocating backup partitions, an attacker who can interrupt an erase or programming operation can leave the ECU partially programmed, which translates into an inoperable vehicle. Once the update package is delivered, the OTA master must perform the first level of digital signature verification before deploying it to the target ECUs. The OTA master is expected to perform several validation checks, such as checking the freshness of the update, the compatibility of software modules within the update with the target ECU, and the size and content of the update. Some of these actions can be delegated to the target ECUs where possible. By following this systematic approach to OTA security, we can ensure that at each step of packaging, transferring, and installing software, security weaknesses are eliminated to ensure an end-to-end secure solution.

In-vehicle network protection

As we saw in *Chapter 1*, in-vehicle networks play a critical role in modern automobiles, enabling different systems to communicate and work together efficiently. The CAN network is a standard protocol that allows ECUs to exchange data in real time. However, the openness of the CAN protocol makes it vulnerable to malicious attacks, which can compromise the safety and security of the vehicle.

Before applying cryptographic measures to secure in-vehicle networks, it is important to consider all external access points that may be abused to directly tap into the in-vehicle network. It is common for vehicle network architects to leave easily accessible network ports to help in quickly troubleshooting network issues during development. Unfortunately, these also enable attackers to easily tap into the vehicle network after the vehicle is in operation. Easy access to the internal network means an attacker can install CAN sniffing tools that can inject malicious CAN messages while the vehicle is operational. This is a serious problem if the vehicle is, for example, used to transport high-value loads, such as the case with heavy commercial trucks, which may be a desirable target for theft or sabotage. The simplest control is to remove external access to CAN ports by increasing the difficulty of physical access. Additional controls can be added, such as tamper detection measures, which alert the driver through a dashboard warning if a locking mechanism is unlatched.

When the availability of the in-vehicle network message is critical, the usage of redundant networks can reduce the risk of loss of communication, assuming the compromise of both networks is harder than a single network. In addition to this, redundant CAN should be implemented to mitigate DoS attacks, such as zero ID message flooding. To further enhance security, GPIO configuration locking can be used to prevent reconfiguration of security-relevant settings (such as GPIO multiplexing). This is typically done during ECU initialization for each boot cycle to eliminate the risk of reconfiguration to an insecure state during mission mode. Lastly, ECU-level whitelist filtering can be implemented to drop unwanted messages and ensure that only trusted messages are accepted. By implementing these security measures, in-vehicle networks can be made more secure, minimizing the risks of cyberattacks on modern automobiles.

Besides these measures, network authentication can be a stronger measure that prevents a malicious network node from being able to spoof or tamper with network messages.

CAN message authentication

To address the risk of tampering, spoofing, and message replay, AUTOSAR **secure onboard communication (SecOC)** (introduced in *Chapter 2*) is a commonly used control.

> Note
>
> SecOC, also known as the secure onboard communication protocol, was defined by AUTOSAR and is a popular protocol for protecting the authenticity, integrity, and freshness of CAN messages.

The protocol relies on the use of shared symmetric keys between ECUs that need to exchange messages and makes use of truncated MAC and freshness counters to protect frames. SecOC can protect both CAN 2.0 and CAN FD frames by authenticating each frame, including the CAN ID, DLC, and payload field. A freshness value embedded in the payload allows a receiving node to detect if a frame with a valid MAC is being replayed. Challenges with SecOC are mainly the performance impact and the synchronization of freshness values between ECUs. Since safety-critical CAN messages must be received within a specific maximum latency time, performing the cryptographic functions to verify the MAC may exceed such limits. Typically, an HPSE is leveraged to accelerate the MAC generation and verification, but even with hardware accelerators, the overhead to fetch the keys and transfer data in and out of a crypto engine still poses a challenge to performance constrained devices. Therefore, careful design of the HPSE and crypto engines is needed to support the maximum number of CAN frames that must be processed within the allotted time. For example, the use of DMA and fast key memory can help maximize cryptographic engine usage to ease the switching between one crypto job context and the next. When a truncated freshness value is used, the receiver must apply a synchronization strategy that ensures that errors in the network link do not result in permanent loss of synchronization.

Ethernet

As mentioned previously, the use of Ethernet as an in-vehicle communication protocol has gained significant popularity due to the increased need for high throughput and bandwidth for use cases such as sensor data fusion and media streaming. To mitigate the risks of Ethernet frame spoofing, tampering, disclosure, and replay, automotive manufacturers can enable the Layer 2 security protocol known as MACsec. When coupled with network segmentation through VLANs backed by a robust Ethernet switch configuration, the in-vehicle Ethernet network can effectively block unauthenticated or replayed frames. Moreover, it is important to protect the Ethernet switch firmware, configuration, and routing tables from tampering by ensuring that the firmware is securely booted and configured at startup. To minimize the risk of tampering with the switch configuration, there should be only a single authorized party that can manage the switch and, preferably, disallow reconfiguration after initial setup. Now, let's take a deeper look at how MACsec can be leveraged to protect Ethernet traffic in vehicles.

MACsec

MACsec offers a range of security features that are well suited for point-to-point communication between vehicle ECUs and sensors. Each node has at least one unidirectional secure channel, which is identified by a **Secure Channel Identifier (SCI)**. As the vehicle network is static, the network architect configures matching receive and transmit secure channels between nodes with the corresponding SCIs. Within each secure channel, secure associations are defined, each having a **secure association key (SAK)** for encryption and authentication. These associations are identified by the association number field of the SecTAG header (as shown in *Figure 8.11*) and are configured to have a limited lifetime before a new session key must be established:

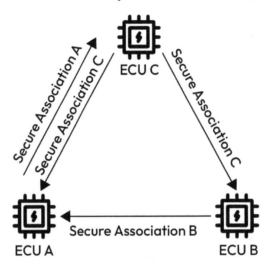

Connectivity Association (CA)

Figure 8.10 – Establishing multiple secure channels within a single connectivity association

Replay protection is also provided within each secure association through the packet number field of the SecTAG header. While MACsec supports a replay window that allows some frames to be accepted even if they have a lower packet number than expected, we recommend setting the replay window to zero. Note that encryption in MACsec is optional and for automotive use cases, data authentication is usually sufficient. When frames are received with an incorrect authentication tag, the frame must be dropped. To further increase the robustness of the MACsec protocol, the Ethernet switch can be configured to only forward traffic through the port after a secure MACsec session has been established. MACsec can further protect against MITM attacks by detecting when a frame source or destination MAC address has been changed:

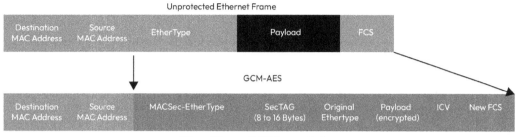

Figure 8.11 – Ethernet frame with MACsec enabled

One of the challenges of deploying MACsec in vehicles is managing MACsec keys between the various nodes before a secure session can be established. First, the **connectivity association key (CAK)** must be shared between MACsec nodes that need to establish secure channels. There are two common methods by which MACsec nodes can share the CAK according to the IEEE 802.1X standard. In the manual key distribution method, the CAK is provisioned on each MACsec node – for example, during the vehicle assembly. This approach is the simplest but requires a secure manufacturing environment to protect the confidentiality and integrity of these keys before they are provisioned in each node. Dynamic key distribution, on the other hand, automatically distributes the CAK among MACsec nodes using the **MACsec key agreement (MKA)** protocol. This protocol relies on a central authentication server, such as RADIUS, to authenticate nodes and distribute the CAK. For many automotive systems, this solution may not be desirable due to the added complexity and cost of deploying a trusted authentication server in the vehicle.

A deciding factor for deploying MACsec is the hardware support for line-rate encryption and authentication. Without it, significant CPU runtime resources will have to be consumed to perform the cryptographic functions in software. Moreover, the storage and handling of the MACsec keys must be protected, preferably with the help of an HPSE. In a system that supports multiple distrustful applications or virtual machines, it should not be possible for one application to transmit Ethernet frames on a secure channel reserved for another application or VM. This restriction can be achieved through a mixture of software and hardware isolation techniques.

Securing diagnostic abilities

During development and maintenance, diagnostic and debug services are seen as lifesavers when it comes to identifying and troubleshooting vehicle issues. However, with this ability comes the risk of abuse. Diagnostic services in the hands of an attacker can pose serious risks to the vehicle data and control functions. This can cause unsafe actuation while the vehicle is in motion or tampering with diagnostic records or settings such as mileage manipulation or emission records tampering.

There are two strategies to protect the vehicle from the misuse of diagnostic services:

- **Disable diagnostic services where they are not needed**: The first type of control entails accounting for all diagnostic service protocols and features in the vehicle. This includes ISO 14229 UDS-based diagnostics, XCP calibration and flashing, and any proprietary diagnostic routines that an ECU supplier may enable during development or manufacturing. Services that can be eliminated after the vehicle is in production must be removed through build-time configuration. An example of such a service is the remoteDownloadandExecute UDS routine. This routine allows external parties to download a code payload and request that it gets executed. If that does not raise a red flag, just reading the name of the service should, as it provides the ability to remotely execute code in the vehicle. Even if such a request required authentication, it is hard to see why such an ability should be necessary in a production vehicle.

  Plausibility checks are an essential part of secure diagnostics and flashing in automotive systems. By applying plausibility checks to reject actuation diagnostic routines while the vehicle is moving, we can ensure that the diagnostic routines are only executed when it is safe to do so.

> **Note**
> Functional safety also requires that such plausibility checks be performed to avoid accidental execution of diagnostic routines that result in unsafe actuation while the vehicle is moving above a certain speed.

  Normally, diagnostic commands have to be routed through a central gateway before reaching a target ECU. Implementing pre-checks in the diagnostic gateway to enable such routing can be especially effective in preventing DoS attacks that abuse the diagnostic protocol. Even if the target ECU rejects such requests due to the vehicle being in motion, having the gateway block the requests in the first place minimizes the risk that a deeply embedded CAN network will become unavailable or disrupted due to a malicious network participant abusing the diagnostic protocol.

- **Enforce strong diagnostic client authentication**: The second type of control is based on cryptographic means of client authentication. The objective of this control is to authenticate the diagnostic client to prevent illegal access to privileged diagnostic routines or services. The next section will demonstrate two main methods that UDS-based diagnostics offer client authentication.

Security access control via UDS service 0x27

First, we will look at the original method of securing the diagnostic protocol through Security Access Service Identifier (0x27). This service partitions access across multiple levels to lock access to a set of diagnostic services. For example, a client that can unlock level 0x02 will gain access to flash programming abilities, while a client that can unlock level 0x03 will gain access to routines that can trigger actuation functions. To unlock an ECU in a vehicle, the client sends a request for a "seed." The ECU replies by sending the random seed in the form of a challenge back to the client. The client then generates a "key" based on the "seed" using a pre-determined algorithm, and then responds with the key. If the client generated the "key" correctly, the ECU will respond that the "key" was valid and will unlock diagnostic services mapped to the requested level. On the other hand, if the client produces an invalid key, the ECU will deny the access request and will reject any attempts to trigger the protected diagnostic services. Additional controls can be enabled to extend the period before the client can make another request if multiple security access requests fail. So long as the "seed" is a cryptographically random challenge with sufficient length, and the algorithm for producing the "key" relies on a NIST or BSI-approved cryptographic method with sufficient cryptographic key strength, the mechanism can be considered effective in protecting access to restricted services. However, due to the locking being done based on levels only, this protocol suffers from a lack of fine-grained access permissions and the need for using shared symmetric keys to perform the challenge verification. To deal with these shortcomings, service 0x29 was introduced, as shown next.

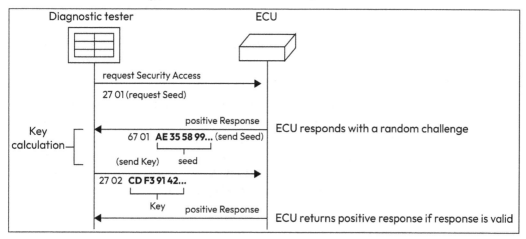

Figure 8.12 – Security access-based protocol

Role-based access control via UDS service 0x29

UDS service 0x29 was added to provide role-based access controls, giving OEMs more control over how to assign diagnostic service privileges for different actors, such as shops, manufacturing personnel, developers, or even owners. With this service, a PKI is used to issue certificates that specify the diagnostic abilities of each client. It is also possible to restrict the validity of that role through the certificate's validity period:

Certificate Mask	Third Party Diagnostic Client	OEM	Tier 1 Supplier	Dealer	After market
Certificate Configuration Bits	☐	■	■	☐	☐
Read Data By Id	■	■	■	■	■
Write ECU Serial Number	☐	■	■	☐	☐
Request Download	☐	■	■	☐	☐
Erase Routine	☐	■	■	☐	☐
Enter Extended Session	☐	■	■	☐	☐

Figure 8.13 – Role based access controls through the use of digital certificates

Figure 8.13 shows a certificate role configuration that grants an authenticated Tier 1 supplier role access to all the listed diagnostic services, while it restricts after-market users to only performing the Ready By Identifier service.

The preferred method to support service 0x29 is by leveraging a PKI infrastructure to issue and revoke certificates as needed. Before gaining diagnostic privileges, a diagnostic client can request a certificate from the PKI infrastructure that assigns them their allowed roles. The diagnostic client then provides their certificate to the ECU, which verifies that the certificate is valid by checking the certificate signature using a pre-provisioned root public key. The ECU then sends a challenge to the diagnostic client to prove possession of the matching private key. The latter computes a signature over the challenge using their matching private key and responds to the ECU. The ECU then verifies the signature using the public key provided in the client's certificate, verifying that the tester is indeed authorized to perform the diagnostic functions that were assigned in the certificate:

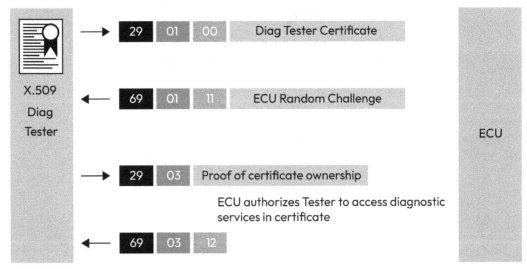

Figure 8.14 – Certificate based authentication with service 0x29

Securing flash programming services

Flash programming over the UDS protocol is a special use case that allows a diagnostic client to erase and reprogram a new software image in a target ECU. Securing the flash programming protocol is partially achieved by securing the diagnostic protocol itself. For example, before switching to a flash programming session, the flash programming tool must authenticate itself and gain access to services such as requestDownload (0x34), requestUpload (0x35), and transferData (0x36). Beyond diagnostic client authentication, it is important to implement plausibility checks that prevent regions that should not be updateable from being erased or programmed. Additionally, the requestUpload service should preferably be removed to eliminate the risk of software exfiltration by an attacker who gains access to an authenticated diagnostic client. Besides these controls, the flash programming protocol should require digital signature verification before marking an updated image as valid to prevent tampering with the ECU software, firmware, or calibration data. Furthermore, the flash programming protocol must be robust against malicious interruptions that can leave the ECU in a partially programmed state. In no case, should a programming event leave the ECU completely unbootable.

Secure decommissioning

There are several events in which a single ECU or the whole vehicle needs to be decommissioned.

Such events include replacing a defective ECU, disposing of a vehicle involved in a major accident or simply when it reaches end-of-life. Besides decommissioning scenarios, having the ability to securely erase user private data arises in events such as the transfer of vehicle ownership and returning a rented car.

To ensure that user private data and intellectual property of the OEM or supplier is not exposed during these events, the vehicle needs to support routines for the deletion or destruction of such confidential data. A common technique to support secure decommissioning is to ensure that all such data is encrypted. Then, by destroying the encryption key, the data becomes practically unusable. Another technique involves securely deleting all private data by identifying and then erasing all copies of the data inside an ECU. This option is harder to achieve as data records can be duplicated and persisted over multiple devices, making it difficult to account for all records that must be deleted. Furthermore, in typical cases, erasure involves modifying metadata rather than physically erasing the storage device. Therefore, care must be taken when choosing this method to rely on erase routines that truly set the device in a state where persisted data is wiped. Of course, the ability to erase all memory contents permanently can be seen as an attractive attack vector by someone who wants to disrupt vehicle operations when the vehicle is not intended to be decommissioned. Therefore, such abilities must be protected through the enforcement of strong authentication mechanisms, preferably by requiring an external trusted party to authorize the erase. One way to implement a secure erase method is by making it part of the HPSE firmware, which, in turn, should require proof of authorization through a mutual authentication step before the service is executed.

Summary

In this chapter, we delved into the essential role of security controls in establishing robust and secure automotive systems. By employing a defense-in-depth strategy, we showed how to deploy multiple layers of protection within the vehicle architecture, making it exceedingly challenging for attackers to bypass these safeguards and accomplish their malicious objectives. To do so, we focused on security measures that apply to various layers of the vehicle architecture, beginning with the backend and extending to the in-vehicle network layer. We emphasized that developing effective security controls necessitates a continuous process of risk assessment to ensure that these protective measures are resilient and resistant to tampering or disablement. This comprehensive analysis of security controls should inspire automotive organizations to invest in the development of security control catalogs and recognize the significance of implementing appropriate measures based on a risk-based approach. By embracing such a method, organizations can create a robust and multi-layered foundation for their automotive systems, ultimately safeguarding their vehicles and the individuals who rely on them.

In the next and final chapter, we will continue with the defense-in-depth strategy but this time with a focus on the internal architecture of the ECU.

Further reading

To learn more about the topics that were covered in this chapter, take a look at the following resources:

- [1] ISO, I., & FDIS, S. 21434-2021, Road Vehicles – Cybersecurity Engineering.

- [2] National Highway Traffic Safety Administration. (2020). Cybersecurity Best Practices for the Safety of Modern Vehicles. National Highway Traffic Safety Administration: Washington, DC, USA.

- [3] Automotive Intrusion Detection Systems | Vector.

- [4] Schmidt, K., Zweck, H., & Dannebaum, U. (2016). Hardware and software constraints for automotive firewall systems? (No. 2016-01-0063). SAE Technical Paper.

- [5] Overview of Unified Diagnostic Services Protocol: `https://nvdungx.github.io/unified-diagnostic-protocol-overview/`

- [6] Uptane Standard for Design and Implementation: `https://uptane.github.io/uptane-standard/uptane-standard.html`

- [7] 802.1AE: MAC Security (MACsec).

- [8] AUTOSAR Intrusion Detection System: `https://www.autosar.org/fileadmin/standards/R22-11/FO/AUTOSAR_RS_IntrusionDetectionSystem.pdf`

- [9] AUTOSAR Secure Onboard Communication: `https://www.autosar.org/fileadmin/standards/R22-11/CP/AUTOSAR_SRS_SecureOnboardCommunication.pdf`.

- [10] ISO 14229-1:2020 Road vehicles — Unified diagnostic services (UDS).

- [11] Protecting Information and System Integrity in Industrial Control Systems.

- [12] Environments: Cybersecurity for the Manufacturing Sector: `https://nvlpubs.nist.gov/nistpubs/SpecialPublications/NIST.SP.1800-10.pdf`.

- [13] Vega, Augusto, Pradip Bose, and Alper Buyuktosunoglu. Rugged Embedded Systems: Computing in Harsh Environments. Morgan Kaufmann, 2016.

9
ECU-Level Security Controls

In the preceding chapter, we delved into security controls at the vehicle level. To maintain our stance on the principle of **defense-in-depth** (**DiD**), our focal point now shifts to the establishment of resilient vehicle components at the **electronic control unit** (**ECU**) hardware, software, and physical component layers. However, before implementing any security controls, an understanding of their potential challenges and pitfalls is crucial. As we walk through each class of security controls, we will share hints on ways to securely deploy them. In the first section, we explore hardware security mechanisms, specifically at the **microcontroller** (**MCU**) and **system-on-chip** (**SoC**) levels. These controls are fundamental building blocks upon which higher-layer software security controls are established. They include controls such as hardware **root of trust** (**RoT**), secure storage, cryptographic accelerators, chip-level isolation techniques, and **trusted execution environments** (**TEEs**). In the second section, we explore software security controls leveraging hardware security primitives such as multi-stage secure boot. Furthermore, we discuss the criticality of isolation techniques in multi-compute environments, by exploring how hypervisors and client-server architectures can be harnessed to achieve this. Additionally, we delve into OSs' roles in enforcing process isolation, access controls, and temporal isolation. In the third section, we touch upon physical-level security controls that aim to reduce the impact of attackers with physical access to the ECU. As we explore these three sections, we'll uncover the competing priorities that emerge between performance improvement, advanced connectivity features, and the need to maintain a secure system. By the end of this chapter, readers will have gained a thorough understanding of the most commonly used security controls in automotive ECUs and how to evaluate future controls as new threats emerge.

Overall, we will cover a range of topics relating to hardware-, software-, and physical-layer controls, including the following:

- Understanding control actions and layers
- Exploring policy controls
- Exploring hardware controls
- Exploring software security controls
- Exploring physical security controls

Understanding control actions and layers

As with vehicle-level cybersecurity controls, ECU-level controls aim to detect, protect, and recover the ECU to a safe and secure state in response to ECU-level threats. As we mentioned in *Chapter 7*, in terms of the controls' effectiveness in risk treatment, the control actions can be classified in this order:

1. **Protect**: These controls prevent the attack from happening in the first place. For example, encrypting filesystems prevents private data exposure.

2. **Detect**: These controls can effectively detect abnormal behavior. For example, authenticating the filesystem image allows the system to detect when it has been tampered with.

3. **Recover**: These controls allow the system to recover to a secure state when an anomaly is detected. For example, upon detecting that a filesystem has been tampered with, a backup image is used to avoid an inoperable system.

4. **Log**: These controls log the event to enable user notification and **root cause analysis** (**RCA**). For example, when filesystem tampering is detected, the event is logged in secure storage for later analysis.

Figure 9.1 shows a breakdown of all the cybersecurity controls to be presented in the following sections, grouped by control family: *policy*, *hardware*, *software*, and *physical* cybersecurity. After that, we will walk through each cybersecurity control and show how it solves a specific security problem to strengthen the security of the ECU:

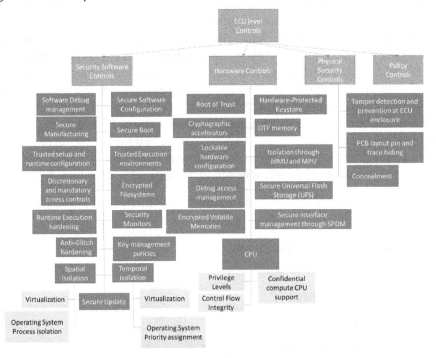

Figure 9.1 – The breakdown of ECU-level controls

Exploring policy controls

Just as with the vehicle-level analysis, **policy controls** must be applied at the ECU level to prohibit design decisions that unreasonably increase the attack surface and significantly alter the threat model of an ECU. Examples of attack surface reduction policy controls are the requirement that all debug interfaces are either locked or disabled, the removal of code profilers, and the elimination of security log traces from production intent builds. The removal of such tools and abilities lowers the attack feasibility related to reconnaissance and the discovery of ECU weaknesses and has a significant **return on investment** (**ROI**) in terms of risk elimination. An organization can also enforce policy controls to prohibit certain design choices that would alter fundamental assumptions made during threat modeling. For example, assume the threat model considers that all external network connectivity is filtered through a central gateway. For improved customer experience reasons, a feature request is submitted to add direct Wi-Fi access to an **advanced driver-assistance system** (**ADAS**) ECU. However, a policy control that prohibits direct external connectivity in components that provide sensing and actuation would prohibit the acceptance of such a feature. Having a central document that captures such policy controls is critical to ensure teams can remain aligned and avoid committing to high-risk changes.

> **Tip**
> When design decisions are made repeatedly to prohibit insecure features, consider abstracting those to a security policy control that can be added to your policy control catalog. This eases the conversation with teams to avoid repeating past arguments as to why certain actions must be disallowed.

It is noteworthy that in some cases, commercial decisions can override security policy controls. In such cases, the risk must be clearly captured, and additional controls must be incorporated from the technical cybersecurity controls space.

In the remaining sections, we will focus on technical controls that can be applied at the hardware, software, and physical layers.

Exploring hardware controls

When it comes to building a secure ECU, **hardware security controls** are king, earning them the first spot among cybersecurity controls to consider. This family of controls forms the foundation upon which software-based cybersecurity controls become possible. This becomes evident when vulnerabilities in hardware are discovered, creating challenges for software developers due to the complexity of crafting and deploying workarounds. In the same vein, if the performance needs of hardware security controls are overlooked, their deployment in time-sensitive automotive systems can become a significant hurdle. Even when implemented correctly and with adequate performance, lack of attention to the usability factor can make such controls hard to deploy, which in some cases results in the user disabling them altogether. Thus, hardware controls should be seen as critical security enablers that must be carefully selected to ensure they can achieve their intended cybersecurity goals within the performance and usability constraints of the system.

In the following subsections, we take a look at a sample of the most commonly employed hardware cybersecurity controls in automotive systems.

RoT

The hardware RoT is a crucial component for establishing trust in the firmware, software, and calibration data used within an ECU. Also known as a **hardware trust anchor** (**HTA**), it can be based on either an external discrete component such as a **Trusted Platform Module** (**TPM**) or an embedded secure enclave such as the **Hardware-Protected Security Environment** (**HPSE**), as shown in *Figure 9.2*:

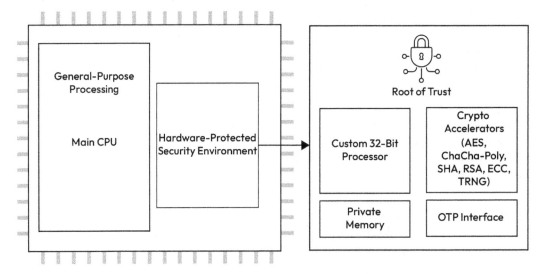

Figure 9.2 – Simplified architecture of an embedded RoT

These components provide dedicated storage space for protecting critical security parameters such as cryptographic key material and chip configuration parameters, which are used during the secure boot process (more on secure boot in a dedicated section of this chapter) and other security protocols. The two fundamental properties of the hardware RoT are the immutability of its firmware and its exclusive control of critical security parameters. To act as a RoT, this hardware component must be resilient to tampering—for example, by having additional circuitry that can detect glitching and temperature abnormalities as well as abnormal clock and voltage input profiles. Additionally, the critical security parameters must be strictly managed by the RoT to prevent replacement or rollback, which can result in the booting of tampered software.

As shown in *Figure 9.3*, in a typical HPSE architecture a dedicated CPU executes the firmware that coordinates cryptographic job requests with the user application environment:

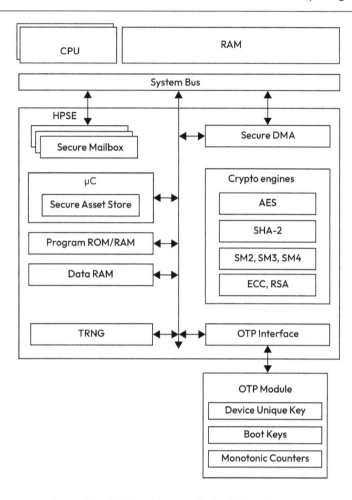

Figure 9.3 – HPSE architecture for building a keystore

Usually, a mailbox mechanism allows the application to signal requests and receive notifications when a response is ready. A shared memory space allows the application to provide data to the HSPE, which in turn performs the requested operation and returns the result back to the shared memory space. This can be facilitated by the usage of a **direct memory access** (**DMA**) controller that transfers the data in and out of the cryptographic accelerators inside the HPSE boundary. A hardware-backed random number generator allows the HPSE to harvest randomness to seed a **deterministic random bit generator** (**DRBG**). Additionally, a dedicated **one-time-programmable** (**OTP**) memory region contains cryptographic secrets and critical security parameters that are exclusively accessible by the HPSE. For example, such secrets may be used to derive cryptographic keys that can then be used to build a secure keystore in normal **non-volatile memory** (**NVM**). The OTP may also store monotonic counters to allow the HPSE to build security protocols for detecting when data or code has been rolled back to a prior version. Even though the HPSE is considered a TEE, it is common to block access to certain cryptographic keys from the HPSE CPU by creating data paths directly from OTP memory into the cryptographic accelerators to prevent the possibility of a key being extracted through compromised firmware.

> **Note**
>
> Hardware-backed random number generators are often referred to as **true random number generators** (**TRNGs**) by silicon vendors. When choosing a TRNG, make sure to pick one that is compliant with *NIST SP 800-90C*. Similarly, when evaluating a DRBG solution, make sure to pick one that complies with *NIST SP800-90A* to ensure that the random numbers are generated with sufficient entropy.

Due to the likely advancements in quantum computing within the lifetime of the vehicle, it is important to build RoT solutions that support quantum-secure cryptographic algorithms.

> **Note**
>
> Recall from *Chapter 2* that we discussed the need to prepare for post-quantum secure cryptographic algorithms. Ignoring such support in the hardware means that a software-only solution will be needed, which has significant impacts on the overall system performance as the computing resources will need to be reallocated to cryptographic operations rather than normal application functions.

Finally, designing the RoT to support root key revocation in the field is essential to enable the update of ECUs in the unlikely but dangerous event that the private signing key is exposed on the automotive manufacturer side. Since the RoT's role in secure boot is highly intertwined with firmware and software aspects, we have dedicated a section to secure boot when we discuss software security controls later in this chapter.

OTP memory

OTP memory refers to a distinct category of NVM that allows data to be programmed only once. Once programmed, the data in OTP memory cannot be altered or erased, making it immune to unauthorized modifications or tampering attempts. This attribute ensures the integrity and reliability of the stored information, making it ideal for storing write-once system configuration data. Due to its resistance to physical attacks, such as probing, tampering, or reverse engineering, OTP memory is also used to store device-unique cryptographic keys and root public key hash values. OTP-based secrets can be leveraged to derive keys that can have various purposes, such as encrypting a keystore, while the hash of a root public key can be used to establish a chain of trust during the secure boot process. **Fuse arrays** are another technology that is commonly used in automotive ECUs to protect secrets and immutable configuration data. OTP memory has some advantages over fuse arrays due to its relative ease of programming and better security properties regarding the difficulty of data extraction and reverse engineering.

Hardware-protected keystore

A hardware-protected keystore is a fundamental building block for enabling security protocols that rely on confidentiality and tamper prevention of cryptographic secrets. In MCU-based ECUs, the keystore is typically located in an embedded flash region that is exclusively accessible by the HPSE. If the main application core attempts to access that region, an exception is triggered. The HPSE firmware can buffer the keys in dedicated RAM regions that are only addressable from the HPSE cores before loading into the cryptographic engines. A set of immutable device-unique keys is additionally programmed in the factory without the possibility of read access from the HPSE CPU. These keys can only be directly loaded into the cryptographic engines of the HPSE by specifying the key index, without the possibility of buffering into the HPSE RAM. This added layer of security is necessary to ensure that even if the HPSE firmware itself is compromised, the keys cannot be directly extracted. These device-unique keys can be used, for example, to wrap other keys for storage in normal flash memory when more key storage is needed.

In an SoC-based ECU, the keystore can either be located in a dedicated external flash device that is only accessible by the HPSE or implemented in a dedicated partition in normal external flash memory.

In either case, the keystore contents must be encrypted to mitigate the risk that an attacker with physical access can extract the flash contents. With a dedicated secure flash memory chip, read and write transactions with that memory are normally encrypted using a device-unique key that is generated during the initial phase of the device setup and configuration. This provides an added protection layer to prevent physical snooping over the address and data bus lines from exposing secrets stored on the device.

Resisting rollback attacks

An additional requirement of any keystore is its ability to resist **rollback attacks** where a snapshot of the keystore can be replaced with a set of keys that may have been cloned from another device. To do so, the hardware must support rollback protection—for example, through monotonic counters. These counters are impossible to roll back by virtue of the way they are implemented. For example, dedicated OTP memory can be used to construct counters that can only increment through an OTP write operation. A **replay-protected memory block** (**RPMB**) is another rollback prevention technology that is supported in certain storage devices for the same purpose.

Physically unclonable functions

A stronger method to secure the contents of a keystore is to rely on a **physically unclonable function** (**PUF**) that is embedded within the HPSE. A PUF is a physical entity that is easy to evaluate but hard to predict. It relies on the inherent randomness and uncontrollability of physical systems to generate unique and random cryptographic keys. The primary purpose of a PUF is to ensure secure key storage and to prevent cloning of/tampering with the device. Unlike keys stored in OTP or flash, which could potentially be extracted by an attacker, a PUF generates a unique key only when required and does not store it, making it extremely difficult for an attacker to discover or duplicate it. This key, generated by the PUF, can be used in various security functions such as encrypting and authenticating a keystore that is stored in flash memory.

Secure Universal Flash Storage

Universal Flash Storage (**UFS**) is a high-performance NVM standard that comes with a set of hardware security controls for protecting data at rest. UFS supports hardware-based encryption using the **Advanced Encryption Standard** (**AES**) algorithm. This ensures that sensitive data remains protected even if the physical memory is compromised or removed from the ECU. To minimize the impact on the application CPU, a dedicated encryption engine is implemented in the host controller, eliminating the need for software to interfere during each read-and-write operation. As of the writing of this book, UFS only supports AES-XTS mode, which offers encryption only, making it an inadequate choice to protect data authenticity and integrity. Therefore, it is important to incorporate additional security mechanisms such as digital signatures to provide data integrity protection. In addition to data encryption, UFS also provides configurable write protection features to prevent unauthorized modification of stored data. This can be applied to specific regions of the memory or to the entire memory, which can be useful to prevent unauthorized erasure of the flash contents. Another important security mechanism of UFS is the support for RPMBs. The RPMB partition is a separate secure area of the memory designed to protect against replay attacks and unauthorized access. To protect against replay attacks, the UFS memory maintains a **write counter** for the RPMB partition. This counter is incremented every time a write operation is performed on the RPMB. When a write request is made, the host device includes the current value of the write counter in the **message authentication code** (**MAC**) calculation. The UFS memory verifies the MAC and checks whether the counter value matches its internal counter value. If they match, the write operation is performed, and the counter is incremented. This mechanism ensures that old, previously written data cannot be replayed to overwrite current data in the RPMB.

Figure 9.4 shows one possible implementation of an inline encryption engine within the UFS host controller. Transactions by the host controller driver result in automatic encryption and decryption operations when interacting with the UFS device:

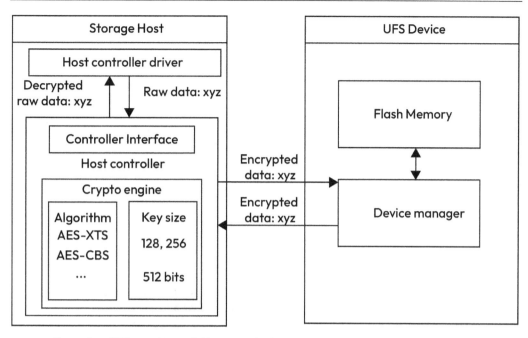

Figure 9.4 – UFS security model between the host and device cryptographic accelerators

Cryptographic accelerators

While designing secure keystores is a fundamental building block to support security protocols, to implement such protocols within the timing constraints of an ECU, cryptographic accelerators are an indispensable and too-often-scarce resource. These accelerators allow the ECU to perform real-time data authentication and encryption in various use cases such as communicating over the **controller area network** (**CAN**) bus and Ethernet, establishing secure sessions with sensors, or establishing **Transport Layer Security** (**TLS**) sessions with backend servers. Without cryptographic accelerators, a software cryptographic library must be used leveraging the application CPU cores. This presents two downsides: first, the application CPU (a precious resource) will be busy performing intensive cryptographic operations, and second, the keys must be loaded in the normal execution environment, adding the risk of key material exposure through illegal memory access and side-channel analysis. It is indeed a good practice to prohibit the implementation of cryptographic services in software outside the HPSE to minimize such risks. This calls for chip designers to be well aware of the security use cases of their systems in order to design the right number of cryptographic accelerators with efficient data pipelining architectures. Without efficient data pipelining in and out of the cryptographic accelerator, the latter becomes a bottleneck that will significantly underperform the application cores. Additionally, hardware mechanisms must be carefully designed to ensure that cryptographic keys can be transported into the cryptographic accelerators without exposure to application software—for example, through indexing by the HPSE.

As the number of security use cases continues to increase, the battle for cryptographic accelerators in automotive ECUs remains a challenge. This is where integrated encryption engines can bridge the gap. Supported in certain hardware interfaces, inline encryption engines are single-purpose engines that perform specific tasks such as encrypting and authenticating **Media Access Control security (MACsec)** frames, UFS read/write operations, or implementing the **Security Protocol and Data Model (SPDM)** protocol over a **Camera Serial Interface (CSI-2)**, **Inter-Integrated Circuit (I2C)**, or **Peripheral Component Interconnect Express (PCIe)** link. By design, these engines perform cryptographic operations at line speed without interference by the software. It is important, however, to pay attention to how the keys are loaded into these engines to protect against tampering and unauthorized access. When strapped for cryptographic engine resources, it is common to fall back to CPU-supported cryptographic instructions such as ones that accelerate AES and hash algorithms. While this can come in handy when cryptographic accelerators are scarce, these methods must be used carefully to avoid leakage of secret keys that are loaded in the normal runtime environment.

> **SPDM to the rescue**
>
> SPDM is a standard that provides a comprehensive set of security features for securing communication between devices such as two SoCs connected via a PCIe link or an SoC and a camera sensor connected over a CSIE link. Rather than relying on proprietary security protocols to protect the control and data planes between these devices, the SPDM is designed to address the need for secure communication between devices through a standardized approach that provides authentication, encryption, integrity protection, replay protection, message sequencing, and certificate management. Furthermore, the standard enables the usage of in-line encryption engines, which are critical for handling the high-bandwidth requirements of such interfaces.

Lockable hardware configuration

Initializing the system in a secure state is one of the fundamental methods to reduce the attack surface at runtime. The support of hardware-enabled configuration locks is a powerful technique that can greatly reduce the ability of attackers to bypass security measures once enabled. One class of lockable parameters is memory firewalls, which can be programmed to deny access to certain runtime execution environments—for example, HPSE access to secure data flash regions. Another class of parameters is chip settings, such as enabling a security mode that enforces certain protections such as the locking of **Joint Test Action Group (JTAG)** ports, forcing the system to boot from HPSE, or locking access to test modes. These locks can be implemented in fuse arrays, OTP, or write-once shadow memory. Building secure life cycle management relies heavily on such mechanisms to prevent an attacker from transitioning the chip to an insecure state. For example, during **return material authorization (RMA)**, blowing a fuse can force a load of test keys and the zeroization of production keys. This prevents leakage of critical secrets to an agent that has been authorized to perform invasive debug operations.

CPU security

The CPU is frequently ignored when considering hardware security controls, although its role in maintaining system security is quite critical. CPU architectures can be both the source of security vulnerabilities and the domain for advanced protection techniques that significantly improve the security posture of the system. Ultimately, the goal of a robust CPU architecture is to protect the computational integrity of the system by providing adequate isolation and runtime execution protections when shared across mutually distrustful applications, as we will see next.

Privilege levels

In MCU-based systems, supervisor and user mode are commonly used to separate the privilege of the **real-time operating system (RTOS)** from user application software. This can be sufficient to ensure that the kernel can configure privileged settings such as **memory protection unit (MPU)** tables and manage system interrupts. In SoC-based systems, a more sophisticated CPU privilege architecture is necessary due to the increased complexity of the software environment. More granular CPU privilege levels determine how the software can manage the access and execution of instructions and resources in a system. These privilege levels provide a hierarchy of access rights that determine what a running piece of software is allowed to do to enable isolation between various software components. You can see an overview of the privilege based on the Arm CPU architecture in the following diagram:

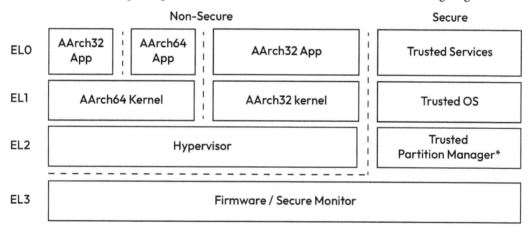

Figure 9.5 – Privilege levels defined in the ARMv8 architecture (credit ARM)

Due to its popularity in automotive systems, we will repeatedly refer to the ARM architecture as a reference throughout this chapter:

- **Secure and non-secure states**: The secure state is designed for executing security-critical code and managing sensitive data, such as cryptographic keys or critical hardware resources. It provides an isolated execution environment that is protected from the non-secure state, which is also commonly referred to as the normal environment. The secure state can be assigned multiple privilege exception levels to provide further access granularity—for example, between the TEE's OS and **trusted applications (TAs)** running within that environment. In the non-secure or normal environment, ARM defines four exception levels, numbered from EL0 to EL3, with higher levels having more privileges and control over the system, as follows:

  - **Exception Level 0 (EL0)**: This is the least-privileged level and corresponds to the user application mode. It is used to run user-space applications that don't have direct access to system resources, such as memory management or hardware control. Software running at EL0 uses system calls to request services from the OS.

  - **Exception Level 1 (EL1)**: EL1 is the level at which most OSs run, including their kernel and device drivers. This level has access to system resources and can manage the execution environment of EL0 applications. The OS running at EL1 is responsible for memory management, task scheduling, and handling requests from user-space applications.

  - **Exception Level 2 (EL2)**: EL2 is used for virtualization and is typically the level at which a hypervisor runs. The latter is a software layer that enables the execution of multiple OSs concurrently, each running in its own isolated virtual environment. The hypervisor running at EL2 has control over the hardware resources and can manage the execution of guest OSs at EL1, providing isolation and resource management between them. Hypervisors are more commonly found in ADAS and Domain Controllers that combine multiple vehicle functions in a single compute environment.

  - **Exception Level 3 (EL3)**: This is reserved for firmware and security-critical functions, such as a TEE and the **Secure Monitor Call (SMC)**, which acts as a gateway between the secure world and normal environment by allowing controlled access to privileged operations and services in the secure world.

This architecture of exception levels aligns well with the **principle of least privilege (PoLP)** by assigning higher privileges and broader access only to the necessary components and levels of system software. This also ensures that each user or component operates with the least privileges required to perform its respective tasks, minimizing the potential attack surface and reducing the risk of unauthorized actions.

Confidential computing

The drive for building central vehicle computers that combine mixed-criticality software under a common computing environment while practicing the principle of zero trust makes confidential computing an attractive candidate for automotive adoption. Confidential computing aims to protect data in use by reducing the number of required trusted parties in the system to achieve the desired data integrity and confidentiality objectives. Through confidential computing, even higher-privileged software such as the hypervisor and the OS should not be able to peak at or tamper with the runtime execution environment of an isolated software instance. Continuing with the ARM architecture, the ARM **Realm Management Extension** (**RME**) is a set of features introduced by ARM to improve isolation between software components running on newer ARM-based processors. Protecting sensitive data while in use is achieved through the creation of Realms, which are isolated execution environments that provide strong separation between software components. Realms can be used to execute security-sensitive workloads, such as handling cryptographic keys, processing users' private data, performing safety-critical functions, or even running proprietary software libraries, all while keeping them isolated from other components of the system (including the OS and hypervisor). Key aspects of confidential computing are set out here:

- **Hardware-enforced isolation**: Realms are implemented with hardware-level isolation mechanisms, providing a higher degree of protection than traditional software-based approaches. Through this isolation, it is possible to protect both the integrity and confidentiality of code and data in use. This further helps to minimize the attack surface and reduce the risk of unauthorized access or data leakage.

- **Minimal trusted computing base** (**TCB**): Realms aim to minimize the TCB by reducing the number of software components that must be trusted to maintain security. By executing sensitive workloads within isolated Realms, the need to trust the OS and hypervisor is minimized, as they do not have direct access to the data or code within a Realm.

- **Hardware-based attestation**: To establish trust in the software running within the environment supporting confidential computing, the **Arm Confidential Compute Architecture** (**Arm CCA**) supports both platform attestation, which checks the status of the underlying firmware and hardware, and Realm attestation, which checks the initial state of the Realm. If attestation fails, the verifier can terminate communication with the attester or apply a customized policy that fits within the vehicle environment.

Software attestation for ECUs

Software attestation is the process of verifying the integrity of software running on the ECU to ensure it hasn't been tampered with or compromised. This is usually achieved by the attester generating a cryptographic signature based on the software's current state, including a challenge provided by the verifier. The latter then compares the provided signature with a reference signature. If the signatures match, the verifier considers the ECU software to be in a trusted state and can proceed to allow more privileged operations such as enabling paid vehicle services that require access to the **original equipment manufacturer** (**OEM**) infrastructure.

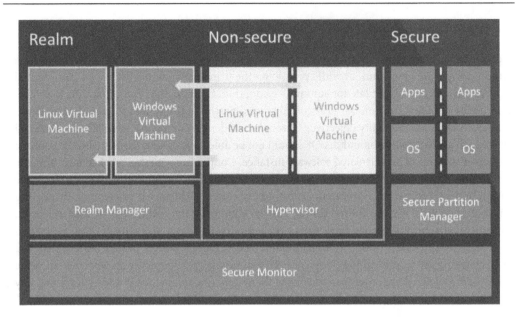

Figure 9.6 – Arm CCA (credit to ARM)

CPU security enhancements

Over the years, CPU architectures have started incorporating hardware security controls to strengthen the computational integrity of the system. One set of enhancements relates to **control-flow integrity (CFI)** countermeasures that make it harder for code injection attacks to take hold of the runtime execution environment. Continuing with the ARM architecture, we will sample some common techniques such as **pointer authentication codes (PACs)**, **memory tagging extensions (MTEs)**, and **branch target identification (BTI)**. Let's look at these in more detail:

- **PAC**: This aims to protect against control flow hijacking attacks, such as **return-oriented programming (ROP)** and **jump-oriented programming (JOP)**, by adding a cryptographically signed authentication code to pointers (such as return addresses, function pointers, or jump targets) when they are stored in memory. This code is generated using a secret key that is only known to the processor. When a pointer is later loaded from memory and used for a control-flow operation, the processor verifies the PAC to ensure that the pointer has not been tampered with. If the verification fails, the processor generates a fault, preventing the execution of potentially malicious code.

ROP and JOP?

ROP and JOP are two powerful attack methods that enable an attacker to execute arbitrary code on a device that has enabled non-executable memory protection. ROP involves finding short sequences of instructions ending in a return instruction (called a "gadget") within the existing program code and chaining them together to form malicious payloads. JOP is a variation of ROP that employs indirect jump or call instructions to chain gadgets rather than return instructions. Mitigations for these attacks fall under the family of CFI protections.

- **MTE**: This aims to mitigate memory safety vulnerabilities, such as buffer overflows and **use-after-free** (UAF) bugs. MTE works by associating a "tag" with each memory allocation, which is stored separately from the actual data. The memory tags associated with each address provide information about the properties or attributes of the memory region. These tags can be used to track memory bounds, indicate memory permissions, or represent other metadata relevant to memory safety. When memory is accessed, the processor checks whether the tag associated with the access matches the tag of the corresponding memory allocation. If there is a mismatch, the processor generates a fault, indicating that the memory access has violated the intended tag purpose.

UAF

This type of attack exploits a bug where a program continues to use a pointer after it has been freed, also known as a dangling pointer. The attacker first identifies a location in the program where the dangling pointer is used after its associated memory has been freed. The attacker then tries to influence what gets placed in the freed memory location by carefully crafting inputs to the system—for example, through heap spraying. If the dangling pointer now contains a function pointer that was supplied by the attacker, then the code execution can be redirected to the attacker's code. Similarly, if the dangling pointer is used to access data, then the attacker can tamper with the supplied data to modify variables containing configuration settings or other sensitive data.

- **BTI**: This helps protect against control-flow attacks by ensuring that indirect branches (jumps or calls) can only target valid destinations marked explicitly by the software. With BTI, software must place a special instruction (a BTI landing pad) at the beginning of any valid branch target. When the processor encounters an indirect branch, it checks whether the target address is a valid BTI landing pad. If it is not, the processor generates a fault, preventing the execution of potentially malicious code. BTI helps mitigate attacks such as ROP and JOP by making it more difficult for an attacker to redirect control flow to arbitrary code locations.

Implementing these mechanisms requires additional checks at various points in the program's execution to ensure that the control flow graph adheres to a predetermined flow. The execution time increases as these extra checks must be performed at runtime—for example, when authenticating the return address with a PAC, which could be frequently executed in a program. Furthermore, storing the information needed for some of these mechanisms, such as memory tags (in the case of MTEs), can also lead to increased memory usage. While these mechanisms add a valuable layer of security, the additional resources needed and runtime checks performed inevitably result in a performance penalty, affecting the overall efficiency of the application. Therefore, it is important to evaluate the performance impact before deciding to enable these mechanisms in real-time constrained automotive systems.

The second set of CPU security enhancements relates to the elimination of side-channel attack paths within the CPU environment—for example, through speculative execution and cache timing attack prevention. This remains a subject of research due to tension between the need to optimize CPU performance and the need to protect the integrity and confidentiality of the runtime execution environment. In the vehicle context, ECUs that support applications with variable levels of security must pay attention to potential data leakage through CPU vulnerabilities. Therefore, when choosing a CPU, observe which CPU vulnerabilities have not been fixed and whether such CPUs offer the option to disable optimizations when data privacy has a higher priority over-optimized performance.

Speculative execution attacks

Speculative execution attacks exploit features in modern processors that were designed to improve performance by predicting the future paths a program may take and executing instructions down those paths before it is certain that the path will be taken. If the prediction is correct, the execution continues seamlessly, but if it's incorrect, the speculatively executed instructions are rolled back, and the correct path is executed instead. While the incorrect speculative execution does not directly affect the program's output, it leaves behind subtle changes to the processor's state and allows an attacker to infer sensitive information such as passwords or encryption keys. In multi-tenant vehicle computers that rely on strong isolation between mixed-criticality applications, these attacks pose a serious risk that must be treated.

Securing the subsystems that are managed by the CPU is essential for completing the hardware security story. This is the focus of the remaining subsections before we switch to software-based cybersecurity controls.

Isolation through MMUs and MPUs

Memory management units (**MMUs**) and MPUs are critical hardware components used in ECUs to achieve **freedom from interference** (**FFI**) objectives through memory isolation and resource access separation.

An MPU is a hardware mechanism that can be configured to allow or deny access to specific memory regions based on the type of access requested, such as read, write, or execute, while considering the CPU privilege level. It is commonly used in MCU-based ECUs to isolate software of mixed safety criticality. While it is primarily used for safety FFI, it can also reduce the risk of unauthorized code execution or data manipulation by configuring data regions as non executable and partitioning software applications.

An MMU, on the other hand, enables memory virtualization by mapping virtual memory addresses used by applications and processes to physical memory addresses. It allows each process to have its own isolated **virtual address** (**VA**) space. To perform the translation of virtual memory addresses to physical memory addresses, it relies on page tables that maintain mappings between VAs and **physical addresses** (**PAs**). When managed by a trusted party (such as the OS), a malicious process can be prevented from writing to the address space of another process. Furthermore, assigning permissions and access rights to different memory pages allows for fine-grained control over memory access. The MMU also detects and prevents unauthorized access attempts, such as accessing memory outside the allocated range or modifying memory configured with the read-only type. In addition to memory, an **input/output MMU** (**IOMMU**) facilitates the virtualization of hardware resources such as I/O devices, interrupt controllers, and other system resources. This allows multiple **virtual machines** (**VMs**) or processes to share and utilize hardware resources based on a predefined access control strategy. MMUs are a fundamental building isolation mechanism in SoC-based ECUs that require isolation at various levels both within a single guest OS and between different VMs running over the hypervisor. Without these mechanisms, an ECU is unable to meet both safety FFI requirements and security isolation expectations.

Encrypted volatile memories

While logical access separation through MMUs and MPUs can be seen as effective measures to protect memory in volatile memory (for example, **dynamic RAM** (**DRAM**) and **system RAM** (**SYSRAM**)) against illegal access, these measures do nothing to prevent the extraction of sensitive data from external volatile memory such as DRAM. Automotive systems that handle highly confidential data and intellectual property may need to rely on encrypted DRAM to prevent interposers from snooping on memory read and write operations. To support encrypted fetch and execute instructions, the CPU must support a lightweight cryptography algorithm that uses a device-generated key for protecting read and write operations without the need for software interference.

Debug access management

As mentioned in *Chapter 3*, abuse of debug interfaces is one of the common attack vectors for extracting ECU data and identifying software vulnerabilities. While completely disabling debug access after transitioning the system into a production state is the most secure option, in most cases developers need a way to re-enable debug access to perform RCA when issues are reported from the field. Hardware controls can be leveraged for both scenarios of debug disablement and debug access locking. Typically, MCU- and SoC-based systems offer a hardware mechanism to permanently disable hardware access either by programming an option byte in shadow flash or by blowing a fuse array respectively. A less strict option relies on a hardware mechanism to authenticate a debug client through a secure JTAG controller using a pre-shared symmetric key or a public key certificate. The latter is more desirable as it simplifies the key management aspect and allows access to be granted for debugging a single device only.

Have a look at the following diagram:

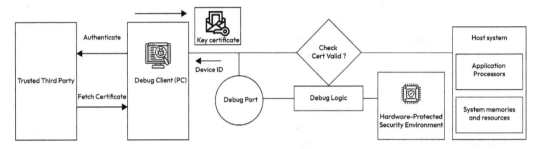

Figure 9.7 – Unlocking debug access through a certificate

In the example shown in *Figure 9.7*, the debug client first reads out a device's unique ID from the target and then authenticates itself to a trusted third party. The latter then generates a certificate signed with a single-purpose debug private key with the allowed debug privileges and the target device ID. The debug client then initiates a debug access request and provides a valid certificate. The SoC validates the certificate using the matching pre-provisioned public key and confirms the debug abilities included in the certificate before unlocking debug access. This limits the debug access to a single device and ensures that only the authorized debug clients get access. A similar mechanism is typically supported in MCU-based systems where the HPSE acts as a gatekeeper for debug access. The process can be adapted in the HPSE firmware to require either a challenge-response sequence based on a shared secret prior to unlocking debug access or the usage of a certificate-based authentication method. It is also possible to create different debug access levels to allow a debug client to gain access to the normal environment versus the TEE or the HPSE itself. Each debug access level must use different key materials to enforce fine-grained access control.

After sampling some of the commonly used hardware security controls in automotive ECUs, it is time to turn our attention to software security controls.

Exploring software security controls

Now that we have previewed some of the commonly used security controls in automotive ECUs, we can switch focus to software security controls. As we will see, many of these controls are built on top of hardware security primitives and aim to provide more sophisticated security mechanisms that hardware alone cannot offer.

Software debug and configuration management

Building on hardware debug access protection, it is equally important to eliminate and/or restrict access to software debug tools. It is common for developers to use a wide range of such tools to aid in troubleshooting and testing the ECU prior to production. A common mistake is to leave these tools in the ECU even after the product is shipped. In MCU-based ECUs, these tools range from proprietary diagnostic protocols that are used in factory mode to trace tools that log extensive error codes to pinpoint the file and line of code where an error occurred, to standard calibration protocols such as **Universal Measurement and Calibration Protocol** (**XCP**). The latter provides an XCP client with the ability to view and alter memory regions in real time for calibration and reprogramming purposes. In SoC-based ECUs, the set of debug tools is much more extensive due to the richness of the execution environment. Examples of such tools are code profilers that identify performance bottlenecks, excessive memory usage, and high CPU utilization. Other examples are **Secure Shell** (**SSH**) and **Teletype Network Protocol** (**Telnet**), which allow developers to gain remote access to an ECU to perform tasks such as configuration, debugging, and even software updates. For reasons that should be self-evident, leaving these tools accessible in a production-intended ECU is a bad practice that will only result in long-term pain when such tools are discovered and exploited. The first step in eliminating this risk is to make an inventory of all software debug tools and interfaces. The next step is to remove these tools from the production build to eliminate any possibility of re-enablement once the ECU is in the field. But what about troubleshooting problems that are reported after production?

The preferred method is to rely on diagnostic protocols that can capture extensive error information in a predefined and approved format without revealing cryptographic secrets and users' private data. Assuming these protocols have adequate authentication protection (as seen in *Chapter 8*), relying on these protocols ensures that there is only a single method for retrieving fault-related data in an access-controlled way. It is also possible to support special debug builds that can be installed in production ECUs in the field, including tools such as the ones listed previously. When choosing this option, two constraints must be observed. First, the method of installing these builds must be done through a secure update mechanism. Second, the debug build must be signed for a single ECU by incorporating a unique device ID into the digital signature generation. The secure boot check can then enforce this binding and reject a build not intended for the device. This prevents the distribution of these coveted debug builds widely across ECUs, which can result in bypassing security controls and essentially jailbreaking devices.

In a similar way, to shrink the attack surface during system configuration, risky interfaces must be disabled if not needed before the system is released in production. These include **Universal Asynchronous Receiver/Transmitter** (**UART**) and **Universal Serial Bus** (**USB**) drivers, as well as network services and ports that should be blocked in a production intended ECU.

Secure manufacturing

The initial device configuration, secret provisioning, and software installation in the factory form the first building block for securing the ECU. Without a secure manufacturing process, we cannot have trust in the integrity and authenticity of device firmware, software, cryptographic secrets, or even the device's life cycle state. The secure manufacturing process combines a mixture of hardware, software, and policy controls, so let's take a closer look.

First, a secure method is needed for provisioning cryptographic secrets and unique device IDs. The simplest and least secure method is to trust the physical security of the factory environment when provisioning these secrets. At a minimum with that option, a **hardware security module (HSM)** must be installed on the factory floor to generate and manage cryptographic keys before delivering such keys to the tools responsible for provisioning devices. In this scenario, such tools will program the secrets in plaintext form, which makes the process vulnerable to insider threats. A more secure way is to rely on a device's unique secret key, which is usually programmed during the chip manufacturing process to allow the delivery of HSM secrets in encrypted form, eliminating any opportunity for cryptographic key material exposure throughout the provisioning chain of tools. Similar to setting up keys, there is a need to provision unique device IDs that will enable OEMs to identify their ECUs in later stages when building security protocols that rely on ECU identification. In addition to secret keys and device personalization, there is also the need to provision public keys that will be used in the enforcement of other security controls such as secure boot and secure update.

The following diagram illustrates such a process:

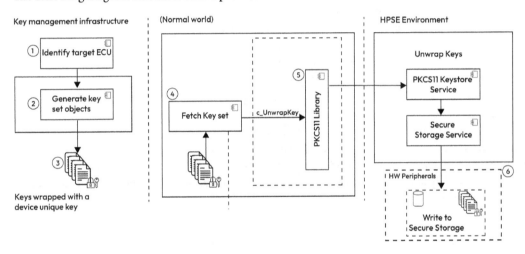

Figure 9.8 – Example flow for installing cryptographic keys using the PKCS#11 standard

The immutability and revocation capability of the OEM root key are both important security measures that work together to ensure the integrity and security of a vehicle's critical systems. The immutability of the OEM root key means that the OEM root public key stored in the trust store of the vehicle's ECUs cannot be modified after production, providing a secure and trustworthy environment for the vehicle's critical systems. Support for revocation of the OEM root public key is desirable to deal with the unlikely event that the matching private key is compromised.

Once the provisioning phase has been completed, we can now install the necessary firmware and software. Leveraging factory-installed root public keys, only signed images must be used to flash the ECU. After software installation, the device itself must be transitioned to a secure life cycle state that restricts abilities that are only required in the factory environment. For example, in the secure state, a secure boot can become mandatory, and debug access can become permanently disabled or locked.

Key management policies

Building on our hardware-protected keystore, it is possible to build more sophisticated key management policies through software that has exclusive access to the hardware keystore.

Whether it is the HPSE firmware or a TEE application, the software can extend key protection by defining policies in the following areas:

- Enforcing access to the keys based on an application and/or VM ID
- Specifying allowed operations that can be performed with the key, such as encryption, decryption, key derivation, or key agreement protocols
- Defining a key lifetime or crypto-period after which the key must be updated
- Determining key attributes such as being erasable, write-protected, or exportable

Key management software can also handle how keys are destroyed once the device enters a decommissioning state—for example, through key zeroization. The *PKCS#11* standard is a good reference when attempting to define your own key management policies.

Multi-stage secure boot

With the hardware RoT immutable code and exclusive control of cryptographic material, it is possible to build security primitives such as secure boot to ensure that only authorized software and calibration data can be executed and consumed within the ECU environment. The primary difference in secure boot implementation between MCU and SoC-based ECUs is the reliance on HPSE firmware for establishing a secure boot chain versus reliance on an immutable boot ROM code. In an MCU-based ECU, the code is fetched directly from embedded flash, therefore the loading part of the code into system memory is not needed. HPSE firmware must be the first code that starts execution after reset to authenticate the flash bootloader and application software. The HPSE firmware typically relies on a root public key that is stored within its exclusive data flash region to verify the authenticity of binaries. Through its ability to keep the MCU application cores in the reset state, the HPSE can prevent application code execution until the respective software binaries have been cryptographically checked for integrity and authenticity. Once the boot check passes, the HPSE can release the application cores from reset. This can either be done in a single stage if the application size permits verification within the expected startup time of the ECU or in multiple stages if an early software partition must start execution before the rest of the application software is verified. Boot-up time is one of the most challenging aspects of secure boot in the automotive environment. In fact, many ECUs forgo this important security feature because they cannot tolerate the delay in startup time. Therefore, it is critical to choose chips that have efficient data pipelining and cryptographic acceleration to support a faster boot-up time.

With SoC-based systems, the software is booted from external storage such as UFS or an **embedded MultiMediaCard (eMMC)** into DRAM and/or internal SYSRAM. Due to the code size and complexity of such systems, the most practical implementation of secure boot is the multi-stage boot process. With multiple cores and separate runtime execution environments, it is possible to verify the authenticity of different software partitions and allow them to start execution in parallel. The key principle for securing multi-stage boot is to maintain the chain of trust from the point of loading the first firmware by the RoT up to and including the loading of applications in the guest OS(s). In an SoC-based ECU, the RoT leverages the boot ROM, which has access to OTP or **electrical fuse (eFuse)** memory where a root public key is stored. After the BootROM performs the first-stage boot check, a second-stage bootloader loads additional software partitions, verifies their integrity and authenticity, performs the necessary hardware setup, and then enables the execution of the loaded software in the relevant execution environments. To maintain the chain of trust, each loaded partition must be signed using the root private key or a private key that is chained to the root private key. If the secure boot check fails, the boot process should be halted, and a reset is issued. Assuming a backup partition is available, a second boot chain should be tried in the hope that it is not also corrupted.

The following diagram illustrates the process:

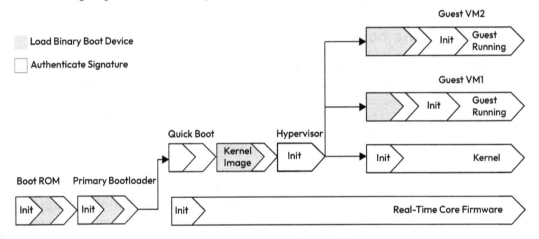

Figure 9.9 – Example SoC multi-stage secure boot flow

There are many ways secure boot can be poorly designed, making it possible to bypass completely. Therefore, once you have decided on a specific secure boot strategy, it is important to perform a design-level threat analysis to identify and eliminate weaknesses in your design. Some best practices for implementing secure boot are set out here:

- Prohibit the start of execution of any software unless the corresponding software image has been authenticated. This can mean holding the corresponding core in a reset state and only releasing it if the authentication is successful.

- Identify and lock access to memory and hardware registers that are exposed to tampering if one execution environment is booted in parallel to another one. This eliminates the risk that software booted securely to memory is tampered with by another runtime execution environment that has already started execution.

- Enable encryption in addition to signature verification. While this can add boot-up latency, since the code is being loaded from flash to system memory, it is possible to perform decryption in parallel to the hash operation.

- When compression is enabled, ensure that software authenticity is verified before decompression is started. This prevents the decompressed software from overflowing the allocated memory (for example, through a zip bomb) or for malicious binaries to exploit the decompression algorithm to perform code injection.

- Apply memory and resource isolation as early as possible in the boot chain setup to eliminate opportunities for interference.

Trusted runtime configuration

Adjacent to secure boot is the secure setup and configuration during the system initialization stage. In an MCU-based system, a trusted setup can be implemented in the startup code and primary flash bootloader. Similarly, **AUTomotive Open System ARchitecture (AUTOSAR)**-based system initialization software can apply a secure configuration—for example, through the setup of CAN acceptance filters and peripheral initialization. In SoC-based systems, each runtime execution environment is expected to be configured by the parent software entity through the allocation of memory and hardware resources. If the hardware supports lockable configuration settings, then it is during this stage that software can enforce such locks to reduce the attacker's ability to tamper with the system configuration after the initial setup. For configuration settings that cannot be locked, fine-grained access controls should be leveraged to ensure that only software entities that need to manage these configurations have access to do so. A trusted setup relies on a trusted third party within the system, which can be in the form of a higher-privileged execution environment—for example, the hypervisor or a TEE.

TEEs

In systems equipped with a singular runtime execution environment, any successful breach within that environment can spread to all other parts of the system. This concern led to the invention of the TEE, a separate and isolated runtime state that remains inaccessible to the normal execution environment.

A TEE leverages CPU privilege-level separation, a feature we introduced earlier, to facilitate the implementation of highly privileged functionalities that must be isolated from the normal execution environment. During the initial phases of system setup, the TEE can be assigned various responsibilities, such as setting up the keystore in protected memory and configuring the power management subsystem in a trusted state. During normal runtime, the TEE can be tasked with critical functions such as arbitrating communication with the HPSE and managing an orderly system shutdown.

A visual representation of a TEE can be seen here:

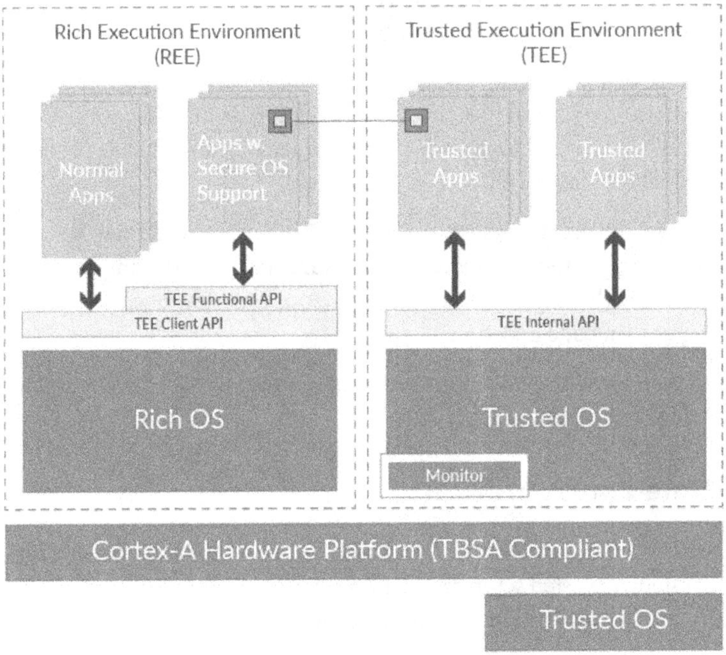

Figure 9.10 – TEE Architecture leveraging the ARM TrustZone (credit ARM)

Additionally, TAs can be deployed within the TEE to perform security-sensitive operations such as **digital rights management (DRM)** for secure content playback. The latter is more commonly found in infotainment ECUs that serve encrypted media—for example, through rear passenger displays. A DRM TA securely handles decryption keys, decodes encrypted content, and ensures that decrypted content isn't accessible to software in the normal environment. Device attestation is another use case to implement within a TEE to securely report the device state to a third party before gaining access to privileged services such as connecting to an OEM backend.

Secure update

In *Chapter 8*, we saw the importance of a secure **over-the-air update (OTA)** as a vehicle-level cybersecurity control. Now, we zoom in on the role of the ECU in protecting how software is updated in persistent storage. Whether the update is delivered over the air or through the **Unified Diagnostic Services (UDS)** diagnostic protocol, the ECU must apply a common set of software cybersecurity controls to prevent the installation of unauthentic software and the unauthorized modification of pre-installed authenticated software. Typically, a primary ECU is tasked with connecting to the OTA backend and receiving the update bundle. After that, secondary ECUs can receive their individual software image updates over the in-vehicle network—for example, through the UDS diagnostic protocol itself. In that case, the primary ECU assumes the role of an onboard diagnostic client, while the secondary ECU behaves as if it is communicating with a standard diagnostic client.

The process is illustrated in the following diagram:

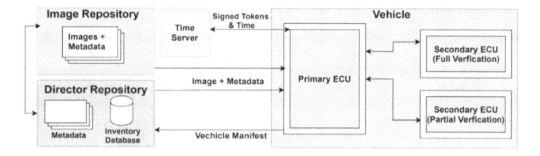

Figure 9.11 – OTA flow based on the UPTANE framework

For simplicity, let's look at each update method regardless of who is initiating the update.

UDS-based flash reprogramming

Prior to executing flash programming routines, the target ECU must authenticate the diagnostic client regardless of whether it is onboard or offboard. This can be done through service 0x29, as we saw in *Chapter 8*, to verify that the client is authorized to update the ECU software. This requires that the ECU is provisioned with a dedicated public key that can authenticate the diagnostic client certificate.

After authentication, the ECU can accept routines that erase memory partitions and download new software blocks; however, a software download will not be considered valid until the integrity and authenticity of the update are verified—for example, through a digital signature verification. Due to the possibility that the update may contain invalid images or may be interrupted, it is highly recommended that ECUs implement a backup partition. This prevents the scenario that the ECU is partially or completely erased due to a failed update and thereby unable to perform its safety-critical functions.

Besides verifying the authenticity of each image, it is important to perform compatibility checks with other software images programmed in the ECU storage to ensure that the update will not result in an undefined behavior after boot. A robust flash bootloader implementation is critical to prevent attackers from successfully modifying ECU software through the bypass of integrity and authenticity checks. For example, the flash routines used to erase and program new images must be treated as critical routines that should be protected from unauthorized access. This can be done by removing such routines from memory after the software update is finished and excluding them from the software build to prevent ROP-style attacks. Additionally, the HPSE can be leveraged to lock the ability to carry out flash programming to prevent an attacker who manages to load their own flash routines from tampering with ECU software without proper authorization.

OTA-based update

When the primary ECU is performing the OTA update, the first prerequisite is to perform a mutual authentication step between the ECU and the OTA backend by leveraging a **public key infrastructure (PKI)**. Here, again, the primary ECU must be provisioned with a root public key to authenticate the backend server certificates. The HPSE can be leveraged to perform the key agreement protocol and protect the integrity and authenticity of the provisioned public key. Upon authenticating each party, a secure session must be established that protects the confidentiality and integrity of data exchanged across the channel. Depending on the OTA process architecture, the primary ECU may be required to verify the authenticity of metadata signed by different private keys that are chained to a common root private key (under the possession of the OEM). The primary ECU must perform the metadata authentication before proceeding to each next step in the update process. For example, an OTA bundle may contain a signed manifest that lists all software images in the bundle. Using the corresponding public key, the primary ECU should validate the manifest and ensure that all software image version information matches the manifest. Similarly, if a time server is used, metadata regarding the freshness of the update must be verified before initiating the update. With each software image update in the packaged bundle, the primary ECU must also use the corresponding public key to verify the corresponding image's digital signature. This ensures that if an attacker manages to sign a bundle containing unauthentic images, the primary ECU can reject such an update. If the primary ECU is receiving an updated image on behalf of a secondary ECU, then it is possible to delegate the image signature verification to the secondary ECU. It is critical that in all cases, the software is not marked as valid and bootable unless all checks have passed correctly. Similar to the UDS case, having backup partitions, especially in the primary ECU, is mandatory to avoid the case that the ECU is left in an unprogrammed state. Without the ability to perform an OTA update, the only option for the OEM is an *expensive mass recall to perform a manual update.*

It is important when implementing any update solution to evaluate the update chain from the point an update is initiated to the point the software is written to storage and marked as valid to identify and eliminate security weaknesses. Even when secure boot is enforced, security engineers should not rely on secure boot to act as a catch-all mechanism as one security layer should build upon the security of another layer and not the opposite.

Spatial isolation

Spatial isolation is a common practice in safety- and security-critical systems that need to ensure that the memory regions and resources allocated for one software entity cannot accidentally or maliciously interfere with those of another entity in the same ECU. When implemented correctly, this practice localizes the impact of an exploitable vulnerability to the affected software entity and its managed resources rather than propagating to other parts of the system. In MCU-based ECUs, spatial isolation relies heavily on the MPU to allocate memory regions with specific access permission rules and attributes that are managed by the RTOS. The latter normally manages the MPU settings during context switches to ensure that one task or OS partition does not interfere with the memory resources of another task or OS partition. In SoC-based ECUs, spatial isolation relies on MMUs to virtualize access to memory and peripherals among multiple guest OSs and virtualized resources. In such systems, spatial isolation is a mechanism that helps achieve effective sandboxing, which is a security technique used to isolate programs, restricting their access only to system resources and sensitive information that they rely on to function properly. By creating a controlled environment or "sandbox," a program can execute without interfering with the broader system. This environment has specific permissions and constraints that limit the program's ability to interact with other applications, access unauthorized files, or perform potentially harmful operations. Moreover, when the program contains malicious code or becomes the target of an attack, potential damage is confined to the sandbox, thereby minimizing the risk to the host system. It is common to allocate different VMs in a single ECU that needs to support software with mixed safety and security criticality to ensure the stability of the system if one VM starts misbehaving. Let's look at techniques for achieving spatial isolation at various levels of the system architecture.

Virtualization and OS-level separation

In a virtualized system, a hypervisor uses an MMU and peripheral guards to partition memory and hardware peripherals among different VMs. The hypervisor manages the distribution of resources such as CPU allocation, memory address space, and hardware resource allocation to each VM and ensures that they remain isolated from one another. As a result, each VM runs its own OS isolated from the other VMs, even though they share the same underlying hardware. This is especially useful in ADAS and vehicle computer use cases where software with varying degrees of safety and security criticality must share the same SoC hardware while minimizing the risk of accidental or malicious interference. Two mechanisms that enable this type of spatial isolation are *Stage 1* and *Stage 2* MMU, outlined here:

- **Stage 1 MMU** is responsible for the translation of VAs to **intermediate PAs (IPAs)**. It is typically utilized by the OS to manage memory, provide memory protection, and enforce memory isolation among different processes running within a single guest OS. Stage 1 MMU supports memory protection mechanisms, such as access permissions (read, write, or execute) at the memory-page level to prevent tampering with certain memory regions or execution of memory intended for data only. The OS is responsible for loading and switching memory mappings for each process when performing context switching. In the example shown in *Figure 9.12*, based on the ARM architecture, the OS kernel running in non-secure EL1 relies on its MMU page table to separate its own memory from the memory of the two other applications and to isolate memory-mapped resources between the two applications.

    OS-level process isolation can be quite effective in reducing the risk that a malicious process interferes with the memory address space of another process when coupled with least-privilege practices. This requires launching processes with minimal privileges (reserving root privilege to a very small set of processes if any) and removing dangerous OS-provided abilities to prevent a compromised process from bypassing process isolation or performing highly privileged operations:

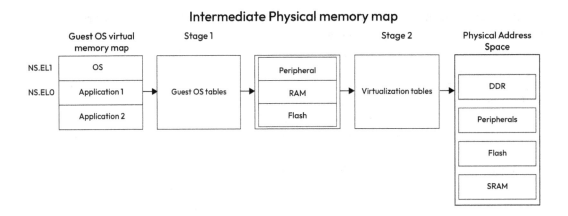

Figure 9.12 – Stage 1 address translation between the OS, and two example applications

- **Stage 2 MMU**, on the other hand, is responsible for translating the IPAs generated by the stage 1 MMU to the actual PAs in the system's physical memory. This allows a hypervisor to allocate and deallocate physical memory pages to VMs.

  Stage 2 MMU allows the hypervisor to enforce memory isolation between VMs by including a **VM ID (VMID)** in the page table entries. It also allows handling memory management tasks specific to the hypervisor, such as maintaining memory mappings for the hypervisor code and data, managing memory pools for VMs, and handling page faults and memory reclamation.

In ARM-based architectures that support hardware-assisted virtualization, the stream ID tagging complements the usage of the MMU address-based translation by restricting access to peripherals based on an ID that constrains a peripheral to a memory region. Stream IDs are IDs assigned to data streams or transactions within a system to uniquely identify the originator of a transaction. IOMMUs use the unique stream ID to map a transaction to a translation context. Consequently, an IOMMU can be configured to filter transactions based on their stream ID by setting up rules that define which VMs are allowed to access specific peripherals based on their assigned stream IDs. This enables the hypervisor to enforce access control policies by examining the stream ID of each transaction and determining whether it matches the allowed stream IDs for a particular peripheral. If the stream ID is in the allowed list, the transaction can proceed; otherwise, it is blocked. Another peripheral isolation technique relies on device assignment where the hypervisor can grant exclusive access of a peripheral to a specific VM. The peripheral can be assigned directly to the VM, bypassing the hypervisor's intervention for most operations and preventing other VMs from having access to the peripheral. By leveraging stream IDs, device assignment, and IOMMU filtering, the hypervisor ensures that only the assigned VM can communicate directly with the designated peripheral. Consequently, other VMs running on the same physical machine are prevented from accessing or interfering with the assigned peripheral's operations. For an in-depth look at how an MMU can be leveraged to achieve VM and peripheral isolation, we recommend studying the *ARM System Memory Management Unit Architecture Specification* [23].

Microkernel versus monolithic kernels

Spatial isolation can be further strengthened through the OS design. SoC-based ECUs rely on **Portable Operating System Interface (POSIX)**-compliant OSs such as QNX and Linux. The first is a microkernel architecture while the latter is a monolithic kernel. The former offers a number of security advantages over the latter. In a microkernel architecture, various entities such as device drivers and filesystems typically operate in user space as separate processes. This isolation ensures that a failure or security breach in one component doesn't directly compromise others, which is a risk in monolithic kernels where all components share the same address space in kernel mode. Microkernels also follow PoLP, only allowing the most essential parts of the OS to run in kernel mode with the highest privileges, thereby reducing the risk of full system compromise. The simplicity and smaller size of microkernels make them easier to verify and audit for security issues, compared to the larger code base of monolithic kernels. Another security advantage is fault isolation and recovery. For example, a failing service in a microkernel can be restarted without impacting the whole system, while the same is not true for a monolithic kernel.

Fine-grained access controls

OSs offer various techniques to control access to system resources such as files, peripherals, and libraries. Both the functional safety and security domains rely on access control mechanisms to limit opportunities for unwanted interference in systems with mixed safety and security criticality. Let's have a look at the different levels of access supported by these techniques:

	File 1	File 2	File 3
Process A	Execute Read Write	-	Own Read Write
Process B	Read	Own Read	Read
Process C	Read Write	Read	Own Execute Read Write

Table 9.1 – Example access permission assignment across processes and files

With discretionary access control mechanisms, a file or resource has associated permissions for the owner or group. Using a permissions model, as shown in *Table 9.1*, different levels of access can be supported, such as **Read (R)**, **Write (W)**, and **Execute (X)**. Furthermore, permission assignment is done through a numeric code; for example, in Linux, a file with permissions 644 means the owner has read and write access (6), and the group and others have read-only access (4). An ownership and group model associates a file or a resource with an owner and a group. If a software entity attempts to access a file without being the owner or belonging to the group, its access can be rejected. Additionally, **access control lists** (**ACLs**) can be constructed to map a user process group ID and the services to which it must be granted access. As long as the ACL remains protected, permission checks can be implemented—for example, through resource managers that check the requester's group ID prior to granting access to a managed resource. In large software projects, maintaining a coherent access control policy requires close cooperation between different teams to ensure access is only granted where needed.

Temporal isolation

Temporal isolation at the ECU level refers to the separation of software components in terms of their access to the CPU and hardware runtime resources. This can be achieved through techniques such as virtualization and OS priority assignment. In the context of cybersecurity, temporal isolation aims to prevent a malicious task, process, or VM from exhausting the runtime resources of the system. This is done through careful priority assignment and limiting abilities to trigger interrupts and exceptions.

Virtualization

Similar to spatial isolation, a hypervisor can control how many CPU resources a certain VM is given. By assigning a VM a lower scheduling priority and disabling its ability to trigger interrupts, the hypervisor can reduce the impact of the VM if it becomes corrupted. This is especially useful when a VM is deemed to be exposed to high risk—for example, due to offering external connectivity. Such a VM can then be enabled only when connectivity is needed, and it can be frequently checked to ensure that any sign of misbehavior can be contained, potentially through an early shutdown to prevent disrupting safety-critical services within the system.

OS priority assignment

OS priority assignment is another technique that can be used to achieve temporal isolation at the ECU level. This technique involves assigning different priorities to different processes running on the same OS. The OS scheduler uses these priorities to determine which process should be given access to the CPU at any given time. This allows for the separation of software components by ensuring that higher-priority processes are given access to the CPU before lower-priority processes. For example, a safety-critical software component responsible for actuating the brakes on a vehicle might be assigned a higher priority than a non-safety-critical software component responsible for updating logs in persistent storage. Even if the latter misbehaves or becomes corrupted, the safety-critical process must continue to be able to perform its functions within the required functional safety timing constraints. Enforcing runtime execution budgets based on a predefined schedule helps in identifying offending tasks or processes and terminating them to ensure overall system stability. Similarly, limiting the usage of interrupts triggered by external events such as network and storage resources can prevent a malicious network participant from initiating interrupt storms to keep the application CPUs busy. It must be noted that temporal isolation is harder to guarantee than spatial isolation due to the existence of side-channel techniques (such as cache-timing attacks) through which a malicious process can disrupt the system. Therefore, at a minimum, systems must be designed with timing monitors that detect drifts in the execution profile to ensure the system transitions to a safe state if certain tasks or processes become starved of runtime resources.

Encrypted and authenticated filesystems

With SoC-based ECUs, one or more filesystems can be leveraged to store software binaries and data files. Due to boot-up performance constraints, such filesystems might not be included in the secure boot process. Instead, their contents must be authenticated and/or decrypted during runtime or after mounting. An OS may offer an out-of-the-box data authentication and encryption solution. If not, then one must be developed to detect the tampering of critical ECU files such as **machine learning (ML)** models or the exposure of confidential data stored in the filesystem, such as user private data. One such solution is dm-verity by Linux, which protects the integrity of data by creating a Merkle tree (hash tree) from the data and storing the hash values alongside the data itself.

Merkle trees are used in many cryptographic systems to efficiently verify the contents of large data structures. They function by hashing individual data blocks and pairing these hashes together, then hashing the pairs, and continuing this process until a single hash remains, known as the root. This structure ensures that even a small change in the data will result in a completely different root hash, which can be efficiently checked to detect data tampering. Let's look at an example Merkle tree with two layers and four leaf nodes, where each leaf node represents a block of data in a filesystem that must be protected against tampering:

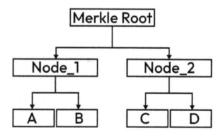

Figure 9.13 – Basic example of a hash tree

First, we calculate the hash value of each block (hash (A), hash (B), and so on).

Then, the hashes of block A and block B together are hashed again to form Node_1, and similarly for block C and block D, as illustrated here:

```
hash(hash(A) | hash(B))=Node1
hash(hash(C) | hash(D))=Node2
hash(Node1 | Node2)=Merkle Root
```

If we wanted to verify that block D has not been tampered with, we'd only need to recalculate the hash value of block D and then recalculate the hash value of Node_2, followed by the hash value of Node_1 and Node_2 together. If the resulting root hash value matched the original Merkle root hash value, then we'd know that block D has not been tampered with without having to recalculate the hash value of all data blocks in the system.

Using this concept, dm-verity generates a Merkle tree from the data stored in a persistent memory device. Building a Merkle tree involves dividing the data into fixed-size blocks and calculating hash values for the content of each block. These hash values are then combined and hashed again to create parent nodes until the root node is reached. This root hash acts as the verification point for the entire dataset. The root hash value of the generated hash tree is stored separately from the filesystem image, typically on a read-only portion of the storage device, and is cryptographically signed to allow for validating its integrity and authenticity. During system startup, the root hash signature is verified using a trusted mechanism to ensure it is authentic and has not been tampered with. Then, whenever a file is requested, dm-verity intercepts read requests to the device and then retrieves the corresponding data blocks and their associated hash values from the device. Next, dm-verity calculates the hash value of the requested data block and compares it with the corresponding stored hash value. If the calculated hash matches the stored hash, the data is considered valid and is passed through to the requesting process. If the calculated hash does not match the stored hash, this indicates that the file has been corrupted or tampered with. In this case, dm-verity reports an integrity verification failure and prevents the potentially corrupted or tampered data from being accessed or used. In this example, only integrity is provided. Supporting encryption requires additional steps to integrate a process for encryption and decryption when files are written and read from the filesystem.

Runtime execution hardening

Building on the CPU security features that aim to reduce the feasibility of code injection attacks, we'll now consider some software techniques that have the same goal. With SoC-based ECUs, these controls include stack canaries, **address space layout randomization** (**ASLR**), and DEP, which are relatively easy controls to deploy with limited to no impact on code size and execution performance.

Stack canaries are used to detect stack memory overflow or corruption by inserting a randomly generated value between a given buffer and the function's return address on the stack. If an attacker manages to inject code into the stack—for example, through a buffer overflow vulnerability—the stack canary will be overwritten. This results in the OS triggering an exception when it performs the stack canary check before popping the return address from the stack.

Have a look at the following diagram:

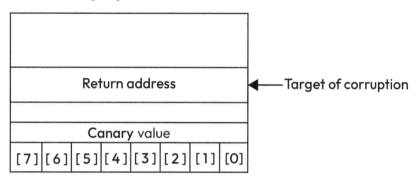

Figure 9.14 – Example stack frame protected by a stack canary

In the example shown in *Figure 9.14*, a function has a local buffer of 8 bytes pushed on the stack. When the function is called, the canary is filled with a known value (for example, a random number generated at the program start). If the function contains a vulnerability that allows an attacker to overflow the buffer, then the canary value will be overwritten as well. Before the function returns, it checks whether the canary has the expected value. If it doesn't, the program knows that a buffer overflow has occurred, and it can halt execution or take other protective measures. If the canary is still intact, the function returns as normal.

ASLR is used to randomize the memory layout of a process. This unpredictability makes it challenging for an attacker to determine the location of specific code or data fragments, thus complicating ROP and JOP gadgets' construction. However, sophisticated attacks might still defeat ASLR if they can leak memory addresses. Both ASLR and stack canaries ideally rely on a secure random number generator to ensure that attackers cannot easily guess what the canary value should be or what the randomized address location with ASLR is.

Data Execution Prevention (**DEP**), on the other hand, is used to prevent the execution of code from non-executable memory regions, such as a stack or heap, as a defense mechanism against buffer overflow and other code injection attacks. Using the MMU or MPU memory protection attributes, such regions can be configured as **Write XOR Execute** (**W^X**), causing any attempt to execute code from regions marked as non-executable to trigger a fault. Together, these techniques form a layered defense against various types of attacks, thereby elevating the security posture of the system and making it harder for attackers to exploit software vulnerabilities.

Security monitors

Security monitors mirror safety monitors in their ability to detect abnormal behavior and enforce an error-handling policy. But for a security monitor to be truly effective, it must run in a TEE to prevent an attacker from tampering with its ability to detect anomalies. Due to the closeness in purpose to a safety monitor, it is recommended to integrate a security monitor with a safety monitor. Unifying safety and security monitors can be an effective way to harmonize the security response when either an attack or a fault is detected. Security monitors can help detect fault injection attacks by monitoring the system for signs of abnormal behavior. For example, a security monitor can monitor the system for unexpected changes in memory or CPU usage, or for attempts to access protected resources in the HPSE. It can also monitor physical properties such as abnormal clock input, voltage swings, and temperature fluctuations. Using an integrated safety and security monitor, the system can choose to terminate security-critical processes such as ongoing cryptographic operations and may even attempt to issue a reset when conditions are safe to do so. Logging faults is also necessary to allow future analysis and troubleshooting.

So far, we have covered a diverse set of cybersecurity controls that can detect and prevent attacks that are carried out through a diverse attack surface, including network interfaces, malicious software applications, and even nefarious insiders. For completeness, it is important to highlight the role of physical security controls in reducing the risk of the tampering and exfiltration of ECU data through physical access-based attacks, which is the topic of the next section.

Exploring physical security controls

Attackers with physical access to the target are normally after high-value assets whose compromise can be leveraged on a larger scale. For example, they may be interested in recovering global secrets, reverse engineering software, or even simply mounting **denial-of-service** (**DoS**) attacks through a physical attack surface. While most physical-based attacks require direct access to the target, some can be carried out by simply being within proximity to the target. In this section, we briefly survey cybersecurity controls implemented through hardware, software, and packaging techniques to raise the difficulty of physical-based attacks.

Tamper detection and prevention

While not the most effective at eliminating risk, physical security measures, such as tamper-evident seals or secure enclosures, can be useful in preventing or detecting unauthorized physical access to the system by raising the difficulty level of carrying out such attacks. For example, attempting to break a seal or open an ECU enclosure at a minimum results in evident tampering that can be noticed through human inspection. It is also possible to trigger a signal to alert the driver if an ECU enclosure has been opened or a restricted compartment has been opened. A more effective policy to handle an opened ECU enclosure is to initiate a lockup of HPSE secrets, effectively rendering the ECU unusable in a real vehicle. With the HPSE in a locked state, cryptographic keys needed to communicate with other ECUs or with the backend become inaccessible or are even permanently destroyed. If the goal of the attacker is to extract cryptographic keys, then this measure can further frustrate their efforts. In some instances, tamper prevention can be as simple as placing physical locks over specific vehicle ports that should not be accessible by unauthorized individuals. For example, an electric vehicle charge port can be locked by default and only unlocked by the driver from inside the vehicle cabin. This prevents an attacker from plugging in fake **electric vehicle supply equipment** (**EVSE**) that may inject malware through the power-line communication interface.

Printed circuit board layout pin and trace hiding

To further increase the difficulty of physical tampering with ECU hardware resources, the **printed circuit board** (**PCB**) layout can leverage pin and trace hiding. This involves hiding the physical connections between different components on the PCB using blind and buried vias, which are small holes drilled into the PCB that allow for the creation of inner layers. This technique can prevent attackers from accessing sensitive information by obscuring physical pathways used to transmit that information. Another technique for hiding traces and pins is one known as via-in-pad, which involves placing vias directly beneath the pads of surface mount components. This technique can hide the connections between the pins of the component and underlying traces on the PCB.

Concealment and shielding

Along the same lines of frustrating attackers is the usage of non-descript component names on the PCB layout. Rather than using the publicly known MCU or SoC vendor names, the OEM may request that these parts be delivered with generic names. This makes it harder for attackers to guess the part used to easily look up the part documentation. In addition to concealment, shielding techniques may be necessary to protect certain vehicle components from **electromagnetic interference** (**EMI**) and **radio-frequency interference** (**RFI**). Shielding involves encasing such components in a conductive material to block or reduce the effects of EMI and RFI.

Summary

In this ninth and final chapter, we looked at the most commonly used security controls applied to the hardware, software, and physical layers of the ECU. With this layered approach, we continued with the theme of DiD, which started at the vehicle interface level in *Chapter 8*. We showed the role that hardware plays in establishing the foundation of a secure system. Hardware security controls included the hardware RoT, secure memory, and authenticated debug ports. Then, we looked at security controls in the software domain that build upon the hardware security controls, such as multi-stage secure boot, virtualization through hypervisors, and process and temporal isolation through OSs. Finally, we looked at controls applied at the physical layer to reduce the feasibility of attacks by agents who have gained physical access to the ECU. While exploring the various security layers, we highlighted areas in which competing priorities emerge between security on one hand and the need for performance optimization and system usability on the other. Especially in performance- and memory-constrained ECUs, we stressed the importance of designing features that can meet the constraints of the system, such as boot-up time, secure communication latencies, and CPU workload impacts. While the reader may get the sense that following all the presented controls should be sufficient to build a secure system, it is important to understand that all defenses suffer from weaknesses. Therefore, it is not sufficient to add a control and assume the job is done. Instead, we must be continuously vigilant in assessing the effectiveness of our controls to eliminate ways in which they can be either bypassed or defeated.

By understanding our systems, staying aware of security standards, following a secure engineering approach, and staying abreast of technical risks and mitigating measures, we now have at our disposal a set of tools, methods, and techniques that should help us build robust and secure automotive systems. This should help you build the systems of the future that will offer greater connectivity and convenience features without compromising the safety and security of consumers. We hope that this book has sparked in you the desire to pursue a journey of lifelong learning in the field of automotive cybersecurity, which—if anything—promises to never give you a dull moment.

Further reading

Studying cybersecurity controls is perhaps one of the most technically interesting aspects of cybersecurity. To further expand your knowledge about cybersecurity controls that can be applied at the ECU level, we recommend the following list of resources:

- [1] *CyBOK, The Cyber Security Body of Knowledge*: `https://www.cybok.org/`
- [2] *Secure Application Programming in the presence of Side Channel Attacks*: `https://www.riscure.com/publication/secure-application-programming-presence-side-channel-attacks/`
- [3] *Development of TEE and Secure Monitor Code*: `https://www.arm.com/technologies/trustzone-for-cortex-a/tee-and-smc`
- [4] *Achieving a Root of Trust with Secure Boot in Automotive RH850 and R-Car Devices – Part 1*: `https://www.renesas.com/us/en/blogs/introduction-about-secure-boot-automotive-mcu-rh850-and-soc-r-car-achieve-root-trust-1`
- [5] *Securing distributed systems: A survey on access control techniques for cloud, blockchain, IoT and SDN*: `https://www.sciencedirect.com/science/article/pii/S2772918423000036`
- [6] *Arm Confidential Compute Architecture*: `https://www.arm.com/architecture/security-features/arm-confidential-compute-architecture`
- [7] *Automotive Security Best Practices*: `https://www.infopoint-security.de/medien/wp-automotive-security.pdf`
- [8] *Maene, P., Götzfried, J., De Clercq, R., Müller, T., Freiling, F., & Verbauwhede, I. (2017). Hardware-based trusted computing architectures for isolation and attestation. IEEE Transactions on Computers, 67(3), 361-374.*

- [9] *Leonardi, L., Lettieri, G., Perazzo, P., & Saponara, S. (2022). On the Hardware–Software Integration in Cryptographic Accelerators for Industrial IoT. Applied Sciences, 12(19), 9948.*

- [10] *S. S. Chung, The Advances of OTP Memory for Embedded Applications in HKMG Generation and Beyond, 2019 IEEE 13th International Conference on ASIC (ASICON), Chongqing, China, 2019, pp. 1-4, doi: 10.1109/ASICON47005.2019.8983654.*

- [11] *MPU Security Part 1: Introduction*: `https://embeddedcomputing.com/technology/security/mpu-security-part-1-introduction`

- [12] *Global Platform, Cybersecurity in Automotive*: `https://globalplatform.org/wp-content/uploads/2023/03/GP-Cybersecurity-in-Automotive-whitepaper-design_FINAL.pdf`

- [13] *Armv8.1-M Pointer Authentication and Branch Target Identification Extension*: `https://community.arm.com/arm-community-blogs/b/architectures-and-processors-blog/posts/armv8-1-m-pointer-authentication-and-branch-target-identification-extension`

- [14] *Universal Flash Storage For Automotive Applications*: `https://ampinc.com/universal-flash-storage-for-automotive-applications/`

- [15] *Reddy, A. K., Paramasivam, P., & Vemula, P. B. (2015, December). Mobile secure data protection using eMMC RPMB partition. In 2015 International Conference on Computing and Network Communications (CoCoNet) (pp. 946-950). IEEE.*

- [17] *The Growing Need for Secure Storage in Automotive Systems*: `https://www.eetimes.com/the-growing-need-for-secure-storage-in-automotive-systems/`

- [18] *Automotive Security: From Standards to Implementation*: `https://www.nxp.com/docs/en/white-paper/AUTOSECURITYWP.pdf`

- [19] *A Comprehensive Guide to Manufacturing Cyber Security*: `https://www.missionsecure.com/manufacturing-cyber-security`

- [20] *Trusted Execution Environments: Applications and Organizational Challenges*: `https://www.frontiersin.org/articles/10.3389/fcomp.2022.930741/full`

- [21] *Recommendation for Random Bit Generator (RBG) Constructions, NIST SP800-90C*

- [22] *Recommendation for Random Number Generation Using Deterministic Random Bit Generators, NIST SP800-90A*

- [23] *ARM System Memory Management Unit Architecture Specification*: `https://developer.arm.com/documentation/ihi0062/b`

Index

packtpub.com

Subscribe to our online digital library for full access to over 7,000 books and videos, as well as industry leading tools to help you plan your personal development and advance your career. For more information, please visit our website.

Why subscribe?

- Spend less time learning and more time coding with practical eBooks and Videos from over 4,000 industry professionals

- Improve your learning with Skill Plans built especially for you

- Get a free eBook or video every month

- Fully searchable for easy access to vital information

- Copy and paste, print, and bookmark content

Did you know that Packt offers eBook versions of every book published, with PDF and ePub files available? You can upgrade to the eBook version at packtpub.com and as a print book customer, you are entitled to a discount on the eBook copy. Get in touch with us at customercare@packtpub.com for more details.

At www.packtpub.com, you can also read a collection of free technical articles, sign up for a range of free newsletters, and receive exclusive discounts and offers on Packt books and eBooks.

Other Books You May Enjoy

If you enjoyed this book, you may be interested in these other books by Packt:

Network Automation with Go

Nicolas Leiva, Michael Kashin

ISBN: 978-1-80056-092-5

- Understand Go programming language basics via network-related examples
- Find out what features make Go a powerful alternative for network automation
- Explore network automation goals, benefits, and common use cases
- Discover how to interact with network devices using a variety of technologies
- Integrate Go programs into an automation framework
- Take advantage of the OpenConfig ecosystem with Go
- Build distributed and scalable systems for network observability

Reconnaissance for Ethical Hackers

Glen D. Singh

ISBN: 978-1-83763-063-9

- Understand the tactics, techniques, and procedures of reconnaissance
- Grasp the importance of attack surface management for organizations
- Find out how to conceal your identity online as an ethical hacker
- Explore advanced open source intelligence (OSINT) techniques
- Perform active reconnaissance to discover live hosts and exposed ports
- Use automated tools to perform vulnerability assessments on systems
- Discover how to efficiently perform reconnaissance on web applications
- Implement open source threat detection and monitoring tools

Packt is searching for authors like you

If you're interested in becoming an author for Packt, please visit `authors.packtpub.com` and apply today. We have worked with thousands of developers and tech professionals, just like you, to help them share their insight with the global tech community. You can make a general application, apply for a specific hot topic that we are recruiting an author for, or submit your own idea.

Share Your Thoughts

Now you've finished *Automotive Cybersecurity Engineering Handbook*, we'd love to hear your thoughts! If you purchased the book from Amazon, please click here to go straight to the Amazon review page for this book and share your feedback or leave a review on the site that you purchased it from.

Your review is important to us and the tech community and will help us make sure we're delivering excellent quality content.

Download a free PDF copy of this book

Thanks for purchasing this book!

Do you like to read on the go but are unable to carry your print books everywhere?

Is your eBook purchase not compatible with the device of your choice?

Don't worry, now with every Packt book you get a DRM-free PDF version of that book at no cost.

Read anywhere, any place, on any device. Search, copy, and paste code from your favorite technical books directly into your application.

The perks don't stop there, you can get exclusive access to discounts, newsletters, and great free content in your inbox daily

Follow these simple steps to get the benefits:

1. Scan the QR code or visit the link below

https://packt.link/free-ebook/9781801076531

2. Submit your proof of purchase
3. That's it! We'll send your free PDF and other benefits to your email directly

www.ingramcontent.com/pod-product-compliance
Lightning Source LLC
Chambersburg PA
CBHW080609060326
40690CB00021B/4634

* 9 7 8 1 8 0 1 0 7 6 5 3 1 *